HELPING PEOPLE HELP THEMSELVES

Evolving Values for a Capitalist World

In most of the world today, the issue is not whether or how to embrace capitalism, but how to make the best of it. The currently dominant capitalist values include competitive individualism, instrumental rationality, and material success. The series explores questions such as: Will these values suffice as a basis for social organizations that can meet human and environmental needs in the twenty-first century? What would it mean for capitalist systems to evolve toward an emphasis on other values, such as cooperation, altruism, responsibility, and concern for the future?

Helping People Help Themselves

From the World Bank to an Alternative
Philosophy of Development Assistance

David Ellerman

THE UNIVERSITY OF MICHIGAN PRESS

Ann Arbor

2008   2007   2006   2005   4   3   2   1

A CIP catalog record for this book is available from the British Library.

Library of Congress Cataloging-in-Publication Data

Ellerman, David P.
    Helping people help themselves : from the World Bank to an
alternative philosophy of development assistance / David Ellerman.
        p.   cm. — (Evolving values for a capitalist world)
    Includes bibliographical references and index.
    ISBN 0-472-11465-4 (cloth : alk. paper)
    1. Economic assistance—Developing countries.   2. Economic
development—Social aspects—Developing countries.   3. World
Bank—Developing countries.   I. Title.   II. Series.
HC60.E433   2004
338.91'09172'4—dc22   2004019094

To Vlasta,
who taught me
a thing or two about
autonomy-respecting assistance,
and to Joe,
who in many different ways
led to my writing this book.

A Note from the Series Editor

Helping People Help Themselves is the fifth volume in the University of Michigan Press Evolving Values for a Capitalist World series. The first volume, *As if the Future Mattered* (ed. Goodwin), describes, and proposes constructive responses to, a deep flaw in the capitalist system, especially in the United States: that considerations of the future are external to most market transactions. The second and fourth books in the series can be seen as a pair. Existing institutions that encourage capitalist firms to act in consonance with social needs and goals are described in *A Civil Economy* (Bruyn); while some of the most antisocial realities of the present system are described in *It's Legal but It Ain't Right: Harmful Social Consequences of Legal Industries* (ed. Passas and Goodwin). The third book in the series, *Rethinking Sustainability* (ed. Harris), takes up the topics of development and how it can be made sustainable for the future. These topics are examined in depth in the present book.

In *Helping People Help Themselves*, David Ellerman focuses on the deepest layer of economic life: the cultural values that determine the institutions that support the economy. In chapter 8, a case study of the disastrously misdirected efforts to smooth the transition to capitalism in the former Soviet Union, Ellerman states that his primary purpose is "to lay the intellectual foundations for an alternative philosophy of development." Economic development is about change; Ellerman starts by inquiring into how change may be fostered on many levels— the most basic being that of individual learning. The answer is a deep and simple truth that has been expounded by a number of thinkers (thoroughly referenced in this book): to be sustainable, change must come from within those who are changing. It must, therefore, be something that they want—not something that the donors (or teachers, community organizers, therapists, or managers) have told them they should want.

We in the industrialized world have not, in fact, done very well at knowing what we actually want—at enunciating acceptable goals for our own economic development. We have been led astray by economic simplifications, which have shown how to maximize that quantifiable thing—wealth—while ignoring the final goal—well-being—that wealth must serve if it is to have human value.

One of the outstanding characteristics of capitalism has been its inexorable spread. Those countries that have successfully adopted capitalism have been vigorous in their attempts to convert others. Unfortunately, economic development, as it has been practiced and preached for the last fifty years, often devolves to transmitting a caricature of capitalism. Standard introductory economics textbooks for high school or college students lay out a simplified understanding of the workings of a market economy. This schematic view is codified and reduced even further in the advice given by development organizations such as the World Bank.

Development assistance, based on an economics in which history does not exist and human psychology is reduced to the most selfish motivations, has too often ignored some essential characteristics on which our own economic system depends. These necessary characteristics include institutions such as legal systems and generally accepted accounting practices—not to mention the educational, health, and social service institutions that support the human beings who run the whole show and for whose benefit (theoretically) it is run. A well-functioning capitalist (or any other) economic system also requires cultural expressions of basic values, such as trust, honesty, and a desire to do a good job or to make a meaningful contribution.

Ellerman describes how much of what has been done in the name of development assistance actually destroys essential culture and values and often fails to support the necessary existing and emerging institutions. He joins a growing chorus in pointing out that efforts to export a version of capitalism based on simplistic, exported goals have in many cases not been sustainable. His evidence supports an emerging consensus that failures in this area arise from the relationship between those who are *doing* the development and those who are having it *done to* them.

One of Ellerman's brilliant innovations is the terminology he uses throughout the book. Insisting on a too-often-ignored reality, that "development will not yield to social engineering no matter how much aid is provided" (chap. 10), he refers to those who are developing some aspects of their own economies as the "doers," while the aid workers, policymakers, and others are, at best, "helpers." This book rests on a deep theoretic grounding in the standard and nonstandard economics of capitalism (including management theory), in philosophy, and in theories of learning and change, for a practical description of how goals can be better set and met. It examines in detail how the relationship between doers and helpers might be better carried out, with specific suggestions such as the use of "parallel experimentation," movement "from a global agency to a global network of local agencies," and encouragement for developing countries to oppose further indebtedness or "addiction" to a kind of aid that enriches a few while further disempowering the rest.

Understanding the reality and the potential of the development relationship between industrialized and other countries is key to understanding capitalism, at its best and its worst. Ellerman not only illuminates many of the values that contribute to more and less successful forms of capitalism; he also suggests a constructive path along which some of these values could evolve.

Neva Goodwin
Co-director, Global Development
And Environment Institute,
Tufts University

Contents

Foreword

This book starts with a quote from John Dewey defining what genuine help to others consists of (and which the author takes as the best one-sentence statement of the idea):

> The best kind of help to others, whenever possible, is indirect, and consists in such modifications of the conditions of life, of the general level of subsistence, as enables them independently to help themselves.

The book uses the interdisciplinary methodology of pointing to similar ideas expressed by a variety of other authors in different fields: management theory by Douglas McGregor, psychotherapy by Carl Rogers, community organizing by Saul Alinsky, community education by Paulo Freire, spiritual counseling by Søren Kierkegaard, and economic development by E. F. Schumacher and myself.

It is important to note the difference between help and perverse, dependency-creating alternatives to self-help. The task is to find forms of help that enable self-reliance and autonomy to come forward. It is time for deep organization experimentation in the ways of development assistance. This can be done by reflecting on the ideas and proposals of the following people:

- Saul Alinsky, with regard to the community organization and the community;
- Paulo Freire, with regard to the relation of the educator and the peasant (or urban poor) community;
- John Dewey, with regard to the relation between teachers and learners;

- Douglas McGregor, with regard to the relation between managers and workers;
- Carl Rogers, with regard to the relation between therapists and clients;
- Søren Kierkegaard, with regard to the relation between teachers and learners;
- E. F. Schumacher, with regard to the relation between the development agency and the country; and
- my own work with regard to the relation between the development advisor and the government.

The aim in all these cases is to design improved or more autonomy-respecting methods of development assistance. The proposals of all these persons are spelled out in detail in chapter 5. The relation between my ideas and those of Paulo Freire is particularly close; so is his relation to Carl Rogers's client-centered therapy.

In the end, the book speaks of a series of ways in which development agencies can experience blocks to learning and singles out the "long confrontation between man and a situation," which, according to Camus, can be so fruitful for the achievement of genuine progress in problem solving. This is the opposite of overconfidence in the solvability of all problems, which Flaubert attacked and named "la rage de vouloir conclure."

Albert O. Hirschman
Professor of Social Science, Emeritus
Institute for Advanced Study

Preface

This book grew out of my collaboration with Joseph Stiglitz as one of his economic advisors and speech writers during his tumultuous tenure (1997–99) as chief economist (and senior vice president) of the World Bank. One of the principal themes of the book, the idea of autonomy-respecting help (assistance that actually helps people to help themselves) was vigorously supported not only by Joe but by James Wolfensohn, the president of the Bank.[1] The idea was expressed as having the "country in the driver's seat" in the statement of principles called the Comprehensive Development Framework, or CDF (Wolfensohn 1999a). I started writing a background paper to put together the intellectual history and support for these ideas for future Stiglitz speeches, and then I got carried away, resulting, years later, in this book.

I owe my biggest thanks to Joe for providing the intellectual stimulation and the organizational environment—indeed an oasis of critical thinking within the Bank—in order for these ideas to be formed and developed. It is important to understand some of the background to Joe's tenure at the Bank. By the early 1990s, Joe had secured a future Nobel Prize in Economics for his work in information economics (he got the prize in 2001 after leaving the Bank) and was already a legend in the community of academic economists. His first foray into the public eye was joining Bill Clinton's first-term Council of Economic Advisors along with Alan Blinder and the chair, Laura Tyson. By the end of Clinton's first term, Joe was the chair of the council and was ready to work on an international scale.

James Wolfensohn, the president of the World Bank, had no love lost on economists. He felt he understood the real-world economy as well as or better than academic economists, but he didn't have all the formal training in economics. Wolfensohn may have feared the fate of Denis Diderot when debating the mathematician Leonhard Euler in Catherine the Great's court. Against the atheist Diderot, Euler asserted "$(a + b^n)/n = x$, therefore God exists"—which left Diderot speechless and defenseless. Hence Wolfensohn wanted an economist of Stiglitz's stature at his side. After the untimely death of the previous chief economist, Michael Bruno, Joe made the move in early 1997 over a few blocks from the White House to the World Bank.

At first Joe may have thought that this would be a time to work out the implications for development economics of his previous work in the economics of information. But events would soon overtake those ambitions. These were tumultuous years for the Bank. The protests against the international institutions, such as the World Trade Organization (WTO), the International Monetary Fund (IMF), and the World Bank, were building up. It was then clear, at least to Joe, that the postsocialist transition strategy based on much advice from Western economists was not going well particularly in Russia and the former Soviet Union. And the East Asian financial crisis began to unfold.

Joe's World Institute for Development Economics Research (WIDER) lecture in January 1998, "More Instruments and Broader Goals: Moving toward the Post-Washington Consensus" (chap. 1 in Chang 2001), squarely took on the "Washington consensus" that had previously been the house orthodoxy in the IMF and the Bank. Over the next two years, Joe took on one shibboleth after another in speeches given around the world. Nine of the most important speeches are republished in Chang 2001, a collection entitled *Joseph Stiglitz and the World Bank: The Rebel Within*. The most barbed attacks were directed against the IMF and the U.S. Treasury, where the chief antagonists were, respectively, Stanley Fischer and Larry Summers, both former chief economists of the Bank.

None of this was what Wolfensohn bargained for. Instead of being at Wolfensohn's side in the perpetual "management meetings" in the Bank, Joe seemed to always be on the road.[2] He had little real interest in the "inside game" in the Bank, and he clearly relished the bully pulpit side of the chief economist's job as well as talking directly to the leaders in the developing countries. But all this created considerable consternation in the Fund, in the Treasury, and even in the Bank itself. Instead of public debate, the Fund and Treasury would express their displeasure directly to Wolfensohn. In the "front office" of the chief economist, we would get the expected phone call: "Please inform Mr.

Stiglitz that Mr. Wolfensohn would like to have a word with him as soon as he returns from his trip." Joe would promise to be more diplomatic, but his natural ebullience kept interrupting.[3]

I do not want to imply that it was all storm and strife between Joe and Jim. Joe was an early collaborator in what Wolfensohn would see as his main intellectual contribution to the Bank and to development, the CDF. For instance, at a major conference in Seoul in February 1999 at which Amartya Sen as well as Wolfensohn and Stiglitz were to appear, Stiglitz's speech "Participation and Development: Perspectives from the Comprehensive Development Paradigm" (chap. 7 in Chang 2001) gave public intellectual support to Wolfensohn's CDF. This was the sort of thing that Jim had hired Joe to do. On the flight together over to Seoul, Jim read Joe's speech and then scolded his own speech writer(s)—he thought that Joe's speech would make his look pale in comparison. At the podium the next day, Wolfensohn pointedly threw away his prepared talk, saying he didn't have all the fancy stuff in Stiglitz's speech, and then he won over the audience with an impassioned off-the-cuff talk about the CDF. The "Joe-and-Jim show" worked well at times like those.[4]

But that was not to last as the complaints mounted—principally from Fischer in the Fund and Summers at Treasury. Wolfensohn's first five-year term as president expired a bit before Stiglitz's three-year term as chief economist was to end in January 2000. There were unconfirmed rumors that Stiglitz's nonrenewal "was the price demanded by the US Treasury for its support for an extra term for Mr Wolfensohn as President of the World Bank" (Chang 2001, 3). But it was clear anyway that Joe and the Bank had arrived at a parting of the ways, so Joe resigned shortly before his term expired.[5]

In Joe's years at the Bank, he represented many of the aspects of autonomy-respecting help developed here such as the basic idea of giving the best arguments on all sides of a question to the counterparts in a developing country so that they could make their own decisions in an informed way. This is in contrast to the usual Bank procedure of trying to give them "the answers" buttressed by an intimidating barrage of one-sided arguments and biased statistics. In the course of the book, this idea is developed into the theme that the Bank in its cognitive role as the "knowledge bank" should take a cue from universities and other scientific institutions and not have "official views" on complex questions of knowledge.

Out of my ten years at the World Bank, the years spent with Joe were my glory days helping him to be "the rebel within" the development establishment challenging the tenets of the Washington consensus.[6] As Joe's advisor, I had the leeway to play the gadfly or attack-dog role, making many of the points contained in this book while still within the Bank. In Joe's post-Bank book, *Globalization and Its Discontents* (2002), he applies his critical analysis more to the IMF than the World Bank. I try to correct that imbalance here.

I am grateful to James Wolfensohn, now ending his second five-year term as president of the World Bank, for taking the initiative to develop the CDF—even if, for the reasons developed in the book, the ideals usually became a travesty when they were processed and implemented by the bureaucracy of the Bank. Jim supported the writing of the book to provide intellectual support for the CDF principles, and he looked at several drafts as the work progressed. After seeing an early first draft, he at one point asked me for the then-current draft to see how it was going. I visibly paused, thought for a moment, and then said somewhat apologetically, "But I am afraid that as the book has developed, it has become clear that the Bank is not exactly the institution to implement your CDF principles." He straightened up, squared his shoulders, looked me straight in the eyes, and said, "You're telling ME that!" While he would probably not agree with my rather negative conclusions about the Bank and my call for alternatives, I felt from that moment on that we at least had a certain mutual understanding. Although my personal views of his leadership at the Bank are quite positive, the rather fatal structural flaws of the Bank (see the last chapter) were there before he came and will, in spite of his best efforts, remain after he leaves.

I am also grateful to Nicholas Stern, Joe's successor as chief economist. Very soon after Nick took the job, he was introduced to an early version of this book when Jim Wolfensohn gave him a copy for comments. Nick read it without at first noting the author, and his response was the start of our positive relationship over the next two years and our mutual appreciation of interdisciplinary scholarship. Joe and Nick had first met doing postdoctoral research in Kenya and were the best of friends ever since then. While they see the world in much the same way, their organizational styles were almost diametrical opposites. Nick is the consummate organizational manager, and Joe, well, was not.[7] Nick kept me on as advisor until the expiration of my fixed-term contract but more as a backroom philosopher than as a frontline gadfly or attack dog.[8] That was fine with me since I had a book to finish and I was by then covered with the isolating "antibodies" that protect the Bank against "alien germs" that by some accident got inside the system.

I greatly appreciated the support of my many colleagues in the chief economist's front office. From my critical viewpoint, my position was an ideal job in the Bank since I got to review, evaluate, and criticize the operational and research work of the Bank. In an organization notorious for its factoid-plus-banality writing style, I tried to write memos and reviews that would be both vivid and stimulating in the hope that they would actually be read. In any case, the content of those internal critiques is the basis for the case study of the Bank developed throughout this book.[9] Halsey Rogers played an important role as my "adversarial-helper." When I played the devil's advocate role vis-à-vis the Bank, he played that role vis-à-vis me (which was not always the same as defending the Bank). In an organization where open debate is not a big part of the culture (although the Bank is a raucous debating society in comparison with the intellectual lockstep of the IMF), this proved to be an important help that often saved me from wasting time analyzing a caricature of Bank policies.

Prior to my five years as economic advisor in the chief economist's front office, I worked for five years as a project manager in the educational or training wing of the Bank known then as the Economic Development Institute (and now as the World Bank Institute). I was originally recruited to EDI and the Bank by Vladimir Kreacic. He went on from EDI to return to operations (the lending part of the Bank), where he showed that one could do excellent work in the Bank in spite of the Bank.[10] Our boss in EDI was Xavier Simon, who exemplified the management theory of McGregor's Theory Y advocated here—get the best people who are intrinsically motivated to do the job and then give them the freedom and support they need to do the job. All of them shaped my years in EDI as a tremendous learning experience—which is the basis for chapter 6.

Over the decade at the Bank, I have been lucky to meet many people who understand how "to help people help themselves" and who have been able to do so even while working in the Bank. Generally speaking, these were people who had matured and gained experience in development before joining the Bank and who then carved out a niche to do good work on their own. Unfortunately their work is more the exception than the rule.[11] My general conclusion—that an organization of some eight thousand people working a few blocks from the White House will not, on the whole, help people in developing countries to help themselves—should not be seen as detracting from the worth or significance of their work.

For intellectual style and content (chap. 9) as well as for the foreword, I owe an obvious debt to Albert Hirschman. He has always been the master of letting each problem determine which intellectual discipline should be brought to bear—rather than trying to fit each problem to the Procrustean bed of one's intellectual formation. In the world of ideas, trespassing is a virtue, not a vice. In a conscious reference to his *Essays in Trespassing* (1981), my last book was entitled *Intellectual Trespassing as a Way of Life* (1995), and I tried to use that style here in a strategy of intellectual triangulation. The basic ideas of autonomy-respecting assistance arise across fields in the helping relationships of teaching, managing, counseling, and organizing as well as in providing development assistance. By liberally snatching testimony for these ideas from the different fields, I have tried to weave together a fabric that has some coherence and strength.

And finally, Vlasta Radan has given me the benefit—whether I asked for it or not—of her sardonic insights based on her life in the former Yugoslavia and on her empathetic observations of life in the developing countries on the receiving end of today's "development assistance."

1

Introduction & Overview

Helping People Help Themselves

The World Bank, the leading multilateral development agency, begins its mission statement with a dedication to helping people help themselves, and Oxfam, a leading nongovernmental organization (NGO) working on development, states that its "main aim is to help people to help themselves."[1] Perhaps the most successful example of development assistance in modern history was the Marshall Plan, which "did what it set out to do—help people help themselves" (Stern 1997). American official assistance to developing countries began with Harry Truman's "Point Four" program in 1949, which was conceived as a worldwide "program of helping underdeveloped nations to help themselves."[2]

John Dewey gave perhaps the best statement of the theme:

> The best kind of help to others, whenever possible, is indirect, and consists in such modifications of the conditions of life, of the general level of subsistence, as enables them independently to help themselves. (Dewey and Tufts 1908, 390)[3]

The idea and the rhetoric of "helping people help themselves" has been with us throughout the postwar period of official development assistance. For instance, we are all familiar with the ancient Chinese saying that if you give people fish, you feed them for a day, but if you teach them how to fish—or rather, if you enable them to learn how to fish—then they can feed themselves for a lifetime.[4] There is broad agreement—at least as a statement of high purpose—that helping people help themselves is the best methodology for development assistance in the developing countries as well as for other types of helping relationships.

Yet, in the course of this book, I argue that the notion of helping people help themselves is in fact a deep conundrum far more subtle than is realized by the many development agencies that routinely use the slogan. Indeed, most of the "helping people help themselves" rhetoric from the development agencies simply takes the idea as being the same as helping people. There is little or no suspicion that most "help" is in fact unhelpful in the sense of overriding or undercutting self-help and is thus quite antithetical to helping people help themselves. Thus much of our discourse must be negative—showing how most help is actually unhelpful in fostering "people helping themselves." On the positive side, genuine help is not something that can be done in a direct frontal way or mounted like an engineering project. You cannot force a person to act spontaneously. You cannot externally supply motivation to a person to act on his or her own motivation. This is often indicated with metaphors like "pushing on a string" or "you can lead a horse to water but cannot make him drink." But the failure of direct frontal help does not mean that external help is impossible. Genuine help is a far more humble and subtle activity that enables self-help in an indirect manner. Our task is to lay the intellectual foundation for the alternative methodology of development assistance that genuinely helps self-help.

The continuing inability of the major development agencies to understand the subtlety of helping people help themselves is evident in the repeated and increasingly frenetic calls for "massively increased aid" and "redoubled efforts" to push through more programs "to help" reach the periodically announced development goals.[5] In a historical perspective, international development assistance has only been a major official organized effort since the end of World War II. It has not been an outstanding success.[6] To some extent this is not surprising since the development of whole societies must surely be one of the most complex tasks facing humanity. It far outstrips the complexity and difficulty of building developmental infrastructure such as highways, power plants, and airports. Dreams that economic development could be engineered in the way that smallpox was conquered or someone was put on the moon have remained dreams. Indeed, I argue that it is not even the same type of task; it is not a task of engineering written large at the level of a society ("social engineering").

The failure is not for lack of money. While one can easily argue that many rich countries have been less than generous in their development aid, I argue that the failure has not been one of insufficient benevolence. The current calls for pouring more money into the conventional channels of development assistance are, unfortunately, not a solution and are not even a move in the right direction.[7] Indeed the approach to development assistance either as a task of social engineering or as an exercise in benevolent aid is part of the problem, not part of the solution. Many of the current forms of assistance not only are ineffective but tend to perpetuate if not exacerbate the problems of development.

I take a different approach, arguing that the problems lie not in the details of the development models nor in the content of the conditionalities imposed by development agencies but in the whole mode and philosophy of development assistance. The intellectual strategy is, in part, to look at the great historical thinkers who have wrestled with the basic conundrum of helping self-help and then to adapt and carry over their ideas and recommendations to development assistance. The results show a strong affinity with the seminal contemporary work in development of Albert Hirschman and Amartya Sen.

This approach exploits the fact that similar subtleties and difficulties occur in all fields of human assistance—in education broadly construed, management, psychology, and social organizing as well as in economic development. For instance, just as most development assistance is in fact unhelpful to self-help, so most schooling has little to do with real education in the sense of awakening and enabling a person's intrinsic thirst for learning. Various thinkers have wrestled with these parallel problems in all areas of human endeavor. Hence my methodology is "to triangulate" on the problems and solutions by bringing out the parallels between the fields in spite of much difference in the terminology and in the particulars. Workers in one vineyard can be heartened when they see workers in other vineyards facing similar problems and perhaps making some progress. Learning to translate between fields—giving due weight to differences—can be a powerful engine of discovery, and it is an engine that I try to exploit.

Across the fields, helping or assistance is a relationship between those offering assistance in some form, the helper or helpers, and those receiving the assistance, the doer or doers.[8] The helpers could be individuals, NGOs, or official bilateral or multilateral development agencies, and the doers could be individuals, organizations, or various levels of government in the developing countries. The relationship is the helper-doer relationship.

The Fundamental Helping Self-Help Conundrum

In every parent-child, teacher-student, manager-worker, or, generally, helper-doer relationship, there is the frustration of the helper wanting the doers to do something—and wanting them to do it for the doers' own reasons. Whatever cajoling, enticements, rewards, or bribes might be offered by the helpers will only supply external reasons. Yes, the doers might be induced to go through the motions in this way, but that is not the desired internally motivated performance. That frustration on the part of the helpers frames our basic problem.

The assumed goal is the doers helping themselves—autonomous development on the part of the doers.[9] The problem is how can the helpers "supply" help that actually furthers rather than overrides or undercuts the goal of the doers helping themselves. This is actually a paradox or conundrum; if the helpers are supplying help that directly influences the doers, then how can the doers really be "helping themselves"? Autonomy cannot be externally supplied. And if the doers are to become autonomous, then how can external helpers have any direct influence? This paradox of supplying help to self-help, "assisted self-reliance,"[10] or assisted autonomy is the *fundamental conundrum* of development assistance. David Korten terms it the "central paradox of social development: the need to exert influence over people for the purpose of building their capacity to control their own lives" (Korten 1983, 220). And Julie Fisher elaborates on this conundrum as the "central paradox of social development" (Fisher 1993, chap. 8).[11] Thomas Dichter refers to the "Classic development dilemma—how can you help people become self-sufficient?" (Dichter 2003, 271).

I have promised to emphasize the parallels between fields. The helping conundrum is always present wherever there is a helper-doer relationship. For instance, it is fundamental not just to social development but to education where it occurs in various forms as the "learning paradox." This learning paradox was clearly posed by the early twentieth-century Socratic-Kantian Leonard Nelson:

> Here we actually come up against the basic problem of education, which in its general form points to the question: How is education at all possible? If the end of education is rational self-determination, i.e., a condition in which the individual does not allow his behavior to be determined by outside influences but judges and acts according to his own insight, the question arises: How can we affect a person by outside influences so that he will not permit himself to be affected by outside influences? We must resolve this paradox or abandon the task of education. (Nelson 1949, 18–19)

The philosopher Gilbert Ryle gave a particularly clear statement of the same conundrum or paradox in education.

> How can one person teach another person to think things out for himself, since if he gives him, say, the new arithmetical thoughts, then they are not the pupil's own thoughts; or if they are his own thoughts, then he did not get them from his teacher? (Ryle 1967, 112)

Or again, the philosopher of science and education David Hawkins has outlined the conundrum in education that his daughter called the "central paradox of social development" (Fisher 1993).

> If we ask how the teacher-learner roles differ from those of master and slave, the answer is that the proper aim of teaching is precisely to affect those inner processes that . . . cannot in principle be made subject to external control, for they are just, in essence, the processes germane to independence, to autonomy, to self-control. (Hawkins 2000, 44)

This educational conundrum is the pedagogical version of the general helping self-help conundrum. Over the years, the seemingly endless debates about aid, help, assistance, and capacity building keep circling around and around the helping self-help conundrum in development assistance.

There is a dangerous bend in the road here that requires special caution.[12] This is a book about development assistance, the helper-doer relationship in development, but the methodology is, in part, to look at the helping conundrum in other fields to get insights into development aid. Thus when education is being examined in the works of Dewey, Ryle, or Hawkins, this is not about "education in development." It is about the helping conundrum in the helper-doer (teacher-learner) relationship in education as an engine of discovery and understanding about the similar helper-doer relationship in development assistance.

The Key Factor in Development Assistance: Autonomy-Respecting Help

Comment is required at this point about the assumed notion of "development." Growth or an increase in wealth (say, in the sense that could come from discovering oil or other natural resources) is not the goal; the goal is development as freedom or autonomy in the sense of the capabilities approach (e.g., Sen 1999; Nussbaum 2000; Alkire 2002) of having the capability and know-how to satisfy one's own needs.[13] But in the idea of development-as-autonomy, there is both autonomy as an end and as a means. In Sen's terms, freedom has both a constitutive and an instrumental role. This dual role of autonomy might be related to the old discourse about the "key" factor in economic development.

In the over half-century of development economics, there has been a parade of "key" factors in development. The initial key was capital formation, particularly the infrastructural capital of transportation, power, and communication networks. After much expensive disappointment, the emphasis shifted to education (the formation of human capital), health, and the satisfaction of basic needs. Without pretending to cover all the development fads, lately there has been an emphasis on governance (e.g., corruption), the atmospherics of the business climate, and the background institutions of a country. Frustration with attempts to specify the key elements has also resulted in vaporous affirmations that "everything is important." But from the viewpoint of development assistance, this focus of development economics on the key elements is "asking the wrong question."

Development agencies do not do development; at best they do development assistance. Perhaps an analogy with the Heisenberg uncertainty principle would be useful. Scientists who work at the atomic level do not have direct contact with the quantum reality; they only have contact with quantum realities as affected by their measurements. In a similar manner, we might say that the development agencies or, more generally, the helpers are not the doers of development. The helpers are involved only through a helper-doer relationship. Thus the question of whether this or that factor is key for the doers is *not* the first question *for the helpers*.

According to the helpers' latest theory of the key factor (e.g., capital, education, institutions, or business climate), the helpers might override or undercut the will of the doers in order to substitute their own will and thus push the doers in the direction of that "what." But this defeats the instrumental role of autonomy on the part of doers. The helpers cannot substitute for it.[14] Thus the first question for the helpers is not the "what" for the doers (which will surely vary from case to case) but the "how" for the helpers in their helper-doer relationship. And that question *does* have an answer; the key "how" is autonomy-respecting help—for the helpers to help in a way that respects, fosters, and sustains the autonomy of the doers. Help that defeats the instrumental role of autonomy on the part of the doers is unhelpful. When the doers have the will, there is a way; the best role for the helpers is to indirectly enable and expedite that way, not to try to substitute their will for that of the doers.

Unhelpful Help

There are many strategies for development assistance that may supply "help" in some form but actually do not help people help themselves. The forms of help that override or undercut people's capacity to help themselves are called *unhelpful help*. There are similar critiques of "help [that] does not help" that emphasize the demeaning psychological effects of most help (e.g., Gronemeyer 1992). The late Ivan Illich developed a general theory of how the "helping professions" (e.g., doctors, nurses, lawyers, psychologists, teachers, ministers, aid workers, and social workers in general), each with its cartel of professional associations, can counterproductively generate "needs" to be administered to by the helpers and thus lead to a learned disability (Illich 1972, 1976, 1978a, and, particularly, "Disabling Professions" in 1978b). These ideas have been further developed by John McKnight (1995) using the notion of "disabling help."

All those who make their living in the helping professions are in the paradoxical position of working to eliminate their own jobs—at least insofar as they actually try to help people help themselves. Hence a minimal requirement on a helping organization is that it views success in the helping relationship as implying a time-limited engagement. Schools that never graduate their pupils cannot be counted as a success. The helping professions are often organized so that they need neediness, disability, incapacity, and helplessness for the continuation of their own livelihood. In spite of the "helping self-help" rhetoric, helpers are often driven by their own organizational imperatives to use "giving-fish" strategies that tend to perpetuate the continuing need for helpers rather than "learn-how-to-fish" strategies that will foster the doers' autonomy—and that will, by the same token, remove the source of income for the helpers.

There are two different ways that the helper's will can supplant the doer's will and thwart autonomy and self-help:

1. the helper, by social engineering, deliberately tries to impose his will on the doer, or
2. the helper, by benevolent aid, replaces the doer's will with her will, perhaps inadvertently.

Override or *undercut* are shorthand for these two conceptually distinct yin and yang forms of unhelpful help (which may be combined as when benevolence hides the desire to control).[15] The two forms of unhelpful help seem to be accompanied by two different types of mental images of the doers in the eyes of the helpers. Social engineering is required when the doers are seen as going headstrong along the wrong path (perhaps for corrupt reasons) and too recalcitrant to follow what the helpers see as the right path. Benevolent aid is sponsored by the imagery of the doers or recipients as being helpless and thus unable to follow the right path. The two forms of unhelpful help lead to the "two Don'ts."

The First Don't: Don't Override Self-Help Capacity with Social Engineering

The First Form of Unhelpful Help

The "overriding" form of unhelpful help is a form of social engineering. Today the intellectual basis for social engineering is usually neoclassi-

cal economics. The helpers supply a set of instructions or conditionalities about what the doers should be doing, and they supply the external carrots and stick "motivation" to follow the blueprint as various
forms of aid to *override* the doers' own motivations. If we use the
metaphor of the doers as trying to work their way through a maze, then
the helpers as social engineers see themselves as helicoptering over the
maze, seeing the path to the goal, and supplying directions (knowledge) along with carrots and sticks (incentives) to override the doers'
own motivation and push the doers in the right direction. The social
engineering approach has had many critics, starting with Adam Smith.

> The man of system . . . seems to imagine that he can arrange the differ-
> ent members of a great society with as much ease as the hand arranges
> the different pieces upon a chessboard; he does not consider that the
> pieces upon the chessboard have no other principle of motion besides
> that which the hand impresses upon them; but that, in the great chess-
> board of human society, every single piece has a principle of motion of
> its own, altogether different from that which the legislature might
> choose to impress upon it. (Smith [1759] 1969, 342–43)

One could illustrate using World Bank experience since it is the leading international finance institution (IFI) and a trendsetter for the
development finance and aid industry. The Bank started after World
War II with financing civil engineering projects to build infrastructure
in developing countries. Soon, diminishing returns set in (only so
many airports or dams were needed), and the private sector proved
quite capable of providing infrastructure finance, so the Bank turned to
what is broadly called *policy-based lending*. That is how the World Bank
started its career as the Vatican[16] in the religion of social engineering.[17]

The object of the lending was the reform of what today we would
call the software of society: the departments of government, the educational and health care systems, the institutions of business, environmental safeguards, transportation and communications systems, and so
forth. The primary external incentive is the loan money with develop-
ment-oriented easy repayment terms that put the costs of the lending
well into the future beyond the political horizons of developing countries' governments. The teeth are in the loan terms and conditions,
which are called *conditionalities*. There might be well over a hundred

specific conditionalities or a smaller number of multipart or general conditionalities. Many loans are only released in a series of payments or tranches to the country, and in theory the country has to be making progress on the conditionalities in order to keep the loan money flowing.[18] The structural adjustment programs particularly in Africa were the most notorious examples of attempted social engineering using development lending as the instrument.[19] Since the countries most in need of development assistance are the least likely ones to pay off the loans, ever larger loans are necessary to create the illusion that the country is staying current in paying off its old loans. Hence, once a country starts down that path, it seems to be locked into that course.

The social engineering vision is that development can be "done" through a series of projects and programs incentivized by development aid (loans and sometimes grants) and executed according to the instructions or plans laid out in the conditionalities, with detailed technical assistance provided by visiting experts. Where there are "good" and "bad" factions in the government, the mental imagery in the agency is that a timely intervention (with a lot of money) can tip the balance in favor of the good guys and push the government over the hump so that deep-lying institutional change will then take place. Where multiple agencies operate in a country, there needs to be "donor coordination" to better channel the government in that right direction. No matter what reasons the opposition had against the changes before, they now have one more, namely that making the changes is kowtowing to an external influence. Hence it is even more likely that the reforms will be perfunctorily implemented or sabotaged and thus short-lived.

There is another reason why this mode of operation of exerting increasing control over the borrowers is built into the organizational structure of the IFIs (e.g., World Bank and regional development banks). As Albert Hirschman argued long ago (1970), there are two polar opposite ways to respond to deterioration in the quality of a relationship (e.g., the helper-doer relationship), namely exit (walk away) or voice (try to fix it). Commercial banks have no fixed relationship to their clients, so they control risks by walking away from bad borrowers—which leaves the responsibility to make improvements in the hands of the borrowers. But the IFIs (global and regional development banks) have a fixed set of members whom they are organizationally obligated to at least minimally service as the members in a financial cooperative. Hence they will gravitate toward the opposite strategy to reduce risk, namely voice—to try to better control and improve the doer-borrower.

Thus the social engineering approach of the IFIs is not just a gratuitous attitude adopted toward the client countries that can be changed by enlightened management. The social engineering vision of development assistance is entailed by the organizational structure of the IFIs. Yet that social engineering approach to development assistance is the vision that has largely failed over the last half century. All the enlightened programs aimed at putting the doers "in the driver's seat" are labors of Sisyphus; the IFIs will always organizationally gravitate back to the strategy of better controlling their borrowers. Our job is to build the theory or intellectual basis for an alternative approach to development assistance—an approach that does not take the current structure of the IFIs and other development agencies as a given.

The Indirect Approach

The notion of autonomy-respecting assistance provides the clue to a new approach. Autonomous action is action based on internal or own motivation. Any action based on the externally supplied motivation of carrots and sticks would be heteronomous. Any attempt to engineer autonomous action with external carrots or sticks would be self-defeating; the means are inconsistent with the motive and thus defeat the end. The inability to externally motivate own motivation harks back to the Socratic point about the unteachability of virtue.[20] This problem is often illustrated using the pushing-on-a-string or horse-to-water metaphors; externally engineered pressures can lead a horse to water (and can remove the obstacles to drinking), but that sort of motivation cannot make him drink.[21]

The whole idea of engineering change with supplied motivation or incentives might be termed the "direct approach." That formulation then points to the alternative as being an "indirect approach." The indirect approach to helping is not *to supply* motivation to the doers but *to find* and start with the existing own motivation of the doers and to supply help on that basis. Such help might take the form of changing the background constraints (breaking barriers) and resources so that the doers are enabled to effectively act on their own motivations.

Such an indirect approach is greatly complicated by the organizational pressures on helpers by their helping agencies and by the gaming strategies on the part of doers who only seek the aid. Aid-seeking doers will try to fake or mimic own motivation for real reforms, so the helpers face a difficult task of judgment.[22] But the difficulties of judgment are little in comparison with the pressures to move the money in the lender and donor agencies. One would expect large "type 2 errors,"[23] particularly as the aid-seeking doers evolve better means of mimicry and the money-moving helpers supply more corroboration for the theory of cognitive dissonance (i.e., judgment bending to be more consonant with self-interest).[24] There is grave doubt that the development agencies with organizational "business plans" based on providing aid by moving money could implement an autonomy-respecting indirect approach to development assistance. The agency must be able to say no without undercutting its own income. This is a paradigm example where—beyond a certain point—the more powerful the agency is, the less likely it is to pursue the indirect methods required to fulfill its mission. More power and money for the helpers leads to less autonomy-respecting help to the doers. Thus for the direct approach, more is less. For the indirect approach, less is more.

The Second Don't: Don't Undercut Self-Help Capacity with Benevolent Aid

The Second Form of Unhelpful Help

The second form of unhelpful help occurs when the helper undercuts self-help by inadvertently supplying the motivation for the doer to be in or remain in a condition to receive help. One prominent form is long-term charitable relief. The world is awash with disaster situations that call for various forms of short-term charitable relief. The point is not to oppose short-term relief operations but to understand how charitable relief operates in the longer term to erode the doers' incentives to help themselves—and thus it creates a dependency relationship. Charity corrupts; long-term charity corrupts long-term.[25] Such help creates a generalized form of "moral hazard"[26]—instead of enabling self-help, it becomes a perverse dependency-creating alternative to self-help. Charitable relief in the longer term is an "undercutting" form of unhelpful help.

Throughout this book, the World Bank is the principal case study. The past practice of the Bank is best understood in terms of social engineering, the "overriding" form of unhelpful help. However, the history of the Bank over the last fifty years is strewn with some recurring failures, particularly in sub-Sahara Africa. In the future, the Bank may be switching more to a disaster relief modality for manmade disasters (e.g., to help "drain the swamp" in collapsed or dysfunctional states as part of the war on terrorism). Hence if the first form of unhelpful help has been its past, its future may be in the second form of unhelpful help.

All aid to adults based on the simple condition of needing aid risks displacing the causality. The working assumption is that the condition of needing aid was externally imposed (e.g., a natural disaster); the aid recipient shares no responsibility. But over the course of time, such aid tends to undermine that assumption as the aid becomes a reward for staying in the state of needing aid,[27] all of which leads to rent-seeking or creates dependency and learned helplessness.

While the World Bank is the main ideologue and practitioner of social engineering, it may now more and more make loans that are more akin to benevolent aid since that also "moves the money." The imagery is that the state of underdevelopment in some countries resembles an ongoing (manmade) disaster so some disaster relief is necessary from the development agencies to attend to the basic necessities in those countries. Jane Jacobs has noted the failures during the 1970s of the World Bank "basic necessities" loans.

> The policy has converted client countries into vast charity wards. While this may or may not be justifiable as philanthropy, it is not my definition of meaningful economic development. Nor is it what was ostensibly offered to poor countries, told as they were that money they borrowed to carry out World Bank programs was money to buy development of their economies. (1984, 91–92)

Today this type of "development aid as disaster relief" reasoning is even stronger due to the AIDS crisis. Over the course of time, this relief becomes the unhelpful help that undermines self-help.[28] The alternative is help based not on needs or deficiencies but on the active initiative to use existing capacities to address problems.[29]

The Time-Inconsistency Problem of "Gap-Filling Aid"

One standard scenario is that *given* a genuine self-help project with a resource gap, gap-filling aid enables the self-help project to go forward. This might actually happen when the project is motivated independently of the offer of aid. But as in the case of continuing charity, there is the time-consistency problem that the continuing offer of aid tends to make the motivation aid driven. In the case of disaster relief, the continuing offer of aid takes the sting out of staying in a needful condition. While the needful condition was initially exogenous or independent of aid, staying in that condition may become an endogenous means for getting more aid. Unless gap-filling aid is rigorously time limited, the continuing offer of aid leads to new projects that are partly incentivized by the aid offer. Instead of self-help projects *that were initially afoot on their own*, doers may create aid-seeking projects camouflaged in a rhetoric of self-help.

Relief Assistance as Generalized Moral Hazard

The first Don't deals with social engineering as a form of unhelpful help that overrides (hopefully temporarily) any self-help capacity in order to get the doers "to do the right thing." The second Don't deals with benevolent aid that, unless very temporary, will tend to undermine self-help capacity. Sometimes aid is sought by a country because of a self-perceived lack of efficacy. Aid granted out of benevolence, even without carrots and sticks, has the adverse effect of reinforcing the lack of self-confidence and doubts about one's own efficacy. Eleemosynary aid to relieve the symptoms of poverty may create a "moral hazard" situation to weaken reform incentives and attenuate efforts for positive developmental change to eliminate poverty (see Maren 1997; Bräutigam 2000).

Moral hazard refers to the phenomenon where excessive insurance relieves the insured from taking normal precautions, so risky behavior might be increased. The phrase is applied generally to opportunistic actions undertaken because some arrangement has relieved the doers from bearing the full responsibility for their actions. Benevolent help softens the incentives for people to help themselves.

In the insurance example, the limit case of no insurance (which means complete self-insurance) certainly "solves" the problem of moral hazard since the individual then has full incentives to take precautions to prevent accidents. Yet the "no insurance" option forgoes the benefits of insurance. There is no best solution of complete insurance without moral hazard, but there are partial solutions in the form of co-payments and deductibles so that the insured party retains some risk and thus some incentive to make investments in normal precautions (e.g., fire alarms or sprinklers).

In a similar manner, the conservative approach of no assistance could be seen as the tough love limit case of autonomy-respecting assistance. It certainly "solves" the problem of softened incentives for self-help, but it foregoes forms of positive assistance that might be autonomy respecting. If aid does not smother the incentives for self-help, then substantial matching payments or first-stage funding by the doers are commitment mechanisms or ways of showing that they are committed *on their own* to the undertaking. This problem suggests the possibility that the post–World War II development assistance effort from the developed countries to the developing world has created a massive generalized moral hazard problem.[30]

Surely one bright spot was the Marshall Plan, which, in many ways, provided a model for later development efforts. Yet it also contained the seeds of moral hazard. Robert Marjolin, the French architect of the Marshall Plan, notes in a 1952 memo that American aid continuing over a longer term could have precisely that effect.

> Although American aid has been a necessary remedy over a period, and will continue to be for a time, one is bound to acknowledge that in the long run it has had dangerous psychological and political effects. . . . It is making more difficult the task of the governments of western Europe trying to bring about a thorough economic and financial rehabilitation. The idea that it is always possible to call on American aid, that here is the ever-present cure for external payments deficits, is a factor destructive of willpower. It is difficult to hope that, while this recourse continues to exist, the nations of western Europe will apply, for a sufficient length of time, the courageous economic and financial policy that will enable them to meet their needs from their own resources without the contribution of external aid. (quoted in Marjolin 1989, 241)

However, the demands of the Korean War and the lack of a permanent aid bureaucracy resulted in the winding down of American aid. If the industrial countries of Western Europe faced moral hazard problems in the short-lived Marshall Plan, one can only begin to fathom the extent of the moral hazard problem today in developing countries that face well-established professional aid providers in the developed countries who must constantly reinvent ways "to move the money"—moral hazard writ large. Today's aid business may therefore be a paradigm example of the counterproductive dependency-creating practices that Ivan Illich wrote about across the various helping professions.

Money is a mixed blessing—to the extent that it is a blessing at all in development assistance. As long as money continues to be the leading edge of development assistance,[31] then the problems of moral hazard will only be compounded. Whenever money becomes the leading edge of assistance, then the supply of aid seems to create and perpetuate the demand for it—which might be labeled as "Say's Law of Development Aid."[32] Aid that might in a few cases be autonomy-respecting assistance ends up "chasing its own tail" by funding needs or projects induced by the offer of aid—all to the detriment of building self-help capacity. What starts as the benevolent impulse thus becomes one of the major problems in the postwar effort toward capacity building and development.

The Scylla and Charybdis of Development Assistance

The "benevolent" impulse to give charitable relief and the "enlightened" impulse to do social engineering are the Scylla and Charybdis facing the benevolent and enlightened leaders and staff of the development agencies. Several major difficulties lie in the path of autonomy-respecting help. The first difficulty to be overcome—the pons asinorum to be crossed—is the simple recognition of the pitfalls of social engineering on the one hand and of benevolent aid on the other hand.

Again and again, one finds social engineering blueprints "to do X" being defended by development agencies on the grounds that the doers should indeed do X. But that is not the question. There seems to be little or no real recognition that if the doers do X only to satisfy conditionalities and thus receive aid, then the motive will falsify the action, the reforms will not be well implemented, and the policy changes will not be sustained. Hence all the arguments about the benefits of doing X miss the point. Paraphrasing Kierkegaard, it is not so much the "what" of reform that counts, but the "how"—if the reform is to take root and be sustainable.[33]

And again and again, one finds benevolent aid being defended as "doing good" in the sense of "delivering resources to the poor" without any real recognition as to how this undercuts the incentives for developing self-reliance. All the arguments about the relief as being help miss the point. It is an unhelpful form of help that in the longer term undercuts capacity building and autonomous development. Developmental processes are rooted in time, not in the ambitions of helpers in a rush to do good.

The other major difficulty to be overcome is the gap between rhetoric and reality. Development agencies are quite adept at adopting the language of being against "charity" and "blueprint-driven social engineering" and being in favor of "helping people help themselves." Whole public relations departments are devoted to the effort. The challenge is that it is a rather subtle matter to overcome the basic conundrum and to supply help in an indirect way that does not override or undercut the development of the capacity for self-help. Again and again, reborn managers in restructured agencies use recycled rhetoric to launch refurbished programs in social engineering or charitable relief or both.

Knowledge-Based Development Assistance

The Cognitive Dimension of Development Assistance

There are always two sides to a person's relationship with the world: the *volitional* side trying to get the world to correspond more to some prescriptive representation or model and the *cognitive* side trying to get one's descriptive representation or model to correspond more to the world.[34] Most of our analysis is concerned with the volitional side of the helper-doer relationship (e.g., actions based on external motives versus those based on internal or own motivation) but sometimes the focus is on the cognitive side (e.g., beliefs based on compliance with external authority versus beliefs based on the exercise of critical reason and rational judgment). There is no question of separation: action should be guided by cognition, and cognition at best arises out of action (as emphasized by John Dewey). But on various occasions, it may add to clarity to make a parallel consideration of the volitional and cognitive sides of a question. For our main case study of the World Bank, the two dimensions are the Bank as a money bank and the Bank as the knowledge bank.

The problems in aid-based assistance tend to be reproduced in their own way in knowledge-based assistance. The main problems lie in the standard theory-in-use (regardless of the espoused theory) that the agency has "development knowledge" in the form of answers that need to be taught, transmitted, and transferred to the target population of doers. That methodology is taken as so obvious that the focus is simply on how to disseminate the knowledge, how to expand the scale of the knowledge transmission in the client country, and how to measure and evaluate the impact of these efforts. In the old Chinese metaphor, it is a matter of "giving out more and more fish."

The Two Don'ts in Knowledge-Based Assistance

The two Don'ts in money-based aid are also reproduced in knowledge-based assistance. Conditionalized monetary aid tries to supply the motivation for the doers to do what the helpers consider as the right thing (i.e., the helpers try "to supply the right will" to the doers). The corresponding problem in knowledge-based aid is supplying biased information, partisan econometrics, and one-sided arguments to supply and induce "the right belief" in the doers (learners). Just as unconditional aid may be avoided for fear that the doers might not "do the right thing," allowing the learners to hear all sides of a question or perform their own experiments may be avoided or discouraged for fear that the learners might not "draw the right conclusions." In both cases, *distortionary* help compromises the autonomy of the doers.

The second Don't focuses on how charitable relief undercuts the doers' incentives to develop the capacity to help themselves. The corresponding problem in knowledge-based assistance is that transmitting or disseminating development knowledge to the doers gives them only borrowed opinions, not knowledge, and undercuts the development of their own learning capacity.

> That real education aims at imparting knowledge rather than opinion, that knowledge cannot be handed over ready-made but has to be appropriated by the knower, that appropriation is possible only through one's own search, and that to make him aware of his ignorance is to start a man on the search for knowledge—these are the considerations that govern and determine the Socratic method of teaching. (Versényi 1963, 117)

Socratic Approach to Doers' Active Learning

The alternative indirect approach in pedagogy as well as knowledge-based assistance starts with Socrates. Instead of having the answers to be disseminated, Socrates displayed the "ignorance" or humility of knowing that he did not know. Instead of the teaching that put the learner in a passive role, Socrates proceeded by getting the learner to actively try to answer questions or resolve problems. Indeed, the key to the indirect approach is for the helper to facilitate the doer taking the active role (be in the driver's seat).

It is rather difficult to imagine elite development agencies adopting this stance of Socratic humility and critical rationality even though it is central to the methodology of science (in contrast to the closed society of a church or party organization that has the answers and has the mission to disseminate the gospel). Applying a similar model to the dialogue between a development agency and a client country would require the agency to exercise Socratic restraint against the arrogant assertion of official views about development issues—perhaps the most complex issues facing humankind. If there are relevant grounds for any views preferred by agency officials, then such grounds should eventually emerge from the dialogue and the country's own learning experiences. Yet one should not underestimate the difficulties of implementing this sort of intellectual humility or Socratic ignorance on the part of elite development officials who justify their own prestige on the basis of their expertise. The more pretentious the agency, the less likely it is to pursue an indirect Socratic approach to cognitive capacity building. Here again, less is more.

The volitional and cognitive dimensions of the two Don'ts are summarized in the table 1.

The Three Dos

The First Do: Start from Where the Doers Are

The *via negativa* of the two Don'ts needs to be supplemented by three Dos. Together the two Don'ts and the three Dos outline the alternative autonomy-respecting approach to both the volitional and cognitive sides of development assistance.

To be transformative, a process of change must start from where the doers are. Yet this is where a common error occurs. Reformers oriented toward utopian social engineering (see Popper 1962) aim to wipe the slate clean. In institutional terms, any attempt to transform the current "flawed," "retrograde," or even "evil" institutions is viewed as only staining or polluting the change process. In the debate about shock therapy in the transition economies, Jeffrey Sachs (1993) and others argued that slate-cleaning shock therapy (doing everything quickly) was needed since "you can't jump over a chasm in two leaps." But the leap of institutional shock therapy fell far short of the other side of the chasm since people "need a bridge to cross from their own experience to a new way" (Alinsky 1971, xxi). It will take the transition countries much longer to climb out of the chasm than it would have taken if a bridge had been built step by step.

Similar considerations argue for an evolutionary and incremental strategy in poor countries rather than trying to jump to new institutions.

Education does not "jump"; it is a gradual process of great subtlety. Organization does not "jump"; it must gradually evolve to fit changing circumstances. And much the same goes for discipline. All three must evolve step by step, and the foremost task of development policy must be to speed this evolution. (Schumacher 1973, 168–69)

Given a choice between helpers using the momentum of bottom-up involvement in flawed reforms and the top-down social engineering of

TABLE 1. Volitional and Cognitive Dimensions of Help

Help	Volitional Dimension	Cognitive Dimension
Unhelpful help 1: social engineering	Helper provides "motivation" for doer to do the "right thing" (aid and conditionalities as "carrots and sticks").	Helper as authority teaches "right answers" based on one-sided arguments to passive doer (student) like "pouring water into a pitcher."
Unhelpful help 2: benevolent aid	Helper provides aid to doer to "solve problem" by relieving symptoms until next time.	Helper gives "answers" to doe save doer the trouble of learning and appropriating knowledge.
Autonomy-respecting help	Enabling helper searches for where "virtue is afoot on its own" in the small and catalyzes social and economic linkages to spread successes.	Socratic helper does not give answers but facilitates doer's own learning (e.g., experiments) and then peer-to-peer learning between doers.

model institutions, the "start from where the doers are" principle (the first Do) argues for the former. Applied to technical cooperation, it would be better (1) for the helpers to train local doers to do the job, even if locals do it poorly at first, so long as there is a learning mechanism than (2) for the helpers to do the job well but with little or no local capacity building. Sometimes the best form of training is for the helper to broker horizontal learning between the would-be doers and those who have already successfully done it under similar circumstances. But, in any case, the organizational pressures on the helpers are to show their bosses that the helpers "did it right" by, in effect, "doing it themselves."

The Second Do: See the World through the Doers' Eyes

Frustrated task managers in the World Bank have been heard to muse about lobotomies or memory erasers that would make their recalcitrant clients wake up the next day and start "doing things in the right way." Then development advice would not need to be tailored to local circumstances. Generic advice would suffice; one message would fit all blank slates. But failing that, it is necessary to acquire a deeper knowledge of the present institutions. This is done by, in effect, learning to see the world through the eyes of the policymakers and people in the country.

An autonomy-respecting interaction between teacher and learner requires that the teacher have an empathetic understanding with the student. If the teacher can understand the learning experience of the student, then the teacher can use his or her superior knowledge to help the student. This help does not take the form of telling the student the answer or solution but of offering advice or guidance, perhaps away from a dead-end path, to assist the student to make "transitions and consolidations" (Hawkins 2000, 44) in the active appropriation of knowledge. The teacher, according to Dewey's learner-centered pedagogy, must be able to see the world through the eyes of the students and within the limits of their experience and at the same time to lend the teacher's viewpoint to offer guideposts. The great mathematician-teacher George Polya emphasized that the Socratic teacher could best foster active learning by asking questions, when necessary, that might have occurred to the student, not questions that show off the teacher's greater knowledge. The questions that involve seeing through the student's eyes and starting from where the student is were called *inside help* as opposed to *outside help*.

> Outside help has very little chance to be instructive—appearing out of the blue, as *deus ex machina*, it can easily be disappointing. Inside help may be the most instructive thing the teacher can offer; the student may catch on, he can realize that the question helps and that he could have put that question to himself by himself. And so the student may learn to use that question; the voice of the teacher may become for him an inner voice which warns him when a similar situation arises. (Polya 1965, 137)

Similarly, in Carl Rogers's notion of client-centered therapy (1951), the counselor needs to enter the "internal frame of reference of the client" in order that assistance can be given that respects the actual capacity of the person. These subtleties in the helping relationship are explored in more detail later.

The Third Do: Respect the Autonomy of the Doers

The third Do summarizes the overall goal of assistance to autonomous development. The tasks of development are fundamentally different from engineering tasks since they focus not on just changing the natural environment but on fostering change in people (i.e., beings capable of autonomy). This book explores a philosophy of autonomous development that provides intellectual background for ideas and themes such as the theme of the developing country being "in the driver's seat" (autonomous) and self-reliantly helping itself.[35] On the negative side, the suspicion is that externally applied carrots and sticks (conditionalities) do not "buy" sustainable policy changes or ownership. Terms like *empowerment, participation, inclusion,* and *involvement* are all fine but tend to be abused to refer to the doers "participating" in a scheme being undertaken by the helpers. These fine phrases will not be heavily used here since the focus is clearly on the doers taking the active role with the helpers having an indirect, enabling role.

The Kantian notion of autonomy is emphasized here ("autonomy-respecting assistance"), although the roots of the emphases on autonomous volitions and critical reason go back at least to Socrates.[36] One of the main themes is John Dewey's notion of active learning writ large and applied broadly to social, political, and economic processes. The broad theme is that people have a natural *ownership* of the results of their own activities (the fruits of their labor) as opposed to what is done to or for them. This book develops this fruits-of-one's-labor idea in terms of *psychological* ownership.[37] The ideas arrived at here also have a considerable overlap with Amartya Sen's emphasis on capabilities, agency, and development as freedom (essentially *autonomy* in my vocabulary).[38] The philosophical congruence with Sen's ideas has increased my confidence in the approach taken here.

Eight Thinkers Triangulate a Theory of Autonomy-Respecting Help

The topic of helping people help themselves is approached by multidisciplinary triangulation[39] (i.e., by looking at the commonalties in different examples of relationships where one party, the helper, is trying to help or enable certain others, the doers, to carry out some activity). The target example of the helper-doer relationship is the relationship between a development advisor or agency and a client country. The method is to look for wisdom about the helping relationship in pedagogy, management theory, psychotherapy, community organizing, and community education. Organized development assistance is a relatively new field of study arising only in the post–World War II period. Hence we turn to older thinkers in these other fields to extract their insights. Eight prominent and relatively modern thinkers are focused on to triangulate on a theory of autonomy-respecting help:

- Albert Hirschman, on the relationship between a development advisor and a government,
- E. F. Schumacher, on the relationship between a development agency and a country,
- Saul Alinsky, on the relationship between a community organizer and the community (or its people's organization),
- Paulo Freire, on the relationship between an educator and a peasant (or urban poor) community,
- John Dewey, on the relationship between a teacher and a learner,
- Douglas McGregor, on the (Theory Y) relationship between a manager and workers,

- Carl Rogers, on the relationship between a therapist and a client, and
- Søren Kierkegaard, on the relationship between a spiritual teacher and a learner.

Representative quotations on the five themes are gathered in the appendix. The argument is not that all these relationships are the same but that there are commonalties when the party in the helper role acts so as to help the parties in the doer role to help themselves. The fact that such diverse thinkers in different fields arrive at interestingly similar conclusions helps to triangulate the results and increases our confidence in the common principles.

This book is an essay in the human sciences where the emphasis is on the coherence of views expressed across a wide variety of disciplines and frameworks so that interconnections may be emphasized. I have taken pains to mark my tracks, not cover them. The text is liberally sprinkled with quotations so that the interested reader can follow the Ariadne's thread of the themes back into the original texts. Often one needs a "handle" or "entering wedge" in order to understand as least a part of some thinkers' works. The quotations may provide a bridge from this work into the works of the many authors who have explored these themes with more depth and supporting arguments in the various disciplines. The point is not to present prepackaged solutions. By seeing a variety of approach roads, the reader may be helped to make the "transitions and consolidations" necessary to make the journey him- or herself.

2

Internal & External Motivation

Beyond *Homo economicus*

Toward a Critique of Agency Theory

In the World Bank, I have heard it said that if economists understand anything, it is incentives. Effective development assistance is supposed to lie in engineering the right motivation—"getting the incentives right." The economic model of *Homo economicus* as a utility-maximizing or incentive-driven creature is, however, incomplete in one basic respect: it leaves out the question of whether the *human source* of the incentives or motivation is external (other people) or internal (own self). It is this matter of source, internal or external, that turns out to be key to the helping relationship.

Development aid laden with conditions can provide the incentives to engineer certain behaviors of the doers. But in the end, it will typically not bring real change because the source of the motivation is external and thus the effort is not "owned" by the doers. In the philosophical language of Kant, the motivation is heteronomous. Autonomous activity is based on the doers' internal or own motivation (i.e., motivation not being manipulated by some external will). Autonomy-respecting assistance must therefore take a different form; it is not a matter of getting the (external) incentives right. This lesson is not unique to development; it is an old theme in education and is increasingly understood in management.

For our purposes, heteronomy must be based on some other human will,[1] not natural events. This dependence on other human wills is familiar in the notions of oppression or coercion.

> "The nature of things does not madden us, only ill will does," said Rousseau. The criterion of oppression is the part that I believe to be played by other human beings, directly or indirectly, with or without the intention of doing so, in frustrating my wishes. (Berlin 1969, 123)

Freidrich Hayek makes the same point about coercion.

> In this sense "freedom" refers solely to a relation of men to other men, and the only infringement of it is coercion by men. This means, in particular, that the range of physical possibilities from which a person can choose at a given moment has no direct relevance to freedom. (Hayek 1960, 12)

Natural events on Robinson Crusoe's island might lead to hardship and suffering but never coercion or oppression. Thus in the juxtaposition of self with "other" as a source of motivation, *other* refers to other human wills. For our purposes, "external" motivation is motivation sourced in the will of others. Thus our basic contrast between external and internal (or own) motivation is relational and thus is not exactly the same as but is closely related to the contrast of extrinsic with intrinsic motivation. Intrinsic motivation could not be external; any external motivation would have to operate through extrinsic incentives. But all motivation for Crusoe would be internal or own motivation (prior to the arrival of Friday) even though much of it was concerned with obtaining food, clothing, and shelter—activities not done for their own sake.

The most sophisticated development of this engineered-incentives view in current economics is in "agency theory," which is relational (unlike the simple notion of *Homo economicus*). The theory is about how a "principal" can design contracts and organizations (or institutions) with the appropriate carrots and sticks so that by following their own interests the "agents" will do the principal's bidding.[2] The problem in agency theory is the neglect of the effects of the human source of the agent's motivation; if the source of the motivation is in the human will of the principal, then it cannot be the agent's own motivation. The alternative to this principal-agent relationship is the autonomy-respecting helper-doer relationship.

The principal-agent language is borrowed from the legal relationship of agency and is used in economics in a much broader context.[3] Douglas McGregor, writing in 1948 before the principal-agent language was established in the economics and management literature, refers to the principal and agent respectively as A and B: "A always refers to the individual (or group) who is attempting to induce a behavior change, and B always refers to the individual (or group) whose behavior is affected" (McGregor 1948; reprinted in 1966, 155).

Agency theory is certainly based on *Homo economicus* or, in Mc-Gregor's terms, on the Theory X view of people (McGregor 1960, 1966, 1967). Positive and negative external economic incentives (carrots and sticks) must be supplied by the principal to induce the appropriate behavior by the agents. Left to their own devices, agents cannot be trusted to act in the manner desired by the principal, so an incentive structure must be externally applied to redirect and channel the agents in the desired manner. The economic theory of agency and its application to institutional design describes a sophisticated *direct* approach. One would be tempted to see the overestimation of external motivation as an occupational disease of economists—if it were not their occupation.[4]

Part of our task is to describe autonomy-respecting indirect approaches to the helper-doer relationship—as an alternative to the economic treatment of the principal-agent relationship. McGregor's alternative Theory Y is an indirect approach. Many of the modern management strategies that have grown out of McGregor's classic formulation of Theory Y will thus have a significant indirect component. The direct approach of Theory X and the indirect approach of Theory Y cannot simply be applied at the same time (although managers often seem to try). The approaches are more substitutes than complements, but it is not simply a matter of choosing one or the other. It is a question of foreground and background. The case in favor of a Theory Y approach is not a case against any human-sourced carrots or sticks per se but a case that the carrots and sticks should be kept in the background as motivational backstops. It is a question of who is in the driver's seat, not who is in the car.

Piece rates and pay-for-performance schemes are examples of carrots trying to get people's attention and thus get in the foreground to channel their actions. An equitable salary more geared to experience and seniority would be an example of keeping the carrot of pay in the background (in which case it is not the determining carrot) so that other more intrinsic motives might emerge in the foreground to guide action. The tight coupling of pay with performance, as implied whenever possible by agency theory, is beside the point when the pay is in the motivational background. For instance, W. Edwards Deming's *New Economics for Industry, Government, Education* recommends, "Abolish incentive pay and pay based on performance" (Deming 1994, 28) (e.g., to pay salespeople by salary rather than by commission, essentially the opposite of what agency theory or the conventional economic approach would suggest). Deming recommends replacing a system based on monitoring and quality bonuses with a system using (for the most part) trust based on self-esteem and pride in the quality of one's work.

In short, this approach to quality relies not on cleverly constructed pay-for-performance schedules but on switching over to a quality system driven largely by intrinsic motivators such as self-esteem and pride in one's work—in short, quality as a calling. The cost-based "low road" relies on controlling production with external incentives, while the quality-based "high road" focuses on developing intrinsic motivation while not ignoring backstop economic incentives.[5] The point is not to eliminate material incentives in place of moral ones (a common mistake in "utopian" design) but to keep the extrinsic incentives in the motivational background so that they are not controlling.

The difficulties many economists have in understanding noneconomic motivation is easily matched by the managers in businesses, organizations, and government who perennially (re)discover "performance-based pay," "output-based evaluations," "results-based management," "stock-option-based management compensation,"[6] and so forth—as if other managers had not thought of such external-measurement-based extrinsic motivators since the dawn of time.

David Hawkins sarcastically makes the parallel with education clear.

> In this way, we have discovered the carrot, the stick, the blinder, the shoe, the collar, the bit, the curb, and many other refinements. . . . We need to remind ourselves that all these kinds of things . . . have been in the public domain for a long time, and that we should replace the patent office with an institute for the study of educational antiquities. (Hawkins 2000, 43)

While educational carrots and sticks can prompt some short-term retention of information and regurgitation on tests, learning that can be sustained and have a transformative effect on the learner needs to be based on more intrinsic motives. And the subtleties of teaching in an autonomy-respecting manner are quickly lost when teachers are subjected to the pedagogical versions of output-based evaluations and performance-based pay. When teachers and students have extrinsic motives in their motivational foreground, then teachers will "teach to the test" and students will see their education only as a way to signal their eligibility for those rewards (see Kohn 1993, 1999).

Nondistortionary Interventions

Nondistortionary Taxes and Subsidies

It is possible to be a little more precise about how the intervention of a principal or helper could distort the original (preintervention) motivation of the agent or doer. It would seem a necessary condition for an autonomy-respecting intervention is that it not distort the original motivation of the doers. The helper should enable the doer without exerting control (in the sense of distorting or "supplying" motivation).

The doer's decision making is assumed to be determined by a relationship between resources and decisions: given the resources available to the doer, the decision is determined. An intervention by the helper is nondistortionary (ND) if it does not change what the doer would do—given sufficient resources. In that sense, the intervention does not distort the original motivation of the doer.[7] It helps the doer to do what the doer already wanted to do but didn't have the resources or was otherwise constrained from doing.

This initial notion looks only to the mode of intervention by the helper, not to the preferences or choices. There is no assumption that the choices of the doer are in any sense autonomous or internal, only that the intervention did not distort them one way or the other. For instance, a lump-sum monetary gift to a drug addict or unrestricted aid to a country addicted to aid or to a corrupt regime would be ND. Choices that are autonomous in the sense of being based on internal or own motivation are considered later.

If we think of the doer as a consumer allocating fixed income between goods, then a lump-sum income tax or subsidy would be an example of an ND intervention. In contrast, an excise tax or subsidy attached to particular goods would "supply" motivation to use less or more of those goods. The relationship between income and consumer choices is the "income-consumption curve," so an ND intervention (e.g., a lump-sum change in income) is one that does not shift the income consumption curve.[8] For instance, a lump-sum grant of income would allow the consumer to buy what she already wanted to buy but lacked the resources for.

For an informal example, suppose one gives fifty dollars bus fare to one's daughter to visit Uncle Henry and Aunt Louise during some college holidays. What if the grant was unrestricted and could have been spent on anything (and without "moral pressure")? If the money was still used for the bus fare, then we could say that the daughter was already motivated to make the visit and just needed the resources. Otherwise, the restricted grant was "supplying" motivation in addition to resources.

The Common Pool Approach to Aid

One form of distortionary development aid (akin to an alcohol tax or a subsidy to stop drinking) is aid accompanied with a conditionality to implement a certain institutional reform. There is no attempt to respect autonomy or internal motivation; the explicit purpose is "to supply" the motivation to make the reform. It has become clear over the decades that this sort of aid is ineffective (e.g., Collier 1997; World Bank 1998a; Gilbert and Vines 2000). How might the lump-sum concept in tax design be applied here?

Since conditionality-based aid is akin to a subsidy only on certain commodities, more independence would be obtained by a lump-sum subsidy to those whose activities can be supported. This is the root idea in what is called the "common pool" approach to development assistance (Kanbur and Sandler 1999; World Bank 2000).[9] Through a national process of consensus building, a government in a developing country would draw up a reform program that makes sense to it independent of and not "distorted" by specific donor intentions (very difficult since donors always find ways to make their desires known). To achieve this independence under this common pool approach, "there would not be discussions about specific sums of money from specific donors for specific projects. Such discussions would detrimentally affect the process of national consensus-building by undermining the country's sense of ownership" (Kanbur and Sandler 1999, 43) When the national plan was thus "given," the donors would then decide how much to fund though a common pool. This approach is designed to decouple the country's plans from the specific donors' intentions so that the country might retain more ownership.[10] Donor assistance through such a mechanism would thus be more compatible with the country's autonomy.

This common pool approach is a many-helpers-one-doer model but the same basic idea could be applied to a one-helper-many-doers situation. Instead of the doer determining plans independent of the helpers' aid, a single helper could supply a fixed envelope of aid to a number of doers who would then have to justify needs and uses to each other and come to a collective decision about the aid allocation. Such a mechanism was part of the original Marshall Plan; the European countries needed to work out amongst themselves how the total aid would be allocated between them.[11] Such a model might be applied in a region where countries have a long history of aid dependency. Instead of each country "gaming" an international aid provider, a fixed envelope of aid could be provided, and then the countries would have to justify to each other how it would be divided and come to an agreement. The funds might be used for loans instead of grants so that the countries would then be more accountable to their peers for the use and repayment of the funds. The dynamics of this South-South peer group monitoring (perhaps arranged through a regional development bank) would be preferable to today's North-South dependency relationships.

Independence Today, "Supply Effect" Tomorrow

A common problem in policy analysis is to ignore time consistency problems. If something makes sense as a one-time-only proposal, would it work on a continuing basis? One common model is to take the actions of the doers as given and then to offer aid or subsidies to assist the doers to complete their given activities successfully. The "independence" assumption is hidden in the assumed "givenness" of the doers' actions. Examples run the gamut from subsidies for infants of unwed mothers to tariffs protecting infant industries. But the independence assumption may fail over a period of time. A simple example: "given" a kidnapping today, paying the ransom may get the loved one back, but it may also lead to the *supply effect* of more kidnappings tomorrow. Across time, the supply of kidnappings is not given.[12]

The questions of reforming aid policy (e.g., welfare, industrial, or development policy) revolve around attempts to establish independence as best as possible—to sterilize as much as possible the effect of the helper's emission of aid on the doer's motivation to remain needy in order to qualify for more aid.[13]

Independence and Moral Hazard

We have already touched on one of the primary examples of nonindependence: "moral hazard" in insurance. In the ideal situation, a party will receive benefits under conditions that are supposed to be independent of the party's conduct (e.g., damages resulting from accidents). The problem of (generalized) moral hazard occurs when these ideal conditions break down and the party by either commissions or omissions can change the conditions to increase the chances of receiving the benefits. In the original insurance example, the intervention of the helper is the issuing of the insurance policy for the doer. The activities of the doer that need to be preserved independent of the intervention are the precautions taken by the doer to prevent insured-against events from occurring. Moral hazard occurs when the insurance is so complete that it dulls the incentives to take precautions so the hazards of the insured-against events actually increase as a result of the insurance. Thus the owner of an overinsured old warehouse might be less careful to keep all the fire-prevention equipment in good working order. A person might drive with less care with a seatbelt or airbag than otherwise.

The general problem of moral hazard in any form of aid is that it may dull the incentives for self-help.[14]

> Communities, especially poor ones, can benefit from external assistance, but to rely very much on it creates a dependency that may prove to be counterproductive. The concomitant paternalism is likely to inhibit self-help and even undermine long-standing patterns of community initiative. (Esman and Uphoff 1984, 77)

Orlando Patterson has noted that the American welfare system has in the past "created serious moral hazards for certain groups" and that "the challenge is to find ways to support individuals in their efforts to reform themselves" (Patterson 2002, 35–36).

This generalized form of moral hazard (opportunism due to weakened incentives to make an effort) is illustrated in a simple game that James Buchanan calls the Samaritan's dilemma. Regardless of whether the recipient or doer makes a high or low effort, the helper or Samaritan (with the payoff listed on the left) is better off by choosing to help. Once the recipient anticipates this, then he or she is better off (with the payoffs listed on the right) by choosing the low-effort option since the adverse consequences of only making a low effort have been masked by the aid.[15]

How is the problem of moral hazard addressed in insurance? Since the nonindependence comes from smothering the precautionary incentives with insurance, the idea is to reduce the insurance somewhat to restore "sufficient" precautionary motives. There is not necessarily a perfect solution to the conflicting goals of insurance and eliminating moral hazard. Eliminating insurance altogether would certainly "solve" the moral hazard problem, but it would sacrifice the original goals of having insurance. Conservatives who are quite attentive to moral hazard phenomena in social welfare policies traditionally favor this "no welfare" solution to the moral hazard problem[16] (which sacrifices the original goals of the welfare program). The older "penal solution" of forced labor in a poorhouse would be akin to not only eliminating safety nets in the form of seatbelts or airbags but putting a spike in the center of the steering wheel.

Commitment Mechanisms to Show Own Motivation

Fortunately there are ways to partially address moral hazard by exposing the insured party to enough risks through co-payments and deductibles to motivate the precautionary investments. With co-pay-

TABLE 2. The Samaritan's Dilemma

Samaritan	Aid Recipient	
	High Effort	Low Effort
No Help	2, 2	1, 1
Help	4, 3	3, 4

Source: Ostrom et al. 2001, 24; adapted from Buchanan 1977, 170.

ments, the insured pays a certain percentage of the costs of each insured-against event. With deductibles, the insured pays all costs of insured-against events up to a certain amount after which the insurance kicks in (perhaps with co-payments) to cover the remaining costs. By exposing the insured party (the doer) to these costs, the incentives to take precautions are substantially restored to make the doer's activity, taking precautions or "self-help against accidents," essentially independent of the helper's intervention (issuing the insurance policy). This is an example where the design of the intervention can effectively (but not perfectly) sterilize it against the distorting dependence-creating effects; it is then more compatible with the autonomy of the doer's activity of self-help against accidents. The intervention provides insurance benefits without overriding or undercutting the doer's own motivation to take precautions.

That original example of addressing moral hazard in insurance can be and has been applied much more broadly. For instance, one old way of trying to ensure that an offer of help does not substantially undercut incentives for self-help or create a perverse "supply effect" is to require a substantial matching payment or cost sharing by the doers as a commitment mechanism. A personal example might be illustrated by Abraham Lincoln's reaction to his stepbrother's request for a loan of eighty dollars (not the first request) to help out on the family farm.

> Your request for eighty dollars, I do not think it best to comply with now. At the various times when I have helped you a little, you have said to me, "We can get along very well now," but in a very short time I find you in the same difficulty again. Now this can only happen by some defect in your conduct. . . . You are now in need of some ready money; and what I propose is, that you shall go to work, "tooth and nail," for somebody who will give you money for it. . . . And to secure you a fair reward for your labor, I now promise you that for every dollar you will, between this and the first of May, get for your own labor either in money or in your own indebtedness, I will then give you one other dollar. . . . Now if you will do this, you will soon be out of debt, and what is better, you will have a habit that will keep you from getting in debt again. But if I should now clear you out, next year you will be just as deep in as ever. (Lincoln 1848 letter quoted in Bennett 1993, 403)

The overall moral hazard charge against the postwar development aid industry is that the aid agencies have kept on supporting many countries with such loans, which, in turn, allow those countries to postpone indefinitely any changes in their conduct.[17] Thus they are now "just as deep in as ever" and hence the need for debt relief programs.

Another commitment mechanism is to only give aid in a second stage so the doers show commitment by entirely funding the first stage in an undertaking. The "train" has to get moving on its own, and then the aid is provided at a second stage to help it go along better.[18]

> As the first tier of effort, the LO [local organization]—whether a cooperative, an LDA [local development association], or a women's association—should identify and diagnose local problems, determine what solutions lie within local means, and carry out such measures. Doing so not only provides direct benefit (or relief) but also demonstrates a serious desire to develop—not merely to attract handouts from the government. . . . The second tier of activity, then—building on the first—is joint action with government or other agencies at the local level to supplement what community members are already doing for themselves. (Esman and Uphoff 1984, 259)

David Korten cites an example of the Bangladesh Rural Advancement Committee (BRAC) applying this deductibles strategy: "To insure against dependence on BRAC and to discourage participation by those only interested in handouts, initial activities developed by the group had to be carried out exclusively with local resources" (Korten 1984, 179). Since the doers have to pay all the costs to get the train moving, the doers must have their own reasons independent of any aid that might subsequently be forthcoming.

Gaming the Safeguards

The design of aid programs will influence the relative success of attempts to approximate independence of the helper's help and the doer's own motivation using the strategies of matching requirements and second-stage aid. Pressure to move the money in the aid agency can lead to trivializing or gutting the matching requirements (e.g., a 5–10 percent match) or the "moving train" criteria. This is usually accompanied by interpreting each possibility of aid as akin to disaster relief for the poorest of the poor who cannot provide matching funds or get their trains moving on their own. Moral harangues are often the prelude to moral hazard.

Since the helpers often want to maintain the semblance of the doers' independence and ownership, there are many games that are played to create that illusion. In the crudest form, the aid givers directly or indirectly (through consultants) draft letters and plans for the potential aid recipients who in turn submit "their" requests for assistance. In a somewhat more subtle form, the aid givers supply suggestive checklists of participative decision-making procedures that the potential aid recipients need to go through in order to generate a "genuine development plan" that can then be submitted to request aid.[19] To the surprise of no one except perhaps those invested in the illusion,[20] the "genuine development plans" bear an uncanny resemblance in conception if not in language to previous development agency documents outlining the programs that the agency wanted to fund.

And in addition to self-deluding games by the helpers, there is gaming by the doers. The more certain the second-stage aid, the more possibility that the first stage of the project (the "moving train") was initiated in order to reap the benefits of the anticipated aid. That is an example of the sort of generalized moral hazard phenomena that arise from the failure of independence between the helper's help and the doer's motivation (i.e., from assistance that is not autonomy respecting). While some forms of gaming can be avoided by clever design, it is perhaps more important for the helper to have enough judgment and selectivity to find internally motivated doers so that it is not necessary to play games.[21]

Let us return to the helping conundrum. If the doers have sufficient own motivation to help themselves, then nondistortionary aid to supply the means would indeed help the doers to help themselves. But if the doers are motivated to seek aid to alleviate the consequences of not changing their own condition, then the aid would subsidize the doers not helping themselves. Thus the aid agencies and international finance institutions "*should help finance the costs of change—and should not cover the costs of not changing*" (Stern 2001; italics in original).

Internal and External Motivation

Moving beyond Homo economicus

There is now a considerable body of literature in psychology, sociology, and organizational behavior on intrinsic motivation as well as the closely related notions of autonomy, self-determination, and internal locus of causality.[22] Although considerations of intrinsic motivation have figured prominently in the Romantic critique of classical economics,[23] the topic has until recently only received sporadic treatment in the economics literature.[24] Bruno Frey's *Not Just for the Money* (1997) and *Inspiring Economics* (2001) are the first book-length treatments of the topic of intrinsic motivation in the economics literature.

The point of the distinction between internal and external motivation is to separate the internal and external levers of control or causality—and thus to separate what activities are "owned" by the doers and which are not.[25] An individual lies at the intersection of many circles or layers of identity (e.g., family, company, community, or country), somewhat like the layers of an onion (except that the circles need not be concentric). Internally motivated or autonomous activities include not only activities done for their own sake (the traditional narrow notion of "intrinsic" motivation) but activities undertaken due to one's identification with a larger social group and one's own judgment about what is best for that community.

Externally motivated activities include not only the usual pecuniary or mercenary activities but actions taken in order to gain social recognition or reputation. The distinction between internally motivated action due to identification with a group and externally motivated action to build one's reputation or social standing as a member of the group might be operationalized by asking: "Would the action be done privately and anonymously?"

Foreground and Background

The relationship between internal and external motivation is represented here using a foreground-background model. By being in the foreground, I mean that that motivation essentially governs decisions, but the other motivation is still present in the background (e.g., the "stick" of punishment might be in the motivational background as a backstop, like a guardrail on a road, without determining one's actions). There are situations where the foreground and background are reversed. Autonomy entails that internal motivation is in the foreground and external motivation in the background. Many of the subtleties in the design of human interventions and organizations arise from the interplay between foreground and background.

The basic model to keep in mind is a simple hierarchy of two systems, a higher system of internal motivation on top of a lower system of extrinsic motivation. We could think of extrinsic motivation as being in the background as long as certain needs are satisfied. However, when a certain threshold is crossed, then a signal is sent (e.g., hunger or pain) that a lower need (subsistence or safety) must be attended to, and then the lower needs are brought into the foreground to command attention.[26] While vastly oversimplified, this sort of a two-level foreground-background model will be sufficient to make most of our points.

Our previous results about nondistorting interventions were in a model with no privileged notion of internal motivation and no distinction between foreground and background. We saw ways to design the carrots and sticks of aid to minimize the distortion of the helper's help on the doer's doings.[27] Now the model is somewhat more complicated by the foreground-background distinction. External carrots and sticks do not directly change internal motivation, although they may trigger a reversal of foreground and background so that carrots and sticks take over the motivational driver's seat. Indeed this is the goal of some development interventions. When internal motivation is in the foreground so that action is autonomous, then an intervention that tries to reverse the field to bring external motivation into the foreground would be autonomy-*incompatible*.[28] If the helper refrains from trying to reverse background and foreground to make the doer externally controllable, then the helper's help must operate in an *indirect* manner.

In summary, an intrinsically motivated activity is an activity carried out by individuals for its own sake. The activity is an end in itself, not an instrumental means to some other end (such as satisfying biological needs). The factors that determine the meaning of "for its own sake" are usually based on the self-identity of the person or persons carrying out the activity. The notion of an internally motivated activity is somewhat broader. An internally motivated activity might even be accompanied by extrinsic motivators if the latter do not take over the locus of causality.[29] For instance, professors typically pursue their professional work for its own sake even though there is a salary and other emoluments in the background. Indeed much of the internal-external story is concerned with the question of the source or locus of causality for an activity. A bribe (carrot) or threat (stick) to get one to do what one would not ordinarily do switches one from an internal to an external locus of causality (reverses foreground and background). The classical sins such as greed, envy, and pride could be rendered in this simple framework as the cancerous growth of extrinsic motivation into passions that take over the foreground of motivation.[30]

Higher and Lower Selves

Much of what I say about internal and external motivation is a reformulation, if not a translation, of older philosophical concepts into modern psychological terminology. There is a very old philosophical theme, often associated with the Stoics, that divides the self into a higher, inner, and noumenal self or "soul"—and a lower, empirical, and phenomenal self. The lower self is typically under the influence of the passions and irrational impulses and sees the world only darkly through a veil of opinion and prejudice, while the higher self can at least potentially be free of being controlled by these external influences and can be guided by critical reason and motivated by autonomous volitions. Much of what is said here about external motivation can be taken as a modern version of the influences of the lower self, while internal motivation represents the volitional side of the higher self.

The narrower and nonrelational notion of intrinsic motivation could be taken as a modern treatment of the Socratic notion of Eros.

> Man, improved by love, is improved by his own work, for, though love is called a *daimon*, i.e. something more than man, Socratic Eros is not something over, above, and beyond man, but rather *his* spirit, *daimon*, and nature, and its gifts are the result of human achievement.
> . . . What [Socratic man] is possessed and driven by is not something alien and external to himself—gods, spirits, external fate—but his own nature and spirit. (Versényi 1963, 133)

In practice, we would expect to find the notions of intrinsic and internal motivation to be largely coextensive.

The economic theory of agency works with extrinsic variables such as monetary rewards or penalties to the agent as the levers that the principal can affect to change the agent's actions. By following the incentives provided by the incentive-compatible reward scheme, the agent will be led to achieve the results desired by the principal. From the agent's viewpoint, such an incentive structure represents an external source of motivation and an external locus of control. By thus appearing "to solve the problem" agency theorists avoid recognizing the inherent motivational inconsistency problems in trying to externally incentivize an activity that would need to be internally motivated in order to succeed (e.g., workers who see quality as a calling, not as a source of bonus payments, or agency task managers who are client oriented as opposed to the boss-oriented ones who strive to appear client oriented.).

> Money is the most obvious [extrinsic motivator] but promotion, praise, recognition, criticism, social acceptance and rejection, and "fringe benefits" are other examples.
>
> "Intrinsic" rewards, on the other hand, are inherent in the activity itself; the reward is the achievement. They cannot be *directly* controlled externally, although characteristics of the environment can enhance or limit the individual's opportunities to obtain them. Thus, achievement of knowledge or skill, of autonomy, of self-respect, of solutions to problems are examples. (McGregor 1966, 203–4)

Pigeons in a Skinner box may respond well to the "piece rates" of being paid a pellet of food each time a lever is pressed. But in the areas of human endeavor using the higher faculties, external motivators may soon fade or may fail to inspire the necessary quality of action. Moreover, the linkage between the desired result X and the external incentive or carrot can always be "gamed." If the system is to do X only in order to get a carrot, then people may soon figure out how only to appear to be doing X or to do X poorly since, after all, the point is to get the carrot.

Western economists sometimes give examples of the untoward results of the Soviet attempts to use various physical indicators of enterprise performance, but they often fail to see the limitations in their own (extrinsic) criterion of market value. From J. C. L. Simonde de Sismondi, Thomas Carlyle, and John Ruskin onwards, there has been a critique of the narrow conception of *Homo economicus*, a critique that is based in part on the limited focus on extrinsic motivation.[31] These questions applied not just to the individual worker but to the enterprise as a whole. There has always been a tradition of thought about management and corporate governance, from Robert Owen (see O'Toole 1995) to Max DePree (1989) and Charles Handy (1989), which has recognized noneconomic motivation (which challenges the primacy of absentee common stockholders interested only in share price and dividends) and has criticized the "tyranny of the bottom line" (Estes 1996)—not to mention the more recent innovations of managerial stock options and the like.

Action = Behavior + Motive

The question can be asked: "Why an indirect approach; why not a direct approach?" Motive is part of action. For our purposes, a highly simplistic model will be used: action = behavior + motive. The same behavior with different motives would represent different actions. If an action has an internal motive, then *that* action cannot be induced by external motivation. This is the old "can't buy love" argument. One can buy loving behavior but not love. The external motivation is inconsistent with the condition of being in love. Any action that involved an internal motive could not be induced by external motivations, only a similar behavior.[32] Bought love is a motivationally inconsistent state: if it is love, then it is not bought (although money may be involved incidentally in the background), and if it is bought, then it is only loving behavior.

In development assistance, a constantly recurring example of the can't buy love problem is the attempt of the major aid agencies to buy "best practices." A successful practice will be based on its own internal reasons and motivations, but its external characteristics (behavior) can be recorded by a development agency as a best practice. Then the agency will use carrots and sticks (aid funds and conditionalities) to get other parties to undertake the best practice (by following the description or checklist of characteristics). When this attempt "to scale up" the best practice has little sustainable success, then the agency concludes that the incentives should perhaps be even stronger. And those being paid to scale up the practice will readily agree with that diagnosis. This problem with scaling up best practices relates only to the motivational or volitional side; there are many other problems (considered later) on the cognitive side about the nonuniversality, the uncodified aspects of the knowledge, the Rashomon effect (description depending on viewpoint), and the ideological predilections in the best practices as captured by the agency.

This "not for *sale*" argument applies to all nonpecuniary motives, not just to internal motivations. McGregor mentions praise and recognition as extrinsic motivators. Yet bought praise or bought recognition would be counterfeit since money payments are not genuine grounds for giving someone else praise or recognition. The lack of decent pay (a local subjective notion) for government workers may bring pecuniary motives into the motivational foreground and lead to corruption. But increasing government pay will not necessarily restore honesty since purchased honesty is another motivationally inconsistent and thus counterfeit notion. In contrast, there is no contradiction in paying someone to undertake a mercenary endeavor, for that motivation is quite consistent with the proposed action.

The motivational component of actions played an important role in Immanuel Kant's ethical theory. A certain behavior could not be counted as ethical if it had external motivation such as avoiding punishment or winning praise. The same behavior motivated internally by reverence for the moral law would count as ethical.[33] It follows, for example, that there would be an inconsistency in the state trying *to make* people act morally or ethically; ethical action requires autonomy (although ethical *behavior* might have prudential reasons). Moral education would have to proceed by Socratic dialogue so that moral insights would grow out of the self-activity of the learner and would thus have what we now call *ownership*.

> Its advantage [i.e., Socratic methods] lies especially in the fact that it is natural for a man to *love* a subject which he has, by his own handling, brought to a science (in which he is now proficient); and so, by this sort of practice, the pupil is drawn without noticing it to an *interest* in morality. (Kant [1797] 1991b, 272)

Kant boldly emphasized that this moral education should *not* be mixed with any religious catechism, for otherwise any "religion that he afterward professes will be nothing but hypocrisy; he will acknowledge duties out of fear and feign an interest in them that is not in his heart" (Kant [1797] 1991b, 272). In the following, we see that Kierkegaard developed these themes with great clarity and force.

Thus one must always match tools to tasks. The direct approach utilizes certain tools such as the carrots and sticks of agency theory, and yet those tools may be inconsistent with the motives of the desired nonpecuniary actions. A carrot cannot motivate a noncarrot-driven action. Such interventions in the context of noncarrot-driven actions require an indirect autonomy-respecting approach.

The application of this simple framework to development aid can now be quickly outlined. Aid agencies have their preconceptions of virtue, in the sense of good policies. They try "to buy virtue" by imposing conditionalities on program aid geared to "virtuous behavior," defined by various outward acts of allegiance to and implementation of "good policies." But if we take virtue as being defined not just by behavior but also by the right internal motives (using the "action = behavior + motive" scheme), then aid can only buy a faux virtue. Such aid is autonomy incompatible as it pushes the external motive of receiving the aid into the motivational foreground and thus establishes external control or heteronomy.

Autonomy-respecting aid would remove impediments and thus enable "virtuous action" where the internal motive was already present and would remain in the motivational foreground (in accordance with the idea of finding out what people are already motivated to do and helping them do it better). However, once it is known that virtue is being rewarded by the donor, then mimicry in the form of virtuous behavior may be elicited in order to also be rewarded—and that virtue does not appear of its own accord. This supply effect of such externally motivated mimicry greatly complicates the provision of aid.

By-products Rather Than Products of Choice

It is noted in the preceding that internally motivated actions cannot be manipulated by external incentives. Jon Elster has considered a large class of mental and social "by-product" states that cannot be brought about by deliberate choice.[34] One cannot "produce" a state that is *essentially* a by-product, just as one cannot machine-produce a hand-made artifact. One can only machine-produce counterfeit handmade artifacts, and food companies can only produce as-if-homemade ice cream.

Imposed autonomy and bought love are among the examples of motive-inconsistent states. The principal cannot pay or threaten the agent to produce such states because the motive contradicts the grounds for such states. The problems arise for cognitive states as well as for volitional states. Belief in some statement P, for example, would be grounded in some reason that could qualify as grounds for belief. Getting paid to believe P or believing P for instrumental reasons such as to attract another person, conformity in a belief-based organization (e.g., a church), or simply to be a team player are not among those grounds,[35] although they may well be reasons for some "believing behavior." A conformity-based rational belief is a cognitive version of the inconsistency involved in oxymorons such as "bought love."

Here again, the answer is clear to the question: "Why not a direct approach?" A direct approach may be self-defeating like shining a flashlight to get a better look at darkness; the approach dispels the goal.[36] A by-product is at best the product of "indirect means" (Elster 1983, 56). Mental states (e.g., volitions and beliefs) have their antecedents or grounds. A direct approach using an instrument that did not fulfill those antecedents or grounds would only produce a counterfeit state or condition. Only an indirect approach that tried to foster or to be a midwife to the right conditions or grounds would have a chance of success. Broadly, this is the recurrent theme that the means often defeat the end; the intervention only elicits the sort of behaviors that are induced by external forces. Such behavioral change is only "outside in," whereas proactive transformation must be "inside out."[37]

The Threat-to-Autonomy Effect

External interventions by other people intended to change a person's behavior pose a threat to autonomy. The threat-to-autonomy or reactance (see Brehm 1972) effect results from using external motivators—carrots and sticks—to shift the locus of causality from internal to external.[38] The effect emerges as a poor quality and low-effort performance, in sullen and perfunctory behavior fulfilling the letter but not the spirit of an agreement, and perhaps even in the urge to defiantly do the opposite just to show one's autonomy. Mark Lepper and David Greene (1978) call these effects the "hidden costs of rewards."

The threat-to-autonomy effect points to a broader complication in accounting for human preferences. An individual's evaluation of an event may be strongly affected by the source of the event (e.g., was a death due to natural causes, an accident, or a murder?).[39] "Hunger and cold cause misery, but men do not revolt against winter or agitate against the desert" (Tawney 1964, 102). A change in a person's choices due to another person's strategic controlling action may give rise to a reactance that would be absent if the change had been necessitated by natural events or by a friendly enabling action by another person.

This complication means that the question of autonomy (e.g., who is in the driver's set?) involves considering the design intentions, if any, embedded in the choice environment facing a person. Is the choice environment freighted with the intentions of another? Is the choice environment like a Skinner box or agency contract designed to elicit certain behaviors and thus be controlling, or is the choice environment noncontrolling in the sense of simply being a neutral "given" or designed with the intention to protect equal freedoms of all? Choices that at first might appear as the same might be quite different when one considers the design intentions embedded in the determination of the available choices. Thus a sharecropper is quite different from an independent farmer even though they might seem to face many of the same choices. The sharecropper operates in a choice environment determined by the landowner to elicit certain behaviors, while the independent farmer operates in a more objectively given choice environment. The standard economic models ignore the *sources* of the constraints and thus overlook these who's-in-the-driver's-seat considerations about the autonomy of the economic agents.

The Crowding-out Effect

The imposition of external motivation may have untoward long-term "by-product" effects. Internal and external motivation might not be additive. Indeed it frequently seems to be the case that external incentives superimposed onto a system involving internal motivation in order to better achieve control will tend "to crowd out" and atrophy the internal motivation.[40]

> It was on the basis of this atrophy dynamic—the less the requirements of the social order for the public spirit, the more the supply of public spirit dries up—that the United States' system for obtaining an adequate supply of human blood for medical purposes, with its only partial reliance on voluntary giving, was criticized by the British sociologist Richard Titmuss. And the British political economist Fred Hirsch generalized the point: once a social system, such as capitalism, convinces everyone that it can dispense with morality and public spirit, the universal pursuit of self-interest being all that is needed for satisfactory performance, the system will undermine its own viability, which is in fact premised on civic behavior and on the respect of certain moral norms to a far greater extent than capitalism's official ideology avows. (Hirschman 1992, 155–56)

This crowding-out or atrophy effect might also be amplified by what Frey calls a "motivational spillover effect." The imposition of controlling external incentives might not only atrophy internal motivators in the given system but in related areas of endeavor where the market-type incentives were not applied.

Frey is also careful to note that intrinsic motivation may be crowded out or overridden not only by external incentives but also by external interventions in other forms such as compulsory laws and regulations. Frey develops a number of illuminating examples of the crowding-out effect:

- a constitution or other system of laws (e.g., tax laws) designed on the assumption that the citizens are Humean knaves bent on trying to break or evade the law may well lead to civic virtue drying up;[41]
- an environmental control system based on market incentives and penalties may lead to the atrophy of environmental morale;
- a system of military conscription ignores intrinsic motivation to serve, and moreover, a system allowing conscripts to buy their way out will quickly undermine any residual motivation of the other conscripts; and
- systems of social actions (e.g., putting waste dumps always in someone's "backyard") where the monetized benefits exceed the losses (Kaldor-Hicks improvements) may operate—without compensating the losers—on the basis of civil virtue if the losers in each case are determined in a fair and transparent manner. But the system may have perverse results if the losers are compensated ("Pareto improvements") because that may dry up the civic virtues and cause adverse spillover effects in other areas (since citizens will then expect to be "compensated" for any adverse effects due to government action).

The history of religions provides interesting examples of the interplay between intrinsic and extrinsic incentives. A poor church, like a poor man or woman, can at least feel assured that "suitors" are not driven solely by economic motives. In the history of Christianity, the early and poor church is often seen as achieving a victory in the conversion of the Roman emperor Constantine and in his massive endowment of the church. Yet a rich church associated with political elites could no longer be assured that acolytes were intrinsically motivated by the love of God or that any such motivation would not be soon crowded out as initiates climbed the internal job ladder.[42] The Puritan writer and poet John Milton makes this point in his tract against "hirelings" in the church, an early work on intrinsic motivation and the crowding-out phenomenon.

> That which makes [hire] so dangerous in the church, and properly makes the *hireling*, a word always of evil signification, is either the excess thereof, or the undue manner of giving and taking it. What harm the excess thereof brought to the church, perhaps was not found by experience till the days of Constantine; who out of his zeal thinking he could be never too liberally a nursing father of the church, might be not unfitly said to have either overlaid it or choked it in the nursing. (Milton [1659] 1957b, 858)

The organizational dynamics of a church are particularly revealing since intrinsic motivation is clearly supposed to be uppermost in a church, but a similar story can told in governments or other large organizations and bureaucracies facing problems of corruption.

The "New Year's Resolutions" and Internalization Theories of Conditionalities

Inside the World Bank and elsewhere in the development aid community, there are two standard counterarguments to the critique of social engineering as external motivation embodied in loan or aid conditionalities: (1) the reforms are really internally motivated and are expressed in the conditionalities simply as a public expression of "New Year's resolutions" that will help strengthen commitment, and (2) the reforms are only initially externally motivated and will eventually become internalized (just as brushing teeth, as children are forced by their parents to do, will be internalized by the time they grow up).

We are not trying to establish a law as in Newtonian physics that can have no exceptions. There could be exceptional cases where these self-promise or internalization counterarguments might apply. Our thesis is that while there might be such exceptional cases, the preponderance of the empirical evidence over the last half century (e.g., Collier 1997; World Bank 1998a; Gilbert and Vines 2000) and the weight of theoretical arguments stand behind the external-motivation critique of conditionality-based assistance.

Both counterarguments seem to embody a fair amount of wishful thinking and self-delusion on the part of the major development agencies that are structurally disposed to operate in the social engineering modality in any case. Aid-seeking doers will, of course, say that they really want to undertake the reforms for their own reasons and be willing to have their "resolutions" expressed in the conditionalities—but that they still need the aid to cover the costs. For a long time, that has been an acknowledged part of the "aid game"; aid-seeking doers try to mimic internal motivation for changes, and helpers who have "to move the money" anyway take part in the illusion so that both parties get what they want. This is the type 2 error of accepting a false-motive project. When the results are predictably disappointing, then the game goes to the next round, with the aid-seeking doers sharpening their mimicry skills and the money-pushing helpers swearing to get tough with tighter conditionalities.

If the doer is not just aid seeking and is genuinely motivated to make the changes, then putting external teeth in the resolutions by making them conditionalities on loans or aid will quickly distort the motivation and insult the doer. It is as if the helper is saying, "We trust you— but you must post bond anyway," which is a rather ambiguous form of trust. But trust or not, the helpers in the form of task managers in large development agencies will opt for the conditionality to cover their own liability if the doer should falter. The effect on the doer might go beyond the resentment to the crowding-out effect that results from the overdetermined motivation (subtle internal plus salient external motivation leading to the atrophy of the internal).

In an autonomy-respecting relationship, a financial helper would have to judge whether or not the doer had own motivation and then, in the case that the judgment was positive, take a risk to be enabling without being controlling. But that strategy requires the possibility of walking away or exiting the relationship when it is discovered that the respect was not reciprocated and that the doer was principally aid seeking. However, that exit is not an organizational possibility for the international financial institutions.

There are always two ways that a helper supplying financial aid can try to control risk: exit or voice. The IFIs are essentially financial cooperatives with various sovereign states as their members. They cannot just "walk away" like a commercial bank would from a bad borrower. Hence they gravitate to the opposite strategy to reduce risk by exerting more control ("voice") over the borrower as in the usual modality of conditionality-based lending.[43] Thus all the well-intended talk of the IFIs putting the client countries in the driver's seat and trying to enable rather than control the borrowers by reducing conditionalities ignores the fundamental fact that an IFI cannot exit the relationship if a country is a bona fide paid-up member.

Turning now to the internalization justification of conditionalities, this is to some extent driven by conscious or unconscious parent-child analogies. Since a parent does not have the option of exit, increasing control over a wayward child is often the chosen option buttressed by the hope that the child will either see the light or at least is plastic and malleable enough to eventually internalize the controls. The educational approach of John Dewey that we explore would not support that strategy, but our concern in the context of development is, in any case, firmly with adults. If it is a cognitive matter of "seeing the light," then the best approach would be to support a scheme of parallel experimentation by the doers so they could find out for themselves what works (see chap. 9).

If it is a volitional matter, then the internalization of motivation is even more implausible for adults. Across many fields—such as management, psychology, education, and development—the use of high-powered external incentives to channel adult behavior creates more resentment and reactance (the threat-to-autonomy effect) than fulsome compliance. There is little alchemy to transmute external incentives into the gold of internal motivation. Yet this is not immediately obvious since external incentives can produce the fool's gold of compliant short-term behavior. Those who are invested in the control provided by such external incentives will interpret the purchased behaviors as signifying long-term changes (internalization) and then will move on to new managerial challenges. But the reform will not stick. As Dewey pointed out almost a century ago, such a reform "has to be continually buttressed by appeal to external, not voluntary, considerations; bribes of pleasure, threats of harm, use of force. It has to be undone and done over" (Dewey and Tufts 1908, 304).

The Universal Solvent Fallacy in the Economic Design of Institutions

Economic recommendations for the "reform" of public bureaucracies tend to recommend raising salaries and benefits to levels competitive with the private sector (where extrinsic motivation is more openly condoned) in order to attract and retain "the best talent." Yet this can be a motivational slippery slope. Such practices will attract and retain the best *extrinsically motivated* talent (the best hirelings) and will tend to crowd out the esprit de corps and dedication to public service of those with such intrinsic motivation.[44] This corruption of the motivational base of an organization may, given the difficulties of monitoring, lead in the end to more, rather than less, of the mundane sort of corruption.

Moreover there is a conceptual "infinite regress" difficulty in designing an institution entirely on the basis of the "solvent" of pecuniary motivation. Pecuniary motivation can be thought of as a type of social solvent; money can dissolve the resistance of others to do our bidding. The economics of pecuniary motivation may be appropriate in its original habitat of the marketplace. But intellectual hubris leads to the assumption of pecuniary motivation as being universal and thus the basis for institutional design, and then we commit the fallacy of the "universal solvent." If a solvent were universal, then it could have no container. If venality were universal, then all the institutional rules and laws that should govern or contain the market could be dissolved into the market. They could become just more commodities to be auctioned off to the highest bidder.[45]

The old question of *Quis Custodiet Ipsos Custodes?* (who is to guard the guardians?)[46] threatens an infinite regress unless it can be stopped by some guardians who will not be seduced by pecuniary motivation. It is precisely here that current economic theory (e.g., agency theory and the new institutional economics) applied to institutional design is somewhat less than helpful. The wisdom of economics is to pay a level of guardians enough carrots so that they will not risk taking a bribe for fear of the stick being applied by a higher level of guardians who, in turn, are paid enough carrots so that they will not risk . . . and so forth. As Aristotle pointed out, to stop a regress, one needs an unmoved mover. To stop this motivational regress, one needs a notion of nonmarket, nonpecuniary, or nonexternal motivation (i.e., internal motivation), and that nonuniversality is what current economic theory (e.g., agency theory) is loathe to recognize because it offers no levers for principals to directly control agents.

> Short of succumbing to comforting but wildly utopian nineteenth-century beliefs in self-regulating social mechanisms . . . , there is a problem of infinite regress. Someone, or some group, must somehow act out of conviction to make any institution function. (Sullivan 1995, 194–95)

In order to contain and govern pecuniary motivation, there needs to be a "container" made of a different material more resistant to that solvent, namely some nonpecuniary intrinsic motivation. Universal venality may be the outcome of "economic reforms" (e.g., in Russia during the 1990s) that ignore intrinsic motivation or that assume extrinsic incentives will simply add to intrinsic ones with no crowding-out effect. The level of extrinsic motivation needs to be "fair" (a locally determined, subjective notion) to those who are oriented to that profession so that such extrinsic matters can recede into the motivational background and so that pride and esprit de corps can then hold the foreground.

3

The Indirect Approach

From Direct to Indirect Assistance

In the opening quotation of the book, John Dewey gives what is perhaps the best one-sentence summary of this book and of helping theory in general where he note that the "best kind of help to others"—helping them help themselves—is indirect rather than direct and is enabling rather than controlling.

The economic approach to structuring incentives (agency theory) so that principals can better control agents is writ large in the development aid industry. Since development assistance became a business that needs to show results and since development agencies as helpers tend to have large power and wealth differentials over the doers, a direct controlling form of help is almost guaranteed. To build a foundation for an alternative approach to development assistance, we must explore indirect enabling methods—no matter how ill suited development agencies are to use these methods. After more than thirty years in development assistance, Thomas Dichter has reached a similar conclusion that the best assistance can only be indirect, not direct.

> The keys to development increasingly lie in the realm of the policies, laws, and institutions of a society, and to change these requires indirect kinds of approaches—stimulating, fostering, convincing—rather than

doing things directly. Why is it, then, that the majority of development assistance organizations continue to "do" things? And why do more and more come into existence every day with funding to do still more things? (Dichter 2003, 7)

To study indirectness, we begin with some less familiar types of indirectness. Three very different examples of an indirect approach serve to introduce the variety and importance of the idea:

- the volitional indirect approach in matters of strategy in military as well as broader human affairs;
- the cognitive indirect approach to learning in the higher animals (in comparison with, say, insects)—the biological version of the Chinese teaching-how-to-fish metaphor; and
- the indirectness of selectionist mechanisms in comparison with instructionist mechanisms.

Then we turn to Douglas McGregor's Theory Y as a prototype indirect strategy for assistance in a managerial context.

The Indirect Approach in Strategy

Liddell Hart's (1895–1970) classic book *Strategy* (1967) evolved from a 1941 book entitled *The Strategy of Indirect Approach*. Hart saw the indirect approach that he recommended in military strategy was in fact part of a much broader indirect approach that could be applied elsewhere in human affairs.

> With deepening reflection, . . . I began to realize that the indirect approach had a much wider application—that it was a law of life in all spheres: a truth of philosophy. Its fulfilment was seen to be the key to practical achievement in dealing with any problem where the human factor predominates, and a conflict of wills tends to spring from an underlying concern for interests. In all such cases, the direct assault of new ideas provokes a stubborn resistance, thus intensifying the difficulty of producing a change of outlook. Conversion is achieved more easily and rapidly by unsuspected infiltration of a different idea or by an argument that turns the flank of instinctive opposition. The indirect approach is as fundamental to the realm of politics as to the realm of sex. In commerce, the suggestion that there is a bargain to be secured is far

more potent than any direct appeal to buy. . . . This idea of the indirect approach is closely related to all problems of the influence of mind upon mind—the most influential factor in human history. (Hart 1941, x)

Hart traces these ideas back to Sun Tzu's *The Art of War* (circa 400 B.C.).

On reading the book I found many other points that coincided with my own lines of thought, especially his constant emphasis on doing the unexpected and pursuing the indirect approach. It helped me to realize the agelessness of the more fundamental military ideas, even of a tactical nature. (Hart 1963, vii)

The Indirect Approach in Biological Learning Mechanisms

A very different area where the indirect approach is prominent is in the comparative biology of learning mechanisms. There are two very different ways in which teaching and learning can take place. Both ways occur biologically if we view what is transmitted through the genetic mechanism from an organism to its offspring as the biological version of what is transmitted from the teacher (helper) to the learner (doer). For many organisms, insects being a good example, the specific behaviors (that are fitted to certain stable environments) are transmitted by the genes from parents to offspring. The individual organism does not engage in learning from the environment because the appropriate behaviors are already determined, or "hardwired," by the structure transmitted through the genes. Thus any learning takes place only at the species level, not at the individual insect level. But evolution eventually leads to a very different type of learning.

The most striking thing about evolutionary history is that the operation of phylogenesis in its generalizing mode created improvements in organism adaptability until it generated learning organisms. Thus, the behavioral reprogramming of organism behavior that is phylogenesis gradually evolved a program (genotype) that provided the organism with the power to reprogram itself—to act as a true learning system at the organism level. In the human species the learning organism reached the point where learning becomes largely socialized because the dominant aspect of the individual organism's learning environment is the presence of and the sharing with other learning organisms. (Dunn 1971, 239)

Norbert Wiener calls the first type of learning *phylogenetic learning* as opposed to the latter type of *ontogenetic learning* (1961, 169). For instance, insects essentially have only phylogenetic learning, whereas the mammals ("higher animals") have both phylogenetic learning and ontogenetic learning.

> [The] very physical development of the insect conditions it to be an essentially stupid and unlearning individual, cast in a mold which cannot be modified to any great extent. . . . On the other hand, . . . the human individual [is] capable of vast learning and study . . . [and] is physically equipped, as the ant is not, for this capacity. Variety and possibility are inherent in the human sensorium—and are indeed the key to man's most noble flights—because variety and possibility belong to the very structure of the human organism. (Wiener 1954, 51–52)

In animals capable of ontogenetic learning, the genes do not transmit only the specific behaviors that might be fitted to a certain environment; the genes also transmit learning mechanisms to the offspring. The animals then interact with, adapt to, and learn from the environment. In this manner, the animals can learn much more complex activities in a wide variety of environments than could possibly be transmitted directly by the genes. Indeed, the adjectives *direct* and *indirect* can be used to describe these two approaches to learning.

> The gene-pattern, as a store or channel for variety, has limited capacity. Survival goes especially to those species that use the capacity efficiently. It can be used directly or indirectly.
>
> The direct use occurs when the gene-pattern is used directly to specify the regulator. The regulator is made (in the embryo) and the organism passes its life responding to each disturbance as the gene-pattern has determined. . . .
>
> The indirect use occurs when the gene-pattern builds a regulator (R_1) whose action is to build the main regulator (R_2), especially if this process is raised through several orders or levels. By achieving the ultimate regulation through stages, the possibility of large-scale supplementation occurs, and thus the possibility of an ultimate regulation far greater than could be achieved by the gene-pattern directly. (Ashby 1963, 270–71)

In the indirect case, the first regulator transmitted by the genes is the learning mechanism, and the second main regulator is the whole set of activities learned by the animal through interaction with the environment.

> [The learning mechanism's] peculiarity is that the gene-pattern delegates part of its control over the organism to the environment. Thus, it does not specify in detail how a kitten shall catch a mouse, but provides a learning mechanism and a tendency to play, so that it is *the mouse* which teaches the kitten the finer points of how to catch mice.
>
> This is regulation, or adaptation, by the indirect method. The gene-pattern does not, as it were, dictate, but puts the kitten into the way of being able to form its own adaptation, guided in detail by the environment. (Ashby 1960, 234)

The direct method (where genes transmit behaviors) and the indirect method (where the genes transmit a learning capacity) are essentially the genetic versions of two basic pedagogies of passive or active learning. In the direct method, the teacher transmits knowledge to the passive student who absorbs and uses the knowledge as needed. For instance, development agencies think they have "development knowledge" and that it is their task to transmit the knowledge to the client countries. In the indirect method, the teacher fosters and awakens an intrinsic desire for learning on the part of the learner who then takes the active role in (re)discovering and appropriating knowledge.

> The aim of teaching is not only to transmit information, but also to transform students from passive recipients of other people's knowledge into active constructors of their own and other's knowledge. The teacher cannot transform without the student's active participation, of course. Teaching is fundamentally about creating the pedagogical, social, and ethical conditions under which students agree to take charge of their own learning, individually and collectively. (Elmore 1991, xvi)

In the indirect method, the teacher does not transmit knowledge but transmits or arranges the learning experience that "puts the [learner] into the way of being able to form [the learner's] own adaptation, guided in detail by the environment." Rousseau says the teacher "ought to give no precepts at all; he ought to make them be discovered" ([1762] 1979, 52). Jose Ortega y Gasset makes a point similar to W. Ross Ashby's: "He who wants to teach a truth should place us in the position to discover it ourselves" (Ortega 1961, 67). Myles Horton of the Highlander Folk School makes a similar point: "one of the best ways of educating people is to give them an experience that embodies what you are trying to teach" (Horton 1998, 68).

These two methods are also described in the old Chinese story that giving a man a fish only feeds him for a day while helping him learn how to fish feeds him for a lifetime. Ashby develops a similar story. Suppose that a father only had ten minutes to teach his child the meanings of English words. Using the direct method, the father would teach the child the meaning of a certain small number of words.

> The indirect method is for the father to spend the ten minutes showing the child how to use a dictionary. At the end of the ten minutes the child is, in one sense, not better off; for not a single word has been added to his vocabulary. Nevertheless the second method has a fundamental advantage; for in the future the number of words that the child can understand is no longer bounded by the limit imposed by the ten minutes. The reason is that if the information about meanings has to come through the father directly, it is limited to ten-minutes' worth; in the indirect method the information comes partly through the father and partly through another channel (the dictionary) that the father's ten-minute act has made available. (Ashby 1960, 236)

The Indirect Approach of Selectionist Mechanisms

If we think of the direct approach as a straightforward causal influence of the helper over the doer, then a new indirect type of connection was discovered in Charles Darwin's (and Alfred Russel Wallace's) theory of natural selection. How does the environment influence the organism and "help" it to increase its fitness? In the Lamarckian theory, the environment directly instructs the organism, which then passes on the learning to its offspring. In the Darwinian selectionist theory, there is no direct or instructive communication from the environment to the organism to tell it the characteristics of greater fitness. Instead, the population of organisms takes the active role and generates a diversity of options (e.g., through mutation and recombination), which the environment passively selects (by allowing the organism to survive and reproduce—or not).

Today the idea of an instructive process versus a selectionist process has been generalized from the original contrast between Lamarckian and Darwinian evolution. Selectionist applications have been discovered in a number of other fields, and ambitious claims (a "second Darwinian revolution") have been made for the wide applicability of selectionist mechanisms (e.g., Cziko 1995; Dennett 1995; Hull 2001; and Heyes and Hull 2001). A number of metaphors have been used to get across that contrast between a direct and an indirect approach. Suppose we want to transmit the name *Charles Darwin* from the helper to the doer. Perhaps the direct approach is to simply say it in a language understood by the doer. An indirect or selectionist method is akin to the game of Twenty Questions. The doer generates a series of questions that the helper can only answer with a yes or no—and the game is to see if the doer can zero in on the answer within a certain number of questions.[1]

The (partial) analogy for our purposes is that the doer generates projects and programs, and the helpers in the form of donors only say yes or no. But over the course of time, this indirect help can become a game where the doers are choosing programs not to address their pressing domestic needs but to guess what will be funded by the donors. This sort of gaming (e.g., Say's Law of Development Aid) breaks down the independence between the doers' choices and the external influence of the helpers, the independence or nondistortion that is a necessary condition for the doers' autonomy. In modern Darwinism, this independence is the "fundamental dogma" that there is only one-way information transmission from genes to the organism. No environmental influence ("learning") during the lifetime of the organism can affect or direct the mutations of the genes—so the doings of the "doers" (changes in genes) are independent of the influence of the external environment (aside from the "message" about the organisms surviving and multiplying).

A particularly striking application of the selectionist approach is to the immune system. The early theories were instructional; the external molecule or antigen would enter the system and instruct the immune mechanism with its template to construct antibodies that would neutralize the antigen. Niels Jerne (1955) proposed a selectionist theory of the immune system: the immune system takes on the active role of generating a huge variety of antibodies, and the external antigen has the passive role of simply selecting which antibody fits it like a key in a lock. As the theory was developed by Macfarlane Burnet (1959), the antibody whose key finds a lock then is differentially amplified in the sense of being cloned into many copies to lock up the other examples of the antigen.

This may seem far from our topic of the autonomy-respecting influence of the helper to the doer, but some of our themes emerge in the selectionist context (based on taking the environment as helper and the organism as doer and the pairings of instructive with direct and selectionist with indirect approaches). For instance, one version of the helping self-help conundrum is the learning paradox—the idea that learning does not involve a direct transmission from teacher to learner that pairs with the "no direct transmission from environment to organism" or "fundamental dogma" condition in a selectionist mechanism. Real learning is based on the activity of the learner, with the teacher playing a more indirect and passive role of the midwife or facilitator. For Socrates, this takes the form of the Meno paradox that learning is recollection. The ideas are in some sense already preformed and innate in the learner. The teacher plays the "selective" role of catalyzing the recollection of certain ideas. Jerne (1967) notes this analogy between the Socratic role of facilitating the recollection of certain preexisting ideas and the antigen's role of selection of preexisting antibodies that are then multiplied.[2] In the next chapter, we see that Søren Kierkegaard developed this indirect approach in Socratic thinking. Jerne's biographer notes that

> in Jerne's view, the action of the mind was always guided from within. We do not learn from others, he thought; we only develop what is already there. He claims that he had come to this understanding through the reading of Søren Kierkegaard, the Danish existential philosopher, . . . and similarly, he reasoned, the immune system must be guided from within, as in the selection theory of antibody formation. (Søderqvist 2002)

Jerne and Burnet both received Nobel prizes for their work on the selectional approach to the immune system, as did Peter Medawar and Gerald Edelman for later work on that approach. One common theme is that, at least in biology, "it appears that wherever a phenomenon resembles learning, an instructive theory was first proposed to account for the underlying mechanisms . . . [but] this was later replaced by a selective theory" (Jerne 1967, 204; see Augustine on this point in the next chapter). In addition to the case of the immune system, Medawar notes ideas of bacteria being "trained" or instructed to become resistant to an antibiotic or to be able to digest a new substrate, but in reality "nothing of the kind occurs: the process of bacterial training is one of evolution . . . and turns upon the natural selection of variant forms already endowed with the new capability" (Medawar and Medawar 1977, 49).

In later chapters on knowledge-based development assistance, the direct approach is typified by the indoctrination of the doer by the helper who has "development knowledge." The alternative indirect approach is to facilitate the doer developing the inborn capacity to learn and acquire knowledge from whatever source. The Medawars evoke the same themes in contrasting the direct instructive mechanism and the indirect selective mechanism in the immune system: "an antigen represents an awakening or activation of some pre-existing potentiality in the responding cell and is not in any sense an indoctrination of the cell by some molecular property of the antigen" (Medawar and Medawar 1977, 103).

After receiving the Nobel prize for his work on the selectional approach to the immune system, Gerald Edelman switched over to neurophysiology and developed the theory of neuronal group selection or neural Darwinism (1992). In extremely simple terms, the brain generates an immense variety of groups of neural circuits (like the variety of antibodies), and then external stimuli only select which neural groups will be differentially amplified. What at first looks like the external environment instructing the brain is seen instead as a selectional process that thus leads to a version of the learning paradox.

> In considering brain science as a science of recognition I am implying that recognition is not an instructive process. No direct information transfer occurs, just as none occurs in evolutionary or immune processes. Instead, recognition is selective. (Edelman 1992, 81)

Augustine gives a clear expression in the neo-Platonist tradition of the point that what first looks like a direct transmission or instruction is really a process of triggering or selecting an internal process to be differentially amplified (see chap. 4).

> According to this analysis, extrinsic signals convey information not so much in themselves, but by virtue of how they modulate the intrinsic signals exchanged within a previously experienced neural system. In other words, a stimulus acts not so much by adding large amounts of

extrinsic information that need to be processed as it does by amplifying the intrinsic information resulting from neural interactions selected and stabilized by memory through previous encounters with the environment. (Edelman and Tononi 2000, 137)

Thus the visual stimulus of a Chinese character can be meaningful to one and meaningless to another "even if the extrinsic information conveyed to the retina is the same" (2000, 138).

My purpose in this chapter and the next is to consider some of the theories behind indirect approaches. What are the basic limitations on direct social-engineering-style approaches, and what are the underlying reasons for the efficacy of indirect approaches?

McGregor's Theory Y: A Prototype Indirect Approach

Surely the best domain for the direct approach of carrots and sticks is the relationship between manager and subordinate. Or, putting it the other way around, the extent to which the direct approach fails in management shows, a fortiori, how much more it may fail in many other helper-doer relationships. Here there are interesting parallels in the failures of traditional management and of conventional development assistance. I take the work of Douglas McGregor as our guide to the parallels between management theory and the other helper-doer relationships.

It is quite instructive to look at the genesis of McGregor's indirect Theory Y. He started not with the traditional manager-subordinate relationship but with the relationship between a staff expert (e.g., in human relations, accounting, finance, engineering, and so forth) who is to help a line manager with a particular problem. It is perhaps because the line manager is not subordinate to the staff expert that McGregor had to explore indirect approaches: "The function of the staff expert in human relations is necessarily indirect."[3] This is the topic in McGregor's 1948 article "The Staff Function in Human Relations," which even precedes the *Theory X* and *Theory Y* terminology. At the end of the article, he muses that this approach might be applied by "the line manager to his own subordinates" (1948; reprinted in 1966, 170). McGregor does just that in his classic presentation of Theory Y in *The Human Side of Enterprise* (1960).

McGregor describes Theory Y as being based on the principle of integration and self-control,[4] where *integration* refers to the situation where an individual "can achieve his own goals *best* by directing his efforts toward the objectives of the enterprise" (1960, 61). Management's task is not to provide incentives or supply motivation; the "task is to provide an appropriate environment—one that will permit and encourage employees to seek intrinsic rewards *at work*" (1967, 14). The contrasting Theory X is based on the principle or philosophy of direction and control using the type of incentives that management can provide (i.e., external incentives).

I outline Theory Y in the broader "principal-agent" setting here called *helper-doer*, where the principal or helper is trying to help the agent or doer to accomplish certain tasks that the doer is own motivated to do. If the motivation is not to be "supplied" by the helper, then it must be "found" in the doer. In an organizational setting, the principal (helper) would have a managerial role, the agent (doer) would be a subordinate (or another manager as in McGregor's staff-line example), and the tasks would be in furtherance of organizational goals. McGregor's early treatment of what became Theory Y could be described in five steps.[5]

Step 1: Starting from the Doer's Problem

The helper starts from the doer's engagement with an organizational problem, a problem that the helper is to help the doer solve. The helper is not to start with what the helper-as-expert thinks is the problem.

Step 2: Seeing the Problem through the Doer's Eyes

The helper explores with the doer the problem as perceived by the doer. How does the doer perceive and conceptualize the difficulty? If the helper sees the situation differently then this should be explained clearly without trying to manipulate the doer's perceptions or impose the helper's view of the problem.

Step 3: Helping the Doer Pursue Their Own Ends to Best Solve the Organizational Problem

This is the core of the indirectness of the approach. Starting with the doer's problem within the organization and seeing the problem through the doer's eyes, the helper can then offer knowledge and experience to help the doer find the best way to further the doer's own intrinsic ends while addressing the organizational problem. The helper is not "to teach" the doer what the helper considers the best solution. This is particularly difficult for engineers and economists who "know" the "one best (or 'optimal') way" to solve the problem. The helper is to create a learning situation so that the doer can arrive at what the doer considers to be the best solution to the problem in view of his or her own ends and capabilities.[6]

> Fundamentally the staff man . . . must create a situation in which members of management can learn, rather than one in which they are taught. . . . A's [helper's] objective is to utilize his skill to create a situation in which B [doer] can learn, and to make his knowledge available so that B may utilize it to augment his own need satisfaction in ways consistent with the achievement of organizational objectives. (McGregor 1966, 161, 163)

Because the arrived-at solution is the fruits of the doer's own labor, the doer has a natural ownership of it that leads to much more effective implementation (e.g., more effective than the typical partial, half-hearted, and sullen implementation of the expert's imposed "solution"). It should be noted that this may conflict with the organizational needs of the expert to show the expert's boss how he or she made a difference and got results.

Step 4: Helping the Doer to Implement, Test, and Refine the Doer's Solution

Having worked with the doer to arrive at what the doer considers the best solution, the helper needs to assist the doer in testing it, refining it, and gaining the skill and self-confidence for full implementation of the refined solution. This at the same time builds trust on the part of the helper that the doer will take responsibility for the problem solving.

Step 5: Helping the Doer Gain Autonomy and Take Responsibility for the Solution

In this final stage, the helper's goal is to assist the doer to achieve independence ("leave the nest") and to take full responsibility for the solution and its implementation—as well as for finding his or her own solutions to similar problems that might arise in the future.[7] There are two sides to this "separation" or leaving the nest problem: getting the doer to avoid dependency and assume responsibility and ownership and getting the helper to have the trust to let go and to avoid trying to take responsibility.[8]

The helper must avoid the benevolent giving of a solution to a grateful doer because that develops dependency and the doer does not learn to help him- or herself. Just as the doer needs to take responsibility, the helper needs to avoid trying to take responsibility. This is particularly difficult since helpers have their own bosses or principals, so the helpers naturally want to take ownership of the solutions to look better in the eyes of their bosses.

> If [the helper's] own need for power is too strong, he will not be able to create or maintain an effective relationship with B [the doer]. If he is overanxious for recognition, he is likely to destroy the results of his work with B by seeking credit for B's accomplishments. (McGregor 1966, 167)

This is the classic ownership problem. If the helper takes ownership of the solution in the eyes of the organization, then we are back in the case where the doers are called upon to implement someone else's plan with the aforementioned lack of effectiveness. The hardest task (helping self-help) requires the lightest touch. The helper is never more successful than when the doer finds the *doer's* solution.[9]

Intrinsic Motivation and Theory Y

Behaviorism, Taylorism, industrial engineering, or, recently, reengineering exemplify Theory X approaches, while humanistic psychology, W. Edwards Deming's approach to quality management, and participative management would be associated with Theory Y. Economists have on occasion not restricted themselves to *homo economicus*.

> A high wage will not elicit effective work from those who feel themselves outcasts or slaves, nor a low wage preclude it from those who feel themselves an integral part of a community of free men. Thus the

improvement of this element in the supply of labour is an infinitely more complex and arduous task than if it depended upon wage alone, but at the same time a task more possible of fulfilment by an impoverished world. (Robertson 1921, 244; quoted in Whyte 1955, 5)

But this is more the exception than the rule. The standard "economistic" treatment of work is essentially Theory X: work is a disutility, people are paid wages to overcome their aversion to work, satisfaction is obtained from consumption expenditure of the wages outside of work, and people are naturally averse to responsibility and risk. There is always plenty of empirical basis for this "economic" viewpoint since sufficient money will usually override intrinsic motivation, at least in the short run, so that one can thus verify that "money talks." Moreover, work organized on the economistic basis of Theory X will cut across any intrinsic motivation that might be otherwise derived from work, and crowded-out motivation will then tend to atrophy. Then the motivation assumed by Theory X will predominate so the theory once applied becomes a self-fulfilling prophecy.

People, deprived of opportunities to satisfy at work the needs which are important to them, behave exactly as we might predict—with indolence, passivity, unwillingness to accept responsibility, resistance to change, willingness to follow the demagogue, unreasonable demand for economic benefits. (McGregor 1960, 42)

Distrust breeds distrust in the Theory X vicious circle.[10] Robert Lane describes the use of what economists call *high-powered* incentives to reverse foreground and background.

The introduction of pay into a task situation, then, moves, or seems to move, the locus of causality from disposition to circumstance, from internal to external; it alters the task from chosen to unchosen, and since people do not work without motives, it transmutes intrinsic motivation into pecuniary motivation. Strangely, it *creates* Skinnerian man where he was missing earlier. (Lane 1991, 379)

Thus conventional economics and Theory X management can usually find short-term (pseudo-) verification for their self-fulfilling *Homo economicus* presupposition that "people respond to (their external) incentives."

Theory Y emphasizes intrinsic motivation that cannot be manipulated by the extrinsic carrots and sticks of Theory X.

> [Intrinsic motivators] are obtained by the individual as a direct result of his own effort; they are inherent in the activity. It is not possible to provide an individual with a sense of achievement, or with the satisfaction associated with the acceptance of responsibility, by controlling extrinsic rewards and punishments. (McGregor 1966, 259)

In this sense of effort, "motivation is not a purchasable input in the marketplace" (Leibenstein 1980, 257) (which is quite a different point from the usual agency theory point that effort is largely unobservable). Since making an achievement or taking responsibility are inherent in the activity of an individual, it cannot be given as an extrinsic motivator from the outside. This places inherent limitations on agency theory insofar as the latter works only with extrinsic motivators. The agency theory emphasis on external motivation tends to override the intrinsic motivators and redirect the locus of control to the extrinsic motivators.

Agency theory may be seen as the most recent form of the old dream that virtue can be rendered unnecessary by well-designed incentive structures in organizations.

> There can be . . . mechanisms within such organisations which harness individualistic self-seeking to the purposes of the organisation—system of material incentives and disincentives. The search for "systems so perfect that nobody needs to be good" has been endless. . . . But ultimately the effectiveness of such systems depends on somebody genuinely caring. There must be enough productive self-fulfilment or a sense of duty rather than acquisitive self-regarding achievement. Otherwise, the rules of the incentive schemes will be stretched; "goal displacement" will turn the organisation into a mere conspiracy for pursuing the individual short-term interests of the members.[11] (Dore 1976, 185)

The usual economic approach (e.g., agency theory) has not been very useful in understanding this sort of organizational behavior. This point is made powerfully by the economics Nobel laureate Herbert Simon.

> Although economic rewards play an important part in securing adherence to organizational goals and management authority, they are

limited in their effectiveness. Organizations would be far less effective systems than they actually are if such rewards were the only means, or even the principal means, of motivation available. In fact, observation of behavior in organizations reveals other powerful motivations that induce employees to accept organizational goals and authority as bases for their actions. . . . The attempts of the new institutional economics to explain organizational behavior solely in terms of agency, asymmetric information, transaction costs, opportunism, and other concepts drawn from neo-classical economics ignore key organizational mechanisms like authority, identification, and coordination, and hence are seriously incomplete. (Simon 1991a, 34, 42)

Simon goes on to identify pride in work and organizational identification as two of the most important motivators, neither of which is controlled by the purse strings of managers.

4

Indirect Approaches

Intellectual History

Background

Our topic is development assistance, the helper-doer relationship when the helper is some individual or organizational promoter of development and the doer is an individual or organization undertaking developmental activities. Since most conventional development assistance or help is actually unhelpful in the sense of overriding or undercutting self-help, our task is to build the intellectual foundation for an alternative philosophy of development assistance—an autonomy-respecting version of the helper-doer relationship wherein help is supplied in an indirect manner that enables self-help. While the organized development assistance business is a relatively recent matter (post–World War II period), similar problems of helping self-help have been discussed since antiquity in other fields of human endeavor. Hence part of our intellectual strategy is to look at the history of thought about the helping self-help problem, or conundrum, from antiquity down to modern times.

The reader should not expect to find the older thinkers talking about development. Their thought is about the subtleties of the helper-doer relationship in other fields (e.g., education or psychology); we have to extract and carry over the lessons to the helper-doer relationship in development assistance.

The reader should recall that there are always the volitional and cognitive dimensions of autonomy that we have tried to keep analytically separate, although they are much intertwined in practice. For instance, the cognitive correlate of a heteronomous action controlled by an externally sourced motive is a heteronomous belief based on the unexamined opinion or authority of others, not on the person's own judgment of weighing evidence and reasoning from other rationally held beliefs. Many of the older thinkers (e.g., Socrates) focused on the cognitive autonomy-respecting helper-doer relationship.

Taoist Antecedents

Direct approaches usually express a controlling and engineering mentality (stereotypically masculine) often associated with the West, while indirect approaches motivated by organic nurturing and enabling attitudes (feminine) are sometimes associated with the East. Eastern religions, particularly Taoism (dated roughly from 600 B.C.), have some clear early arguments against a direct controlling approach to human affairs.[1]

> For those who would like to take control of the world and act on it—
> I see that with this they simply will not succeed.
> The world is a sacred vessel;
> It is not something that can be acted upon.
> Those who act on it destroy it;
> Those who hold on to it lose it.
>
> (Lao-Tzu 1989, chap. 29)

Taoism has the central concept of *wu-wei*, which is variously translated as "action by inaction" or "effortless action." Perhaps wu-wei can be best understood as a general metaphor for the *indirect* approach. Certainly the *inaction* implies refraining from direct controlling actions that, as noted above, may defeat their purpose. A proper indirect approach by the helper will enable and enlist the intrinsic motivation and best energies of the doers so that matters will progress effortlessly on their initiative.[2] A clear example is in learning. Learning externally imposed lessons requires quite an effort, but "when I study a subject which I love,—no matter how many years it takes me to learn it—I never feel that I am making any effort" (Smullyan 1977, 161). When the teacher refrains from teaching a topic (in the sense of "pumping" knowledge into the pupil) and instead awakens the learner's interest in the topic so that learning becomes self-motivated, then that is the wu-wei of the indirect approach on the part of the teacher as helper.

Applied to government, an interfering and overbearing government will stifle and crowd out the initiative and self-activity of the people.

> The more prohibitions there are, the poorer the people become.
> The more sharp weapons there, the greater the chaos in the state.
> The more skills of technique, the more cunning things are produced.
> The greater the number of statutes, the greater the number of thieves
>   and brigands.
>
> Therefore the Sage says:
> I do nothing and the people are reformed of themselves.
> I love quietude and the people are righteous of themselves.
> I deal in no business and the people grow rich by themselves.
> I have no desires and the people are simple and honest by themselves.
>   (Lin 1948, chap. 57 of the *Te-Tao Ching*)

Thus the best wu-wei of the government is that which best enables the people to help themselves (which is not necessarily laissez faire).

The Socratic Method

I begin the history of the indirect approach in the West with Socrates (469–399 B.C.). Socrates did not teach, but those who engaged him in dialogue were engaged in learning. He had no writings, and the systemic doctrines expressed in the Platonic dialogues seem to be more attributable to Plato. Socrates was the quintessential cognitive helper whose aim was to help others, the doers, to learn to think for themselves. Most people think rather passively, reflecting conformity to external opinions and values. Socrates exemplified critical reason that could take up the common opinions and values and critically examine them to see if they could qualify as knowledge and virtue. But he did so in an indirect way by asking questions that would spur the learners to reexamine their own thoughts. Knowledge, for Socrates, was not opinion that happened to be true.

What distinguishes knowledge from opinion is neither its truth nor belief in it but simply the knower's ability to account for the truth of what he holds to be true. For Socrates, to know something means to be able to give reasons for it, to defend it by rational argument and to demonstrate it to others. It means to hold something not as an uncon-nected isolated piece of information unsupported by anything else, but to hold it as a conclusion fastened by a long chain of reasoning to an unshakable foundation in first principles whose truth cannot be ques-tioned. In contrast to opinion (right or wrong), knowledge is something reflected upon, something reasoned, criticized, and argued, something that is not merely accepted on someone else's authority but appropriated by the knower himself through rational reflection, made his own by questioning and accepted on his own authority as a reflective human being.[3] (Versényi 1963, 111–12)

It is only by such critical examination that a true belief can be appro-priated as knowledge and made one's own. And only by the relentless examination of acquired values could one expect to find and appropri-ate the knowledge of virtue. Otherwise, the "unexamined life is not worth living."

As in McGregor's initial steps, the helper should not "preach the Truth" but start where the doer is, see the situation through the doer's eyes, and activate the doer's own energies in addressing the problem.

If education is understood in the Socratic way, as an eliciting of the soul's own activity, it is natural to conclude, as Socrates concludes, that education must be very personal. It must be concerned with the actual situation of the pupil, with the current state of the pupil's knowledge and beliefs, with the obstacles between the pupil and the attainment of self-scrutiny and intellectual freedom. (Nussbaum 1997, 32)

Socrates' direct goal was not the transmission of truth; otherwise the Sophists' lectures or sermons might have been the chosen pedagogical device rather than dialogue. Socrates' goal was not to instill a specific set of doctrines in his pupils (a temptation Plato could not resist) but to enable them to employ their critical reason so that after critically reex-amining themselves during the dialogue and thereafter, the pupils would have "ownership" of the results. By living the examined life of reason, the learners would come to know themselves and to be autonomous.

As Socrates' goal was not to transmit specific doctrines, he (unlike the Sophists) always professed what is now known as "Socratic ignorance." Since he did not "know,"[4] he would have to constantly ask questions to better elucidate the topic.[5] The purpose of the questions was not for Socrates to find answers for himself but to get the pupils to think for themselves. A common perversion is the pseudo-Socratic method employed by someone who has already decided upon the answer and is only trying to ask leading questions to bring the listeners to the same conclusion. As always, the difference is between the helper controlling ("helping") the doers or enabling the doers to better help themselves. Socratic questioning is an indirect method, a method designed not to better control and instruct the student but to self-activate the learner during the dialogue and perhaps thereafter. Socrates aimed not to be the father of truth but the midwife of critical reason.

Samuel Taylor Coleridge's discussion of Socrates' system of education connects the active mind with the autonomy-respecting influence of the teacher.

> We see, that to open anew a well of spring water, not to cleanse the stagnant tank, or fill, bucket by bucket, the leaden cistern; that the EDUCATION of the intellect, by awakening the principle and *method* of self-development, was [Socrates'] proposed object, not any specific information that can be *conveyed* into it from without; not to assist in storing the passive mind with the various sorts of knowledge most in request, as if the human soul were a mere repository or banqueting-room, but to place it in such relations of circumstance as should gradually excite the germinal power that craves not knowledge but what it can take up into itself, what it can appropriate, and re-produce in fruits of its own. To shape, to dye, to paint over, and to mechanize the mind, he resigned, as their proper trade, to the sophists, against whom he waged open and unremitting war. (Coleridge in Coburn 1968, 80)

The Socratic teacher is described not only as a coach, a catalyst, or a midwife but as a "brooder," both in the sense of one who meditates about questions and as a hen brooding over her eggs and chicks. Scott Buchanan, the Socratic architect of the renowned learning program at St. John's College (Annapolis, Maryland), describes the Socratic teacher (following Jacques Maritain)[6] as

> knowing more than the pupil does, yet in some sense not conveying it but seeing that it is made available to the pupil. The great use of supe-

rior knowledge is to understand what the pupil is learning as it is learned. It takes great wisdom to be able to follow a learning pupil sensitively enough to know what the next step is for him, and you don't press the next step. You watch it happen. If it sticks, you help it a bit, but it's not a transmission or an imposition or a filling of a vessel or any of those things. Those are all bad images of the real teaching function: the real one is this penetration of the intelligence, of one intelligence into another. (Buchanan 1970, 51)

The "if it sticks, you help it a bit" advice corresponds to David Hawkins's advice about the teacher helping the learner make "transitions and consolidations" (Hawkins 2000, 44). This view of the Socratic role of the teacher also follows from the constructivist pedagogy of Jean Piaget's genetic epistemology (e.g., Piaget 1955, 1970).

To summarize what Piaget said about active methods, he pointed out that the criterion of what makes an "active" method active is not the external actions of the learner. He said, for example, that Socrates used an active method with language and that the characteristic of the Socratic method was to engage the learner in actively constructing his own knowledge. The task of the teacher is to figure out what the learner already knows and how he reasons in order to ask the right question at the right time so that the learner can build his own knowledge. (Kamii 1973, 203)

The Path of Stoicism

Many paths diverged from Socrates and Plato: Aristotle and his school, the Skeptics, the Epicureans, and the Stoics. For the purposes of understanding indirect approaches, the golden thread runs through the Greek and Roman Stoicism of Chrysippus, Cleanthes, Zeno, Seneca, Epictetus, Cicero, and Marcus Aurelius (although the thread of Neoplatonism is picked up later).

In this example of the helper-doer relationship, Socrates is replaced by the Stoic teacher who functions as a physician for the soul of his interlocutors, the doers who seek to follow this path. Again the teacher must start with the particular situation of the doer and see the situation through the doer's eyes in order to be more helpful.

Just as it is appropriate for the [physician] of the body to be "inside" as they say, the affections . . . that befall the body and the therapeutic treatment that is proper to each, so it is the task of the physician of the soul to be "inside" both of these, in the best possible way. (Chrysippus, quoted in Nussbaum 1994, 328–29)

In order to better engage the self-activity of the student, the teacher focuses on practical problems, not abstract philosophical themes.[7] The use of concrete examples and stories serves the same end.

Yet a problem did arise in the transition from Socrates to the Stoics, a problem that has and perhaps will always tend to undermine the strengths of the indirect approach. Epigrams, sayings, and writings accumulated from the sages of the past. Instead of developing their own critical facilities or the autonomy of their wills, students could now memorize the "lessons" of Socrates and the previous Stoic philosophers (e.g., like the "checklists" or "blueprints" for "doing the right thing") and then regurgitate them with flourish and skill to become "sages" themselves. For this modus operandi, no indirect pedagogy was needed; the direct approach of indoctrination in the lessons and great books of the past would suffice. Thus one finds Epictetus (A.D. 55–135) going to great lengths verbally lambasting his students for these pretensions. Seneca (A.D. 1–65) likewise chides his correspondent Lucilius on the desire to accumulate sayings:

> It is disgraceful that a man who is old or in sight of old age should have a wisdom deriving solely from his notebooks. "Zeno said this."And what have you said? "Cleanthes said that." What have you said? How much longer are you going to serve under others' orders? . . .
>
> To remember is to safeguard something entrusted to your memory, whereas to know, by contrast, is actually to make each item your own, and not to be dependent on some original and be constantly looking to see what the master said. (Seneca 1969, letter 33)

In the same spirit, Martha Nussbaum today chides those who would erect "The Great Books" as authorities to be learned, revered, and deferred to and suggests a "more Senecan title, such as 'Some useful and nourishing books that are likely to help you think for yourself'" (Nussbaum 1997, 35).

The goal of the indirect method is the self-transformation of the learner, not to make the learner into "an instrument for what others have to say" (Seneca 1969, letter 33). But the written word (or remembered spoken word) always provides the temptation to revert to the easier direct method of teaching so that the pupils might at least display some of the outward behavior that might accompany self-transformation. The first mover or first doer has no problem with ownership since there was no prior source of the belief or volition. The problem is to foster and enable ownership on the part of subsequent doers. Therein lies the rationale for indirect methods since a direct transmission would violate the basis of ownership (being the fruits of the doer's activity).

Learning in Neoplatonism

There is a stream of thought supporting indirect methods that comes from Plato more than Socrates. Plato argues that, as is seen most clearly in mathematics, concepts do not come from experience but arise within the mind itself. The Platonic Ideas or Forms are innate in the mind and arise in consciousness through a process of recollection or reminiscence perhaps prompted by our sense experience. The theme of innate mental structures and mechanisms triggered—but not controlled—by experience has percolated down through Western thought (e.g., Plotinus, Augustine, the Cambridge Platonists, René Descartes, Gottfried Wilhelm Leibniz, Kant, and Wilhelm von Humboldt) to find modern expression in the pedagogy of constructivism (e.g., Piaget 1955, 1970) and the school of generative linguistics (e.g., Chomsky 1966).

For our purposes, it is sufficient to see how the theory of the mind as an active, generative organ supports the indirect approach, while the opposing theory of the mind as a passive tabula rasa, or wax block, supports the direct approach. Plato has some passive images of the mind as a wax block (*Theaetetus*, 191–95) or a mirror or reflector (*Timaeus*, 71). But Socrates (Plato, *Symposium*, 175d) notes that wisdom was not the sort of thing that could flow as through pipes "from the one that was full to the one that was empty." In a direct statement about education, Plato uses the cave allegory where the soul turns away from the shadows to see the Forms.

> If this is true, then, we must conclude that education is not what it is said to be by some, who profess to put knowledge into a soul which does not possess it, as if they could put sight into blind eyes. On the contrary,

our own account signifies that the soul of every man does possess the power of learning the truth and the organ to see it with; and that, just as one might have to turn the whole body round in order that the eye should see light instead of darkness, so the entire soul must be turned away from this changing world, until its eye can bear to contemplate reality and that supreme splendour which we have called the Good. (Plato, *Republic*, 518)

According to Plotinus the Platonic process of recollection becomes an explicitly active process represented by metaphors such as an overflowing fountain or a radiating light.

In discussing the human perception of the divine overflow, Plotinus explicitly rejected the concept of sensations as "imprints" or "seal-impressions" made on a passive mind, and substituted the view of the mind as an act and a power which "gives a radiance out of its own store" to the objects of sense. (Abrams 1953, 59)

The opposing metaphors of the mind as a passive mirror or as an active lamp correlate with two opposite pedagogies. The supporters as well as the critics of the mirror pedagogy used various models of the student as being essentially passive: a wax tablet on which knowledge is stamped, a mirror or reflector for knowledge (Plato and John Locke), a vessel or cistern into which knowledge is poured (Ralph Cudworth,[8] Coleridge, and Dewey), a phonographic record onto which knowledge is recorded (Dewey, Antonio Gramsci, and Ryle), and now in the computer age "a sort of printout in the minds of students" (Hawkins 2000, 2). The teacher supplies the knowledge that is imprinted onto the student, crammed into the student as into a bag (Maritain), forced into the student through a funnel (Martin Buber), drilled into the student as into hard and resisting rock (Dewey), or forced into the student using a grease gun (McGregor).

The other, lamp, pedagogy sees the student's mind as taking a more active role represented by metaphors such as a lamp, fountain, or projector—or often by organic metaphors of a growing plant. The teacher then has a more subtle indirect role of a guide, coach, or midwife to foster and nurture the student's active search for and appropriation of knowledge. Some of the subtlety of the teacher's indirect role can be expressed using the metaphor of the internal fountain. Impediments can obscure or block the flow of the fountain (like turning off a faucet or hose). External enabling help can then unblock the fountain or open the faucet, but the subtle point is that external help cannot directly supply the pressure to make the fountain flow. That pressure has to come from within.[9]

The Learning Paradox and Augustine

The insights of a philosophical tradition are sometimes expressed in a deliberately provocative slogan, epigram, or paradox. One of the striking epigrams of Neoplatonism is the thesis that "no man ever does or can teach another anything" (Burnyeat 1987a, 1). This epigram is a variation on Meno's paradox, or the learning paradox. In the *Meno* dialogue, Socrates attempts to indirectly "teach" a slave boy some truths of geometry. Socrates claims that people cannot be directly taught such truths, they must recollect them.

> *Meno:* I see, Socrates. But what do you mean when you say that we don't learn anything, but that what we call learning is recollection? Can you teach me that it is so?
> *Socrates:* I have just said that you're a rascal, and now you ask me if I can teach you, when I say there is no such thing as teaching, only recollection. Evidently you want to catch me contradicting myself straight-away. (Plato, *Meno* 81e–82a)

One interpretation of Meno's paradox is that a priori truths such as the truths of geometry must be recollected since no amount of empirical investigation can verify the truths of mathematics. But that is a paltry interpretation; Augustine (who "Christianized" Neoplatonism) and others gave a stronger interpretation to the claim that "no man ever does or can teach another anything."

In *De Magistro* (*The Teacher*), Augustine develops an argument (in the form of a dialogue with his son Adeodatus) that as teachers teach, it is only the student's internal appropriation of what is taught that gives understanding and knowledge.

> Then those who are called pupils consider within themselves whether what has been explained has been said truly; looking of course to that

interior truth, according to the measure of which each is able. Thus they learn, ... But men are mistaken, so that they call those teachers who are not, merely because for the most part there is no delay between the time of speaking and the time of cognition. And since after the speaker has reminded them, the pupils quickly learn within, they think that they have been taught outwardly by him who prompts them. (Augustine, *De Magistro*, chap. 14)

The basic point is the active role of the mind in *generating* understanding. This is clear even at the simple level of understanding spoken words. We hear the "auditory sense data" of words in a completely strange language as well as the words in our native language. But the strange words "bounce off" our minds with no resultant understanding, while the words in a familiar language prompt an internal process of generating a meaning so that we understand the words.

Nothing can be present in the mind (*Seele*) that has not originated from one's own activity. Moreover understanding and speaking are but different effects of the selfsame power of speech. Speaking is never comparable to the transmission of mere matter (*Stoff*). In the person comprehending as well as in the speaker, the subject matter must be developed by the individual's own innate power. What the listener receives is merely the harmonious vocal stimulus. (Humboldt [1836] 1997, 102)

This simple example provides one of the most accessible examples of an autonomy-respecting intervention. Instead of transmitting or disseminating understanding from the helper to the doer, the actions of the helper (speaker) stimulate and catalyze internal processes in the doer to reproduce the understanding. The direct approach misrepresents this process using the metaphor of "transmitting" the material from the first to the second person.[10]

There are many variations on this theme of the active mind in understanding. John Dewey makes a point about ideas that is similar to the learning paradox, a point that supports Dewey's active learning pedagogy.

It is that no thought, no idea, can possibly be conveyed as an idea from one person to another. When it is told, it is, to the one to whom it is told, another given fact, not an idea. The communication may stimulate the other person to realize the question for himself and to think out a like idea, or it may smother his intellectual interest and suppress his dawning effort at thought. (Dewey 1916, 159)

The common element in the various interpretations of the general learning paradox "no man ever does or can teach another anything" is that the external transmission from the speaker-teacher to the listener-learner does not itself account for the active role of the mind in generating an understanding of what was received. The external transmission prompts and guides the internal process; the internal processing appropriates what is received in terms of prior experience and makes it our own.[11]

The Augustinian point is that what is often taken as a direct process (e.g., transmitting or disseminating knowledge) is actually a more indirect process. Today, "knowledge management" in organizations is constantly designed and implemented using "transmission" images of direct methods when in fact a more subtle understanding and implementation of indirect capacity-building methods would yield a better chance of success.

Jean-Jacques Rousseau's Copernican Revolution in Pedagogy

Ortega y Gasset (1883–1955) asks what has been the "great historic advance in pedagogy," and he answers that it was the turning inspired by "Rousseau, Pestalozzi, Froebel, and German idealism." Before, pedagogy had focused on the teacher and on the subject matter, but with Rousseau the themes known today as self-direction, autonomy, active learning, and learner-centered education came to the forefront. "The innovation of Rousseau and his successors was simply to shift the center of gravity of the science from knowledge and the teacher to the learner, recognizing that it is the learner and his characteristics which alone can guide us in our effort to make something organic of education" (Ortega 1966, 46).

The helper's assistance to the doers is unlikely to be autonomy respecting if the help is undertaken in the spirit and conception of social engineering. The success of the natural sciences from Galileo and Newton through the Enlightenment to understand and control Nature inspired attempts in the developing psychological, social, political, and economic sciences to similarly "engineer" social outcomes.

Although ancient civilizations had their "social engineers," the new aspect was "that the engineering paradigm now becomes a highly conscious, central paradigm. There is the growing conviction that the only *real* problems of men are precisely those amenable to an engineering approach" (Schwartz 1978, 194). The Romantic reaction to this technocratic strand of Enlightenment thought can be traced to Rousseau.

Here again we see the two theories of the mind represented by the two metaphors of the mirror and the lamp (Abrams 1953). The mirror approach lent itself easily to social engineering, as seen for example in the later development of behaviorism. Descartes, following the Platonic tradition, saw the mind as a lamp endowed with innate structures that unfold and mature under the impact of experience and through the stimulus of action. Rousseau developed a version of the lamp theory, although he was more given to organic metaphors of natural growth assisted by appropriate care.

Learning is an active growth, not the accretion of layers as in the "growth" of a pearl. Pedagogy based explicitly or implicitly on the engineering approach sees the teacher as depositing new layers of knowledge rather than seeing the learner as taking the active role growing new layers of understanding. A teacher might take pride in explaining everything thoroughly for the student, but that crowds out an active role for the student.

> Talent at instruction consists in making the disciple enjoy the instruction. But in order for him to enjoy it, his mind must not remain so passive at everything you tell him that he has absolutely nothing to do in order to understand you. The master's *amour-propre* must always leave some hold for the disciple's; he must be able to say to himself, "I conceive, I discern, I act, I learn." (Rousseau [1762] 1979, 248)

This problem is repeated manyfold when administrations in schools and other organizations want their staff (teachers or task managers) "to show results," which in turn leads to those helpers taking an instrumental or engineering approach in their assistance to the ultimate doers (see McClintock 1982). The end result is that the doers' amour propre, pride, and ownership is crowded out and overridden so they cannot say, "I conceive, I discern, I act, I learn."

Ortega also mentions Johann Heinrich Pestalozzi (1746–1827) and Friedrich Froebel (1782–1852) as continuing to emphasize a learner-centered pedagogy in Rousseau's tradition. Indeed, Pestalozzi's work "contains ideas not yet realized in our time, namely, that education of both young and adults is ineffective unless it grows out of the initiative of the people themselves, unless it speaks their language, and unless it influences not only isolated individuals but the life of the whole community" (Ulich 1954, 480).

In addition to being known as the founder of kindergarten, Froebel has been hailed as "the prophet of the active nature of the learning process" (cited in Lawrence 1970, 244). Froebel made the self-activity of the learner the central theme of his pedagogy: "To stir up, to animate, to awaken, and to strengthen, the pleasure and power of the human being to labour uninterruptedly at his own education, has become and always remained the fundamental principle and aim of my educational work" (Froebel 1954, 525). With Froebel, we also see the emphasis on intrinsic motivation for autonomous learning activities. "Froebel's self-activity is necessarily coupled with joy on the part of the child. To him joy is the inward reaction of self-activity" (translator's note cited in Ulich 1954, 557). The role of intrinsic motivation in active learning foreshadows the modern literature on the limitations of external motivators in education (e.g., Kohn 1993, 1999) and in work (e.g., McGregor and Deming, not to mention Ruskin)—a theme that helps account for the general ineffectiveness of direct methods in fostering mental transformation.

John Dewey and the Active Learning Pedagogy

John Dewey's (1859–1952) theory of education was based on the autonomy-respecting actions of the teacher and the activist role of the learner. As noted above in the context of the learning paradox in Augustinian Neoplatonism, Dewey notes that no idea "can possibly be conveyed as an idea from one person to another," and he evokes the horse-to-water metaphor. The reliance on extrinsic rewards or punishments, not to mention physical control, may yield conforming behavior and a rote learning but has little educative or transformative effect. Indeed, the threat to autonomy may lead to an adverse reactance effect. "His instincts of cunning and slyness may be aroused, so that things henceforth appeal to him on the side of evasion and trickery more than would otherwise be the case" (Dewey 1916, 26). An autonomy-respecting educational program needs to engage the person's more natural and intrinsic motivation.

When we confuse a physical with an educative result, we always lose the chance of enlisting the person's own participating disposition in getting the result desired, and thereby of developing within him an intrinsic and persisting direction in the right way. (Dewey 1916, 27)

The students' active interest and involvement is a necessary component, so one must consider the roots of engagement. Students do not construct knowledge in a void. Learning is contextual; it builds upon the context of previous knowledge, experience, and problems. Hence Dewey's "pragmatic" emphasis was placed on learning in the context of the "social environment," albeit simplified and ordered in a school, so that the student would have a natural or intrinsic incentive to learn. Hence Paulo Freire's emphasis on dialogue as the prelude to, as well as the means of, learning (1970). By formulating a literacy campaign in terms of the peasants' daily concerns, the peasants are motivated to be involved and take ownership of the process. The cases, examples, and questions can be couched in terms that make sense from the student's viewpoint and are relevant to the student's interests. With this preparation, the student can take responsibility for actively reconstructing and appropriating knowledge with occasional prodding and questioning from the teacher as midwife. Knowledge obtained in this active way is more the student's own; it is neither an imposition nor a gift. In general, one may try "to give" help to others or to impose "help," but in neither case are the others helping themselves.

The most common error in an educational effort is for the one with superior knowledge (the teacher) to try to impose or imprint knowledge on the one with less knowledge of the relevant sort (assisted by manipulated rewards and punishments). Another common error is to think that the alternative role for the teacher is passivity (leaving the children to "free play"). Between these poles lies the autonomy-respecting modes of interaction that are Dewey's "direction by indirection" (Westbrook 1991, 107). Martin Buber also tries to capture the subtlety of direction by indirection in his description of the relationship between educator and pupil.

For if the educator of our day has to act consciously he must nevertheless do it "as though he did not." That raising of the finger, the questioning glance, are his genuine doing. Through him the selection of the effective world reaches the pupil. He fails the recipient when he pre-

sents this selection to him with a gesture of interference. It must be concentrated in him; and doing out of concentration has the appearance of
rest. Interference divides the soul in his care into an obedient part and a
rebellious part. But a hidden influence proceeding from his integrity has
an integrating force. (Buber 1965, 90)

Such an indirect autonomy-respecting interaction is even more subtle
when all parties concerned are adults with their own past education
and formative life experiences.[12]

Carl Rogers's Nondirective Therapy

The next example of an indirect approach comes from Carl Rogers's
notion of client-centered therapy (Rogers 1951)—which was also
called *nondirective therapy*, echoing Dewey's notion of direction by
indirection and other indirect approaches. The temptation for the
therapist, as for the teacher and manager, is to take charge and to try
"to produce" the right results. And as in the other cases, this overbearing approach cuts across the other person's internal resources for self-
directed activities. On the other hand, a complete laissez-faire, or
hands-off, approach would lead to no interaction rather than an autonomy-respecting interaction (a charge sometimes leveled against nondirective therapy). One key for the therapist, as for the educator, is to see
the world through the client's eyes.

> This formulation would state that it is the counselor's function to
> assume, in so far as he is able, the internal frame of reference of the
> client, to perceive the world as the client sees it, to perceive the client
> himself as he is seen by himself, to lay aside all perceptions from the
> external frame of reference while doing so, and to communicate some-
> thing of this empathic understanding to the client. (Rogers 1951, 29)

The client-centered therapist must guard against this empathy being
used as a gimmick to control the patient "while pretending to let him
guide himself" (Rogers 1951, 30) just as the Theory Y manager needs to
avoid seeing participation as a tool to get worker "buy-in" to management decisions. The basis in all cases is the respect for the autonomy of
the client (student or worker):

the sincere aim of getting "within" the attitudes of the client, of entering the client's internal frame of reference, is the most complete implementation which has thus far been formulated, for the central hypothesis of respect for and reliance upon the capacity of the person. (Rogers
1951, 36)

The therapist's role is to be a "catalyzer of change, rather than a director,
controller, or external motivator. . . . In terms of causality . . . , the goal
of therapy is to be a strengthening of one's autonomy orientation, that is,
one's capacity to be self-determining" (Deci and Ryan 1985, 291).

Rogers applies the client-centered approach to education where it
becomes "student-centered teaching" (Rogers 1951, chap. 9), which
acknowledges the debt to Dewey and develops the same themes and
even some of the same metaphors ("you can lead a horse to water, but
. . ."). Rogers also points out the connection to management theory.

The grounds for the theory of administration which McGregor calls
"Theory Y" have been exemplified in all of the preceding chapters of
this book. The assumptions on which this theory is based, the kinds of
evidence from the behavioral sciences which support it, the view of
human nature which permeates it, constitute the backbone of what I
have set forth. (Rogers 1969, 207)

Rogers also notes the application of these principles to community
development. How would an external expert or leader be able to best
help in the development of a community? "If the leader was a catalyst,
a person genuinely able to accept the neighborhood as it existed and to
release the group to work toward its real purposes and goals, the result
was in the direction of socialization" (Rogers 1951, 59). If, however,
the expert tries to give the community the answer based on knowledge
of "best practices" or whatever, then this is incompatible with its own
autonomous development. Rogers quotes at length from a 1944 memo
by Clifford Shaw, a sociologist working on problems of social disorga-
nization and delinquency (the young Saul Alinsky once worked in one
of Shaw's projects), about Shaw's experience in a Chicago-area community project.

[A]ttempts to produce these changes *for* the community by means of
ready made institutions and programs planned, developed, financed, and
managed by persons outside the community are not likely to meet with

any more success in the future than they have in the past. This procedure is psychologically unsound because it places the residents of the community in an inferior position and implies serious reservations with regard to their capacities and interest in their own welfare. What is equally important is that it neglects the greatest of all assets in any community, namely the talents, energies and other human resources of the people themselves. . . . What is necessary, we believe, is the organization and encouragement of social self-help on a cooperative basis.[13] (Shaw 1944; quoted in Rogers 1951, 59)

Our methodology emphasizes the parallels in the autonomy-respecting helper-doer relationships between different fields and the representative eight thinkers. Many of the parallels were recognized by the eight thinkers themselves as when Carl Rogers refers to John Dewey or to Douglas McGregor. Moreover in describing the process of an aid agency trying to help a developing country, Albert Hirschman recommends a process of familiarization—of walking in its citizens' shoes and seeing through their eyes to see the array of problems facing the country.

Little by little, after getting committed and "seeing," that is, learning about the country's problems, some hypotheses should emerge about the sequence in which a country is likely to attack successfully the multifarious obstacles. In the search for the best hypothesis, those who administer aid programs should use what Dr. Carl Rogers, the psychotherapist, calls "client-centered therapy."[14] (Hirschman 1971, 185)

Søren Kierkegaard and Ludwig Wittgenstein on Indirect Communication

Søren Kierkegaard (1813–55) was the philosopher of the indirect approach par excellence. His approach to philosophical persuasion was steeped in indirect Socratic irony, and his main message was that all direct objective approaches to spiritual insight must fall short; only subjective inwardness could appropriate the truth about questions of moral or spiritual value. For example, can one directly inform and persuade a conventional Christian that he is only under an illusion of being a Christian? After "loving and serving the truth" one must withdraw rather than press the point so that the other can make an embarrassing admission in private.

Kierkegaard's main point was not just about the indirectness of persuading others but about the subjectivity of moral or spiritual insight even for oneself so that all direct objective or intellectual ("speculative") approaches were doomed to fail and could only produce a counterfeit approximation to insight. He poses the learning paradox about the extent to which truths, spiritual Truth in his case, can be learned from others. He reviews the old doctrine of recollection according to which "the Truth is not introduced into the individual from without, but was within him all the time" (in Bretall 1946, 155). Hence these matters need to be communicated indirectly or maieutically (as by a Socratic midwife).

> The fact that several of Plato's dialogues end with no conclusion has a far deeper reason than I had earlier thought. For this is a reproduction of Socrates' maieutic skills, which activate the reader or listener himself, and therefore end not in any conclusion but with a sting. This is an excellent parody of the modern rote-learning method that says everything at once and the quicker the better, which does not awaken the reader to any self-activity, but only allows him to recite by heart. (Kierkegaard's journals VII I A 74; quoted in Storm 1999, 11)

Kierkegaard also gives a spiritual interpretation of "Socratic ignorance" as the recognition that this inward subjective truth cannot be obtained objectively or speculatively.

We note in the preceding that actions have motives and beliefs have grounds. Kierkegaard is making the point that intrinsically motivated actions and inwardly subjective beliefs cannot be extrinsically or objectively obtained just as love cannot be bought. "But to be a lover, a hero, etc. is reserved specifically for subjectivity, because objectively one does not become that. . . . And . . . piety is rooted precisely in subjectivity; one does not become pious objectively" (Kierkegaard 1992, 132). It is not the "what" of one's beliefs that counts—as that can be learned by rote—but the "how" of the beliefs (i.e., how the beliefs were subjectively appropriated). For instance, Kierkegaard satirizes an orthodox "Christian" gentleman who

> does everything in the name of Jesus and uses Christ's name on every occasion as a sure sign that he is a Christian and is called to defend Christendom in our day—and he has no intimation of the little ironic secret that a person, just by describing the "how" of his inwardness, can

indirectly indicate that he is a Christian without mentioning Christ's name. . . . If anyone says, "Yes, but then one can in turn learn the 'how' of faith by rote and recite it," the answer to that must be: That cannot be done, because the person who states it directly contradicts himself, ... [O]ne human being cannot directly communicate this something else to another. . . . All ironic observing is a matter of continually paying attention to the "how," whereas the honorable gentleman with whom the ironist has the honor of dealing pays attention only to the "what."[15] (Kierkegaard 1992, 613–14 and footnote)

In this sketch, no attempt is being made to capture the richness and scope of Kierkegaard's philosophical psychology or the particulars of his treatment of Christianity. For our purposes, he was the quintessential philosopher of the inner life; indeed he was obsessed with the juxtapositions of the outer to the inner, the external to the internal, the objective to the subjective. In terms of our scheme "activity = behavior + motive" (and "belief = proposition + grounds for belief"), the first part (i.e., behaviors or propositions) was Kierkegaard's objective or external "what," while the second part (i.e., motives or grounds for belief) dealt with the subjective and internal "how." He saw clearly that the usual direct methods for dealing with the outer, external, and objective aspects of the world would not extend to the other side; indirect methods were needed to deal with the inner, the internal, and the subjective. Attempts to apply the direct methods to subjective transformation would only produce inauthentic counterfeits.

Kierkegaard is widely considered as one of the founders of existentialism, but it is quite relevant to our theme to see the influence on Ludwig Wittgenstein (1889–1951). By analyzing Wittgenstein's intellectual and social background in early twentieth-century Vienna, Stephen Toulmin and Allan Janik have persuasively argued for a more Kierkegaardian interpretation (with significant influence also from Arthur Schopenhauer and Leo Tolstoy) than the conventional interpretations of the early Wittgenstein as a logical positivist or the later Wittgenstein as an ordinary language philosopher. This Kierkegaardian reading is important for understanding the enigmatic ending of the *Tractatus Logico-Philosophicus* (1922): "Whereof one cannot speak, thereof one must be silent." Wittgenstein, like Kierkegaard, strictly separated the objective world of facts from the subjective world of moral and aesthetic values.[16]

In separating reason from fantasy, the mathematical representation of the physicist from the metaphor of the poet, straight-forward descriptive language from "indirect communication," Wittgenstein was convinced that he had solved "the problem of philosophy" [that is, in the *Tractatus*]. . . . The implication of the model theory was that the "meaning of life" lay outside the sphere of what could be said. . . . So the model theory corroborates Kierkegaard's notion that the meaning of life is not a topic which can be discussed by means of the categories of reason.

Subjective truth is communicable only indirectly, through fable, polemics, irony, and satire. This is the only way that one can come to "see the world aright." Ethics is taught not by arguments, but by providing examples of moral behavior; this is the task of art. It is fulfilled in Tolstoy's later *Tales*, which explain what religion is, by *showing* how the truly religious man lives his life. (Janik and Toulmin 1973, 198)

In a December 1929 conversation, Wittgenstein made the explicit connection to Kierkegaard.

Nevertheless, we run up against the limits of language. This running-up-against Kierkegaard also saw, and indicated in a completely similar way—as running up against the Paradox. This running up against the limits of language is *Ethics*. I regard it as of great importance, that one should put an end to all the twaddle about ethics—whether it is a science, whether values exist, whether the Good can be defined, etc. In ethics people are forever trying to find a way of saying something which, in the nature of things, is not and can never be expressed. We know a priori: anything which one might give by way of an definition of the Good—it can never be anything but a misunderstanding. (reported in Waismann 1967, 68–69; quoted in Janik and Toulmin 1973, 194–95)

In the turn from the early to the later Wittgenstein, his doubts about the efficacy of direct communication in ethical and aesthetic matters spread, albeit for different reasons, to descriptions of the world. Instead of mirroring or picturing facts, language acquired its meaning by its use in inherently social forms of life. When removed out of its embedding in such a language game, an expression might have many interpretations and might cause undue philosophical problems when it is assumed to have a meaning in a very different game. Wittgenstein would use indirect methods of stories and fables to dissolve philosophical problems resulting from lifting language from one form of life to another.

What Tolstoy's *Tales* had done for the unsayable in ethics, these fables of Wittgenstein's did for the unsayable in the philosophy of language. So, in philosophy as in ethics, Wittgenstein believed, teaching could bring a man only to a point at which he recognized what you were getting at, for himself; and it was no good attempting to draw an explicit conclusion for him. (Janik and Toulmin 1973, 229)

This is again expressed in the warhorse aphorism about the indirect way that "you can lead a horse to water."

Wittgenstein's theory of meaning as use embedded in a form of life also gives a version of the Augustinian learning paradox that "no man ever does or can teach another anything."

> No-one can achieve my understanding for me, not for the trivial reason that it is mine, but because to internalize the requisite connections is to go beyond what is presented on any occasion of so-called teaching. Augustine does not have Wittgenstein's subtle arguments to bring out the multiplicity of ways in which I might seem (to myself and others) to understand and later turn out to have missed the point, which in turn demonstrates the multiplicity of connections in understanding itself. But we might read Wittgenstein as reviving the ancient understanding of the complexity of understanding. (Burnyeat 1987a, 23)

Understanding comes from the listener's integration into the form of life where a linguistic expression is ordinarily used and where the "meaning is the use." This interpretation of Wittgenstein's use of indirect methods meshes well with our next topic—which takes us from Kierkegaard's unsayable "how" to Ryle's inarticulate "knowing-how."

Gilbert Ryle and Michael Polanyi on Uncodified Knowledge

Knowledge that can be directly communicated has already been codified, but much knowledge has the uncodified form of practical or tacit knowledge or know-how. Gilbert Ryle (1900–1976) and Michael Polanyi (1891–1976) have in different fields, using various terminologies, explored the special problems of uncodified knowledge, including alternatives to the naïve pedagogy of direct teaching as if all knowledge were the technical, explicit, codified, or knowing-that type of knowledge.[17]

Michael Polanyi (1962, 1966) made the notion of tacit or personal knowledge into the centerpiece of his philosophical viewpoint. When one focuses on another face and recognizes it, the features of the face necessary for recognition are only attended to in a *subsidiary awareness* (1962, 55), and one will be hard put to articulate them. In one's *focal awareness* of the face, these features are brought together in a *gestaltlike* way so that the face is seen as a familiar one. One has a commitment to that tacit knowledge and relies on it for the recognition. If one tries to articulate the separate features of the face that make it recognizable, then one loses the gestalt. Polanyi generalized these aspects of tacit knowledge being utilized in a unifying way in all human actions including rigorous scientific activity.

The bringing together or integrating of the underlying tacit knowledge is a creative mental action, and thus it is reminiscent of the active (Kantian) role of the mind in Augustine's Neoplatonism and in modern generative linguistics. In Polanyi's analysis, the problem with direct methods of teaching or transmitting knowledge is not simply that they neglect the tacit component but that they do not supply the active integration of the tacit knowledge into the focal act of knowing. This is the Augustinian point that what is naively seen as direct transmission is really the more indirect prompting of internal gestalt processes of learning and knowing.

Gilbert Ryle (1945–46) made an early distinction between knowing that (propositional knowledge) and knowing how, the latter being his treatment of practical and personal knowledge. How does Ryle's treatment of the different types of knowing illuminate the direct and indirect approaches to acquiring knowledge? Is the problem with the direct approach simply that it tends to leave out tacit knowledge that might be picked up by indirect means? Or does it relate back to the more passive role of the student under the direct method of teaching in contrast to an indirect approach that casts the learner in a more active role? For Ryle, the important thing was not the explicit/implicit or codified/tacit distinction but the difference between learning propositions (e.g., 7 × 8 = 56) essentially by rote and learning how *to do* something (e.g., to multiply as well as to ride a bike). And when the student learns by doing, then that inextricably active component in the student's role implies a more indirect approach, whereas the direct approach is based on a "semi-surgical picture of teaching as the forcible insertion into the pupil's memory of strings of officially approved propositions" (Ryle 1967, 108).

In a by-now-familiar manner, Ryle poses the learning paradox.

> How can one person teach another person to think things out for him-
> self, since if he gives him, say, the new arithmetical thoughts, then they
> are not the pupil's own thoughts; or if they are his own thoughts, then
> he did not get them from his teacher? Having led the horse to the water,
> how can we make him drink? (Ryle 1967, 112)

Ryle's answer is along the lines of the motive inconsistency argument;
there is no way to heteronomously impose autonomous action.

> How can the teacher be the initiator of the pupil's initiatives? the
> answer is obvious. He cannot. I cannot compel the horse to drink
> thirstily. I cannot coerce Tommy into doing spontaneous things. Either
> he is not coerced, or they are not spontaneous. . . .
>   How in logic can the teacher dragoon his pupil into thinking for
> himself, impose initiative upon him, drive him into self-motion, con-
> script him into volunteering, enforce originality upon him, or make him
> operate spontaneously? The answer is that he cannot—and the reason
> why we half felt that we must do so was that we were unwittingly
> enslaved by the crude, semi-hydraulic idea that in essence to teach is to
> pump propositions, like "Waterloo, 1815" into the pupils' ears, until
> they regurgitate them automatically. (Ryle 1967, 112, 118)

Ryle makes the case for the indirect approach crystal clear. The
point is not the distinction between codified propositions and tacit
practical knowledge; even to actually use and apply codified knowledge
requires a knowing how that needs to be acquired actively. Thus the
problem with the direct approach is the inconsistency of trying to
impose active learning. The teacher can open the faucet but cannot
supply the pressure for the water to flow (to use a Neo-platonic variation on the horse-to-water metaphor). At best the teacher uses an indirect approach to bring the learner to the threshold; the self-activity of
the learner must carry the process the rest of the way.

Gandhi and Satyagraha

An indirect approach is central to Mohandas Karamchand Gandhi's
philosophy. In the case of Gandhi's method of social action called
satyagraha (truth-force), the relationship between the first party, A

(helper), and the second party, B (doer), is openly antagonistic. The first party is an aggrieved person or group who feels that his or her or its rights have been violated by the second party who is typically an established political or economic authority. With these caveats in mind, the helper-doer terminology is still used here—particularly in view of Erik Erikson's analogy between the method of satyagraha and the therapeutic relationship (1969, 413 and 439).

It should be noted that this section does not focus on Gandhi's writings directly about development but about the autonomy-respecting helper-doer relationship embodied in the method of satyagraha and how it might give us insight into the helper-doer relationship in development assistance. The latter might sometimes also be rather antagonistic, as when the doer is a corrupt government who resents any such imputation.

In the relationship of mind to mind, the main problem of direct methods of influence is motive inconsistency. Means are employed to bring about a change of mind in the doer when the motives are inconsistent with the desired change. Often the motive inconsistency is of little concern. If one were being attacked, then one would like the attacker (doer) to desist, and one might not be fastidious about how the attacker's mind was changed. Ideally one might want a potential attacker to refrain out of recognition and respect for one's rights, and one's defense might do little to bring about that recognition and motivation. This motivational inconsistency in one's defense would be of little practical consequence if the attack was a one-time matter. But if the situation was repeated as it would be in the case of a group of people with a long-standing grievance against an economic or political power, then one might want to consider the motivational dynamics of one's method. Is there an alternative to the vicious cycle of tit for tat or eye for an eye?

The first criterion for an alternative strategy is that it be motivationally consistent with the desired actions on the part of the other party. That is the minimal basis for the passive "turning the other cheek," for not feeding the vicious cycle of attack and counterattack dynamics. The next step is to design an active response strategy that will not only be consistent with a desired motivation but will try to elicit a motive on the part of the doer that will lead to a mutually acceptable state of affairs. That goes beyond turning the other cheek to

"Love your enemies and pray for those who persecute you" (Matthew 5:45).

> Prior to reading Gandhi I had about concluded that the ethics of Jesus were only effective in individual relationships. The "turn the other cheek" philosophy and the "love your enemies" philosophy were only valid, I felt, when individuals were in conflict with individuals; when racial groups and nations were in conflict a more realistic approach seemed necessary. But after reading Gandhi, I saw how utterly mistaken I was. Gandhi was probably the first person in history to lift the love ethic of Jesus above mere interaction between individuals to a powerful and effective social force on a large scale. (Martin Luther King Jr., *Stride toward Freedom*, quoted on dust jacket of Gandhi 1961)

These strategies at the individual or social level go beyond the reach of direct carrot and stick methods. As Dewey remarked, "while we can shut a man up in a penitentiary we cannot make him penitent" (1916, 26). The stick at best deters and does not reform, and that may be the best that can be expected against a Tamerlane or a Hitler. But in most social situations, there are other possibilities that might be obtained by more subtle, indirect methods.

By using indirect methods, mind can affect mind in ways that would be motivationally impossible with direct carrot and stick methods. Indirect strategies are designed not just to get the doer to change his or her behavior (e.g., for prudential reasons) but to change his or her "heart and mind" and perhaps to set off a more positive dynamic to the benefit of both parties. Changes at that deeper motivational level cannot be forced, and any attempt to crudely force such changes will only lead to resentment, resistance, and intransigence from the doer. Thus indirect methods operate on the basis of respect for the integrity of the doer.

After exhausting conventional channels to resolve the conflict, the aggrieved party may decide to resort to satyagraha. This party (the helper trying to help the doer change) believes it has been wronged on certain grounds by the doer; that is its "truth." The "truths" asserted by the helper must be heartfelt and not just tactics. To show that the claims are made for authentic reasons, the helper must be vulnerable to rational counterarguments or new facts that might come to light and must under such circumstances change his or her mind.

> A devotee of Truth may not do anything in deference to convention. He must always hold himself open to correction, and whenever he discovers himself to be wrong he must confess it at all costs and atone for it. (Gandhi 1957, 350)

In this manner, arguments on the helper's side about these beliefs are kept on authentic grounds, not on the level of strategy and tactics, and the doer can then be authentically invited to reexamine his or her beliefs in the light of reason and evidence, not just self-interest.

The conflict is social and is carried out in public. In line with the old strategy "fight a war to secure a peace" the actions of the aggrieved party must be compatible with the doer changing his or her mind while maintaining self-respect and self-esteem. While pressure will be brought on the doer to provide motivational backups, the pressure should not take the form of injuries that will derail the motivation for authentic change. That is the basis for the Gandhian doctrine of non-injury, or *ahimsa*.

> Under the Babul Tree Gandhi announced the principle which somehow corresponds to our amended [Golden] Rule: "*That line of action is alone justice which does not harm either party to a dispute.*" By harm he meant— and his daily announcements leave no doubt of this—an inseparable combination of economic disadvantage, social indignity, loss of self-esteem, and latent vengeance. (Erikson 1964, 239)

In Joan Bondurant's authoritative treatment of satyagraha, she notes: "If there is dogma in the Gandhian philosophy, it centers here: that the only test of truth is action based on the refusal to do harm" (1958, 25). Thus Truth and ahimsa were two fundamental prongs in satyagraha.

> *Ahimsa* and Truth are so intertwined that it is practically impossible to disentangle and separate them. They are like the two sides of a coin, or rather of a smooth unstamped metallic disk. . . . Nevertheless *ahimsa* is the means; Truth is the end. (Gandhi 1961, 42)

A third component is the self-suffering, or *tapasya*, which works to elevate the motivation of the helper in the eyes of public opinion, if not in the eyes of the doer.

> Self-suffering, the third element of satyagraha, guarantees the sincerity of the satyagrahi's own opinions, the while it restrains him from propa-

gating uncertain truths. The objective of satyagraha is to win the victory over the conflict situation—to discover further truths and to persuade the opponent, not to triumph over him. (Bondurant 1958, 33)

This last point—about winning the victory over the situation, not over the person—is particularly important as a means of maintaining respect for and the self-respect of the doer. When actions face constraints, it is very important whether or not the constraints are human caused or natural. As previously noted, this is Rousseau's point: "The nature of things does not madden us, only ill will does" (quoted in Berlin 1969, 123). Thus the doer will change his mind more easily if the conflict can be reframed as a depersonalized "situation" so that he or she is reacting to the situation rather than to specific pressure from the aggrieved party. In management theory, this is Mary Parker Follett's indirect method, the "law of the situation."

> Our job is not how to get people to obey orders, but how to devise methods by which we can best *discover* the order integral to a particular situation. When that is found, the employee can issue it to the employer, as well as employer to employee.[18] (Follett [1926] 1992, 70)

Thus unilateral command and pressure from another person is replaced by mutual recognition of the law of the situation.[19]

In the context of development assistance, if a government undertakes reforms for its own motives (e.g., fighting corruption as an end in itself), recognizing its pressing problems and the "law of the situation," then it is not kowtowing to pressure from development agencies. One of the temptations of great power in the development business (as in the World Bank) is to yield to the use of a conventional arm-twisting direct approach to ensure behavior change. I have time and again seen cases where governments were trying to make changes on their own and then the World Bank task managers would say:

> Just to be sure, we need to have the conditionality there. If they should falter, I don't want to be in a position of having my boss say "What!? You didn't even have language [i.e., conditionalities] about that in the loan agreement?"[20]

Thus the Bank uses its power because it has the power to use extrinsic motivation levers to force (superficial) change. That in turn creates resentment (the threat-to-autonomy effect) and a longer-term crowding-out effect. Instead of the government saying, "Now we have two reasons to make the changes, our own higher self motives and the Bank's conditionalities on the loans," it is resentful that the Bank is twisting its arm to do what it was already trying to do for its own reasons. This crowds out the better reasons so that the government ends up going through the motions to satisfy the conditionalities (if that) and the real reforms are sabotaged by the Bank's impatient steamroller methods induced by its power. Like a "religious conversion" at the point of a sword, the "reform program" probably won't amount to much.

Direct carrot and stick methods on the part of the aggrieved party, the helper, are motivationally inconsistent with the motives that would bring about changes in the heart and mind of the doer. To keep the space open in the doer for those transformative motives to develop and come into the motivational foreground, the aggrieved party's actions should also be motivationally compatible. That means that those actions should be clearly based on shared principles, not tactical self-interest (a point dramatized by the self-suffering or tapasya of the aggrieved party), and that the arguments should appeal to shared reason and evidence. Then it is possible for the doer to yield to principles and reason with self-respect intact, not to be "defeated" by the other party.[21]

However, in view of the human powers of self-righteous rationalization, particularly on the part of those doers who hold power, these appeals by themselves are not sufficient to bring about transformative changes in the doer. The point must be emphasized that just because external pressure should not be in the motivational foreground to force the change in the doer, that does not mean that external pressure should be absent. It is again a question of foreground and background. The basic idea of ahimsa is that the external pressures (e.g., economic boycotts) should be kept going in the background but should be designed so that they do not take over or crowd out the appeals to the better motives of the doer. Otherwise, the pressure might come into the foreground and ignite the downward spiral of retaliatory dynamics.

What if the circumstances of the doer should change so that the doer would have to yield to the extrinsic pressure alone, as was essentially the case while England was involved in World War II? In spite of pressure from his lieutenants, Gandhi put the drive for India's independence on hold until after the war. In general, the aggrieved party might reduce or temporarily suspend the pressure to help ensure that the eventual changes on the part of the doer were made for the right reasons. This belies the common misconception that satyagraha is the weapon of the weak. While the weapon of the strong is to try to push through a direct approach, satyagraha is an indirect approach to bring about change for the right reasons on the part of the doer. When Gandhi had the external power, he refrained from using it.

In summary, Gandhi's satyagraha—abstracted from the particulars of the Indian case—is the development of the indirect method into a full-fledged methodology of change in the context of an antagonistic helper-doer relationship, and as such, it is a social invention of the first order.[22]

Summary of Common Theme: B-ing and Non-B-ing

My purpose has been to try to discern the theoretical basis for the indirect approach by looking for the common themes in the use of the indirect approach in a wide variety of human endeavors over a long period of intellectual history. A common theme has emerged, once one allows for the many different vocabularies and diverse settings.

A simple model suffices to make these points. Actions have motives just as beliefs have grounds. An activity B (B-ing) can be analyzed as a B-like behavior plus a B-appropriate motivation. The behavior is the observable part of the activity, while the underlying motivation is not externally observable (although there may be telltale clues in the behavior—which, however, may also be faked). A direct intervention then attempts to induce activity B by supplying some motivation for the B-like behavior. But the motivation may be quite different from and inconsistent with the B-appropriate motivation. Thus the direct intervention produces not the activity B as intended but an inauthentic pseudo-B activity (non-B-ing),[23] which could be modeled as B-like behavior plus B-inappropriate motivation.[24] The attempt to buy love is the classic example, where loving behaviors may be purchased with inappropriate motivation so that only some inauthentic (non-loving) pseudolove is obtained. Ryle highlights the inconsistency between motive and activity in the context of teaching: "How in logic can the teacher dragoon his pupil into thinking for himself?"

For some "economic" activities, the motivations that can be supplied by a direct intervention are quite appropriate, and thus they will produce the authentic activity. Paying someone to undertake a mercenary activity will produce an authentic mercenary activity. No motivational inconsistency is involved since the pecuniary motivation is an appropriate motivation for a mercenary action.

The fundamental problem with social engineering or the direct approach can be easily demonstrated. Some sequence of desirable activities A, B, and C is identified as a "best practice" to be reproduced by a government, development agency, or other organization engaged in the attempted social engineering. A checklist is developed giving the observable behaviors associated with A, B, and C, and incentives are provided to implement the checklist. But the external incentives supplied by the agency are inappropriate to the activities, so the efforts at best produce pseudo-A, pseudo-B, and pseudo-C activities. This unhelpful help fails to yield the desired results with the doers. Since the agency still has to move the money, it rededicates itself to improved efforts with "increased incentives," "redoubled efforts," and "better monitoring for output-based results" without realizing that the problems are in the whole approach.

This basic problem in the direct approach runs across the political spectrum: socialist development planning (top-down attempts to reproduce bottom-up development activities),[25] technocratic attempts to use checklists to be checked off ("checklistitis"), matrices to be filled in, and blueprints to be followed in order to fabricate discovered best practices, and more right-wing attempts to improve educational outcomes in the schools with standardized tests and results-based performance bonuses.

In the wide spectrum of human endeavor, there is only a fairly small bandwidth where the motives can be supplied by the carrots and sticks of the direct approach (including market-driven activities as special cases of the direct approach to affect behavior described in agency theory). For some stroke-of-the-pen reforms, physical engineering projects, or "such physical tasks as vaccinating children" (Dichter 2003, 191), reproducing the right behaviors is sufficient regardless of motivation. Outside the spectrum of pecuniary and prudential behavior, the attempt to use direct methods in a controlling manner contradicts the internal motives for actions (and the grounds for beliefs). As in trying to shine a flashlight to get a better look at darkness, it is self-defeating to try to buy virtue or impose autonomy.

All this is not to argue that "economic" or external motivation should be eliminated: it is a question of foreground and background. When for whatever reason the self-direction of an automobile driver breaks down, it is quite useful to have curbs, guardrails, or other physical barriers to keep the car on the road. The "economic" design of institutions (e.g., agency theory) is more like the metaphor of a train guided by rails (or sheep being herded along a narrow chute into a sheep-dip) than a car freely driven on a road edged by curbs or guardrails. The externally supplied carrots and sticks should have a role in the motivational background as a backstop or curb for when there is a breakdown in the intrinsic motivation in the foreground. For instance in a well-functioning society, people would be motivated to refrain from committing crimes against others not by their fear of detection and punishment but by their sociability—Adam Smith's moral sentiments [1759] (1969). But when that sociability breaks down, then inauthentic sociable behavior based only on the stick of threatened punishment is still better than antisocial actions violating the rights of others.[26]

For the "higher" human activities, the motives must come from within, as rational beliefs need to be based on the exercise of our own critical judgment. People then have an active role to make the actions their own—or to make the beliefs their own. It is a psychological variation on the old juridical principle that people have a natural ownership over the fruits of their own activity. The helpers cannot externally supply the doers' own motives or own reasons. The helpers can at best use the indirect approach to bring the doers to the threshold; the doers have to do the rest to make the results their own.

5

Autonomy-Respecting Development Assistance

Development Intervention as a Principal-Agent Relationship

After our Cook's tour of indirect autonomy-respecting methods across disciplines and across time, this chapter focuses on elaborating the five themes (the three Dos and two Don'ts) in the context of economic development. Direct quotations are gathered together in the appendix on the five themes by the eight thinkers: Albert Hirschman, E. F. Schumacher, Saul Alinsky, Paulo Freire, John Dewey, Douglas McGregor, Carl Rogers, and Søren Kierkegaard. The assumed setting is an external development organization (the helper) trying to help economic development in a less-developed country (the doer). I am concerned with development projects or programs that involve changing human institutions, not with physical construction projects. The standard implicit or explicit model of the relationship between the development organization and the client country is the principal-agent or agency relationship (e.g., see Killick 1998 or Gilbert, Powell, and Vines 2000). How can the development organization, as the principal, design a package of incentives—carrots and sticks—to induce the desired actions on the part of the client country as the agent?

The economic theory of agency is one of the most sophisticated forms of the social engineering approach to human affairs, so it is worthwhile to examine it in a development context. The terms *principal-agent relation* and *agency relation* have been imported into economics (see Ross 1973) from legal theory but are then used to denote contractual relationships that are not agency relations in the original legal sense. Agency relations tend to arise from large asymmetries in knowledge so the principal cannot contractually specify the detailed actions of the agent (e.g., doctor or lawyer). Instead the agent takes on a legal or institutional fiduciary role involving the trust "to act for or in the interest of" the principal. Since information is always imperfect and each party to a contract would like to influence the behavior of the other concerning unspecified actions, economists have applied the "agency" phraseology to the general economic theory of contractual incentives. For example, Tony Killick applies agency language to the relationship between an international financial institution and a developing country where the IFI is the principal and the country is the agent (Killick et al. 1998).

The first mistake in this approach is the model itself. In an agency relationship, "one person [the agent] acts for or represents another by [the] latter's authority" (Black 1968, entry under "Agency"). Yet the client country has no such agency relationship to the development organization; the client country does not have a legal or institutional role to act for or represent the development agency. If we analogize with, say, the doctor-patient or lawyer-client relationship, then it is reversed. If the development organization is seen more as a "doctor for countries," then it should be noted that the doctor is ordinarily considered the agent in the doctor-patient relationship,[1] not the principal. The doctor or the lawyer is supposed to use specialized expertise and knowledge in the interests of the patient or client by the latter's authorization.

Leaving aside the tellingly mistaken characterization of the relationship, the development agency might be viewed as a doctor, therapist, or helper who would promote certain changes in the patient, client, or doer. The standard tools are economic incentives such as loans on favorable terms or grants, both only if certain conditions or "conditionalities" are satisfied. Here we see the second dubious assumption in the standard relationship between development agency and client country—namely that certain changes can be well implemented regardless of the source of the motivation. There are, of course, certain stroke-of-the-pen reforms that are within the domain of a government's deliberate action (e.g., setting exchange rates, reserve ratios, and other discretionary macroeconomic variables).[2] But the hard part of development assistance is concerned with social and institutional reforms.

> Institutional reforms lie at the opposite end of the simplicity-complexity spectrum by comparison with currency devaluations: they are not for the most part amenable to treatment as preconditions; donor agencies are liable to have difficulties in keeping track of the extent of compliance; and such reforms are often imperfectly under the control of the central authorities, take time, typically involve a number of agencies and are liable to encounter opposition from well-entrenched beneficiaries of the *status quo*. (Killick et al. 1998, 40)

The main determinants of economic development lie deep in the institutional infrastructure and cultural makeup of the country.

The institutions, not to mention the mind-sets, norms, and culture, of a country are based in part on the country's collective self-identity. To carry over the notions of internal and external motivation from an individual to the people who make up a country as a collectivity, we might say that the culture and basic institutional habits are expressions of "internal motivation" based on the country's self-identity. Short-term behaviors can be "bought" with sufficient external incentives to temporarily override the more internal incentives of governmental policymakers, but that by itself is not transformative in the sense of changing the institutional and cultural roots of long-term behavior.

A common form of this error is the confusion between "changing laws" and "building institutions." For instance in Russia, once Western laws are passed or decreed, then won't everyone wake up the next morning and start acting "like in the West"? The economic historian Richard Tawney put it well after visiting China in 1930.

> To lift the load of the past, China required, not merely new technical devices and new political forms, but new conceptions of law, administration and political obligations, and new standards of conduct in governments, administrators, and the society which produced them. The former could be, and were, borrowed. The latter had to be grown. (Tawney [1932] 1966, 166)

Institutions are more written "in the hearts of the people" (which cannot be changed overnight) than in the pages of the law books.[3] Changing the de jure institutions does not by any means imply a transformative change in the de facto institutions and norms that govern long-term behavior. This is particularly true when the changes in the laws are due to external leverage such as loan conditionalities that at best only override rather than change internal motivation and at worst lead to a negative reactance, resentment, and "pushback" that will impede any real institutional change. In terms of the warhorse metaphor, trying to force the horse to drink may make it all the more "mule headed."

Who has "ownership" of a reform program? On the side of the development agency, the reasoning is often to apply resources only where there is a positive marginal effect—where a positive reform program would not have otherwise taken place without the extra resources. Thus the agency feels it made a difference and can rightfully claim ownership of that reform. But that tends to be precisely the situation where the government may feel it is just being "paid" to do the reform and thus have little or no ownership of it—with the usual perverse results.

On the other hand, if the government is going to do the reform for its own internal reasons (but perhaps could use some funding) and thus it has ownership, then the agency may say: "Why should we put resources there? They were going to do that reform anyway one way or another. We want to have a development impact." How can the agency make a difference without thereby taking ownership and thus eventually not making much of a difference after all? That is again the basic dilemma, conundrum, or paradox of "assisted autonomy" addressed by the notion of autonomy-respecting assistance.[4]

We have been considering the helper-doer relationship in development assistance with the agency as the helper and a client government as the doer. Needless to say, the same problems occur between development agencies (e.g., development donors) and Third World or South NGOs. The methods of supplying resources used by the donor-helpers could defeat the ownership on the part of the NGO-doers. After surveying a number of examples, an Oxfam handbook concludes: "Hence, the very mechanisms which donor agencies use to protect their own resources are thereby denied to those whose independent capacity or autonomy they want to promote" (Eade 1997, 140). The natural desire of the donors is to give project-tied funding so that they can see the results, whereas more effective capacity building of the NGO might be obtained by lump-sum funding of the NGO's core budget.[5] Capacity building might also entail helping the NGO to diversify its funding base and to develop its own sources of income, but these activities might also be seen by the donor as "weakening its influence."

We have also discussed the rather general model of a development agency using a package of extrinsic incentives—carrots and sticks—to induce development-enhancing behavior on the part of a client country. Perhaps better models and more refined theorems about incentive-compatible mechanisms in the economic theory of agency would allow the development organization to design a more effective package of economic incentives to push the country along the right path. But that progress through such refinements might be rather limited. Indeed, I have argued that the whole approach is seriously flawed as an instrument of institutional reconstruction and transformation.

In short, the standard model of development "assistance" is heteronomous, and therein lies its ineffectiveness. Long-term economic and social transformation grows, in the last analysis, out of autonomous activity. One way or another, a country must find the internal loci of causality necessary for autonomous development. External development assistance—"to do no harm," not to mention to be effective— must be autonomy respecting.[6] With today's powerful development agencies, this means "less," not "more." It is now time to examine the five themes of autonomy-respecting assistance in the specific context of economic development.[7]

First Do: Starting from Present Institutions

To be transformative, a process of change must start from and engage the present endowment of institutions.[8] Otherwise, the process will only create an overlay of new behaviors that is not sustainable (without continual bribes or coercion). Yet this is a common error.

An unwillingness to start from where you are ranks as a fallacy of historic proportions;. . . . It is because the lesson of the past seems to be so clear on this score, because the nature of man so definitely confirms it, that there has been this perhaps tiresome repetition throughout this record: the people must be in on the planning; their existing institutions must be made part of it; self-education of the citizenry is more important than specific projects or physical changes. (Lilienthal 1944, 198)

There are a number of reasons why development interventions are often not designed to begin with existing institutions. Revolutionaries and reformers oriented toward utopian social engineering (see Popper 1962) aim to wipe the slate clean in order to install a set of "ideal" institutions.

> Everyone has heard the story of the man who was asked by a stranger how he could get to Jonesville; after long thought and unsuccessful attempts to explain the several turns that must be made, he said, so the anecdote runs: "My friend, I tell you; if I were you, I wouldn't start from here." Some planning is just like that; it does not start from here; it assumes a "clean slate" that never has and never can exist. (Lilienthal 1944, 198–99; quoted in Alinsky 1969, 77)

Any attempt to evolve out of the current "flawed," "retrograde," or even "evil" institutions is viewed as only staining or polluting the change process. In spite of a rather moralistic outlook, Woodrow Wilson nevertheless made a case for an incremental approach in his first inaugural address.

> We shall deal with our economic system as it is and as it might be modified, not as it might be if we had a clean sheet of paper to write upon; and step by step we shall make it what it should be, in the spirit of those who question their own wisdom and seek council and knowledge, not shallow self-satisfaction or the excitement of excursion whither they cannot tell.[9]

The moralistic frame of mind was particularly prevalent in the first generation of West-supported reformers in the postsocialist countries who constantly used cold war rhetoric to preclude and rule out any transitional institutions that would start with the actual initial conditions. Any such bridging institutions would rest in part on the communist past (since a "bridge" has to have a foot on each side of the chasm). Instead, the reformers thought they could use shock therapy methods ("market bolshevism") to engineer a clean break with the past and jump over the chasm in one great leap forward.[10]

Similar considerations argue for an evolutionary strategy in poor countries rather than trying to jump to new institutions. Another reason for not starting with the status quo ante is a simple lack of famil-

iarity with existing institutions and cultural habits in the developing
country on the part of those who seek to act as change agents.

> The beginning of wisdom is the admission of one's own lack of knowl-
> edge. As long as we think we know, when in fact we do not, we shall
> continue to go to the poor and demonstrate to them all the marvellous
> things they could do if they were already rich. This has been the main
> failure of aid to date. (Schumacher 1973, 199)

In the transitional economies as well as elsewhere, development
agencies often face the stark choice of (1) starting from the present
institutions and working with existing homegrown but imperfect institutional reform initiatives led by "embedded" reformers or (2) trying to
wipe the slate clean, work with clean reformers (e.g., returning expa-
triates educated in the West), and install clean model institutions ("use
aid money to draft a new model law and put in a conditionality to pass
it!"). Given a choice between the momentum of bottom-up involvement in "flawed" reforms and top-down imposition of what reformers
see as "model" institutions, the "start from where the doers are" principle would argue in favor of using knowledge and experience to work to
improve flawed reforms using the bottom-up approach to transformation—rather than throwing it overboard in favor of utopian social
engineering based on the false hope of imposed ideal models (see chap.
8 for more analysis of the transition).

The renowned military historian and strategist Liddell Hart argues
in general for the indirect approach not just in military matters but in
"all problems of the influence of mind upon mind—the most influential factor in human history" (Hart 1941, x). When reflecting on
Gandhi's strategies, J. Nehru quotes (1956, 457–58) much of the preface to Hart's book, which includes the idea of starting where the doers
are and presenting any innovations as evolving from that starting
point.

> Looking back on the stages by which various fresh ideas gained accep-
> tance, it can be seen that the process was eased when they could be pre-
> sented, not as something radically new, but as the revival in modern
> terms of a time-honoured principle or practice that had been forgotten.
> This required not deception, but care to trace the connection—since
> "there is nothing new under the sun." (Hart 1941, xii)

This leads to the next theme. The helper must not only put him- or herself empathetically in the doer's shoes; the helper must then see the world—including a way forward—from that vantage point.

Second Do: Seeing the World through the Eyes of the Client

If a utopian social engineer could perform an "institutional lobotomy" to erase the present institutions, then development advice would not need to be tailored to present circumstances. Generic advice would suffice; one size would fit all "blank slates." But failing that, it is necessary to learn to see the world through the eyes of the policymakers and people in the country.[11]

There is a clear parallel with educational theory. As shown previously, an autonomy-respecting interaction between teacher and learner requires that the teacher have an empathetic understanding with the student. If the teacher can understand the learning experience of the student, then the teacher can use his or her presumably superior knowledge to help the student.[12] This help does not take the form of telling the student the answer or solution but of offering advice or guidance, perhaps away from a dead-end path, to assist the student in the active appropriation of knowledge.

In a recent metastudy on learning research, one of the main findings was that

> Students come to the classroom with preconceptions about how the world works. If their initial understanding is not engaged, they may fail to grasp the new concepts and information that are taught, or they may learn them for purposes of a test but revert to their preconceptions outside the classroom. (Donovan et al. 1999, 15)

Thus the teachers "must draw out and work with the preexisting understandings that their students bring with them" (Donovan et al. 1999, 15). In Eleanor Duckworth's development of Piagetian pedagogy, she emphasizes how this requires some skill in listening.[13]

> A good listener, or a good understander of explanations, is aware that his first interpretation of what is being said may not be the right one, and he keeps making guesses about what other interpretations are possi-

ble. This ability is singularly undeveloped in little children but it should
be highly developed in good teachers, who try to listen to what children
are trying to say to them. (Duckworth 1973, 142)

This pedagogical point then carries over to development assistance as
a form of social learning.

> Like a teacher who tries to "give reason" to her pupils, seeking out the
> sense that underlies their apparently senseless questions, policy makers
> have a rational interest in giving reason to the apparently perverse
> behavior of their intended beneficiaries.
>   But in order to "give reason" to the patterns of behavior manifested
> by other actors in the environment, policy makers must be able, again,
> to put themselves in their shoes, entering into their ways of framing the
> policy situation and constructing meaning for the policy object.[14]
> (Schön and Rein 1994, 185)

In the context of adult transformation, how does the educator/inves-
tigator find out about the client-student's world? That is the role of
Paulo Freire's notion of dialogue. In the nondialogical notion of education, the teacher determines the appropriate messages to be delivered
or "deposited" in the students, as money is deposited in a bank. Instead
of ready-made best-practice recipes, Freire, like Dewey, saw the educational mission as based on posing problems, essentially the problems
that were based on the students' world.[15] Yet often to development
"professionals, it seems absurd to consider the necessity of respecting
the 'view of the world' held by the people" (Freire 1970, 153–54). In
Robert Chambers's terms, it is a reversal that means "putting the last
first."

> Respect for the poor and what they want offsets paternalism. The rever-
> sal this implies is that outsiders should start not with their own priorities
> but with those of the poor, although however much self-insight they
> have, outsiders will still project their own values and priorities. (Cham-
> bers 1983, 141)

Jane Addams's settlement workers tried to gain an empathetic
understanding of people's situation by living in their midst. Yet there
are other ways to gain some measure of an empathetic understanding,
or *Verstehen*, as was the great insight of the historian Giambattista Vico

(1668–1744). The idea is to apply the old maxim that "one can fully know only what one has made" to the realm of cultural and historical experience.

> [Vico] uncovered a sense of knowing which is basic to all humane studies: the sense in which I know what it is to be poor, to fight for a cause, to belong to a nation, to join or abandon a church or a party. . . . How does one know these things? In the first place, no doubt, by personal experience; in the second place because the experience of others is sufficiently woven into one's own to be seized quasi-directly, as part of constant intimate communication; and in the third place by the working (sometimes by a conscious effort) of the imagination. (Berlin 1980, 116)

It would seem to be a corollary that an empathetic understanding of a people can best be obtained by others who have some proximity of experience and some desire for "intimate communication" or dialogue. Maurice Friedman (1960) emphasizes the importance of seeing through the eyes of the other in Buber's notion of dialogue.

> Particularly important in this relationship is what Buber has variously called "seeing the other," "experiencing the other side," "inclusion," and "making the other present." This "seeing the other" is not . . . a matter of "identification" or "empathy," but of a concrete imagining of the other side which does not at the same time lose sight of one's own. (Friedman 1960, 188–89)

First Don't: Transformation Cannot Be Externally Imposed

We choose according to our preferences and beliefs, but we do not simply choose our preferences or beliefs. Transformation is the indirect byproduct of one's authentic activities, not the direct object of choice. External incentives can buy loving behavior, assertions of belief, or gestures of faith—but being in love, believing in a principle, and having a faith all come by the "grace" of transformation, not by the vagaries of consumer choice.

> This much seems clear: effective change cannot be imposed from outside. Indeed, the attempt to impose change from the outside is as likely

to engender resistance and barriers to change, as it is to facilitate change. At the heart of development is a change in ways of thinking, and individuals cannot be forced to change how they think. They can be forced to take certain actions. They can be even forced to utter certain words. But they cannot be forced to change their hearts or minds. (Stiglitz 1998, in Chang 2001, 73)

The idea that one person cannot simply change a judgment or preference at the behest of another has an old and venerable tradition. Indeed, Martin Luther's principle of liberty of conscience was one of the root principles of the Reformation and one of the main sources of the theory of inalienable rights (which placed limits on the reach of the market).[16] It is impossible for a person to alienate his or her decision-making power to the Church on matters of faith.

Furthermore, every man is responsible for his own faith, and he must see it for himself that he believes rightly. As little as another can go to hell or heaven for me, so little can he believe or disbelieve for me; and as little as he can open or shut heaven or hell for me, so little can he drive me to faith or unbelief. (Luther [1522] 1942, 316)

Authorities, secular or religious, who try to compel belief can only secure external conformity.

Besides, the blind, wretched folk do not see how utterly hopeless and impossible a thing they are attempting. For no matter how much they fret and fume, they cannot do more than make people obey them by word or deed; the heart they cannot constrain, though they wear themselves out trying. For the proverb is true, "Thoughts are free." Why then would they constrain people to believe from the heart, when they see that it is impossible? (Luther [1522] 1942, 316)

Francis Hutcheson, a teacher of Adam Smith and a previous holder of the chair in moral philosophy in Glasgow, developed this inalienability argument as a part of the Scottish Enlightenment.[17] He followed Luther in showing how the "right of private judgment" or "liberty of conscience" was inalienable.

Thus no man can really change his sentiments, judgments, and inward affections, at the pleasure of another; nor can it tend to any good to make him profess what is contrary to his heart. The right of private judgment is therefore unalienable. . . .

A like natural right every intelligent being has about his own opinions, speculative or practical, to judge according to the evidence that appears to him. This right appears from the very constitution of the rational mind which can assent or dissent solely according to the evidence presented, and naturally desires knowledge. The same considerations shew this right to be unalienable: it cannot be subjected to the will of another: tho' where there is a previous judgment formed concerning the superior wisdom of another, or his infallibility, the opinion of this other, to a weak mind, may become sufficient evidence. (Hutcheson 1755, 261–62, 295)

Thus a person's sentiments (preferences) and judgments (beliefs) are not the subjects of choice in the marketplace. Development agencies that try "to buy" policy changes "cannot do more than make people obey them by word or deed; the heart they cannot constrain, though they wear themselves out trying."

The opposite of an agency's autonomy-respecting interaction with a client is a heteronomous (external compulsion) intervention based on the theory that the coerced client will then see the light, internalize the motivation, and continue along the reformed path without further externally applied carrots or sticks. The standard model for this internalization strategy is the parents "coercing" children to do something for their own good (e.g., brushing their teeth) and then the children eventually internalizing the activity and continuing it when they are grown. But will this strategy work between development agencies and organizations or governments in the developing world?

Development agencies often have a short time horizon, so they tend to interpret the purchased outward performance as evidence for sustainable change (i.e., successful internalization) and long-term transformation. Thus the internalization theory is constantly pseudoverified and reapplied again and again by a development agency—much as a Theory X manager may as necessary "buy" outward obedience in the "spot market" for compliant behaviors and then interpret that as successful organizational development.

Moreover, we have seen how the attempt to buy or force transformation with carrots and sticks can lead to the threat-to-autonomy effect—a negative reactance, resentment, and pushback. Rousseau points out that the teacher will teach students "to become dissemblers, fakers, and liars in order to extort rewards or escape punishments" ([1762] 1979, 91). Dewey notes that extrinsic incentives administered in a controlling manner would arouse the "instincts of cunning and slyness." McGregor saw that such incentives would lead to "passive acceptance" at best and more likely to "indifference or resistance."

Eventually the reliance on external carrots or bait can induce the atrophy effect when the original internal motivation dries up and the party becomes an aid-dependent marionette responding only to external strings—a condition perhaps approximated in some countries of the former Soviet Union or Africa (see Van de Walle 2001). In contrast, Japan from the middle of the nineteenth century and South Korea and China more recently have developed and modernized without losing their national autonomy.

Many powerful development agencies are, at least in principle, aware of the problems of trying "to buy" local policy initiatives by using external carrots or sticks but are simply unable to do otherwise (what is power for if not to be used?). There is perhaps less appreciation that similar problems arise concerning the cognitive (as opposed to incentive) element in the client country's decision making. The imposition of beliefs in the form of best-practice recipes can temporarily override local judgment but will probably not lead to any sustainable change in conviction. As Hutcheson puts it, to a "weak mind" the "superior wisdom of another" may provide "sufficient evidence" for credible belief (particularly when baited with the offer of aid),[18] but such tutelage seems a slim basis for long-term policy changes. This carries us back to the activist pedagogy and the reasons why the Socratic guide or Deweyite teacher does not simply give the "answers" (even assuming the answers are available).

> Learning is *not* finding out what other people already know, but is solving our own problems for our own purposes, by questioning, thinking and testing until the solution is a new part of our lives. (Handy 1989, 63)

Through investigation of any sources (perhaps with hints from the teacher/guide), direct observation, and structured experiments, adult learners may actively rediscover and reappropriate knowledge with "ownership" (see chap. 6 on the idea of knowledge-based development assistance)—which at the same time will be adapted to local circumstances. This pedagogy puts the learner in the active role (i.e., in the driver's seat).

Second Don't: Addams-Dewey-Lasch Critique of Benevolence

We have focused mostly on how the help might not be autonomy respecting by being an imposition that is controlling in a quasicoercive sense. However, there is also a "soft" form of control through "gifts," paternalism, and benevolence that is even more insidious.[19] "*It tends to render others dependent,* and thus contradicts its own professed aim: the helping of others" (Dewey and Tufts 1908, 387). This is the self-reinforcing cycle of "tutelage"[20] and dependency.[21]

One imagines a standard scenario where the poor undertake some initiative to help themselves but they lack a key resource to implement the plan. But then an international or domestic development agency arrives with timely aid to fill the gap, save the day, and empower the poor to better their condition. What is wrong with this picture? Nothing today. The problem comes tomorrow as others learn that if they likewise satisfy certain criteria, then they will also receive aid. The original scenario was, *given* the problem, the aid is helpful to solve the problem. But the presence of the offer of aid then *creates* a new scenario where the problematic situations are partly incentivized by the aid offer. The order of the causality is reversed. The well-intended aid may even tend to perpetuate the situations requiring the aid by postponing the need to work out real solutions. The supply of aid seems to create and perpetuate the demand for it—in what was called "Say's Law of Development Aid."

This problem is illustrated by the debate about social funds (e.g., Tendler 2000) that seems to recapitulate some forms of North-South unhelpful help at the community level. Many of the arguments for social funds could, perhaps uncharitably, be called *charity arguments.* Social fund advocates seem to often imbue the funds with the moral urgency of disaster relief—indeed the funds might be viewed as a disaster relief mechanism repackaged as a means of "community-driven development." One of the better-known funds (Bolivia) started out providing aid in a disaster situation and then, as organizations are wont to do, reinvented its mission to sustain itself. Many funds started out in a package along with structural adjustment loans to mitigate the social impact of such loans. Charitable relief and "social work" seem to be close to the mission of the funds (e.g., in one fund, the definition of "eligible vulnerable groups" was persistent juvenile offenders, victims of abuse, alcoholics, drug abusers, the disabled, and AIDS victims). There is no question that the charity work of arranging for other people's money to be given to needy people can be morally satisfying, but it should be questioned as a means of development assistance.

Social funds (SFs) are currently something of a policy fad; they are often described using the imagery of promoting self-help with gap-filling aid. The funds are typically set up by national governments "to quickly deliver resources to poor people," bypassing the perhaps corrupt and unresponsive national ministries and regional or local governments. They are funded by grants from donors or by hard currency loans with a payback beyond the political horizon of the central government. One of their main activities is to make grants (or near-grants with trivial matching requirements) to fund small infrastructure projects. Lenders and donors tend to like the social funds since they "move the money" with tangible outcomes (more schools, tube wells, health clinics, warehouses, and so forth), which in turn rewards the benevolent impulse in the lender and donor agencies.

The problem is that social funds are more instruments of relief in the sense of "quickly delivering fish to poor and hungry people," rather than instruments of capacity building and development in the sense of "helping poor people learn how to fish for themselves." There is disagreement less about the facts than about the choices between short-term aid and long-term capacity building.

By using a new, separate, and "clean" organization of the central government, supporters argue that SFs bypass unresponsive, incompetent, and perhaps corrupt ministries and regional or local governments to quickly help satisfy the needs of poor people (table 3). Critics see the same reality as central government largess buying or rewarding local support, as an elite special agency (often outside civil service) attracting good talent out of the ministries, and as bypassing sustainable reforms and capacity building in the lower levels of government. Since no one argues that SFs should actually replace the ministries or local and regional governments, the net result is a plus for short-term relief and a minus for long-term government reform.

Supporters see local people choosing their preferred local infrastructure project from a menu to be funded by the social fund as being "bottom-up, demand-driven community empowerment." Critics see the same reality and argue that local people soliciting and receiving largess from an agency funded by and solely accountable to the central government is more top-down paternalism than bottom-up community empowerment. Eliciting "demand" for grant-funded projects is hardly demand driven in the sense of projects that are afoot on their own (e.g., with doers covering enough of the costs to indicate that they wanted to do the project anyway).[22] "Empowering" people to buy outcomes with an external grant is rather different from building the community's own capacity to reach those outcomes in a fiscally sustainable manner.

The social fund debate illustrates one important fact in recent debates about development assistance. Public relations is very much in the saddle, and language has become quite Orwellian in the sense that "fine phrases" such as *bottom-up*, *demand driven*, and *community empowerment* can be used to describe almost the opposite reality. Even *helping people help themselves*. The public-relations-driven disconnect with reality has become so large that the use of these phrases has become quite shameless.

All good policy fads seem to have self-reinforcing loops that keep them rolling. To close the loop, social funds need to be "scientifically evaluated." Supporters argue that they have done the research and have the impact evaluations to show that SFs have a good impact.[23] Critics argue firstly that impact evaluations are independent of cost. A true *project* evaluation would have to look at whether the impact was obtained with ten dollars or ten million dollars. Secondly, the impact evaluations compare communities that receive social fund grants with otherwise similar, "counterfactual" communities that receive no

TABLE 3. Social Funds as seen by Supporters or by Critics

Summary of arguments	SF Supporters	SF Critics
Separate organization from civil service and local governments	Bypass corruption in ministries and in regional and local governments	Central government (ruling party) largess buying or rewarding local support
People choose which grant project from menu	Bottom-up, demand-driven community empowerment	Top-down paternalism ("you choose which gift")—no capacity building
Evaluation	Positive impact evaluations with matched pairs of communities: money vs. no money	Impact evaluations ignoring costs. Phony counterfactual. Real alternative with same money spent next best way

grants. Not surprisingly, the studies tend to show that the communities that receive the funds have better facilities (more "impact") than the communities that don't receive funds. Sometimes the difference is not that significant, but the real point is that a well-specified counterfactual would be a community that had the *same* resources available for the best alternative approach to community development (e.g., see the eighteen cases of assisted self-reliance in Krishna et al. 1997).

How can we differentiate the forms of help that are compatible with the autonomy of the beneficiary from those forms that are paternalistic and controlling? Jane Addams, John Dewey, and Christopher Lasch (among others) have developed a critique of benevolence and compassion along these lines. Dewey expresses the argument as a critique of oppressive benevolence,[24] and Lasch juxtaposes the "ethic of respect" to the "ethic of compassion" (Lasch 1995).

Dewey's thinking about the controlling aspects of paternalistic employers was prompted by the Pullman strike of 1894 and by the critique of Pullman's paternalism in the essay "A Modern Lear" by the Chicago reformer Jane Addams (1965), an essay that Dewey calls "one of the greatest things I ever read both as to its form and its ethical philosophy" (quoted by Lasch in Addams 1965, 176).

> As its title suggests, Addams's essay was based on an extended analogy between the relationship between King Lear and his daughter Cordelia and that of Pullman and his workers. Like Lear, Addams suggested, Pullman exercised a self-serving benevolence in which he defined the needs of those who were the objects of this benevolence in terms of his own desires and interests. Pullman built a model company town, providing his workers with what he took to be all the necessities of life. Like Lear, however, he ignored one of the most important human needs, the need for autonomy. (Westbrook 1991, 89)

Jane Addams's Hull House in Chicago was one of the leading examples of settlement houses in the turn-of-the-century settlement movement. The settlement workers, by living with and working with the poor, tried to use an ethic of respect in contrast to the ethic of benevolence exemplified by the charity organizations of the day.

Respect, starting with the self-respect of the poor, is related to their working to improve their own affairs, not being a target for "betterment."

Self-respect arises only out of people who play an active role in solving their own crises and who are not helpless, passive, puppet-like recipients of private or public services. To give people help, while denying them a significant part in the action, contributes nothing to the development of the individual. In the deepest sense it is not giving but taking—taking their dignity. Denial of the opportunity for participation is the denial of human dignity and democracy. It will not work. (Alinsky 1971, 123)

Dewey develops at some length his critique of "oppressive benevolence." According to Westbrook, Dewey holds that

self-realization was a do-it-yourself project; it was not an end that one individual could give to or force on another. The truly moral man was, to be sure, interested in the welfare of others—such an interest was essential to his own self-realization—but a true interest in others lay in a desire to expand their autonomous activity, not in the desire to render them the dependent objects of charitable benevolence. (Westbrook 1991, 46–47)

Too often social workers and reformers treated the poor as an inert or wayward mass to be improved or bettered. An incapacity for beneficial self-activity was assumed to be part of the poor's condition, so reformers would treat them accordingly.

The conception of conferring the good upon others, or at least attaining it for them, which is our inheritance from the aristocratic civilization of the past, is so deeply embodied in religious, political, and charitable institutions and in moral teachings, that it dies hard. Many a man, feeling himself justified by the social character of his ultimate aim (it may be economic, or educational, or political), is genuinely confused or exasperated by the increasing antagonism and resentment which he evokes, because he has not enlisted in his pursuit of the "common" end the freely cooperative activities of others. (Dewey and Tufts 1908, 303–4)

Thus an autonomy-respecting interaction would work to establish the conditions "which permit others freely to exercise their own powers from their initiative, reflection, and choice" (Dewey and Tufts 1908, 302). A quarter of a century later, Dewey reiterates these themes in the revised edition.

History shows that there have been benevolent despots who wished to bestow blessings on others. They have not succeeded except when their actions have taken the indirect form of changing the conditions under which those lived who were disadvantageously placed. The same principle holds of reformers and philanthropists when they try to do good to others in ways which leave passive those to be benefited. There is a moral tragedy inherent in efforts to further the common good which prevent the result from being either good or common—not good, because it is at the expense of the active growth of those to be helped, and not common because these have no share in bringing the result about. (Dewey and Tufts 1932, 385)

Third Do: Respect Autonomy of the Doers

This theme (the third Do) is our overall point about autonomy-respecting assistance. One route to this result is by applying the activist philosophy of education to social learning. Instead of being externally imposed, transformation can only come from within as a result of activities carried out by an individual—or a larger organization, government, or country. As Tawney observes about China in the early 1930s, "Salvation could not be imported from the West, even if the West possessed it; it is not an article of commerce. It must come from China herself, if it is to come at all" (Tawney [1932] 1966, 186).[25] While compliant behavior can be elicited from the outside, a country must be in the driver's seat in order to undergo a sustainable transformation. Similarly, ownership of an outcome comes from the outcome being the fruits of the activities of the individual, organization, or country, not from being a gift or an imposition.

If the client country should take the initiative and be in the driver's seat, then how should a development agency initiate a project? In order to be rooted in the local soil, projects should not be initiated; embryonic projects should be found. This strategy is expressed in Schumacher's favorite themes:

The first task is to study what people are already doing . . . and to help them do it better. . . .
    The second task is to study what people need and to investigate the possibility of helping them to cover more of their needs out of their own productive efforts. (Schumacher 1997, 125)

See where water is flowing in a good direction on its own accord and then widen and deepen the channel so that the stream might grow into a river. Look for the positive changes already starting to take place in the underlying institutions (a "moving train") and then apply development incentives ("jump on board") to strengthen those preexisting tendencies.[26] The development aid should not be controlling in the sense that the train should be moving anyway (i.e., by virtue of the country's internal motivation). That is, the moving train should not be extrinsically motivated as a means to get the aid. If no trains are moving, then motion induced by "bribes" is unlikely to transform the underlying institutions.

These points may be illustrated by juxtaposing two very simple models of change. In a top-down or planning model, an agency offers incentives to mobilize agents of change to bring about a certain desired transformation. This may work if the transformation only concerns various stroke-of-the-pen reforms that can be implemented by external motivation. But for most structural or institutional reforms, changes in short-term behavior incentivized by the agency will be quite insufficient to induce a transformation. This sort of transformation can only come out of the internal motivations embedded in the processes of the society. An external helper can at best locate, not create, the agents of change and then perhaps help them along. But "one thing leads to another" by virtue of horizontal pressures and linkages within a society, and eventually the desired reforms may take place as a result of these strengthened internal processes of change. Faced with certain obstacles to development, an advisor might try to locate agents of change and would explore "how, by moving the economy forward elsewhere, additional pressure (economic and political) could be brought on the obstacle to give way" (Hirschman 1971, 184).

Autonomy-respecting development assistance is on a different timescale than the imposed development projects of an impatient development agency whose staff need to show results for their career purposes.

> Moreover, the method of awakening and enlisting the activities of all concerned in pursuit of the end seems slow; it seems to postpone accomplishment indefinitely. But in truth a common end which is not made such by common, free voluntary cooperation in process of achievement is common in name only. It has no support and guarantee in the activi-

ties which it is supposed to benefit, because it is not the fruit of those activities. Hence, it does not stay put. It has to be continually buttressed by appeal to external, not voluntary, considerations; bribes of pleasure, threats of harm, use of force. It has to be undone and done over. (Dewey and Tufts, 1908, 304)

Projects that are imposed and are not based on domestic consensus and initiative only seem to be more efficient. Such projects are much more likely to fail, fall victim to the vicissitudes of the political process, and have to be repeatedly undone and done over.

Development agencies may try to transplant a "best practice" backed up by conditionalities on policy-based lending to motivate the country to implement the best-practice recipes. Yet this policy reform process is designed to promote neither active learning nor lasting institutional change. It will undermine people's incentives to develop their own capacities and weaken their confidence in using their own intelligence. There is a real danger that a development intervention, instead of acting as a catalyst or midwife to empower change in an autonomy-respecting manner, will only short-circuit people's learning activities and reinforce their feelings of impotence. The external incentives may temporarily overpower the springs of action that are native to the institutional matrix of the country and will probably not induce any lasting institutional reforms. As these reforms are externally imposed rather than actively appropriated by the country, there will be little ownership of the reforms. Compliance may be only perfunctory; the "quick" transplant may soon wither and die—to then be reinstalled in an "improved" form by the next generation of energetic task managers anxious to prove their worth by taking another spin around the hamster wheel of conventional development assistance.

6

Knowledge-Based Development Assistance

The Standard Methodology and Its Problems

The Standard Theory-in-Use

In this chapter and the next, the focus is on the cognitive side of autonomy-respecting assistance. The helper is a development agency, and the doers are some group in need of development assistance (e.g., policymakers and government officials in a developing country). One prominent case of knowledge-based development assistance is the vision of the World Bank operating as the "knowledge bank."[1] How do the three Dos and two Don'ts translate into guidelines for knowledge-based development assistance?

The main problem in knowledge-based development assistance is the standard, default, or naive theory-in-use (regardless of the self-help rhetoric in the "espoused theory")[2] that the agency has "development knowledge" in the form of answers encapsulated in standard core courses that need to be taught, transmitted, and transferred to the target population of trainees. That methodology is taken as so obvious that the focus is simply on how to deliver the knowledge, how to scale up the knowledge transmission belt into the client country, and how to measure and evaluate the impact of these dissemination efforts.[3]

This standard view of knowledge-based development assistance is based on the pedagogy that sees the learners as essentially passive containers into which knowledge is poured. It is the theory that Paulo Freire calls the "banking" theory since teaching was seen as depositing knowledge into a bank account (1970). The standard theory is also captured by the old Chinese simile of help as "giving out fish."

The Volitional and Cognitive Sides of Helping Theory

First we need to revisit and make more explicit the analogies between the volitional and cognitive sides of helping theory. Karl Marx juxtaposed changing the world to (merely) describing the world. In the one case (volition), the idea is to change the world (action) to match some desired representation, and in the other case (cognition), the idea is to change the representation (judgment) to match the world. In most examples of the helper-doer relationship, the volitional and cognitive elements are thoroughly intermixed. But there are limit cases that are concerned with volitional action (e.g., lump-sum financial aid) or cognition (e.g., Socratic teaching). Each topic is developed in its own terms, but here it is perhaps helpful to summarize the analogies and comparisons (table 4).

Ownership Problems

In accordance with the principle of people owning the fruits of their labor, the doers will have ownership when they are in the driver's seat (indeed, the term *doers* would not be accurate if they had a passive role). In the standard view of knowledge-based assistance, the helpers are teachers or trainers taking the active role to transmit knowledge for development to the passive but grateful clients.

Since this knowledge for development is offered below cost or for free as an "international public good," it is quite tempting for the developing countries to accept this sort of knowledge-based development assistance. There are even positive incentives such as extensive travel, pleasant accommodations, generous per diems, and other vacation-like benefits offered to those who undergo the training. From the agency side, management pushes task managers or trainers "to show results"—particularly results that can be observed and evaluated back at headquarters (such as the head count in training programs). The task managers need to show that they have "given out a certain number of fish" or even better that they have helped set up a "fish distribution system" to scale up the delivery of the knowledge to the client country. Thus the helpers need to take ownership of the process of assistance in order to show results, and the clients are agreeably induced to go along.[4]

This is not a new problem. It is a version of the organizational tendency of schools to hold teachers responsible for the students' learning. For instance, one would hope that the substantive goal of schoolteachers is to awaken a self-starting learning capacity in the students—but that goal is difficult for a third party to objectively certify. Hence the measurable proxy goal of passing standard tests is used, and then teachers are pushed by educational administrators to fulfill the results-based

TABLE 4.   Volitional and Cognitive Version of Themes

General theme in helper-doer relation	Volitional Side	Cognitive Side
First do: Helper starting from doer's position	Help in actions that start from the doer's present situation in the world	Help that starts with the learner's present knowledge, not from a tabula rasa
Second do: Helper seeing through doer's eyes	Help with actions guided by doer's own perceptions of the world	Help with learning that starts with how the learner sees the world (e.g., helper "giving reason" to learner)
First don't: Distortionary assistance	Conditional aid to induce a certain action by doer.	Giving biased information and one-sided arguments to induce a certain belief in learner
First don't (restated positively): Nondistortionary enabling assistance	Giving lump-sum aid to enable own motivated doer action.	Giving unbiased information, both sides of arguments (e.g., through Socratic dialogue), and neutral knowledge tools to learner
Second don't: Giving results to doer as a gift	Doing action for the doer so results are a gift	Giving the answers to the learner so beliefs are at best borrowed opinions, not knowledge
Third do: Autonomous activity of doer	Own motivated action resulting in owned product of doer's autonomous action	Self-directed learning resulting in owned knowledge (able to give reasons, arguments, and evidence)
Third do (restated negatively): Externally determined actions/beliefs	Making choices according to externally supplied incentives—like a marionette	Adopting externally supplied "opinions" on the basis of conformity to authority or fashion.

requirements by drilling students to pass the standard tests. In this way, the shoehorning of education into the Procrustean bed of results-based contracts—as recommended by agency theory—would probably do more harm than good to the original substantive goals of education.

> In a way, it is all quite ironic. Parents, politicians, and school adminis-trators all want students to be creative problem-solvers and to learn material at a deep, conceptual level. But in their eagerness to achieve these ends, they pressure teachers to produce. The paradox is that the more they do that, the more controlling the teachers become, which . . . undermines intrinsic motivation, creativity, and conceptual under-standing in the students. . . . The same is true for managers and others in one-up positions. The more they feel pressured to get results from their employees (or children, or athletes, or students) the harder they push. Unfortunately, in the process, they typically sabotage their own efforts. (Deci 1995, 158)

Indeed, educational and developmental organizations face very sim-ilar pressures. The educational thinker Robert McClintock has master-fully described the way in which ancient self-directed study was slowly displaced by teacher-centered instruction in modern times.

> As passionate causes wracked human affairs, . . . people found it hard to maintain restraint, they ceased to be willing merely to help in the self development of their fellows; they discovered themselves burdened, alas, with paternal responsibility for ensuring that their wards would not falter and miss the mark. . . . Pressures—religious, political, social, eco-nomic, humanitarian pressures—began to mount upon the schools, and it soon became a mere matter of time before schools would be held accountable for the people they produced. (McClintock 1982, 60; quoted in Candy 1991, 32)

A similar history could be given for the whole modern "industry" of development agencies; the more the agencies take responsibility for developmental outcomes, the less ownership on the part of the devel-oping countries. Judith Tendler (1975) develops a particularly power-ful version of this thesis that organizational ownership undermines and crowds out client ownership. Without working to generate its own sup-ply of good projects, a development agency would have insufficient "deal flow" to justify its own budgets.

The initial position of the Bank was that preparation of a project was the responsibility of the borrower; if the Bank became involved, it could not thereafter be sufficiently objective in appraising the project. Though buttressed by logic, this position soon gave way to the pressure of events. "Experience has demonstrated that we do not get enough good projects to appraise unless we are involved intimately in their identification and preparation." (quoted sentence from Mason and Asher 1973, 308; quoted in Tendler 1975, 87)

The pressure was generated by the low quality as well as small quantity of projects. The development agency is like a company that receives inputs (project proposals) of such a poor quality that the company cannot produce its own product (funded projects). Hence the company needs to vertically integrate the production of the input into its own operations.

This taking over of project generation by development assistance institutions is like the backward vertical integration of firms in the private sector. The organization expands "backward" into the task environment and starts to "manufacture" project applications itself. It thereby lessens the high degree of uncertainty of the environment from which it must get its inputs, assuring itself of a more reliable source of supply. (Tendler 1975, 103)

Thomas Dichter (2003), writing over a quarter of a century later, shows powerfully that this tendency of organizational imperatives in the "Dev Biz" to subvert development continues unabated if not strengthened today. This *Tendler effect* shows how the organizational imperative to take responsibility for the "product" crowds out the ownership of the clients and leads to passivity and dependency.

That is, the more that donor organizations are able to impose order on the outside decisionmaking that affects their product, the better they can perform their task. In so doing, however, they bring dependency to those whose decisionmaking has been so ordered. Seen in this light, dependency is the result not necessarily of design but of an organization's attempts to do well. (Tendler 1975, 109)

Yes, "it is all quite ironic." The same logic ramifies through every level of educational and developmental organizations.[5] Those who teach or help must show results in order "to do well," so more and more responsibility and ownership is taken over to the detriment of the learners or doers of development.

Self-Efficacy Problems

The standard view of delivering knowledge for development leads to an impairment in the self-confidence, self-esteem, and self-efficacy of the clients. The message behind the "main messages" is that the clients are unable to organize their own learning process and to find out these things in their own way. They need to be helped—to be shown the way. But the way in which the standard methodology shows them the way only reinforces the clients' passivity and perceived lack of self-efficacy.

Economists think of an "externality" as an effect that one party has on another outside of a market interaction—like a nonmarket interaction a person might have with family members, relatives, friends, neighbors, and workmates. But there is another use of the word *externality* in psychology that is relevant here. Externality is the psychological condition of seeing whatever happens to oneself as having external causes. The locus of control over one's life is seen as external; one's own actions are seen as being ineffectual. At best, there is only a highly circumscribed sphere of personal or mental life where one might be able to exercise some internal locus of control. Externality leads to a "why bother?" condition of learned helplessness, apathy, and fatalism. In contrast, "internality" is the condition of seeing one's actions as having a real effect—of having an internal locus of control over what happens to oneself.[6]

Amartya Sen in his capabilities approach to development as freedom (1999; recall that we are using *autonomy* in much the same sense as his *freedom*) uses the notion of "agency" in an Aristotelian sense to describe the freedom of the doers to choose, act, and exercise capabilities. This is another terminological conflict within economics since *agency* in the economic theory of the principal-agent relationship (agency theory) has a quite different connotation. In agency theory, the agent is seen as maximizing his or her preferences or utility according to the incentives established by an external human source, the principal. This is quite different from and, indeed, opposed to Sen's use of *agent* to describe the active party as opposed to the passive "patient" who is acted upon.[7] The agent of agency theory has little agency in the sense of Sen. That agent is a motivational marionette responding to the externally sourced incentives provided by the principal and thus has little Aristotelian agency and little internality in the psychological sense.

The conditions of externality and internality each tend to be self-reinforcing. Externality leads to resignation and fatalism so individuals will not make a concerted effort to change their condition, little will thus change, and their fatalism will be confirmed in a continuing vicious circle. If, however, individuals believe their efforts will make a difference, then they are more likely to make a concerted effort, and thus they are more likely to succeed so their internality may be confirmed in a virtuous circle.

The poor, unless their condition is deliberate (like a monk), already have a history of ineffectual action to better their condition, so any kind of assistance that reinforces that perceived inability to help themselves is simply the wrong kind of assistance, no matter how well intended.

Cognitive Dependency Problems

Self-efficacy or the lack of it is usually considered as a matter of volition, but a similar problem arises with cognition. A party might lack self-confidence in their own intelligence, judgment, and other cognitive skills in addition to lacking self-confidence about the efficacy of their actions. In an extreme state of dependency, they might be like a marionette not only in their actions but also in their opinions, views, and knowledge. This cognitive aspect of dependence is clearly very relevant to understanding the detrimental forms of knowledge-based development assistance.[8]

With the standard methodology of knowledge-based assistance, the "best learners" are often the most marionette-like trainees who quickly learn the new jargon to parrot the main messages. Those best learners are then qualified to staff the local missions or missionary outposts that are the staging areas and repeater stations for scaling up the transmission of the main messages to others in the target population. Here is the language from the Bank's training wing, the World Bank Institute, describing to the Bank's board this process of going from retail to wholesale training.

These relationships evolve as follows. The partner institutions send some of their faculty to attend the course that they propose to replicate. Then WBI trainers and partner staff work together in the design, joint delivery, and adaptation of the course. Initially, the partner institution receives strong support, followed by a gradual reduction over three years, by which time it is expected to take up full responsibility for program delivery. From this point on, WBI limits its role to supervision, monitoring quality, network facilitation, and updating training materials.

Thus they learn "to replicate"; they don't learn to learn. To people from postsocialist countries, this is a COMINTERN transmission belt style of operating but with the Bank's partner institutions presumably parroting the Right Messages.

Those local outposts might also be the gatekeepers for other aid and resources flowing from the development agency to the client country. A version of this scenario has played itself out in the debacle of Western aid to Russia and the other post-Soviet countries during the decade of the 1990s. The most ambitious and "quick learning" of the old elite or near-elite (e.g., the group associated with Anatoli Chubais, largely from St. Petersburg) rapidly acquired the ability to parrot the main messages and thus to qualify as the gatekeepers for great wealth flowing into the countries as loans and aid. While this created a state of extreme dependency and disempowerment on the part of the country as a whole, it was enormously empowering to the small clan of gatekeepers whose real power base was not in the country but in the sources of the external resource flows. Ironically, an example of an all-too-similar phenomenon was the gatekeeper role of the Communist parties installed in the central European countries occupied by the Soviet army after World War II.

The cognitively dependent recipients of the main messages will also play a role in perpetuating the dynamics of stifling critical reason in favor of bureaucratic reason in the development agencies. As such clients have become cognitively dependent, they would be distressed if they should hear the "authorities" arguing among themselves about development knowledge and strategies. They are accustomed to being told the "best practices" to follow, so it weakens their faith in the prestigious authorities with the global purview to determine best practices if there is any public disagreement. How can the patient have faith in the doctors if the patient is exposed to arguments among the doctors about the best treatment? Thus the complaints (real or imagined) of the cognitively dependent, cue-seeking clients are used as arguments within the agencies to keep any real debate about development strategies well behind closed doors.[9]

A more genuine approach to capacity building might start with a gedankenexperiment. One takes a client country as it is and then envisions how it might—without the WBI or Bank—develop the knowledge capacity to deal with the policy challenges it is facing. How might the key local institutions, from what sources and experiences, develop their knowledge, and how would the knowledge be converted into policy decisions in the country? Once one sees how these things are starting or trying to develop anyway from indigenous roots, then one can design assistance to help those institutions do it better.

And how to help them do it better? The best way is to stop the "training" for the replication of Bank courses and instead to send over someone from a successful institute to walk around with the institute director for several weeks to learn to see the world through the director's eyes and thus to see what type of help would actually be helpful. This hooking up with another institute director is an example of knowledge brokering and of fostering peer-to-peer learning.

The conventional approach to capacity building does not seem to incorporate the idea of fostering knowledge institutions in the developing countries that can construct from any sources and their own experience the relevant training programs and public information campaigns. In such a conception, Bank-provided materials would have to compete against all others on the grounds of quality and relevance—instead of the client institute being *paid* to replicate the World Bank's course.[10] Let us examine the conventional approach to capacity building more closely.

Examples of Building "Incapacity"

Core Courses

It will be said that surely there is some basic knowledge that international development agencies could usefully deliver to developing countries to build their capacity. But a small dose may set up a self-reinforcing dynamic with quite untoward consequences. Passive dependence for basic knowledge sets the stage for increased dependency in the future on the part of the client country. From the agency side, it is the foot in the door for ever larger programs with the well-known supply-driven dynamics that perpetuate cognitive dependency.

What then is the solution? The problem is that any specific suggestion will more likely lead to a new gaming strategy on the part of those on both sides who benefit from the standard methodology.

For instance, how might the purveyors of knowledge for development ensure that their programs are less supply driven? The ideal, of course, is that the doers of development undertake their own learning programs and then, as appropriate, request outside assistance—for instance in the form of a letter requesting a specific training program. Aha! A specific suggestion: give (free) training programs in response to client requests so the programs will then be demand driven. Of course, the specific suggestion can be gamed. The most cognitively dependent client can still put together a letter of request or, at least, can sign a letter drafted by the training agency.[11]

Training of Trainers

Perhaps the solution is to get beyond just training to capacity building. But capacity-building strategies lead to a new set of games. By far the simplest game is to rename the trainees as potential trainers so that the program can be called "training of trainers" (TOT is the usual acronym) and presented as a form of capacity building. Anyone who attends a course "could" train others in the future. Indeed, often the agency might hire their best (i.e., best at parroting the messages) trainees as trainers in future agency courses. All this directly competes with and crowds out any local training institutes that cannot afford to pay participants to come, to hold their courses in resort locations, and so forth. This form of capacity building in fact damages rather than builds local training capacity.

The justification given for these programs is that independent local training organizations might have "low-quality" programs and send the "wrong messages" so the agency needs to keep control of the indigenous capacity-building process.[12] It is an enduring "problem" that autonomous training programs might go "off-message." Since the post-socialist countries were only recently freed from the thought control of communism, it is incumbent on the agency to see that they don't stray down some "wrong" path again.[13] Quality control is a frequent rationale for this sort of enlightened control of training programs and (wherever possible) of the intellectual agenda in developing and transitional countries. Given the organizational structure of a global knowledge-based training agency, the outer limit of any probing questions is about the quality of the knowledge being poured into the heads of the clients, not about the entire methodology.

Training Networks

Another simple capacity-building strategy is to continue the usual program of training courses but to relabel every individual who has attended a course as a "member" and every group that provided a classroom and coffee as a "partner organization" in the (virtual) Agency Training Network (insert name of the appropriate agency). There is no actual funded and staffed organization; it is only a manner of speaking (like referring to all the people who ever attended a course on underwater basket weaving as the Network of Underwater Basket Weavers). Every training course held by the agency can then be described as a "meeting" of the Agency Training Network.

Eventually some of the alumni-trainees can be hired as consultants to repeat the standard courses without a task manager from headquarters being present (a "remote control course" in agency argot)! Thus "local knowledge capacity" is created and leveraged by the Agency Training Network to broadcast the main messages on a wider scale in the client country (all paid for by the agency in competition with local training institutes trying to run their own courses on an indigenous basis without foreign subsidies). To publicize such capacity-building successes, brochures describing the work of the Agency Training Network are designed and printed at the agency headquarters to be distributed by the proud task managers and their superiors. Such games are ways that knowledge-based development agencies get beyond mere training to "genuine capacity building."

These games can also have quite an adverse effect on actual capacity building. Here is an example. In Russia, the Morozov Project (http://www.morozov.ru/) has a national center in Moscow and had at its peak sixty-five staffed and self-supporting training centers throughout Russia. The project had some initial assistance from the European Bank for Reconstruction and Development (EBRD) and the U.S. Agency for International Development (USAID), but it was largely self-funding from user fees and local Russian funds. The Morozov Project was a natural partner for WBI (and the Bank as a whole) for training programs that would have impact all over Russia. Yet in the mid-1990s, when an attempt was made to hook up WBI (then EDI) with the Morozov Project, it was strongly (and successfully) resisted by task managers who wanted to continue delivering their own courses in Russia as before. The argument was that EDI had already built a "Training Network" in Russia, so there was no need to support the *rival* Morozov network that was not built by EDI (being the result of largely Russian efforts).

Fees for Service

To help ensure that the standard courses are not supply driven, an agency might put the courses to a market test by charging fees. Often the courses are given in Washington, DC, Paris, or Vienna, and many top officials and policymakers are suddenly able to find the time and money to quench their thirst for knowledge in these locations. Agency task managers justify this as a way to directly educate the top policymakers. What is wrong with this picture?

One of the hardest tasks in building the capacity of training institutes in developing countries is finding the money for them to be self-sustaining. The countries have little or no domestic sources of philanthropic funds, and government officials are not accustomed to paying for training courses or seminars (junkets to foreign cities may be another matter). When a prestigious development agency (or institutes associated with top universities such as Harvard and Princeton) offers courses for fees in cities of developed countries, then that deprives the local training institutes of potential income. Their local offerings are easily crowded out by the prospect of such a prestigious educational or, at least, hobnobbing experience in an elite setting. This practice is bad enough for organizations in advanced countries that do not pretend to be concerned with capacity development (e.g., semiprivate, university-affiliated training institutes), but it is especially pernicious for development agencies with a clear capacity-building mission.

Evaluations

But, it will be said, if the standard methodology of transmitting development knowledge is ineffective, then it will show up in the evaluations. Suppose that government officials and other policymakers are given full-expense-paid trips to attractive foreign cities or resorts to attend training programs or conferences.[14] Naturally, the evaluation forms filled out by the participants will show that the participants "learned a lot" and that they want "to repeat and deepen the learning experience" in the future, perhaps in a different resort. From the agency side, such junkets are justified "to attract high-level officials" and thus "to leverage the impact of the training expenditures."

Or suppose there is a program costing tens or hundreds of thousands of dollars to train a certain set of businesspeople in the rudiments of running a market-based business. The agency needs to evaluate the program and to learn from its mistakes. Naturally, the evaluation needs to be "scientific," so the business results of the group of trainees are compared over a period of time with the results of a counterfactual control group that received no training.[15] And, sure enough, the trained group gets better results than the untrained control group! Thus the training program is classified as a success (never mind the costs), the training managers and their supervisors get a pat on the back, and budget increases are requested for the next year.

Such impact evaluations leave something to be desired. Even though development training agencies are often run by economists, such evaluations ignore one of the most basic concepts in economics, the notion of opportunity cost. The opportunity cost of plan A is the benefit foregone by not applying the same resources to the best alternative plan B. The pseudo-evaluation described in the preceding compares the results of the resources applied to plan A with the results of applying no resources, and lo and behold, plan A usually seems to win. A real evaluation would compare the benefits of plan A with the benefits of the best alternative plan B *using the same resources.* The nature of that best alternative plan B would usually be quite controversial and subtle (e.g., how might the same resources be applied in an autonomy-respecting manner?). And the e-con-ometricians (with the accent on the "con") carrying out the scientific evaluation would plead "no data" about plan B.

Since in theory an evaluation of plan A is a comparison of its benefits with those of the best alternative plan B, the attempt to delineate such a plan B cannot be ruled out on the grounds that plan A gets positive evaluations. An evaluation of the direct training programs, international conferences, and junkets would mean considering how the same resources might be used in capacity building in the client country itself. The multitude of people who might have benefited from such a plan B would, of course, not be around to fill out evaluation forms for the evaluation of plan A.

One of the great benefits of competition (in the sense of rivalry) is that some alternative plans are actually carried out so plan A is thus subjected to more of a real evaluation. Since the training programs of the development agencies typically do not take place in a competitive environment, their evaluations will tend to confirm the efficacy of the standard forms of knowledge-based development assistance—as compared with no training (see chap. 7 for the role of devil's advocacy in outlining competitive alternatives within an organization).

Public Relations and Other Influence Activities

Thoreau said that firewood warmed him twice, once when he cut it and once when he burned it. Publicity-conscious task managers and their supervisors also design training programs to warm themselves twice, once as events in the field and again in the publicity generated from the event back at headquarters in slickly produced reports, photos, videos, and self-serving pseudo-evaluations. In the economic theory of agency, these are "influence activities" by the agents to better the image of their work in the eyes of the principals. As in the case of advertising and public relations, the influence activities are always justified as providing information. Eventually these influence activities become "the tail wagging the dog," as, for example, a training event becomes the occasion for a self-advertising campaign within the bureaucracy about what a great job is being done.[16]

Influence activities may exhibit increasing returns to scale due to lumpiness in the schedules of the top agency managers. Suppose for a given amount of budget, ten or fifteen capacity-building activities can be held in developing countries. The top managers cannot split their scheduled visits into ten small parts, and no single event will not warrant their attention. Hence the events will not appear on the radar screens of the top management. The top managers may remark that they don't see the training division doing anything (i.e., it is not showing on their radar screen). This will throw the middle management into a panic: "How can our activities become visible on top management's radar screen?"

If the same budget is rolled into one megaconference, then that will warrant a place on some top manager's schedule to visit the megaevent and perhaps ennoble it with an important speech. The top manager can then say to the middle manager: "Now I see you're doing something" and "Thank you for providing me the forum so that I could get across some of our Main Messages." The attendance of the top manager and some other celebrities in the globe-trotting "development set" will, in a self-reinforcing way, help build the attendance (often subsidized) at the megaevent to make it a big success. Informative talks and seminars coupled with general networking and schmoozing will yield a good time for all. And a few locals will be shipped in from the client countries to provide authentic color. Evaluation forms will be filled out enthusiastically by attendees in the hope of "doing it again next year." All the foregone small capacity-building events in the local institutes will be quickly forgotten amidst the general self-congratulatory euphoria and back patting of the development set. All the people who might have benefited from that alternative use of the megaevent budget will not be filling in evaluation forms, so there will be little or no dissent regarding the brilliant new strategy.

One could go on to describe other ingenious ways that the standard methodology of "knowledge transmission" and "learning delivery" can be relabeled, repackaged, and gamed to better suit a rhetoric of local capacity building, indigenous knowledge development, autonomous development learning, and the like.[17] One should not expect to find here some foolproof rules that cannot be gamed.

Economic and Sector Work: A "Jobs Program"
for Bank Economists

Any country that is able to manage its own affairs will have researchers in universities, institutes, bureaus, and think tanks that will study the economy and be able to research policy options. An important task of development agencies is to help build that research capacity in economic and sector work (ESW) in developing countries. A development agency has an internal need to research a country that might be borrowing money or receiving aid. This is "due diligence" or fiduciary ESW. However, the main function of ESW is to better inform policymaking in the country. ESW reports emanating from development agencies are ill suited for this role for a number of reasons. One set of reasons has to do with the strong policy filters applied in the agency. Another has to do with lack of local knowledge. Yet another is the lack of competition. Local institutes and think tanks are in competition to provide accurate readings of the economic situation and useful policy advice, while multilateral development agencies tend to have a monopolistic position vis-à-vis the country with the expected consequences. But the most basic reason is the violation of the cognitive autonomy of the country. Cognitive capacity building does not mean turning the government into a marionette that will believe and do what it is told as long as the aid or loan is forthcoming. A government in a country with a modicum of political opposition would deservedly be the object of ridicule if the best reasons it could marshal for making tough reforms were essentially that the reforms were based on the research done by the World Bank, IMF, or other agencies—and that the agency-promoted reforms were lubricated by aid or loans.

Yet the major development agencies rarely do any genuine capacity-building work with the research institutes, bureaus, or think tanks in the countries they work with. Why is that? It is not for lack of means. For instance, an agency could easily subcontract most research work to domestic institutes (perhaps in competition with one another). Yet there is an obvious reason why this is rarely done. The researchers in the elite development agencies need to justify their own jobs by writing the ESW reports themselves (with locals employed to fetch data). Of course, this dominant practice is not publicly justified as a "jobs program" for agency researchers. Insofar as agencies even bother to publicly justify the practice, the discourse is always "quality control."[18] Somehow only the reports prepared by the agency's own staff can have the necessary quality to warrant their funding. Work done by researchers in a developing country unfortunately does not measure up the "high standards" exacted by the elite development agencies.

This is not some newly discovered problem that needs to be brought to the attention of the development agencies to be resolved.

> Why is it that so many of these countries are still being treated as if they had learned very little in these years of tutelage and guidance? Surely this isn't true. If it isn't true, then why do the technical staffs of aiding agencies, national and multinational, and outside experts, so often continue to conduct exhaustive and repetitive reviews and to pass judgments on these countries with the same particularity exercised a decade

before? A school in which pupils never seem to be eligible for promotion to a higher grade would not seem to be a very good school. (Lilienthal 1967, 55)

This was written when the World Bank had been around for about twenty years. Now it is well over fifty years, and the "school" still has precious few graduates, and the practice is as strong or stronger than ever.

We may reasonably assume that managers and staff in the World Bank and other development agencies are interested in capacity building in the client countries. However, that rather abstract interest is nowhere near as salient and strong as the organizational need for the staff to justify their jobs in such agencies. Every attempt to reduce the amount of ESW done in the Bank is met with an explosion of new ESW products that the Bank should provide.[19] As in project preparation, so in research work, the organizational imperative of the Tendler effect is far more powerful than the other nice goals periodically enunciated by development agencies. Out of their dedication to project and research quality, the development agencies have to do this work themselves until the developing countries are ready to do it themselves. Since this process somehow never seems to lead to the countries being able to do it themselves with sufficient quality, the agency needs to constantly redouble its efforts and rededicate itself to "quality assurance"—and thus the ESW hamster wheel keeps the hamsters gainfully employed.

I have shown how the ordinary organizational imperatives in a powerful training and research organization lead to building or preserving incapacity rather than capacity in the developing countries. This is not due to some personal failing on the part of the managers and staff. Here and there a heroic individual may find the courage and organizational space to try something different, but sooner of later the organizational forces will grind down and smooth out such aberrations. The flaw lies in the very idea that capacity building in developing countries can be engineered by powerful external development agencies.

External Aid Agencies Co-opting Local Talent

Aside from their training programs, there is another way that external assistance agencies in a developing country can thwart capacity building, namely by providing an alternative career path for some of the best and brightest local people. The expatriate staff in the international and multilateral aid agencies in a country need the best local staff they can find to help sell the agency programs in the country. The salaries, benefits, and prestige of these "international sector" jobs in a developing country are usually incomparably better than what is available locally in government, universities, think tanks, or local NGOs.

From the side of the agencies, the rationale for this practice is that they are building local capacity rather than thwarting it. For example, a local person may be hired to work on project X so that when the funding for the project ends, the country will then have a local expert on X for work in the government, universities, think tanks, or NGOs. But the local person has now shown his or her competence and skills to work in the international sector and is not about to take the huge reduction in rewards and prestige of a domestic job. And the other locals who remained in government or other domestic jobs will not gladly receive an already privileged person jumping over them on the domestic job ladders. Hence as the funding for project X draws to a close, the local expert is strongly lobbying inside the agency either to extend the funding to a longer-term basis or to allow them to use their experience on some new project Y. All the while, the local expert's resume is circulating among all the other international agencies in the country (or perhaps elsewhere). One way or another, it is like a one-way trapdoor. Once the best and brightest make it into the international sector, they will not return (if they can help it) to a domestic job.

Unsustainable Missionary Outposts

A variation on the theme is for the foreign agency to provide first-stage funding for a new institute, think tank, or organization in the country where the domestic government may make a "matching contribution" of unused building space. The salaries in the organization are comparable to the international standard in order to attract the best and brightest of the local talent and thus to embellish the agency's success story in the country. Here is a tangible result of the agency's work in the country; it would not have otherwise happened. Accordingly the agency's clear sponsorship and "ownership" over the organization limits its influence in the domestic debates (imagine an EU-, Russian-, or Chinese-funded think tank in Washington, DC, churning out position papers on American political issues). Since the helper-agency is using its direct power and resources "to make things happen," the resulting local organization will have few domestic roots and less sustainability if weaned off the international funds. Although the World Bank does not make grants, there are various ways that multiyear institutional development projects can be funded from Bank resources and other international donor funds.

The idea, of course, is that the external initiative of the "missionary outpost" will eventually be internalized in the country, will be funded through internal sources, and thus will be successful at local capacity building. But years later, these organizations are still annually knocking at the door of the Bank or U.S., European, or Japanese foundations or agencies to fund their activities. Domestic funding will probably not be anywhere near the expected "international" level or will have unacceptable strings attached. Any local private wealth will probably rather fund its own initiative. Rather than face up to taking a fundamentally wrong approach, the preferred approach of the international agencies is to redefine *sustainability* as meaning not moving to domestic funding but moving to cofunding by some other sources in the international sector. Thus the international agencies can pick up some third-stage cofunding on each other's projects and thereby show that their projects are "sustainable."

Types of Development Knowledge

Universal versus Local Knowledge

So far the focus has been on the "how" of knowledge-based assistance (transmitting development knowledge from agency to clients) and how that methodology undercuts the ownership, self-efficacy, self-direction, and capacity-building efforts of the developing countries. The standard methodology is, however, also flawed in its implicit assumptions about the "what" of crucial development knowledge.

Can a money bank also function as a "knowledge bank"? Money travels a lot better than knowledge. General knowledge is knowledge that holds across countries, cultures, and times; local knowledge takes account of the specifics of place, people, and time. "Every man is mortal" is general knowledge, while "every vegetarian is a foreigner" is local knowledge in Greenland or Mongolia. A "best practice" might work well in some countries but fail miserably when recommended in other contexts. One size does not fit all.[20] In questions of institutional development, it is very difficult to know a priori just how general is a best practice. Global best practices usually need to be locally reinvented.

> The significance of this point of view is that contrary to the simplistic use of the term by many economists, there is, in principle, no such thing as diffusion of best practice. At best, there is only the diffusion of best practices, practices that evolve in the course of their diffusion. Contrary to popular wisdom, there are times when it pays to reinvent the wheel! (Cole 1989, 117)

Prudent counsel is to scan globally for best practices but to test them locally since local adaptation often amounts to reinventing the best practice in the new context. This is not a new insight.

> What makes modern industry is ultimately not the machine, but the brains which use it, and the institutional framework which enables it to be used. It is a social product, which owes as much to the jurist as to the inventor. To regard it as an ingenious contrivance, like a mechanical toy, or the gilded clocks in the museum at Peiping made by London jewellers for the amusement of Chinese emperors, which a country can import to suit its fancy, irrespective of the character of the environment in which the new technique is to function, is naïve to the point of absurdity. It is like supposing that, in order to acclimatise Chinese script in the West, it would be sufficient to introduce Chinese brushes and ink. (Tawney [1932] 1966, 130)

Many foreign experts have painfully discovered that the devil is in the (local) details. It is the local component of knowledge that requires adaptation—which in turn requires the active participation of those who know and understand the local environment. Local adaptation cannot be done by the passive, cognitively dependent recipients of development knowledge; it must be done by the doers of development in the course of their self-activity.

There are two points here: the necessity that knowledge be made locally applicable and that the adaptation be done by the local doers of development (not given as a gift or imposed as a conditionality from the outside). It is by the local selection, assimilation, and adaptation of knowledge that local doers make it their own. By taking a machine or device apart and putting it back together again, one can make it one's own even if there is little adaptation or redesign.

Contrary to the superficial arguments of the supporters of globalization driven by the powerful developed countries, it is not a matter of being open or closed to outside knowledge. It is a matter of being open to outside knowledge in a way that reaffirms one's autonomy. For Gandhi, this was intellectual swaraj (self-rule or autonomy). "I do not want my house to be walled in on all sides and my windows to be stuffed. I want the cultures of all lands to be blown about my house as freely as possible. But I refuse to be blown off my feet" (quoted in Datta 1961, 120). Only by remaining "on their feet" from an intellectual standpoint can the local doers have the self-confidence to select, assimilate, and adapt the external knowledge—instead of being overwhelmed and rendered intellectually dependent and subservient.

Considerable effort is required to adapt development knowledge to local conditions and culture. Policy research institutes (think tanks) are examples of local institutions that can play that important role. In the developed countries, think tanks have proliferated and have become important agents to introduce and adapt new policy initiatives. Think tanks or similar research institutions are no less needed to transplant social innovations to new contexts. The Japanese use a metaphor based on the gardening technique called *nemawashi* of slowly preparing and wrapping each root of a tree in order to transplant it.[21] The chances of a successful transplant are much larger than if the tree is pulled up in one place and planted in another.

Development institutions might try a quicker transplant method. Experts come in (physically or electronically) to give a senior policy seminar to local government officials, and then the experts return home hoping that their sound advice will take root. Yet this policy reform process is designed to promote neither active learning nor lasting institutional change. As these reforms are externally imposed rather than actively appropriated by the country, there will be little ownership of the reforms. Compliance may be only perfunctory; the quick transplant may soon wither and die.[22]

Local think tanks can be seen as nemawashi institutions who carefully adapt and prepare a transplanted policy initiative to survive and perhaps thrive in the local environment. It takes longer, but the roots are better prepared for the local soil. The political process of changing policies and implementing new ideas is usually rather messy and in need of high-maintenance support. The officials or parliamentarians constantly need more information and advice—more backup and hand-holding—in order to carry out the policy reforms. A thick report prepared by "high-quality" researchers from elite development agencies in the North will not do the job. As a result of this process of adaptation, which often involves virtually reinventing the idea, the government officials see the policy reform not as a foreign imposition but as a local product that addresses their needs and that they can sponsor. Scan globally; reinvent locally.[23]

When advocating a certain type of organization (e.g., local policy research institutes), it is necessary to indicate what is *not* being advocated.[24] In the relationship between the center (e.g., the multilateral development agency) and the periphery (e.g., the developing country), there may be certain organizations in the country that are "legitimized" not by their role in the country but by their role as local gatekeeper for the central authority. The center judges the local organization by its ability to faithfully clone or parrot the "universal" messages from the center, not by the organization's ability to adapt the experiences of others to the local situation and to thus earn an embedded legitimacy in the country.

If anyone in the center doubts the applicability of the central messages, then the local accommodating elite will always be more than willing to supply "local positive feedback" about the applicability of the central messages—which also serves to vouchsafe the intermediary role of the local counterpart elite as gatekeepers for the resources and influence emanating from the center.[25] This mutual reinforcement locks in the relationship, so the center ends up having little transformative effect on the more embedded and indigenous local structures, all the while receiving positive feedback on "the wonderful job it is doing." In some cases, the international agency even hires (directly or through the local counterpart) a public relations firm to publicize "Potemkin villages" so the rest of the world will also hear about the wonderful job it is doing.[26]

Those in the center who are legitimated in their expertise, prestige, and privileges by the "universality" of their messages are disinclined to recognize limitations or subtleties in the local applicability of their technical expertise.[27] Novel complexity, genuine uncertainty, conflict of values, unique circumstances, and structural instabilities are all downplayed or ignored since they might diminish the perceived potency of the center's expertise and undercut the client's faith in that potency. The client often wants the childlike security and comfort of being in the hands of the professional expert who will solve the perplexing problems.[28] Thus the center and periphery may well agree on establishing a "transmission belt" between the "wholesale" source and the local "retailers" for all the universal expert messages and best-practice recipes (i.e., the standard knowledge transmission methodology). These are some of the strong institutional forces to underappreciate the subtleties of local knowledge, to hamper the growth of autonomous client ownership, and to stymie the development of indigenous, local knowledge institutions.

Codified versus Tacit Knowledge

Explicit or codified knowledge is knowledge that can be spoken, written, and codified to be saved on a computer disk or transmitted over a telephone line. But we know more than we can say. We know how to ride a bike, to recognize a face, and to tell a grammatical sentence in our native language, but we would be hard put to turn this knowledge into explicit or codified knowledge. As explained in the previous chapter on the intellectual background for indirect approaches, Michael Polanyi (1962) pioneered the distinction between tacit (or personal) and explicit knowledge in the philosophy of science, and the distinction has since proven important to understand problems in the transfer of technologies, not to mention the "transfer" of institutions.[29]

There is much more to a technological system than can be put in an instruction book. The same holds a fortiori for "social technologies" or institutions. In a codified description of a best-practice case study, the uncodified tacit knowledge is often "the rest of the iceberg."[30] Some tacit knowledge might be transformed into codified knowledge (see Nonaka and Takeuchi 1995) so that it could be transferred by conventional methods. But the remaining tacit knowledge needs to be transmitted by special methods such as apprenticeship, secondments, imitation, twinning relations, and guided learning by doing. These methods of transferring tacit knowledge will be called "horizontal" methods of knowledge transfer—in contrast to "vertical" methods where knowledge can be codified, transmitted to a central repository or library, and then retransmitted to students.

Cargo Cult Reforms: Where Is the Road That Leads to Cargo?

The idea of appropriate technology also needs to be applied to institutions. There is a certain self-reinforcing vicious circle that leads to attempts to install inappropriate "advanced" institutions in developing and transitional postsocialist countries. Let us begin with the supply side of this unhappy transaction.

People from developed countries are, in effect, "born on third base and think they hit a triple."[31] Often such "natural-born development experts" are graciously disposed to teach developing countries how to hit a triple.[32] According to these experts, the developing country should redraft its laws to describe the institutions as seen from the vantage point of third base, and then after passing these new laws, everyone should wake up the next morning as if they too were born on third base. Unfortunately, societies tend to operate on the basis of their de facto institutions, norms, and social habits, not their formal laws—and particularly not formal laws "pulled out of the air" with little relation to past experience. When such a gap between formal and de facto institutions is introduced, then the bulk of the population can rarely jump over the chasm to suddenly start living according to the new formal laws—so the rule of law is weakened. Semilegal ("gray") and illegal ("black") activities become more prominent as the connection between legal and actual behavior is strained to and beyond the breaking point (see chap. 8 on the post-shock-therapy situation in Russia and the former Soviet Union). The advice from the natural-born development experts thus becomes more part of the problem than part of the solution. More relevant institutional information could be provided by people who were only on first or second base since they might actually know how to hit a single or a double.

I now turn to the demand side—the demand for impossible jumps to institutions copied from technologically advanced developed countries. The people and the politicians of the developing and the transition economies are constantly bombarded by the mass media with images of life in the First World. They want to get there tomorrow (if not yesterday). Consultants and academics from elite universities with no real development experience—and thus with only a third-base perspective—badger the government officials to have the political courage and will to undertake a shock-therapy-style change in institutions, to jump over the chasm in one leap (i.e., to jump directly to third base)—as if such institutional change were actually possible.[33] Those locals who caution against radical leaps are dismissed as only trying to protect their privileges and "rents" from the past regime. "How dare you think you know better than professors from Harvard!" The idea is to escape the past (not to study the past to better design incremental change strategies). If the scientific experts from the First World give this advice, how can the benighted officials from the Third World or the postsocialist countries resist?[34] All people have to do when they wake up the next morning is to start behaving according to the new laws drafted by the experts!

For instance in a southeast European postsocialist country that had been particularly isolated in the past, government officials wanted to jump to modern corporations like those in Europe. This was an example of an "iceberg" institutional reform; the "above-the-water-line" laws could be quickly changed, but the problem was the "below-the-water-line" long-term changes in behavior. The officials located a European foundation that was willing to fund an "adaptation" of the corporate laws of a West European country. The new draft laws were quickly passed by the parliament so that the government officials and legislators could brag that they now had European corporate statutes. All they needed now was a few lawyers, a few judges, a few accountants, a few regulators, a few businesspeople, and a few decades of institution-building experience so that the new statutes could actually be used. Any attempt to get the country to adopt laws similar to those in neighboring countries that had incrementally evolved toward a market economy for several decades was angrily rejected. "Why do you try to get us to use these second-best or third-best laws when we can adopt the *best* European statutes?" Surely the natural-born development experts from the First World want to provide the best laws for their clients?

Thus the government officials demand that they do not want some second-best "halfway house," some first-base or second-base model; they want the very best for their people—like in the advanced countries. The third basers in the international aid bureaucracies then can reap the fruit of the seeds they have sown by listening to the clients and responding to the clients' desires by trying to set up public joint stock companies in Albania, a stock market in Mongolia, defined contribution pension plans in Kazakhstan, modern self-enforcing corporate laws in Russia, and so forth. Thus the circle is completed; supply responds to demand in a self-reinforcing vicious circle to waste untold aid resources on the attempted instant gratification of a nonevolutionary "great leap forward" to First World institutions.

The first Do of autonomy-respecting assistance is that the helpers start from where the doers are, not from the helpers' or doers' fantasies. As an institutional change strategy, this is incrementalism as opposed to a shock therapy or blitzkrieg strategy of jumping over an institutional chasm in one leap. Those who promote a shock therapy approach are given to the self-serving misinterpretation of the debate as being about gradual versus rapid change. But incremental change can be quite rapid (e.g., the Chinese agricultural reforms), and it can take quite a long time to climb back out of the chasm after failing to jump over it in one leap.

The failed attempts at utopian social engineering might be usefully viewed from an anthropological perspective. Many of the First World institutions such as the stock market have a certain totemic or "religious" significance. The Wall Street mentality found in the postsocialist world is reminiscent of the cargo cults that sprung up in the South Pacific area after World War II.[35] During the war, many of the glories of civilization were brought to the people in the southern Pacific by "great birds from Heaven" that landed at the new airbases and refueling stations in the region. After the war, the great birds flew back to Heaven. The people started "cargo cults" to build mock runways and wooden airplanes in an attempt to coax the great birds full of cargo to return from Heaven.[36]

Peter Berger has pointed out the cargo cult mentality in development that promises a great magical leap to modernity:

> Indeed, one recurrent assertion of revolutionary propaganda is that its program can deliver the "cargo" more surely or more swiftly than the gradualistic development models. (Berger 1976, 21)

Postcommunist countries, with hardly a banking system worthy of the name, nonetheless opened up Hollywood storefront "stock exchanges" to supposedly kick start capitalism. Government officials in Eastern

Europe, the former Soviet Union, and even Mongolia proudly show the mock stock exchanges, complete with computers screens and "big boards," to Western delegations (with enthusiastic coverage from the Western business press) in the hope that finally the glories of a private enterprise economy will descend upon them from Heaven. An earlier generation of misguided development efforts left Africa dotted with silent "white elephant" factories, and the present generation of revolutionary reforms in the postsocialist world have left the region dotted with dysfunctional cargo cult institutions—the foremost among them being "stock markets" promoted by USAID, the World Bank, and the IMF.

Knowledge Assistance: Brokering between Experiments, Not Disseminating Answers

Since we don't know how "to do development" as an engineering project, what is a development agency to do? Much of what is now clear is negative—for example, the unhelpful forms of help such as social engineering and benevolent aid. Agencies, like Socrates, do not know the answers, and in questions of development, there would be little irony in that admission. Autonomy-respecting help is essentially indirect; it cannot be reduced to a set of "do this" and "do that" instructions.

There is a saying in education that a teacher should be "more like a guide by the side than a sage on the stage." The sage on the stage image fits the agency that pretends to have the answers in the form of development knowledge so that the main problem is dissemination and local absorption. As the guide by the side, the agency works to guide the development of local learning capacity in government and in think tanks that play a key role in gathering and adapting knowledge to local conditions. The agency might play a role in brokering peer-to-peer learning. If we think of development assistance being provided more by a global network of smaller and less powerful local agencies rather than powerful global agencies, then a knowledge-brokering agency would help connect people trying to undertake a reform with other groups in somewhat comparable circumstances who have already done so. The Internet is particularly helpful to facilitate networking (e.g., user groups of people all involved with trying to solve the same sorts of problems).

Where there is little available prior experience, then the agency can turn to experiments. An experimentalist strategy is to sponsor a program of parallel decentralized experiments with discussion, benchmarking, and horizontal learning among the experimenters—all of which will tend to ratchet up the performance of the whole group. The agency plays more of a broker role between the experimenters than a center disseminating the truth to the periphery.

Many development strategies implicitly assume (or desperately hope) that a country already has a central planning and implementation capacity to make institutional reforms from the top down and/or that institutional reforms can be somehow pushed through with the external pressures of aid conditionalities. In a decentralized social learning strategy, developmental transformations are induced not by governmental fiat but by releasing and channeling local energies in smaller projects that will in due course spread by forward and backward linkages as well as through horizontal learning, benchmarking, and imitation (see chap. 9 on Hirschman and others for more on these ideas).

7

Can Development Agencies Learn & Help Clients Learn?

Introduction: A "Church" versus a Learning Organization

In this chapter, our focus is on the organizational structure of the helping agency from the cognitive point of view. In the modern world it is now commonplace to accent the importance of intellectual capital and knowledge management. Most organizations want to be seen as learning organizations. Yet many old habits persist that are directly opposed to learning and to the advancement of knowledge. The new rhetoric of "learning" is applied as a veneer onto a churchlike organization proselytizing its own dogmas—an organization that shuts its eyes to the sun so that it can see better by the glow of its own moon.

In the previous chapter, I consider questions about the methodology of knowledge-based development assistance and the subtleties introduced by different types of development knowledge. Now I focus on the organization or agency involved in knowledge-based development assistance. There are two different sites of learning: within the organization and within the client country or group being assisted. How can such an agency function as a learning organization, and how can it foster active learning on the part of the clients? These questions are approached by considering some of the major roadblocks in the way of organizational and client learning.

The case in point for this chapter is the World Bank. President James Wolfensohn raised the idea of the Bank as a "knowledge bank" in addition to being a money bank. In addition to all the accumulated development experience of the Bank's operational staff, the Bank has several hundred PhDs (mostly in economics) in its research department—a vice presidency called Development Economics (DEC) with the chief economist at the head of it. It is the largest concentration of researchers on development issues in the world. Moreover, the researchers have inside access to World Bank experience and can even, in theory, move in and out of operational positions to gain firsthand experience at doing what the Bank does (which is sometimes called *development experience*). In this chapter, we examine whether or not such an organization can be expected to function as a learning organization—as a "knowledge bank."

Roadblock to Learning 1: Official Views as
Dogma, with Examples

To put it simply, the basic problem is that in spite of the espoused model of a learning organization, the theory-in-use of a development agency is often a model of a "development church" giving definitive *ex cathedra* Official Views on all the substantive questions. As with the dogmas of a church, the brand name of the organization is invested in its views. This is true for any large powerful organization that enunciates Official Views, but I concentrate here on my primary case study, the World Bank. Once an Official View of the Bank has been announced, then to question it is an attack on the Bank itself and on the value of its franchise, so subsequent learning is in fact rather discouraged. Thus when licensing an Official View in the first place, the Bank authorities need to have what Milton calls the "grace of infallibility and incorruptibleness" since any subsequent "learning" would be tantamount to disloyalty.[1] The end result is what Milton calls the "laziness of a licensing church"—an organization populated with intellectual clerks dutifully producing the statistical factoids and politically correct banalities that pass through the filters.

When the Bank takes Official Views, then the discussion between the agency staff and the clients is a pseudodialogue since the agency staff are not free to unilaterally change Official Views (just as missionaries are not free to approve local variations in church dogmas). In fact, the staff are not even free to publicly state their personal views *as personal views* if they differ from the Official Views. Here is the current official language from the External Affairs Department instructing Bank staff.

> All staff should recognize that journalists assume that whatever statements they make on Bank Group activities or development issues reflect the institution's policy or thinking. Accordingly, staff members making such statements have a responsibility to be fully informed about the Bank Group's position. Expectations of staff in their dealings with external audiences are explained in the Administrative Manual, under Section 14. Crucially, staff contemplating a speech, article, opinion/editorial, or letter to the editor must realize that a disclaimer that the speaker or writer is expressing personal views is unconvincing and usually ineffective. It also does not exempt the staff member from following procedures, or from recognizing that they speak for the institution.

It is an astonishing fact that the same senior management that makes these medieval-church-like regulations also expects the public to view the published results of the Bank's research staff as being of comparable objectivity and quality as the research published by, say, university researchers—when universities do not take official stands on the issues and would not dream of similarly gagging their researchers (e.g., try substituting *Harvard University* for *Bank Group* in the preceding regulations).

One important event in this glorious history dates back two decades. After Robert McNamara retired as president, one of his key advisors, Mahbub Ul Haq, had a rather rocky relationship with the next president, Tom Clausen. Ul Haq was asked by the Mexican organizers of the upcoming Cancun summit in 1981 to attend in personal capacity a nonpublic meeting with a number of other prominent development thinkers to talk about what ideas might be usefully discussed at the summit. Ul Haq took personal leave from the Bank for the trip, which was paid for by the Mexican organizers, not the Bank. In his oral history interview after leaving the Bank, Ul Haq said what transpired when he returned.

> I came back and Mr. Clausen asked for my explanation; how could I do this when he, himself, had not been involved in the Cancun Summit? When I told him that I was doing it in a personal capacity, he made a

remark which I think he believed in very strongly and I respect his phi-losophy. I disagree with it violently, but I respect it. What he said was that when you are in the service of the Bank, there can be no distinction between an official capacity and a personal capacity. Nobody has a personal capacity in the Bank. He followed up his philosophy by telling even the External Relations Department that those articles which appeared in "Finance and Development" where it was indicated that these were the personal views of staff, by saying, I can never believe these are any personal views, you can not have any staff having personal views and a directive should be issued to the staff to the effect that they can only have official views which have to be cleared first in a forum. (Ul Haq 1982)

Ul Haq left the Bank in a matter of months.

The "tradition" goes on. As one of Joseph Stiglitz's advisors and speechwriters, I was careful to add a personal disclaimer to Stiglitz's more controversial speeches (see Chang 2001), but Stiglitz was constantly called into President Wolfensohn's office to account for the heresies.[2] Stiglitz eventually resigned shortly before the end of his three-year term as chief economist. The External Affairs view quoted in the preceding that a personal disclaimer is "unconvincing and usually ineffective" is remarkably presumptive about what other people understand—as if journalists were not well aware that Stiglitz's views were not the Official Views. Moreover, the "thought police" could make the personal disclaimer quite effective when they wanted to. For instance, in Stiglitz's last public speech as chief economist (the last chapter in Chang 2001), he impishly "announced" that the Bank had finally reversed itself and supported the International Labour Organization's fourth labor standard on the rights of workers to organize and collectively bargain. On the next business day, the Bank issued a statement saying that the speech represented only Professor Stiglitz's personal views.

A respected Bank economist, Ravi Kanbur, had left the Bank to take a chair at Cornell University, and then he returned as a consultant to lead the important World Development Report (WDR)—the Bank's flagship research publication—for the millennium year 2000. There was an unprecedented yearlong consultation process with groups around the world, and the early drafts of the report were posted on the Web for public comment. In the last stages of finalizing the report, Kanbur felt there was quite inappropriate pressure from the U.S. Treasury (which oversees the U.S. role in the Bank) and from some top Bank managers to change some of the crucial conclusions. It was an abridge too far, so he publicly resigned, thereby embarrassing the Bank and forcing it to keep the report more or less intact.

And there is the notorious case of William Easterly. Easterly was a widely respected and "tenured" economist in the Research Department of the Bank. In 2001, he showed great intellectual and personal courage in publishing a book, *The Elusive Quest for Growth*, which cat-alogued the failures of the official development strategies over the last half century. While there might be some wiggle room if unwelcome results are published in suitably obscure books or journals, Easterly committed the cardinal sin of publishing his conclusions (labeled *per-sonal*) in an op-ed article in the *Financial Times*. Since this was most certainly not cleared by the "thought police" of the External Affairs Department, Easterly was charged with an ethical violation. In a short while, he took a leave and then resigned to start a new career as a uni-versity professor.

After the Stiglitz-Kanbur-Easterly resignations, the rest of the research staff in the Bank presumably took the object lesson in profes-sional ethics from the public relations department: that being allowed to publish results entails having the results agree with the party line and that feisty independence of thought can quickly lead to an ethical violation. Surely such a regime of thought control in a Soviet research organization would have brought a swift condemnation and a swift dis-crediting of the intellectual integrity of the organization. Yet, to this day, it is unclear to me which part of the norms of modern intellectual life—not to mention the methodology of science—that the intellec-tual leadership of the World Bank does not understand or does not accept and that thus would account for its behavior. Or is it simply that power corrupts (like the Church in the Middle Ages), and the leader-ship thinks the power of the Bank allows it to give short shrift to the norms of intellectual integrity and the methodological rules of science? In contrast, these norms are on the whole respected by universities that have no monopolistic power (called *global role* in the case of the Bank) and plenty of competition.

Perhaps part of the reasoning is that the Bank will have better cog-nitive control over the clients if the clients don't hear all sides of an argument. The slogan is something like "Give the clients an inch of nuance, and they'll take a mile of status quo" (Kanbur and Vines 2000,

101). The Bank wants the clients to be like Henry Ford's Model T customers who were free to choose any color so long as it was black. The clients who wish to receive assistance are free to learn and to make up their own minds so long as they arrive at the Right Answers.

There is little motivation for the staff to actively appropriate or understand any deeper rationale for the Official Views since they must advocate the Official Views to the clients in any case. The views are generally not those that the staff members individually decided upon based on evidence or argumentation. In project design, the herd instinct takes over. If a project manager designed a project in conformity with Official Views and the project failed, then the individual could hardly be faulted for being a good team player. If a project of innovative ("deviant") design should by some happenstance be approved and then fail, then the culpability of the individual project manager would be inescapable. If, on the other hand, the deviant project showed signs of succeeding, then this recognition would be opposed by the higher-ups who determine the Official Views and by the other project managers who are well-accustomed and "committed" to doing projects in the approved way. Any evidence of success would need to be double- or triple-checked by researchers selected by the higher-ups. If, after all this, the success was undeniable, then it would presumably be due to some unique, unreplicable circumstances, and the higher-ups would in their wisdom see no reason to modify the Official Views.

If the higher-up officials identified with an old Official View have retired,[3] then perhaps a new view can be announced with minimal internal resistance and embarrassment. But there can be no publicly aired debate within the agency on its Official Views. The reasoning behind this strategy is standard: parents should not argue in front of the children, and doctors should not debate in front of the patients. How can a developing country put itself in the hands of the development agency if the agency is openly debating about the One Best Way? Without firm guidance from the development experts, the developing country may be put in the uncomfortable and unaccustomed position of having to make up its own mind and take responsibility for its own decisions.

The root problem is not simply the content of the Official Views but the adverse dynamics set in motion by an agency taking Official Views in the first place. We must still ask why the Bank, the IMF, and some other agencies enunciate Official Views. It is important to understand the self-reinforcing symbiosis or vicious circle between the helpers and doers in this case. It is not just the corruptions of power or the self-confidence of textbook solutions in neoclassical economics that lead to the hubris of licensing Official Answers. The agencies are responding to demand. The governments of developing countries are facing daunting problems. They genuinely yearn for some magical solution from abroad—particularly from the experience and the science of the advanced industrialized countries—along with the long-term money to apply the magical solution or, at least, to alleviate some of the politically troublesome symptoms. If it seems to work, the government is a hero; if it fails, who can blame it for trying the solution proffered by the best and the brightest in Washington, DC? And money can buy some short-term behavior change and some symptomatic relief—all of which is interpreted by the agency and the government as "success."4 Agency managers are promoted for their "successful" programs to positions of greater bureaucratic power, which facilitates ensuring that future unwelcome evidence about the "successes" will be lost down the organizational memory hole. A new generation of project managers arrive to prove their mettle. The governments of the developing countries are even more desperate for magical solutions and for the longer-term money to finance today's solutions and to service the loans that financed yesterday's solutions.

The church model of the development agency also fits perfectly with the standard default methodology of knowledge-based development assistance. Isn't it the job of the teacher to supply the answers to the pupils? And what would students expect from teachers if not to be supplied with the answers? Luckily the Bank has distilled the true "knowledge for development" from its decades of global experience as well as from the textbooks of economic science, and it takes its mission to be transmitting this knowledge through various forms of aid-baited proselytization to the passive clients in the developing world.

The organizational opposite to a church might be taken as a university. "[A]mong contemporary social arrangements the modern Western university is the main one that has endeavored to make intellectual criticism and innovation a legitimate and regular aspect of the prevailing social order" (Moore 1972, 91). The university sets itself up not as an arbiter of truth but as an arena within which contrary theories can be examined and the "collision of adverse opinions" can occur in open debate.[5] When an agency takes Official Views on questions or considers its views as branded knowledge, then the genuine collision of adverse opinions and the rule of critical reason will tend to give way to the rule of authority and bureaucratic reason within the hierarchy of the organization (e.g., the "Soviet theory of genetics" or the "University of Utah theory of cold fusion").

One example of this was the internal conflict within the World Bank, described by Robert Wade (1996), between the emerging conclusions of a team putting together the *East Asian Miracle* report (World Bank 1993) and the conclusions of an earlier 1991 *World Development Report* on development strategy. This is plausible behavior in a church, but one would hardly expect a university administration to interfere with the publication of the results of one group of scholars because the results did not agree with those of a prior publication of another group of scholars from the same university. The question "But what about the reputation of the institution?" might be answered by arguing that such interference in fact damages rather than enhances the intellectual integrity of the institution and its researchers. The other publications of researchers from such an institution are then thrown under the shadow of being the product of such bureaucratic "smoothening" (called "coordination of messages" in bureaucratese). In any case, material left out of the *East Asian Miracle* was developed and published by the Brookings Institution by one of the team members and a colleague, Jose Edgardo Campos and Hilton Root (1996).[6]

The authorities in an organization would naturally decide the Official Views of the organization that would be expressed to the world and would tend to shut off any feedback loops that might expose any errors in their Official Views and thus might subtract from the franchise value of the brand name.

> Can the social scientist serve two masters—Truth and the Corporative Sponsor? When he has rendered unto the corporation that which is the corporation's, how much is left to the idols of the laboratory? Is the scientist's allegiance to truth only an obligation to obey the ground rules and observe the amenities of something called Scientific Method— selectively perceiving all the trees within his field of vision, while selectively overlooking the forest? (Matson 1966, 78)

For instance, publication of experimental results contradicting Trofim Lysenko's official Soviet theory of genetics would be anti-Soviet behavior.[7] Learning from errors, which involves changing Official Views and modifying branded knowledge, is minimized, so the organization tends to function more as a secular church or organized priesthood than as an open learning organization—regardless of the espoused label.

The church model of proselytizing directly contradicts autonomous or self-directed learning in the client countries. The project manager from the agency wants the clients "to learn"—so long as they learn "the right thing." The gardener wants only her own seeds to grow; all else are weeds.

For example, one of my first assignments at the World Bank was to conduct a seminar on privatization in Kazakhstan since the country had not yet decided on a privatization strategy. I organized the last session of the weeklong seminar as a debate in front of the officials and staff struggling with privatization issues. A consultant from one of the Big Six accounting firms argued in favor of voucher privatization (see the next chapter), and I argued against it and in favor of various alternatives. When word of this debate reached headquarters in Washington, DC, the country manager in the Bank was outraged that I had used a World Bank seminar to present arguments against voucher privatization, which the Bank had already decided was best for the country. Since approval by the country manager was required for travel by Bank staff to a country, I was banned from the country for several years.

With the help of stock market boosters and the "families" (i.e., tribal groups) that realized the possibilities for corruption, the Bank was successful in pressuring Kazakhstan to adopt voucher privatization. But as I had argued, it turned out to be a debacle. The Bank has a quasi-independent Operations Evaluation Department (OED), which is supposed to harvest lessons from the Bank's past experience. I say *quasi-independent* since OED is a department within the Bank answering to the board of directors but its draft results are debated with the operations staff before being finalized. All the OED staff except the top director will eventually rotate back into other parts of the Bank so there is inevitably some "smoothing" of the conclusions. In the case of the OED report on the Kazakhstan country program including the voucher mass privatization program, the penultimate draft had some quite unusual words about the debacle.

> IPFs [Investment Privatization Funds] themselves operated without regulations that would have protected voucher holders. The OED audit of

the Rehab loan in mid-1997 suggested that asset stripping, "off-book" transactions, embezzlement and improper or postponed plant mainte- nance have reduced firms' worth. During OED's 1999 audit mission for the SAL [Structural Adjustment Loan], no IPF could be contacted. The rapid decline in gross fixed investment and limited access to bank credit reflect continued weak corporate governance. In hindsight, the IBRD [International Bank for Reconstruction and Development, the official name of the World Bank] should not have supported the mass privatiza- tion strategy although this strategy got broad support in Kazakhstan at the time. (OED 2000, 13)

In the final version of the report, made public, the wording was much toned down and the above sentence saying that the Bank "should not have supported the mass privatization strategy" was deleted. In addition to being a little more forthright seven or eight years after the fact, the Bank would have done better at the time by ensuring that the government heard the arguments on all sides of an issue from the lending staff and even that the government tried some parallel experimentation of different options on a topic with so little prior experience. Instead, the Bank had decided on its Official Views, and the staff was expected to duly support them with the client.[8]

Any genuinely self-directed learning process in the client country might veer off in the "wrong direction" in opposition to the Official Views. For example, if the project manager had returned to headquar- ters with a country-approved privatization program quite different from voucher privatization, then by contradicting the Bank's Official Views it would probably not be funded, and the project manager's career in the Bank would be in trouble. Therefore the flow of knowledge must be "managed" in the name of "quality control." The clients must be kept from being distracted by alternative views. Knowledge-based develop- ment assistance should transmit the expert-determined official truths to the clients. The standard methodology of dissemination to passive clients (discussed in the previous chapter) is a corollary of the church model.

Roadblock to Learning 2: Funded Assumptions as Dogma

Why is it so necessary for a development agency to take an Official View on the One Best Way to solve a development problem? One common answer is that a development agency is not a university; the agency puts money as loans or grants behind projects based on various assumptions. University professors do not "put their money where their mouth is," so they are free to debate questions forever. Once an agency has committed significant resources to certain assumptions, then it is time "to join the team," "fall in line," and support the funded assumption.

This remarkable doctrine is one of the marvels of bureaucratic reason. There are obvious bureaucratic reasons why individual project managers and their superiors would like a funded project assumption to be treated as gospel, but they are not reasons why the whole institution should take such a stand. The commitment of funds and prestige even seems to alter perceptions.[9] For instance, subjective assessments of winning probabilities tend to increase after bettors at a racetrack have placed their bets. But horses do not run faster when bets are riding on them. It does not take much understanding of the sciences to know that theories are corroborated by evidence, not by commitments of funds. Even in the business world, many firms have come to grief because managers would not revisit strategies after initial costs were sunk. In view of the record of international development aid, there is little evidence to support the similar practice of seeing project assumptions as hardening into gospel because of the commitment of funds.

Roadblock to Learning 3: "Social Science" as Dogma

Today, science has long since replaced religious authority (the Church) as the source of dogmas that one can appeal to without further reason or corroboration. That style of argumentation completely misrepresents the scientific method, not to mention the role of critical reason, but it is none the less quite common given the intellectual herd instincts prevalent in the aid bureaucracies. The all-too-human factors that previously led to an appeal to church dogma have not suddenly disappeared in today's scientific age, so one should expect the appeal to science to be thoroughly abused. This is nowhere more true than in the social sciences (see Andreski 1972). Economics is the "rooster ruling the roost" in the social sciences,[10] so one should expect much to be passed off in the name of "the science of economics." Yet many of the theses imposed by bureaucratic power as the "truths of economics" would not pass without serious challenge in any open scientific forum—particularly when one goes beyond academic model building to policy applications. Thus many of the Official Views that are presented as truths of economics usually have some other less-than-scientific basis—as becomes evident years later when economists finally arrive at a "nuanced appreciation of the complexities of the situation" (e.g., in the transition economies such as Russia or Kazakhstan).[11]

It is particularly unfortunate when a Tayloristic One Best Way (Kanigel 1997) mentality creeps into development policy-making in the name of "science."[12] The problems of the developing and transition countries are much too complex to yield to formulaic best practices and magic bullets. Many different approaches need to be tried on an experimental basis, so when a major development agency stakes its reputation on some One Best Way, then the development effort as a whole is impoverished.

Roadblock to Learning 4: The Rage to Conclude

Hirschman has often noted the problems created in developing countries by the tendency that Gustave Flaubert ridiculed as "la rage de vouloir conclure," or the rage to conclude.[13] But the same attitude is rampant in development agencies. Indeed, this is another self-reinforcing lock in between development agencies and their client countries.

> [Policy-makers] will be supplied with a great many ideas, suggestions, plans, and ideologies, frequently of foreign origin or based on foreign experience. . . . Genuine learning about the problem will sometimes be prevented not only by the local policy-makers' eagerness to jump to a ready-made solution but also by the insistent offer of help and advice on the part of powerful outsiders. . . . [S]uch practices [will] tend to cut short that "long confrontation between man and a situation" (Camus) so fruitful for the achievement of genuine progress in problem-solving. (Hirschman 1973, 239–40)

The questions that face development agencies about inducing economic and social development are perhaps the most complex and ill-defined questions facing humankind. Donald Schön (1971, 1983) notes the novel complexity, genuine uncertainty, conflict of values, unique circumstances, and structural instabilities that plague such problems of social transformation and that preclude definitive blueprint solutions. Yet one must marvel at the tendency of the major development agencies to rush forward with universal "best practices"[14]—a tendency based not on any methods resembling social science but on a bureaucratic need to maintain elite prestige by having an answer for the client.

In contrast, every field of science is populated by competing theories, and scientists do not feel the need to artificially rush to closure just "to have an answer." Any university president who asked the members of a department to at least come to an agreement among themselves before publishing ("coordination of theories") so as not to embarrass the university would, one hopes, soon be out of the job. Yet such pressure for the "coordination of results" is *routine* in the World Bank, the IMF, and presumably the other major development agencies.

Consider, for example, the complex problem of fighting corruption. Economists might approach the topic by trying to minimize government-imposed discretionary regulations that present rent-seeking opportunities to officials who might offer to relax a restriction for appropriate consideration. Accountants might emphasize transparency and uniformity of data and the independence of auditing. Civil servants might emphasize codes of ethics, organizational morale, and disclosure requirements. Lawyers might encourage civil discovery procedures and criminal sanctions. Others would promote a free and independent press, a high standard of public ethics, and a vigorous civil society. There are clearly many ways to approach the topic, and there seems to be no One Best Way, so a multipronged approach seems advisable. Yet there was alarm and dismay within the Bank at the lack of coordination of messages when different Bank groups took different approaches to fighting corruption and aired these different views at an international conference. Why couldn't the Bank "get its act together" and tell the client the One Best Way to address the corruption problem?

When journalists try to build a story by pointing out differences within a development agency, then agency bureaucrats should point out to the opportunistic journalists the necessity of the open clash of adverse opinions to intellectual advance. They should point out to the journalists that the real story is the intellectual honesty and integrity of an agency that would have such open discussions that are the lifeblood of intellectual and scientific progress. Instead public-relations-oriented bureaucrats are more typically alarmed at the lack of coordination of messages and rededicate themselves to better vetting the public statements of agency officials and researchers (recall the previously quoted staff rule issued by the Bank's External Affairs Department), a tragicomic effort usually carried out in the name of quality control. How can the passive, dependent clients put themselves in the hands of the international experts if the latter cannot agree on the One Best Way to fight corruption or to address other complex development issues?

The church approach has implications for the question of client-centered versus paternalistic approaches to client learning. What would be wrong with two different parts of an international development institution expressing at an international conference two different views on a complex question? What would be wrong with the listeners or readers realizing that affiliation with an elite institution is not the touchstone of truth just as publication in an elite journal is not the imprimatur of infallibility? Indeed, such a realization might have the rather positive effect of leading the listeners or readers to think the matter over and thus to take some responsibility in forming an opinion for themselves.[15] In short, it would foster active learning rather than promote passive acceptance of the "truth" promulgated by a churchlike organization.

Often the argument is "Yes, there are doubts and differences within the agency, but the agency must show a united front in order to steel the resolve of the clients trying to implement a difficult program of social and economic change." Perhaps the clear resolve of the agency's Official View and the possibility of aid conditioned on acceptance of that view will tip the domestic balance in a developing country and bring the internal advocates of that view to power. Firstly, this argument implicitly assumes a Jacobin (or Bolshevik) rather than adaptive and experimentalist strategy of change. Yes, a Jacobin strategy does assume a fanatical resolve that cannot publicly entertain doubts, but that is one of the many problems with that philosophy of social change. An adaptive, experimentalist, or pragmatic approach requires no such certitude, and indeed it welcomes a variety of parallel experiments in various regions or sectors to see what works (e.g., as in the Chinese reforms).[16] Secondly, this argument assumes that the government is deriving its reform motivation from the agency, not from within—an assumption that by now requires no further comment. Thirdly, while Hirschman notes that this imagined sequence is not impossible, "it is our conviction that this picture of program aid as a catalyst for virtuous policies belongs to the realm of rhapsodic phantasy" (Hirschman and Bird 1971, 205).

The Open Learning Model

Surely much has been learned about economic development. What is wrong with espousing the best practices from successful development as well as promoting the underlying guiding principles (perhaps plied with aid so that "need can do the work of reason")? Should international development organizations just be agnostic on the questions of development and treat all opinions as having equal weight? To approach these questions, it is useful to consider the methodology of science. Science as a loosely structured international open learning organization is hardly agnostic in any given area. All opinions are not given equal weight. Certain theories are the received or current theories in a field. The difference from a church lies in the methodology used to sustain or overturn the hypotheses. In mathematics, it is published and intersubjectively verifiable proof, not authority, that is the basis for theorems. In the empirical sciences, hypotheses are developed on the basis of intellectual coherence and factual cues and are then openly subjected to experiments that can be intersubjectively verified and reproduced. As long as intersubjective verification remains the touchstone of any scientific theory, then no theory needs, in principle, to be accepted on the basis of authority.

As an aside, we can now see the connection between (cognitive) autonomy and universality in Kant's thought. By grounding a belief in an autonomous manner (e.g., on empirical evidence and logical argument) as opposed to an heteronomous manner (e.g., based on some authority or on voices in one's head), the belief thus becomes universalizable since anyone can in theory perform the same experiments or follow out the same arguments.

> To employ one's own reason means simply to ask oneself, whenever one is urged to accept something, whether one finds it possible to transform the reason for accepting it, or the rule which follows from what is accepted, into a universal principle governing the use of one's reason. Everyone can apply this test to himself; and when it is carried out, superstition and zealotry will be seen to vanish immediately, even if the individual in question does not have nearly enough knowledge to refute them on objective grounds. (Kant [1786] 1991, 249).

In a similar manner, Kant tried to connect volitional autonomy and universality in his moral thought.

This methodology of science shows, at least in general terms, how an open learning model of a knowledge-based development agency might operate. The important thing to teach a client country is not the "truth" (e.g., propounded by zealots in neoclassical economics) but the active learning methodology to find and corroborate or disprove "truths" (i.e., hypotheses and theories).[17] Thus it could arrive at the knowledge autonomously rather than just be taking it on authority. That means capacity building in the knowledge institutions of the country.

This is again the Socratic principle that even if the teacher has the "answers" the goal of teaching is not to transfer the answers to the students but to develop the students' capabilities for learning on their own.[18] In describing the Danish folk schools, Joseph K. Hart notes that a real teacher is one "who is capable of learning, and who can teach, not so much by his teaching, as by his capacity to learn." Our adult educational institutions "have plenty of men and women who can teach what they know; we have very few who can teach their own capacity to learn."[19]

Learning processes in a country are encouraged by experiments "to see what works." Indeed, there are usually different decentralized experiments going on in a country—*processes of growth and change already under way* (sometimes called *moving trains*) often unbeknownst to government officials. Where the train of reform is already moving on its own, then reformers can jump on board to help it go better. The moving trains can be held up as models and benchmarks for other reform efforts in the country.

For instance, if a knowledge-based development agency wants to promote the One Best Way of reforming or changing certain institutions (e.g., the "best" model of fighting corruption or the "best" form of privatization), then it should be willing to share the source of that "knowledge," to promote or discover some experiments in the country to corroborate such a hypothesis or to validate a local adaptation, and to encourage horizontal cross-learning from similar experiments documented in the organization's knowledge management system—all before the reform is accepted as anything like a blueprint for the country as a whole. In short, the intersubjectivity and reproducibility that are key to scientific knowledge translate into local experimentation and verification in the case of development knowledge. The message to policymakers is

To the best of our accumulated experience (which we deem to call *knowledge*), here is what works best in countries like yours. Why don't you study this experience (by researching good practice success stories), take a look at these case studies, contact these people who designed those reforms, set up horizontal learning programs with those best-practice cases, and try some experiments to see what works in your own country? After carrying out this learning process on your own, you might call us back if you feel we could help by partially but not wholly funding the reform program you have decided upon.

The most important thing is to get away from the model of teaching as the transmission of knowledge from the development agency to the developing country.

When asked how he tried to persuade people, Noam Chomsky focused on how to get them to think for themselves.

> I don't try to persuade people, at least not consciously. Maybe I do. If so, it's a mistake. The right way to do things is not to try to persuade people you're right but to challenge them to think it through for themselves. . . . In complicated areas, like human affairs, we don't have an extremely high level of confidence, and often a very low level. In the case of human affairs, international affairs, family relations, whatever it may be, you can compile evidence and you can put things together and look at them from a certain way. The right approach. . . . is simply to encourage people to do that. . . . You shouldn't believe what I say is true. The footnotes are there, so you can find out if you feel like it, but if you don't want to bother, nothing can be done. Nobody is going to pour truth into your brain. It's something you have to find out for yourself. (Chomsky 2000)

To impose a model (e.g., by aid-baited dissemination of development knowledge) without this local learning process would be to short-circuit and bypass the active learning capability of the local policymakers, to substitute "authority" in its place, and thus to perpetuate the cognitive passivity of tutelage.

Competition and Devil's Advocacy in the Open Learning Model

Devil's Advocacy and Countervailance

How might a large bureaucratic agency advance from the church model toward an open learning model? One way is for the agency to take some of its own medicine in the sense of fostering competition within the agency.[20] For instance, the defendant's right to an attorney in an American courtroom takes away from the prosecutor the monopoly right to present evidence and arguments. A judge may not go to the jury before both sides of the arguments have been heard, and a patient should not go to surgery before getting a second opinion.[21] Even the Roman Catholic Church gets beyond the church model when considering someone for sainthood; it has a "devil's advocate" (*Advocatus Diaboli*) to state the other side of the candidate's story. A development agency should not pretend to greater authority or infallibility when it canonizes a good practice success story as the One Best Way. Thus devil's advocacy might not only be tolerated but be fostered in a development agency functioning as an open learning organization.[22]

This idea of the constructive role of public criticism goes back at least to the role of Socrates in Athens as a gadfly.

> For if you kill me you will not easily find a successor to me, who, if I may use such a ludicrous figure of speech, am a sort of gadfly, attached to the state by God; and the state is a great and noble horse who is rather sluggish owing to his very size, and requires to be stirred into life. I am that gadfly which God has attached to the state, and all day long and in all places am always fastening upon you, arousing and persuading and reproaching you. (Plato, *Apology*, 30–31)

The penchant for competition and debate seems to be one of the key features of Athenian Greece that distinguished it from other societies of antiquity, and Socrates represented the use of dialogue and contestation as the road to improving knowledge. "The form Socrates' teaching took—intellectual dueling before a sportive audience—looks much odder to us than it did to Athenians, whose whole culture was based on the contest (*agōn*), formal and informal, physical, intellectual, and legal." (Wills 1994, 163) This also relates to the broader theme of democracy as being based on government by discussion.

> The traditional theory of the contest and interplay of group interests was not so much a scientific description as a normative injunction; in fact it contained the moral basis of liberal democracy. In order for the truth to be known, this theory argued, speech must be free; in order for wise decisions to be made, all the interests must be in the field and all the values articulated. The ancestry of this liberal pluralism might well be traced, beyond Mill and Madison and Montesquieu, all the way to the dialecti-

cal principle of Socrates: the method of verbal contest or discussion grounded on the faith that there was indeed a truth to be reached, through mutual deliberation, on which reasonable men could agree. (Matson 1966, 107)

Immanuel Kant recognized that the "means which nature employs to bring about the development of innate capacities is that of antagonism within society," and he represented the insight with the analogy of trees competing in a forest:

In the same way, trees in a forest, by seeking to deprive each other of air and sunlight, compel each other to find these by upward growth, so that they grow beautiful and straight—whereas those which put out branches at will, in freedom and in isolation from others, grow stunted, bent and twisted. All the culture and art which adorn mankind and the finest social order man creates are fruits of his unsociability. (Kant [1784], 1991a, 46)

Similarly, there is the oft-quoted line:

In Italy, for thirty years under the Borgias, they had warfare, terror, murder and bloodshed, but they produced Michelangelo, Leonardo da Vinci, and the Renaissance. In Switzerland they had brotherly love, they had five hundred years of democracy and peace, and what did they produce? The cuckoo clock. (Orson Welles in *The Third Man* [1949], screenplay by Graham Greene)

Of course, not all antagonism or unsociability is helpful, so Hirschman (1995) has investigated which forms of social conflict are beneficial (see also Coser 1956), a question that also goes back to the contrast between Socrates' provocative dialogues to improve knowledge and the Sophists' eristic methods to simply defeat an opponent.

But, for our purposes, the focus is on the difference between an organization that incorporates (hopefully beneficial) antagonism and one that aims at a nonantagonistic idea of agreement, cooperation, and "playing with the team" of intellectual clerks—a small society like that is dryly satirized by Kant as the Arcadian ideal where men would be "as good-natured as the sheep they tended."

Some modern research (Lloyd 1996) has used this contrast to address the question of why, after such a promising beginning in ancient China, science developed strongly in ancient Greece but not in China. The key feature in ancient China was the intermixing of power with questions of empirical truth—a feature shared with the role of the Church in the Middle Ages or with Lysenkoism (and the role of the party in general) in the Soviet Union. The emperor's mandate of heaven was based on a view of the world that pictured the emperor in the central role of maintaining the harmony between heaven and earth. The views of philosophers and scientists needed to accommodate that basic scheme. In contrast, the Greek intellectual life exhibited "radical revisability" (Lloyd 1996, 216) where the masters would offer theories completely at odds with those of their rivals—a practice that would not be allowed where the mandate of heaven was seen as being based on the "official theory." Chinese intellectual life put the emphasis on accommodation and harmony, while the Greeks thrived on antagonism and adversariality. The differences extended throughout social and legal affairs.

> Differences between individuals or groups that might well have been the subject of appeal to litigation in Greece were generally settled [in China] by discussion, by arbitration, or by the decision of the responsible officials. The Chinese had, to be sure, no experience that remotely resembled that of the Greek dicasts [large public juries], nor, come to that, that of Greek public participation in open debate of political issues in the Assemblies. (Lloyd 1996, 109)

Given the rather clear historical verdict of the mixing of power and knowledge in ancient China, the medieval Church, and the more recent Communist Party, there seems to be little reasoned basis for a development agency dedicated to promoting development knowledge to adopt Official Views on some of the most complex and subtle questions facing humankind.[23]

Indeed, the arguments for not taking official institutional views seem so clear that perhaps one should try to explain why the leaders of the major development agencies stick with the old Official Views policy. But this leads to asking why someone in a position of power would oppose a regulation that would weaken that power for fear that it might be abused. While the power holders might abstractly agree with a regulation for others who might abuse the power, they might not feel it is needed while they are in power. Paraphrasing Augustine, their reply is: "Yes, the churchlike policy should be changed—but not yet."

Aside from not licensing Official Views, how might an agency promote internal adversariality? Devil's advocacy is one practice that might be fostered in a development agency functioning as an open learning organization. The political scientist Alfred De Grazia recommends such a countervailance system as a part of any large bureaucracy. "The countervailors would be a corps of professional critics of all aspects of bureaucracy who would be assigned by the representative council of an institution to specialize as critic of all the subinstitutions" (1975, 168). The devil's advocacy concept can also be applied to written documents. When Thomas Jefferson complained about the one-sided press, James Madison half-seriously asked: "Could it be so arranged that every newspaper when printed on one side, should be handed over to the press of an adversary, to be printed on the other, thus presenting to every reader both sides of every question, [so] truth would always have a fair chance" (quoted in Smith 1988, 41). Perhaps the op-ed page in a newspaper could be seen in this light. Although all development agencies have various newsletters and bulletins from management to communicate to staff, I am unaware of any which allow independent "op-eds" to be published in it by staff or outsiders.

Another example is the systematic inclusion of dissenting opinions in higher-court decisions made by a panel of judges. The concept could be applied widely to written reports recommending a specific policy or course of action. A well-constructed options paper will not just argue the virtues of the preferred option but will present the best alternatives—or better yet have those alternatives be presented by their advocates. Conference volumes often present the main papers along with written comments and criticism by the discussants. Some journals (e.g., *Behavioral and Brain Sciences* and *Journal of Economic Perspectives*) are organized in the powerful and rewarding format of invited papers followed by criticism, commentary, and counterarticles all in the same issue. The Opposing Viewpoints series of Greenhaven Press is an excellent example of a book series that focuses on giving point and counterpoint on the major issues (e.g., Rohr 1989). The preface in each volume cites John Stuart Mill in *On Liberty*:

> The only way in which a human being can make some approach to knowing the whole of a subject, is by hearing what can be said about it by persons of every variety of opinion, and studying all modes in which it can be looked at by every character of mind. No wise man ever

acquired his wisdom in any mode but this. (quoted in preface to Rohr 1989, 10)

Such a format of point and counterpoint would seem quite appropriate for institutions that want to foster intellectual inquiry and knowledge development. Yet development agencies operating on a de facto church model want to bombard the client with one-sided arguments leading to uniform advice and do not want "to confuse" or "distract" the client with conflicting ideas (particularly when coming from within the agency). Instead of functioning as a church enunciating a canonical view, an institution could allow multiple viewpoints, each argued passionately by its advocates, while adopting none as its official viewpoint. The client would have to decide and take responsibility for that decision.

The General Case for Devil's Advocacy

The general case for a more systematic devil's advocate or countervailance role in an organization is much the same as the case for genuine debate and open discussion. The classical statements for that argument are in John Milton's *Areopagitica* (1644), Thomas Jefferson's *Bill for Establishing Religious Freedom* (1779), Tunis Wortman's *A Treatise Concerning Political Enquiry* (1800), John Stuart Mill's *On Liberty* (1859), and John Morley's *On Compromise* (1928).[24] If little is known on a question, then real debate and the clash of adverse opinions are some of the best engines of discovery. Since "each rooster likes to crow on top of his own dungheap" the dung heaps are more likely to be objectively appraised if there are many other roosters in the barnyard. If partial truths are known, then it is better to allow the half-truths to collide since intercourse should produce an offspring closer to a whole truth. Mill argues that even in cases of settled opinions, debate and discussion serve to disturb the "deep slumber of a decided opinion" so that it might be held more as a rational conviction rather than as an article of faith.

> So essential is this discipline to a real understanding of moral and human subjects, that if opponents of all important truths do not exist, it is indispensable to imagine them, and supply them with the strongest arguments which the most skillful devil's advocate can conjure up. (Mill [1859] 1972, 105)

Intellectual liberty and tolerance is fundamental to the heritage of the Reformation and Enlightenment. Rather than a "church" to protect "truth" and suppress "error," free discussion and debate fueled by the collision of opposing opinions is the best security against error.

These principles of philosophical liberalism were first hammered out in the battle for religious freedom. Jefferson asked that his tombstone record only three deeds. In addition to the Declaration of Independence, he was the author of Virginia's 1779 *Bill for Establishing Religious Freedom*, which argued in part that truth "is the proper and sufficient antagonist to error, and has nothing to fear from the conflict unless by human interposition disarmed of her natural weapons, free argument and debate; errors ceasing to be dangerous when it is permitted freely to contradict them."[25] The toleration for dissent and debate is fundamental to the spirit of a university, not to the spirit of a church. The third deed was being founder of the University of Virginia.

Problems in Implementing Devil's Advocacy

What can go wrong in trying to implement a devil's advocate role? One problem is the domestication of the devil's advocate. A "domesticated" devil's advocate maintains a role in the councils of power by keeping dissent well within the bounds of certain spoken or unspoken assumptions (which are often part of the problem) and by not getting "carried away" by going public or appealing to the opposition (see Janis 1972, 120). The devil's advocacy function can become ineffective by being ritualized, taken for granted, or restricted to minor approved variations on the groupthink status quo.

Intimidation is a related problem. Arguing against the conventional or received wisdom is more akin to a battle than a tea party.

> Recognition of dynamic conservatism [i.e., the self-reinforcing nature of status quo] explodes the rational myth of intervention pervasive in official rhetoric, which envisages social change as a process made up of analysis of objectives, examination of alternatives, and selection of the most promising routes of change. . . . [T]he rational myth assumes implicitly that transformation occurs in a vacuum rather than in the plenum of self-reinforcing systems . . . [or] that rational plans will implement themselves, or they leave the question of implementation to a mysterious process of sales, persuasion, or politics.

> Actual patterns of transformation center around crisis and reveal variations of invasion and insurgency. (Schön 1971, 59)

The devil's advocacy role should be a protected part of "programmed conflict" role-playing to improve decision making and should not be attributed to the personal "perversity" of the individual in that role. This brings within an organization the role of and the protections for opposition political parties.

The devil's advocate functions as an intellectual ombudsman, shop steward, or public defender for alternative viewpoints. Those who oppose a strategy may be too prudent or vulnerable to speak out individually, and the difficulties of collective action may hinder coordinated opposition. An institutionalized devil's advocate role can serve as a lightning rod to collect and aggregate opposing views and thus resolve the collective action problem.

Rotation of the devil's advocate function can help to prevent domestication and intimidation. To implement the rotating devil's advocate function, temporary teams can be assigned to prepare the cases for the alternative policies. Individuals identified with one position can be asked to present the case for the opposition (just as authors at some academic conferences are asked to give each other's papers). Rotation also helps to keep a specific individual from being sidelined or dismissed for being only a naysayer, for not being a team player, or even for being disloyal.

And finally there is the problem that if there is an official devil's advocate, then this may be seen as relieving other staff members from exercising their critical reason in public so that they can take the path of least organizational resistance with a clear conscience. It isn't "their job" to publicly argue against the vanities and inanities of the high officials in the organization. But a well-implemented devil's advocacy role would be part of a general democratization of the organizational culture that would change the usual penalties attached to the public exercise of critical reason.

Devil's Advocacy as the Qualitative Version of the Opportunity Cost Doctrine

In economics, the opportunity cost doctrine evaluates an option or good by comparing its value with the value of best alternative. If plan B is the best alternative to plan A (and the plans are mutually exclusive), then the opportunity cost of choosing plan A is the value fore-gone by not choosing plan B. Plan A is preferable if its value exceeds its opportunity cost. The application of the opportunity cost doctrine requires the analysis and evaluation of the best alternative—and that is the more general role of devil's advocacy even when quantitative values cannot be assigned to the alternatives. By eliciting plan B, devil's advocacy generalizes the opportunity cost doctrine from cost-benefit analysis to general policy analysis in the marketplace of ideas. In a rivalrous market, competition provides the B plans, so organizational devil's advocacy could be seen as an attempt to provide the benefits of benchmark competition *within* an organization.

One pseudoscientific method of evaluation is to see if the benefits of expending resources on plan A exceed the benefits of the "untreated" or "control" plan B (namely, doing nothing). But a genuine evaluation of plan A would compare its benefits to the benefits of expending the same resources on the best alternative plan B (not an untreated control sample of doing nothing). The design of the best alternative plan B is usually devilishly difficult. But it is the job of the devil's advocate in the sense of constructive criticism since it is usually beyond of the inclinations of the sponsors of plan A.

Evaluation = Retrospective Devil's Advocacy

Evaluation might be seen as the retrospective devil's advocate role.[26] It is this role of considering the best alternative use of the resources that is so often overlooked when organizations congratulate themselves for projects that "have a positive impact" and "succeed in fulfilling their objectives." There are enormous groupthink pressures of conformity to be a team player by "celebrating our successes" rather than "dwelling on hypothetical counterfactuals" (about what might have been done with the resources). Economists often seem to be as allergic as anyone to dwelling on what might have been even though that is the underlying logic of the opportunity cost doctrine.

Without the backward-looking devil's advocate, the most informative negative feedback and learning may be lost, and the organization is condemned to repeat its "glorious" past.

Progress, far from consisting in change, depends on retentiveness. When change is absolute there remains no being to improve and no direction is set for possible improvement: and when experience is not retained, as

among savages, infancy is perpetual. Those who cannot remember the
past are condemned to repeat it. (Santayana [1922] 1962, 184)

There is something like this present mindedness where "experience is
not retained" in large technocratic organizations like the World Bank
or IMF. Seeing the mistakes of the past is a double-edged sword—the
two edges being learning and blame. Since avoiding blame is a paramount bureaucratic imperative, learning is also avoided as the mistakes
of the past are quickly lost down the organizational "memory hole."

But that is not the only reason why experience is not retained in a
technocratic organization. There is a superficial view that science
advances along a well-defined frontier so that knowledge of past theories and ideas is only of antiquarian interest. All that was useful or valid
in the older theories has been supposedly swept up and incorporated in
the latest theories. This is a common view in "development economics"
and particularly in the large development bureaucracies such as the
World Bank. Thus intellectual life in the field is seen as keeping up
with the latest econometric studies and digesting the latest intellectual
fads. Within a churchlike organization, this intellectual life entails
keeping up with the latest fads sponsored by the organization's leaders
along with the accommodating econometric studies produced by the
intellectual clerks who play with the team. It is quite daunting to try to
follow the rush of "bold new initiatives" all described in breathless new
rhetoric—like trying to drink from a fire hose. And it is all very "scientific" since all this new thinking surely represents the ever-advancing
frontier in the science of development. In this manner, there is an all-
too-modern version of Santayana's savages who do not study the past.

Amidst this exciting march of science into the future, there is no
room for backward-looking thinking that might discover uncanny similarities between the bold new initiatives of today and the failed bold
new initiatives of yesteryear that were clothed in different rhetoric.
Thus the lack of institutional memory is not just a means of organizational self-protection; it is the very epitome of "scientific" advance.

Variations: Adversarial Legal Process, the Loyal Opposition, Separation of Powers, and Civil Society

There has been some incorporating of a general devil's advocacy role
into various institutions. The state requires significant prima facie evi-

dence to charge a person with a crime. In spite of that evidence, the adversarial system gives the defendant the right of legal representation to have access to the evidence, to call witnesses, and to contest the charges in an open court before the judge and jury. For an individual viewpoint this could be seen as a matter of individual rights, but from a social viewpoint, the adversarial system of legal proceedings seems to increase the quality of social decision making on the important questions of guilt or innocence.

In a multiple-party democracy, the main party out of power forms the institutionalized "loyal opposition" that plays the political devil's advocate role (see Ionescu and de Madariaga 1972). The loyal opposition forms an independent power base of those who seek to express opinions and policies at variance with the party in power. Without such a protected role, those out of power can be isolated, atomized, and silenced, and the iron law of oligarchy will hold full sway (see Michels 1962; Ellerman 1988a).

The separation of powers within a government or an organization is intended to diminish or prevent the problems that arise from the exercise of unified and unopposed power.

> This policy of supplying, by opposite and rival interests, the defect of better motives, might be traced through the whole system of human affairs, private as well as public. We see it particularly displayed in all the subordinate distributions of power, where the constant aim is to divide and arrange the several offices in such a manner as that each may be a check on the other—that the private interest of every individual may be a sentinel over the public rights. (Hamilton, Madison, and Jay, *Federalist Papers* No. 51)

Centralized power can be abused in private and public bureaucracies as well as in democratic government. The general idea of separation of powers, with one interest checking the overextension of another interest, has a broader applicability in organizations.

Public evaluation of government policies and actions requires a protected public space for ideas to be discussed, for views to be aired, and for opposing opinions to collide. This requires a free press, access to the electronic media, and a tradition of tolerance for open discussion in spite of adverse impact on vested interests. Courageous and outspoken individuals are not enough; it takes a multitude of vigorous nongovernmental organizations and associations to sustain the sphere of civil society. Thus in the broadest sense, civil society, and the traditions of public discussion that undergird it, support the devil's advocacy function in liberal democratic countries.

Nondogmatism and Socratic Ignorance in Organizations

I have argued that organizational learning can best take place if open competition, devil's advocacy, and the collision of ideas is allowed— instead of being suppressed in favor of an outward show of allegiance to Official Views. This openness is now taken for granted in the institutions of higher learning as well as in the informal communities of the scientific disciplines, but development agencies still operate on the basis of the church model regardless of the espoused theory.

I now turn to the cognitive helper-doer relationship between an organization aspiring to be a learning organization and its clients. I have taken pains to develop helper-doer themes both volitionally and cognitively. One theme was that the helper should not impose actions on the doer. In the cognitive version of that theme, the helper needs to refrain from trying to teach or impose a certain representation or view on the doer. The Socratic-Kantian Leonard Nelson emphasizes this aspect of the Socratic process of instruction.

> Philosophical instruction fulfills its task when it systematically weakens the influences that obstruct the growth of philosophical comprehension and reinforces those that promote it. Without going into the question of other relevant influences, let us keep firmly in mind the one that must be excluded unconditionally: the influence that may emanate from the instructor's assertions. If this influence is not eliminated, all labor is vain. The instructor will have done everything possible to forestall the pupil's own judgment by offering him a ready-made judgment. (Nelson 1949, 19)

That will call for the helper to display a nonassertiveness, nondogmatism, cognitive humility, tolerance, "egolessness,"[27] or Socratic ignorance.[28] This Socratic humility or ignorance is the cognitive counterpart to the forbearance of material assistance in a way that would override or undercut the volition of self-help on the part of the doers. Karl Popper's critical rationalism based on the principle of fallibility gives an appropriate answer to "How do you know?"

I do *not* know: my assertion was merely a guess. Never mind the source, or the sources, for which it may spring—there are many possible sources, and I may not be aware of half of them; and origins or pedigrees have in any case little bearing upon truth. But if you are interested in the problem which I tried to solve by my tentative assertion, you may help me by criticizing it as severely as you can; and if you can design some experimental test which you think might refute my assertion, I shall gladly, and to the best of my powers, help you to refute it. (Popper 1965, 27)

In debate and discussion, there is a spirit that shuns intellectual vanity, "scientific" dogmatism, and what Michel de Montaigne calls "that tiresome and wrangling arrogance which believes and trusts entirely in itself, and is the chief enemy of learning and truth" (Montaigne [1595] 1958, 356). Indeed, it is a spirit that welcomes a strong counterargument or new evidence as an opportunity to improve one's knowledge, not as a defeat for one's pride or embarrassment of one's organization.

It is from my own experience that I emphasize human ignorance which is, in my judgement, the most certain faction in the school of the world. Those who will not be convinced of their ignorance by so vain an example as me—or themselves—let them acknowledge it through Socrates. (Montaigne [1595] 1991, 1221)

Thus Socratic ignorance is interpreted as the exercise of restraint against the prideful assertion that demotes dialogue to a battle of egos and "is the chief enemy of learning and truth."

In chapter 4 I discuss Mary Parker Follett's "law of the situation," which is based on a restraint against the attempt to directly control a person by issuing a command in favor of the indirect method of getting the other person to understand that the action is required by the situation. Applying the same idea cognitively, one party to a dialogue would refrain from directly asserting a proposition so that the other party might be led indirectly by the dialogue and the evidence to arrive at the proposition. And the second party might do likewise with his or her prior beliefs. In such a two-way dialogue, learning can take place without any price being paid in one's pride or self-esteem.

Applying a similar model to the dialogue between a development agency and a client country would require the agency to display a humility born of experience and to exercise Socratic restraint against the arrogant assertion of "truths" or Official Views. If there are relevant grounds for any views preferred by agency officials, then such views, unless divinely revealed, should eventually emerge from the dialogue and the country's own (perhaps arranged) learning experiences. Yet one should not underestimate the difficulties of implementing this sort of intellectual humility or Socratic ignorance on the part of elite development officials who justify their own prestige—along with its material accoutrements—on the basis of their "expertise."

It is perhaps some of the same spirit that puts the emphasis on being one's own worse critic. In this spirit, the worst intellectual sin is not in being wrong and changing one's views but in being so slack in self-criticism (or auto-error-checking) that the realization of error came from someone else who had no special knowledge that was not available to oneself. "[I]f we respect truth, we must search for it by persistently searching for our errors: by indefatigable rational criticism, and self-criticism" (Popper 1965, 16). Intellectual autonomy implies the vigorous self-discovery of error wherever possible.

The late mathematician and philosopher Gian-Carlo Rota of MIT (my mentor in mathematics) lamented that so many presentations of mathematical theorems gave no hint of how the results were in fact obtained. He argued for the full intellectual honesty that entailed giving the actual approach to arriving at the ideas including the previous errors and dead ends.

> The truth of any piece of mathematical writing consists of realizing what the author is "up to"; it is the tradition of mathematics to do whatever it takes to avoid giving away this secret. When an author lets the truth slip out, the accusation of being "sloppy," "philosophical," "digressing," or worse, is instantly made. (Rota 1997, 215)

Such a self-admission of one's strategies, errors, and previously missed opportunities would not only show the student how mathematics (or science) is actually done, it would humanize the all-too-human writer and check the growth of the intellectual hubris that can so poison intellectual discourse.

John Holt recounts a story of a graduate student who suggested to a noted professor that there should be a publication where the researchers

> would write about their mistakes, the hunches that had not worked out, the experiments that had not proved what they were meant to prove, or

didn't prove anything. The professor agreed that such a publication would teach students a great deal . . . [but], he said, there was no use even thinking about such a publication, because no one with a reputation to defend would ever put anything in it. So we find it hard to find most of our mistakes because we are so rarely told how the do-ers of the past came to make and later find theirs.[29] (Holt 1976, 96–97)

If we carry Gandhi's notion of satyagraha or Buber's notion of dialogue over into scientific discourse, then we see that this type of "reputation" is inimical to dialogue and learning. Rota and Holt are arguing for a more honest and thus more humble mode of intellectual discourse (and thus a very different notion of reputation) that is more compatible with genuine learning. The argument here is that the same considerations apply to organizations such as development agencies that are often tempted to arrogantly assert the One Best Way to approach some of the most complex questions of the day.

Rethinking the Agency-Country Relationship

The idea of learners taking the active role in rediscovering and reappropriating knowledge as their own—that idea transposed to the task of development assistance means the country taking the driver's seat and taking charge in the development learning process. Development agencies often do not have "the answers" even when they think they do. But the point is that even if they did have "international standard best-practice recipes," the agencies should not feed or give that formulaic knowledge to the developing countries. The task is to help build the learning capacity for the countries to (re-)discover and to appropriate as their own the development "answers" that work for them. As a practical matter, the more powerful the agency, the less likely it is to adopt such a Socratic stance—but let's set aside that for awhile by assuming a subtle and humble agency.

Conditionalities are a blatant form of the external motivation—an intervention that we have seen can actually impede development transformation in a country. The problems lie with conditionalities that conspire to induce transformation in mind-set, norms, and institutions. What if the agency relaxes conditionalities so that a country can "climb into the driver's seat" and then the country promptly "takes a wrong turn"? The freedom required for a country to develop its own policies is also the freedom to take a wrong turn. In the dialogue with the country, the agency must plumb the country's rationale. Is it a genuine attempt to find its own path, or is it only a cover story for rent-seeking and theft behind the scenes? In the latter case, the assistance should be terminated, which, however, is most unlikely since the agency "lives off" the delivery of assistance. If the country is genuine in its experiment, then it should be willing to specify reasonable benchmarks and criteria for success. If the criteria are not satisfied, what are the lessons and the next steps in view of those outcomes? The agency should support such a genuine country-directed learning process—even if it starts off with what seem like false steps.

There seems to be an analogy with parents paying for a son's or daughter's college education. Everything is fine as long as the student is engaged in a genuine learning process. But the process can go wrong in one of two ways. The offspring may have more interest in not working than in learning, so the "studying" is only a cover story to keep the parents' money flowing. A more subtle problem is when the student studies what he or she thinks the parents want—taking the parents' desires as a conditionality for the financial support—even though the topic has little intrinsic interest. Then the student runs through the money and graduates all without knowing what he or she really wants to do.

Perhaps a development agency like the World Bank finds itself in a similar situation—except that the countries are not offspring, there seems to be no time limit on life as a student (since the agency lives off keeping the students in school), and the Bank may aspire to be both professor and provider of financial aid. In spite of those differences, the basic idea is again to financially support a *genuine learning* process—in this case to transform mind-sets, norms, and institutions. Again there are two ways to fall off the knife-edge. The process may fail to be a *learning* process at all when it is a cover for living off the loans or aid. Or the process may not lead to *genuine* learning and transformation when the government is only going through the motions to satisfy the financial conditionalities.

How might one try to judge the genuineness of beliefs or commitment to learning and reforms? The standard bureaucratic question is, "What's the checklist?" While there is no checklist, there are few pointers that may be used to directly judge "whether or not a person's beliefs in proposition (P) are autonomously, as opposed to nonreflectively, held" (Krimerman 1972; quoted in Candy 1991, 106).

Krimerman gives some cognitive guidelines concerning a person, but they can be extended by analogy to a country.

- Has the ability to explain P to others using words and in circumstances substantially unlike those in which P was first encountered
- Has tested and evaluated P against alternatives, even when there are no extraneous rewards (social, psychological or physiological) for doing so
- Is willing to relinquish or decrease belief in P when relevant counterevidence is presented
- Is not angered, threatened or incapacitated when objections or alternatives to P are presented (Krimerman 1972, 334–36; quoted in Candy 1991, 106–7)

Moving from the cognitive to the volitional version, Krimerman states guidelines to test whether a person's goal (G)—in our case the goal of carrying out a certain set of reforms—is autonomously held.

- Has the ability to explain (in terms and circumstances different from those in which the goal was first encountered) what G consists of, how it differs from other goals, and how it might be achieved
- Has personally experimented with alternative goals without the threat of sanctions, or hope of rewards, for such experimentation
- Is willing to curtail or eliminate the pursuit of G when autonomously held beliefs concerning G alter, or when it becomes apparent that attainment of G is incompatible with other, more highly valued goals
- Is not angered, incapacitated or threatened when exposed to criticisms of the value of G, or when temporarily prevented from pursuing or attaining G (Krimerman 1972, 334–36; quoted in Candy 1991, 106–7)

To explore alternatives to the conditionalities that generate adverse, if not self-defeating, effects, let us consider an example of a controlling boss. Suppose you planned on performing some difficult task because it was necessary in order for your job to be done well and thus you wanted to do it out of your self-esteem and pride in your work. But before you could do it, your boss publicly told you that you had better do the task or else there would be negative consequences. Do you say, "Now I have two reasons to do it," and cheerfully perform the task? Many people would resent being forcefully told to do what they were going to do for their own good reasons. They would have a negative "reactance" effect due to the boss's attempt to externalize their locus of causality. The boss hijacked their motivation and took over "owner-ship" of the task either to influence a higher-level boss or out of amour propre.

Let us now slightly change the example. Suppose that you, the staff member, wanted to perform the task for your own intrinsic reasons but that you needed some additional resources. If the boss said that you could have the resources but only on the condition that you perform that task, then while not as blatant as a direct command, this would also tend to highjack your motivation and diminish your ownership of the task. If, however, the boss made the resources available for you to perform whatever task you really thought was appropriate (with agreed-upon evaluation and learning procedures), then the external provision of resources would, in this case, not crowd out the internal motivation or take away your ownership of the task. In the first case, the external intervention by the boss was *controlling*, while in the second case, it was *enabling* and autonomy-respecting.

In this example the staff member and the boss agreed on the correctness of the task. Let us now suppose they disagreed. The staff member wanted to perform the "wrong" task (wrong in the eyes of the boss). The controlling boss would provide the resources only for the "right" task together with carrots or sticks so that it would become mandatory to the staff member and thereby would create even more resentment and nonownership. The enabling boss would provide the resources as before for whatever the staff member sincerely thought was the appropriate action. By dialogue, the enabling boss and staff member would arrive at procedures for evaluation and learning from the member-chosen task.

I have developed the example in the context of management theory,[30] where the helper and doer are the boss and staff member. In table 5, I transfer these examples from management theory to development assistance. In the middle, "controlling," column, we have the example of a development agency like the World Bank driven by a loan approval and money-moving culture that uses its resources to essentially "buy" what it considers to be the "right" reforms. Since the agency imposes the conditionality "just to be sure and to give leverage" even if the government wants to make the "right" reform anyway, the government may be somewhat insulted at the imposition and reduce its ownership of the reform. If the government really wants in its best judgment to make a different reform, then it will be even more resentful to be "forced" to make what the agency takes as the "right" reform just to get the resources. Only if such an own-motivated government with the "wrong" reforms cannot be bought will the controlling agency not provide resources.[31] If the government just wants to get the resources and be "incentivized" to be a "good reformer" then the agency will "buy" some compliant behavior (at least insofar as it is monitorable).

The actions of the controlling agency are not connected to country learning. All the learning has already taken place in the agency to determine the "right" reforms, and it is the country's role "to do the right thing"—with sufficient external motivation for doing it.

In the rightmost column, we have a very hypothetical enabling agency. The important thing is not whether the country agrees with the agency about the "right" reforms but whether or not the agency has through dialogue with the country verified an own- or internal motivation for a reform process guided by genuine learning from successes and failures. Given that *metaconditionality* that is the basis for partnership

TABLE 5.   Controlling versus Enabling Development Agency

	"Controlling" agency provides external incentives and resources conditional on "right" reform.	"Enabling" agency provides resources (meta-) conditional on dialogue and genuine learning.
Country has own motives for "right" reform.	Agency gets "right" reform but with diminished country ownership.	Agency enables country to take "right" reform with full ownership and learning.[a]
Country has own motives for "wrong" reform but needs the loan/aid money.	Agency buys "right" reform behavior but with counterproductive resentment.	Agency enables country to take "wrong" reform with full ownership and learning.
Country has own motives for "wrong" reform and won't be "bought."	Agency does not provide resources, although efforts may continue to find a rationale to move the money.	Agency enables country to take "wrong" reform with full ownership and learning.
Country has no genuine own motives.	Agency "buys" the "right" reform behavior but without country ownership.[a]	Agency does not provide resources, although dialogue may continue.

[a]Represents a type of equilibrium.

and trust, the development agency provides resources even if the agency and government don't agree on the best route as the government takes the steering wheel and starts down its *own* road. If the country dialogue does not verify own reasons (internal motivation) for reforms and only finds the willingness to be rewarded to conduct "reforms," then the metaconditionality (genuine own commitment to a process of reform learning and adaptation) fails, and no resources should be provided—although dialogue might continue with the government and its successors. In this last case, the enabling agency does not enable the country with resources or aid even though the country is "willing" (given suitable rewards) to undertake "reforms" (a virtual impossibility with large money-driven development agencies).

It should also be noted that the metaconditionality is based on the presence of internal motivation that cannot be "bought" or generated on demand. The agency can exercise selectivity in choosing to deal with governments that already have this genuine motivation and commitment; the agency must find it but cannot buy it with aid. I have called this a "metaconditionality" because a government does not have a "choice" to satisfy it. If a government commits to a reform process *in order to get* the resources then it will actually *fail* the metacondition of having its *own* commitment to the reform learning process. That is precisely the case where the controlling agency would provide resources and the enabling agency would *not* (bottom row of table 5).

The use of this metaconditionality would contradict the structure of the multilateral development banks and agencies who have the countries as members. The banks have a "front door" through which a country may graduate, although this rarely happens since development banks, like any banks, love to make loans to clients who don't really need loans.[32] But the development banks do not have a "back door" through which they can kick out a country that shows no genuine prospects for reforms. This is hardly surprising in view of the organizational imperatives. The development banks are as anxious to move the money as such countries are to get the money—letting the future bring what may (e.g., more debt relief). When developmental rationales fail, there are always the political pressures from the major powers to reward certain countries—pressures resulting from the cold war in the past and from the war on terrorism in the present time. And without developmental rationales and without political pressures, the development agencies will still want to move the money for reasons of humanitarian relief. "Think of the children!" Powerful organizations will always try to find reasons to perpetuate themselves, and in the case of development agencies, that means moving the loan or aid money. Hence our example of an enabling agency that would not move the money when a country did not satisfy the metaconditionality of own-motivated reform is very hypothetical.

Table 5 is static, but there might be some interesting dynamics. In the controlling agency column, any own motivation would constantly be crowded out, so we might expect it to atrophy. Thus governments would drift toward the bottom row where they would be motivated largely by the external incentives (that cell is the controlling agency equilibrium). In the enabling agency column, the dialogue and reform experience with the reform-committed government should lead to learning on both sides so there would be convergence toward the case where the agency and government agreed on the right reforms (that cell is the enabling agency equilibrium). Leaving aside noncommitted governments learning how to consistently fake genuine reform commitment or agencies continuing to be conned to alleviate pressures "to move the money," then we should expect movement out of the bottom row only with changes in government and perhaps only with broader changes in a country.[33]

8

Case Study

Assistance to the Transition Countries

The Challenge of the Transition

My primary purpose is to lay the intellectual foundations for an alternative philosophy of development assistance. For concrete examples (mostly negative), I have focused on the "case study" of the World Bank and to a lesser extent the other large multilateral and bilateral agencies (e.g., IMF and USAID). The transition from communism to a private property market economy presented a unique challenge to the major development assistance agencies. A new regional development bank, the European Bank for Reconstruction and Development (EBRD), was also established to help meet the challenge. My purpose in this chapter is to discuss the propensities of the development agencies by examining how they tried to meet the challenge of privatization in the transition countries of Europe and Central Asia during the 1990s.

It is a tale of woe in general and a debacle of historical proportions in Russia and the former Soviet Union. The development agencies after some indecision and shallow debate adopted what became known as a "shock therapy" and "market bolshevik" approach (see Stiglitz 2001; Reddaway and Glinski 2001; Ellerman 2001a, 2003). It was driven by visions of social engineering that massively violated the precepts of starting where people are, seeing the world through their eyes, and respecting their autonomy (the three Dos).

China by contrast largely rejected Western advice and chose an incremental homegrown (internally motivated) approach, so the contrast between Russia and China provides a remarkable natural experiment to compare two strategies of institutional change. The difference in results could hardly be more striking. Since the Chinese reforms started with government support in the early 1980s, China has had around 8 percent per capita annual growth (McMillan 2002, 204), perhaps the largest growth episode in history.

Russia, using the shock therapy strategy, went the other way. In the first year of shock therapy (1992), production fell by 19 percent with a further 12 percent and 15 percent in the ensuing two years (McMillan 2002, 202). In all, the country bottomed out at about a 50 percent drop in gross domestic product (GDP). Experts can argue about the interpretation of the economic statistics, but the demographic trends tell an even more worrisome story. The population has actually declined over the 1990s in such a precipitous manner—now for every 100 babies born, 170 Russians die—that the government projects a 30 to 40 percent drop by 2050 (Feshbach 2003b). In her preface to Feshbach (2003a), Laurie Garrett notes:

> There have been few times in human history when a vast region, encompassing a militarily, if not economically, powerful nation has been depopulated to the extent Russia has—and will. It is difficult to find a precedent from which to draw a comparative reckoning about Russia's future.

The causality behind these trends is very hard to disentangle—which is why the side-by-side comparison with China is so revealing. The apologists for shock therapy are quick to offer one-liners like "Russia is not China." But it is hard to see how the other differences aside from the opposite institutional change strategies and the ensuing disruption could account for the diametrically opposite results for the two neighboring countries making the transition from communism to a market economy.

The Privatization Debates: Did History have a "Timeout" under Communism?

While the transition countries faced large challenges on many fronts, I view this history through the lens of privatization. This was not a matter of privatizing a few state-owned companies. All companies of any size had some form of state or social ownership, so it was more a matter of systemic ownership transformation rather selling off a few dinosaurs.

In the debate about privatization, one of the basic determinants of one's position was one's view of history. Many held the ideologically driven view that history essentially stopped in Central and Eastern Europe when the Iron Curtain descended across it after World War II. History was then restarting after the Berlin Wall fell and the other liberations of the 1989–90 period. History in between was like a timeout during a sporting match. Whatever people may have constructed or accomplished positively during that time period was like a goal scored during a timeout; it didn't count. Starting from where people were by recognizing their positive accomplishments was seen as tantamount to validating communism.

This view is held with particular vehemence by political and economic exiles. History stopped inside the country when the exiles left. After communism collapsed, they expected to return with the historical clock reset to the time they left. Everything that happened in the interim was the result of communist coercion, so it should not be validated by recognizing any changes in the initial conditions prevailing before communism.

On this view of history, the aim of the privatization policies should be to reposition the players (or their descendants) as they were when the timeout occurred and then to restart the game. Of course, they know that time does not stand still, but they view history in the sense of human agency as having been frozen by totalitarian coercion. Anything accomplished starting from the old property was viewed like the natural growth of a forest and thus belonging to the rightful landowner. Insofar as this "return and restoration" was not feasible, then history should be restarted from a blank slate that treated everyone equally. This view rejected the principle of starting where people are since that was based on "fouls" that were committed and "goals scored during the timeout."

The alternative view was that history has no timeouts. Crimes were committed on the negative side of the ledger, but generations of people had positive achievements that should not be treated as goals scored during the timeout or as the achievements of an undifferentiated mass. On this approach, the aim of privatization policies should be to find the

best socially acceptable approximation to the de facto rights representing the positive accomplishments of the citizens while trying to com-
pensate for the crimes of the past without pretending that history could
be stopped and restarted. If the de facto rights representing people's
accomplishments in spite of communism had been recognized in Russia as they were in China, then the people would have met the market
as something that further empowered them to build upon their
achievements. Instead the so-called market reforms swept away what
people had and allowed new oligarchs and mafiosi to pour into the
social and economic void in Russia. Our task is to try to understand
what happened and what can be learned from the striking natural
experiment of the Russian versus the Chinese transitions.

Voucher Privatization

The Ideas behind the Scheme

Those tending to the ahistorical view had to face the reality that the
countries were emerging from communism after periods ranging from
over forty years to over eighty years. Only a very limited amount of
return and restoration was feasible. Hence they tended to view most of
developed industry as an undifferentiated and state-owned mass to be
privatized in a way that would treat all citizens equally. Since the
development agencies were familiar with the idea of selling off a few
state-owned enterprises in Thatcher's England or in a developing
country, that was the first idea. The proceeds would go into the state
coffers and thus, in theory, benefit all citizens equally. Since the citizens of the transition countries did not have the cash to buy more than
small shops, this strategy could mean selling off all enterprises of any
size to foreigners who had cash. Something like this strategy was only
possible in the very special case of selling East German enterprises to
West Germans in a unified Germany. Elsewhere, aside from a few special firms, the sell-off strategy was not feasible for the bulk of the firms.
Sellers did not appear with offers to buy the companies at any prices
that were politically feasible (not to mention guarantees about investment and employment).

It was at this juncture that the voucher privatization schemes were hatched.[1] The basic idea was that each citizen of a transition country would get vouchers according to some measure of equality (e.g., equal per person or equal per year of age). All firms would be turned into state-owned corporations (more on this later), and then most would be auctioned off in return for vouchers. Thus most firms would be privatized to the citizens as general "stockholders" independent of their involvement in any particular firms. Anything people might have accomplished in their workplace under socialism was like goals scored during a timeout and thus irrelevant.

But this initial voucher scheme had a "governance" problem in the sense that the far-flung shareholders would not be able to coalesce together to provide governance over the firm by owners. Hence a new variation was hatched: investment funds would serve as intermediaries between the citizens and firms. The voucher investment funds (VIFs) would be somewhat like mutual funds in the West except that the VIFs were supposed to have real control over the firms. They would acquire sizable chunks of shares (20–30 percent) in the firms using vouchers that the VIFs had acquired from the citizens in return for the shares in the VIFs. Thus the citizens would end up being the far-flung owners of the VIFs, which, in turn, would have some sort of working control over the firms.

This scheme of voucher privatization with investment funds was presented as solving the governance problem—although a moment's thought showed that it only transferred the problem to the VIFs, which had an even larger set of far-flung shareholders (since there were relatively few VIFs in comparison with firms). The VIFs were set up and run by fund management companies under contract to the VIFs, and the fund management companies could be privately owned by a few individuals or could even be owned by state banks. I have described the first-implemented model, that of Czechoslovakia. After some initial weak resistance to the model from the World Bank and other development agencies, they quickly succumbed to the public relations blitz that declared the Czech model a success. They also succumbed to the arguments in favor of such a model made by prestigious American academic economists such as the "Harvard wunderkinder."[2] Then the agencies promoted variations on the model across the transition countries from Slovenia to Mongolia, and many countries adopted some version of the model.

The Arguments for the Scheme

The arguments given by the development agencies for the VIF scheme are of interest to intellectual history largely because they are so remarkably inane. The initial (hypothetical) scheme had the citizens' vouchers being invested directly in the thousands or tens or hundreds of thousands of firms (depending on the country). This was considered as having too many shareholders in a company for them to coordinate together to govern as "real owners." But the alternative with the VIFs had the same citizens' vouchers being invested in dozens or a hundred or so VIFs so there would a much *larger* set of shareholders in each VIF with a correspondingly *worse* governance problem.

How could the "experts" in the agencies think that a concentration of industrial control into a few dozen "trusts" with effectively no governance from the far-flung private "owners" would be an improvement in governance? The result was to transfer industrial power without industrial ownership to the "new nomenklatura" who ran the fund management companies.

Another set of remarkably implausible arguments put up by the agencies concerned the potential of the VIFs to use their control to restructure the firms. But it was rather clear from the beginning that the VIFs had neither the expertise nor the capital nor the incentives to undertake industrial restructuring.

If the people who set up the VIFs and the fund management companies had any expertise, it was a genius in advertising, as in the case of the "Harvard funds" in the Czech Republic.[3] Many groups were trying to gather pledges of citizen vouchers to pass a certain threshold before they could qualify as a VIF to enter the auctions of companies for vouchers. Those with the most genius for advertising and the most advertising money would win the race. How could the agency "experts" think that these advertising whiz kids would be able to engineer the massive industrial restructuring necessary to turn around the failing companies left over from the socialist period? Since the VIFs "sold" their shares in return for vouchers, the VIFs were very thinly "capitalized" and had little or no capital to undertake restructuring in their several hundred or so portfolio companies.

And if we assume that the VIFs miraculously had enough turnaround expertise and restructuring capital to invest, they still had almost no incentive to do so. The VIFs were limited by law to owning no more than 20 or 30 percent of a portfolio company. The decision-making power was in the hands of a fund management company whose annual return was typically fixed at 2 percent of the value of the shares under management. Suppose that the fund managers invested enough time, expertise, and capital to bring about an increase in the value of a portfolio company. What would be their annual gross part of the increase? It would be 2 percent of, say, their 30 percent of the company or .6 percent of the increase. If we generously capitalized that annual .6 of 1 percent of the increase into a present value, then we would arrive at something in the vicinity of 3 percent of the increased value.

Thus the economic "experts" in the World Bank and other development agencies promoted a privatization scheme that foresaw the massive job of restructuring being undertaken by parties that had neither the expertise nor capital to do the job. And if those parties somehow did the job anyway, they would only get at most about 3 percent of the increased value, with the other 97 percent going to free riders. And that is the gross return to the actual decision maker. You have to subtract off the explicit costs and implicit opportunity costs of the time and effort to get the actual net return to the fund management company. Thus there is negligible or negative ownership returns (a.k.a. the "incentives" that the Western economic advisors were supposed to understand so well) from restructuring.

This lack of incentives for restructuring was not some secret; the percentage going to the fund management companies (e.g., 2 percent) and the legal maximum of ownership in a portfolio company (e.g., 20 to 30 percent) were all public knowledge. It is thus unclear why the "top-notch economists" should be so surprised when it was finally revealed that the Czech and other fund management companies had found more "efficient" ways to extract or tunnel value out the back door of their portfolio companies. Since the lack of restructuring incentive was clear all along, why did the Western advisors and reformer counterparts strongly promote voucherization with voucher investment funds? Here is one case where they just had to do the math to really understand the incentives.

It is sometimes argued that voucher privatization was necessary to irreversibly get the state out of the economy. Yet that is not an argument for voucher privatization as opposed to other forms of privatization. Moreover much of the thrust of the voucher-oriented schemes was to first recentralize power by reversing and undoing earlier reforms (see the following) that had decentralized power away from the state—all of which revealed the underlying political motive rather than a single-minded drive to get the State out of the economy.

Voucher Privatization was a *Political* Strategy

We have seen, time and again, that the arguments for voucher privatization were blatantly poor—indeed quite unworthy of the most worthy elite advisors from the West and their reformer counterparts from the East. What was going on? The holes in the Swiss cheese arguments are akin to Sherlock Holmes's "dog that didn't bark"—the absence tells the story. The advisors and reformers were following another logic that was less defensible in public.

The effort to pull power and ownership back to the state to be "properly" redistributed revealed the underlying political battle. It was not the battle between Light and Darkness presented to Western onlookers; it was the conflict between two very different strategies out of communism. The battle was between

1. the new, "clean" postsocialist revolutionaries, those from internal or external exile—relatively untainted by the old system, armed with free market rhetoric, and well connected to Western aid sources—who emerged to take over after the democratic revolutions of 1989–90, and
2. the old, "embedded" decentralizing reformers, those who worked against the old system from within and who generally had social democratic views but were dismissed as "communist nomenklatura" by the new, clean revolutionaries.

In a nutshell, voucher privatization was essentially the cover story for the power plays of the new, clean postsocialist revolutionaries against the old, embedded decentralizing reformers.

In the years and, in some cases, decades before 1989–90, many of the socialist countries had decentralizing reforms with varying degrees of success: self-management in Yugoslavia, goulash communism with the enterprise councils in Hungary, Solidarity with the self-management councils in Poland, and perestroika with the decentralized management, cooperatives, and lease buyouts in Mikhail Gorbachev's Soviet Union. When the dam finally broke in 1989–90, what was the best path to the market? The route that would start where people are and build incrementally on the previous reforms would have been to push the halfway decentralizing reforms in the same direction all the way forward to the market. That would have meant transforming the quasi-ownership of the workers embodied in the various self-management councils into German-style works councils (codetermination) or into management and employee buyouts (MEBOs), perhaps as in the employee stock ownership plans (ESOPs) of the United States and United Kingdom or as in the Mondragon cooperatives of the Basque region in Spain (see Ellerman 1990).

But the clean postsocialist revolutionaries and their Western advisors each had their own reasons for opposing this direct route to the market where worker ownership would have been a major theme. The clean postsocialists had won electoral victory over the older generation of embedded reformers, but the older reformers were still represented in the management of the enterprises and on the worker councils. The new generation, having obtained political power, needed to secure and enrich it by also obtaining economic power. This group needed a grand scheme to stop the drive toward decentralization and the market so that economic power could be pulled back to the state now controlled by the clean postsocialist revolutionaries and then redistributed to their allies (e.g., the people controlling the fund management companies). After some debate and experimentation, voucher privatization with voucher investment funds emerged as precisely that grand scheme—and Western wunderkind economists emerged as the perfect shills with world class credentials to testify that it was the True Path to the Market. Thus the Western economists who were marketing themselves as the intellectual saviors of the benighted East ended up putting the scientific prestige of neoclassical economics behind one of the most cockamamie social engineering schemes of the twentieth century.

But in spite of all the phony economic arguments about restructuring and corporate governance, voucher privatization with investment funds was a brilliant *political* strategy for the postsocialist revolutionaries to reverse the decentralizing reforms of the past and to pull power back to the state—to their new, "clean" state—so that economic power could then be redistributed to the "right people."

Institutional Shock Therapy versus Incrementalism

The institutional debate is not fast versus slow or rapid versus gradual methods. It never was; that was another phony argument. The argument was institutional shock therapy (or blitzkrieg) versus incrementalism. An incrementalist approach would embody most of our themes: starting where the people are, seeing the situation through their eyes, avoiding social engineering, and, overall, respecting the autonomy of the doers. One of the best treatments of this debate about institutional change is in Albert Hirschman's 1973 *Journeys toward Progress*, which far antedated the transition debate. Reform mongers in their strategies and even more so in their rhetoric could be divided into those who take an ideological, fundamental, and root-and-branch approach versus those who take an incremental, piecemeal, homegrown, and adaptive approach.

Intellectual historians, from the perspective of history, will see how little neoclassical economists understood the critique of Bolshevism-Jacobinism by the conservative or "Austrian" tradition of Hayek, Popper, and Edmund Burke. So many of our best and brightest economists seem to have just thought the Bolsheviks had the wrong textbooks. With the right textbooks in their briefcases, the market bolsheviks thought they could fly into the socialist countries and use a peaceful version of Bolshevik methods to make the opposite transition.

But the task was not resetting inflationary expectations with a dose of shock therapy. The task was deep-lying transformation of many complex, interconnected institutions. These institutions had evolved through decades of communism, so the deeply rooted interconnections were not apparent, particularly not to the market bolsheviks parachuting in from the West. The origin of what became known as the shock therapy approach to the transition was not only a bad analogy with inflation-stopping therapies. I fear the origin also lay in the moral fervor of cold warriors who sought to wipe the slate clean of the institutions of communism and to socially engineer in their place (using the right textbooks this time) the new, clean, and pure "textbook institutions" of a private property market economy.

An incremental approach evolving reforms out of existing institutions (e.g., pushing decentralization all the way to the market with lease buyouts) would be an admission that "history matters" and that history was not timed out during the socialist period. But history does not exist in neoclassical economic models, and many people in the transitional countries wanted to escape their past with magical formulas, all in one leap. Hence the embedded incremental route was rejected by the utopian social engineers from the East and West. Western experts argued that only a slate-cleaning blitzkrieg approach during the window of opportunity provided by the "fog of transition" would get all the necessary changes made.

That was the market-bolshevik road to the "democracy" and "market economy" we saw in Russia. This mentality was not new. It was a reincarnation of the spirit and mindset of Bolshevism and Jacobinism. A wise commentator has described these Bolshevik tactics well:

> We have a fearful example in Russia today of the evils of insane and unnecessary haste. The sacrifices and losses of transition will be vastly greater if the pace is forced. . . . For it is of the nature of economic processes to be rooted in time. A rapid transition will involve so much pure destruction of wealth that the new state of affairs will be, at first, far worse than the old, and the grand experiment will be discredited.

These words are as true today as when they were written. And they were written by John Maynard Keynes (1933, 245) about the original Bolshevik transition, not today's market bolshevik transition in the opposite direction.

China: An Incrementalist Transition

What was the alternative strategy? The reform experience in China, which has never had an IMF program and which largely ignored the World Bank's advice to transition economies, represents something like this incremental approach in practice—crossing the river groping for the stepping stones rather than jumping over the chasm in one last great leap forward. As Deng Xiaoping put it in 1986: "We are engaged in an experiment. For us, it [reform] is something new, and we have to grope around to find our way. . . . Our method is to sum up experience from time to time and correct mistakes whenever they are discovered, so that small errors will not grow into big ones" (see Harding 1987, 87). When experiments had positive results, the idea was to then catalyze the process. As Chinese reformer Hu Qili put it at the same time: "We allow the little streams to flow. We simply watch in which direction the water flows. When the water flows in the right direction we build channels through which these streams can lead to the river of socialism."[4]

One of the important misformulations of the transition question was, "Fast versus slow?" *Incremental* might be misleading if it is construed as gradual or slow. The Chinese reforms were neither gradual nor slow, and the Russians will not soon climb out of the chasm they failed to jump over in one leap. The point is to find and build step-by-step upon the reform efforts of the past (which requires taking into account past conditions) rather than trying to wipe the slate clean and legislate ideal institutions in one fell swoop. Peter Murrell (1992) explored the connections between incrementalist strategies and conservative political philosophies. Lawrence Lau, Ying-Yi Qian, and Gerard Roland (2000) analyze the Chinese "two-track" system of reforms, such as the dual pricing system, where a second track, step, or stage is inaugurated and can then grow from where it is to eventually render the earlier stage obsolete.[5] Bernard Black, Reinier Kraakman, and Anna Tarassova (2000) use the word *staged* in much the same sense. In Joseph Stiglitz's "Whither Reform?" (2001), the two "ideal types" were compared in a table as a "battle of metaphors" (table 6).

Another part of the incremental approach, also evident in China, is the willingness to allow experiments in different parts of the country and then foster horizontal learning and the propagation of the successful experiments (see the next chapter). This is an important part of the alternative to the Bolshevik/Jacobin approach of legislating the brave new world from the capital city to be applied uniformly across the country. The transition from socialism to a market economy had not happened before in history, so the situation *clearly* called out for experimentation and pragmatism.[6] Instead the World Bank succumbed out of its own arrogance and "la rage de vouloir conclure" (the rage to conclude) to the social engineering Bolshevik/Jacobin mentality (complete with cold warrior moral fervor to wipe the slate clean of past evils), with help from elite academic advisors, and supported Moscow legislation to apply the dreamed up solutions across all of Russia.

Why an Incrementalist Approach Might Be Successful

One of the important reasons why the incrementalist approach seems to have worked well in China is that it respects de facto property rights. Neoclassical economics tends to follow Ronald Coase and to emphasize the importance of establishing clear, formal property rights (and then perhaps the market will do the rest). And the cartoon picture of the transition used by the IFIs and allied experts is one that hammers away on the importance of respecting private property rights. Unfortunately the "clear-cut private property rights" might be the ownership of junk shares in voucher investment funds on the tail end of many-layered agency chains.[7] And never mind that in the U.S. economy (i.e., the experts' implicit mental model) there has been a "separation of ownership and control" for most of the twentieth century so that the

TABLE 6.   "Battle of Metaphors"

	Shock Therapy	Incrementalism
Continuity vs. break	Discontinuous break or shock—razing the old social structure in order to build the new	Continuous change—trying to preserve social capital that cannot be easily reconstructed
Role of initial conditions	The first-best socially engineered solution that is not "distorted" by the initial conditions	Piecemeal changes (continuous improvements) taking into account initial conditions
Role of knowledge	Emphasizing explicit or technical knowledge of end-state blueprint	Emphasizing local practical knowledge that only yields local predictability and does not apply to large or global changes
Knowledge attitude	Knowing what you are doing	Knowing that you don't know what you are doing
Chasm metaphor	Jumping across the chasm in one leap	Building a bridge across the chasm
Repairing the ship metaphor	Rebuilding the ship in dry dock. The dry dock provides the Archimedean point outside the water, so the ship can be engineered to blueprint without being disturbed by the conditions at sea.	Repairing the ship at sea. There is no dry dock or Archimedean fulcrum for changing social institutions from outside of society. Change always starts with the given historical institutions.
Transplanting the tree metaphor	All at once transplantation in a decisive manner to seize the benefits and get over the shock as quickly as possible	Preparing and wrapping the major roots one at a time (nemawashi) to prevent shock to the whole system and improve chances of successful transplantation.[a]

Source: Stiglitz 2001, 155.

[a]See Benziger 1996 on the Chinese knowing they didn't know "what they were doing," Elster, Offe, and Preuss 1998 for the use of Otto Neurath's "rebuilding the ship at sea" metaphor in this context, and Morita 1986 on nemawashi.

top managers who command the heights in this paradigm private property market economy do so on the basis of their organizational role (not unlike Communist Party officials) and de facto control of the board—*not* on the basis of their private property rights. Neoclassical cartoons tend to ignore such troublesome aspects of reality.

James Scott's book *Seeing Like a State* (1998) argues persuasively that states use simplified pictures of static reality to administer their affairs but that these simplified pictures lead to disaster when they are the basis for large-scale social engineering schemes to change societies. Academic economists and global development bureaucracies have even less contact with local realities than national governments, and thus they tend to be even more driven by stereotypes or cartoon models. Exiles who have not participated in the give and take of politics in a country for years if not decades also tend to have cartoon models. It is the combination of power and abstract or highly simplified models of complex social realities that is particularly lethal. In our case, the power of the IFIs together with the bureaucratic/academic cartoon models—all fueled by cold war triumphalism and its good guy/bad guy simplicities—led to the debacles and disasters of shock therapy in the former Soviet Union.[8]

On the property rights issue, progress has been made recently in Hernando de Soto's book *The Mystery of Capital* (2000). Although this was little noticed by those who wrote blurbs for his book jacket, including Ronald Coase, de Soto argued not just for formal property rights but for the formalization of de facto property rights. That's a horse of another color. After all, all the land occupied and farmed by peasants or occupied and used by slum dwellers already has formal owners; it was not part of some "commons." The idea is that by using and improving these assets (formally but absentee owned by others), people have created (as the fruits of their labor) certain de facto property rights (like easements) that give them the capability to sow and reap. Any reform that would take away those de facto property rights (and the capabilities they represent) to assert absentee formal property rights would in fact be disempowering and antidevelopment. To promote market-driven development, the reforms should find out ways to formalize some socially acceptable approximation to those de facto rights so that the people then encounter the market and the private property system as something that empowers them—rather than the opposite.

Now transpose this argument over to the transition economies. In the decentralizing socialist reforms over the years and decades before 1990, the workers, managers, and local communities had developed a range of de facto property rights (or "use rights") over their enterprises. Central planning never worked well, and as it got worse, forms of decentralization took hold in varying degrees across much of the socialist world. One way or another, in often bizarre ways, people learned to do things in a twilight half-centralized and half-decentralized system. They developed de facto property rights that represented their capabilities to actually get a few things done and to squeak by.

When the spell was finally broken in 1989–90, the alternative to institutional shock therapy and market bolshevism—the counterfactual—would have been "to start where people are" by formalizing the nearest approximation to the de facto property rights that would be accepted as socially fair and thus to continue the decentralizing thrust going "straight to the market" (e.g., through the lease buyouts discussed later). If that alternative approach had been taken, then people would have encountered the market as something that would recognize and formalize the capabilities they had already developed and would allow them to do even better.

Instead the market bolsheviks designed the so-called market reforms with the exact opposite purpose to deny the de facto property rights accumulated during the communist past, to righteously wipe the slate clean by renationalizing all companies of any size, and to start afresh with formal property rights deliberately unrelated to the previous vestiges of communism. Sometimes these "ideal reforms" were compromised in getting legislation passed, but by and large, the "reforms" were successful in sabotaging the de facto property rights acquired during the earlier decentralizing reforms. For instance, outside of a small elite, most Russians encountered the market not as something that strengthened their capabilities and empowered them to do more but as something that took away what they were capable of doing and left them in a position where the rational choice was to grab what they could in the face of a very uncertain and uncontrollable future.

These points are perhaps easier to understand when applied to dwellings. Here pragmatism tended to prevail over market bolshevik ideology. People also acquired various de facto property rights over their flats in the socialist countries (analogous to squatters' rights in de Soto's work). Since the distribution of housing also partially reflected the power relationships under communism, one might pursue the same logic to suggest that the slate should be wiped clean of the communist past and all apartments should be put on the market and auctioned off to the highest bidder. Just think of the efficiency gains by jump-starting the housing market! Instead most of the postsocialist countries figured out ways to arrive at formal rights that were the closest socially fair approximation to the de facto rights.

Moreover, this analysis and critique is not just hindsight. I wrote the following long quotation over a decade ago in 1992, and it was published (outside the Bank) in 1993. It contrasts the two institutional strategies that emerged after the collapse of the socialist idea in the late 1980s, the big bang approach and the incremental approach.

The Big Bang approach advocated just drawing a big **X** over the old half-reformed institutions and then legislating new "ideal" institutional forms. . . .

The old *de facto* property rights embodied in the half-reformed institutions would not be recognized in any significant way, and the new *de jure* property rights would be legislated by the new "revolutionary" democratic government.

. . . People will resist and "drag their feet" in countless ways when their *de facto* property rights are canceled or trivialized. The imagined great leap breaks down in chaos. Instead of disappearing overnight in favor of the new ideal institutions, the de-legitimated old institutions break down in favor of a shadowy anarchy of *ad hoc* opportunistic forms. The Big Bang becomes a Big Bust.

The alternative is a strategy of incremental institutional change. Instead of an imagined great leap forward over the chasm between socialism and capitalism, incentives would be devised to move people incrementally but irreversibly from the existing quasi-reformed institutions towards the "ideal" institutions. Instead of just negating the *de facto* property rights of managers and workers, they can arrive at a nearby set of legitimized *de jure* property rights by moving in the right direction. . . .

For instance, the privatization-by-liquidation program in Poland is based on an incremental strategy while the Polish mass privatization plan originates from a Big Bang approach. The Czech voucher plan is a Big Bang strategy, while small business privatization in the Czech Republic (and in most other countries) is based on an incremental approach. Aside from the lease buyouts and other MEBOs, the Russian mass privatization program is a Big Bang program, while the Chinese reforms in agriculture and industry are the clearest example of a thoroughgoing incremental approach. (Ellerman 1993, 27–28)

The Lease Buyout Counterfactual

What are the forms of privatization that try to move to a set of formal property rights that are a socially acceptable approximation to the de facto property rights that resulted from the earlier reforms during the socialist era? In Stiglitz's "Whither Reform?" the general strategy was called *stakeholder privatization*. Look at the parties who actually have to cooperate in order for an enterprise to succeed regardless of the ownership structure. This includes the workers, managers, and local authorities. It does not include voucher fund managers sitting in Moscow. Then "shrink-wrap" the ownership structure around those stakeholders to arrive at a minimal agency-chain structure where the owners have to cooperate on a day-to-day basis.[9] In the preceding passage written over a decade ago, I pick out the Polish privatization-by-liquidation (also called *Polish-leasing*) program, the Soviet lease buyouts, and the Chinese reforms in agriculture and industry (i.e., the household responsibility system and township-village enterprises, or TVEs) as examples of this strategy to strive for formal rights close to de facto rights and to minimize the distortions of information and effort involved in long agency chains and absentee ownership.

What was a counterfactual or alternative to the market bolshevik program in Russia? If the logic (minimizing agency chains and building on de facto property rights) is sound, then the Soviet lease buyouts and related experiments seem to be the closest thing to a counterfactual to grow out of the reform experience in the former Soviet Union.[10] As noted in the preceding, this option was argued for at the time and on the basis of roughly these arguments. Martin Weitzman also at the time gave a pragmatic argument for the worker ownership version of stakeholder privatization.

> Under worker ownership, the workers themselves, or their agents, will have to control pay and negotiate plant shutdowns. The most acute 'us vs. them' stalemates may be avoided. Ownership is more concentrated relatively close to management decisions and can put more immediate pressure on performance. Regulatory capture may be avoided. Hard budget constraints may be more acceptable. There is less opportunity for financial manipulation. (Weitzman 1993, 267)

Note Weitzman's version of the minimal agency chain and shrink-wrapped ownership argument: "Ownership is more concentrated relatively close to management decisions and can put more immediate pressure on performance." Unfortunately, the IFIs chose to promote privatization in the way that Soviet expert Weitzman recommended "How Not to Privatize."

Moreover, the IFI specializing in the region, the European Bank for Reconstruction and Development, was not only aware of the leasing option but sponsored a set of pilot projects in Russia to show how lease buyouts could be done using modern corporate forms (Lloyd 1993). The structure of these deals and a host of other examples were presented in an EBRD technical note (EBRD 1993), so all these ideas were known in the early 1990s to those in the IFIs who wanted to know.

Here is another "dangerous bend" in the argument that is liable to be misunderstood. The incremental counterfactual is often caricatured by the defenders of shock therapy as arguing that institutional and regulatory reform should have preceded privatization. While it might be nice to have a nicely ordered historical sequence, they argue that the economic crisis in Russia forced them to proceed with (voucher) privatization and institutional development simultaneously. However, the point is that stakeholder privatization minimizes the need for the institutions to police long agency chains (which takes decades to develop) so that the *appropriate* forms of privatization can go forward as those institutions are being developed and can, indeed, drive that institutional development through the endogenous Hirschmanian linkages (in contrast to the IFI conditionalities).

For instance, it might be argued against the Russian lease buyouts that "Russia did not have a sufficiently well developed national or regional institutional environment, as in Poland, to prevent large-scale managerial expropriation of assets under such a scheme."[11] But the stakeholder theory did not depend on a "well-developed national or regional institutional environment" (such as securities and exchange commissions and auditing agencies) to protect the self-interest of those who have to cooperate together on a daily basis to earn their economic livelihood. The stakeholders are all "mutual hostages" to the success of the enterprise, so they can exercise their de facto property rights directly, not by trying to get national or regional institutions to enforce any formal rights.

Unfortunately, the "experts" did not seem to have understood the argument then—or now.[12] When the "experts" have a quasireligious faith in ersatz national or regional watchdog institutions enforcing long agency chains and fail to see how people will try to enforce their de facto property rights in their concrete day-to-day self-interest, then the "experts" seem to have "failed in their understandings of the core elements of a market economy" (Stiglitz 2001).

There is also the argument that the stakeholder privatization option would have been too slow. In the Bank, we often heard a specious dichotomy of mass privatization (meaning vouchers) versus case-by-case privatization, where the latter meant painstaking negotiation of each deal. Yet the lease buyout schemes were a form of "mass" privatization in the sense that each deal simply had to satisfy certain cookie-cutter requirements in order to go through. Polish leasing was not slow, and the ten thousand or so Soviet lease buyouts before 1992 (when the door was shut) indicate that they were also not slow.

Indeed, one of the "problems" with the lease buyouts is that they were too fast and too popular at the firm level, not that they were too slow. The stream might swell to a river. If the lease buyouts had not been stopped, then the market bolsheviks feared that there would not be any good firms left to go into the voucher auctions. Thus the stream was dammed, and the waters diverted into the Kremlin-preferred channel of voucher privatization.

To conclude the focus on voucher privatization, the major development agencies had alternative advice and alternative practical experiments—so there were alternatives or "counterfactuals." Yet the agencies eschewed pragmatism and local experimentation in favor of what they decided was the One Best Way, which was then imposed, as best they could, all across the transition economies. Nor was this all. When blunders of historic proportions are committed, then one might at least expect some timely or perhaps *ex post* learning by the major agencies such as the World Bank or the IMF. Yet that did not happen. Long after voucher privatization had been a debacle wherever it was tried all across the postsocialist world and even after the collapse of the World Bank and IMF program in Russia in the summer of 1998, the World Bank still imposed a voucher privatization program in war-destroyed Bosnia in 1999.

One of the prerogatives of power is the avoidance of accountability and the learning that might follow. Instead of learning about messy local realities, the powerful agencies prefer to base their policy recommendations on big power politics (including cold war triumphalism), their own internal organizational imperatives, "expert" advice from the best and brightest neoclassical economists, textbook economic theories, and cartoon models of the transition and developing societies. The power differential between a well-heeled global agency and the countries that most need help is so great that there is no real incentive for the agency to learn. As is argued in the concluding chapter, the solution is not to expect the powerful agencies to suddenly reform themselves or dedicate themselves anew to learning but for the agencies to be displaced by more decentralized and local agencies. The less the power differential between the helper and the doer, the better.[13]

Closing Remarks on the Transition Case Study

My purpose in this chapter has been to look at the performance of the major development agencies aided and abetted by the best and brightest of neoclassical economists in facing one of the biggest developmental challenges of our time: the transition of the socialist countries to private property market economies. The experience split into a natural experiment of two opposing cases as clear-cut as history will ever provide: Russia and China. As stated by Gregory Mankiw (a Harvard economist and currently head of the Council of Economic Advisors but not involved in the transition debates):

> According to the 2002 World Development Report, from 1990 to 2000, China's real GDP grew at an amazing 10.3 percent per year. Meanwhile, Russia's output fell at a rate of 4.8 percent per year. Such a shocking contrast cries out for an explanation. (Mankiw 2003, 256–57)

The explanation that I have outlined in this chapter, like the explanation given in the book by John McMillan (2002) and reviewed by Mankiw, is based on the different philosophies, shock therapy and market bolshevism in the case of Russia and incrementalism in the case of China (the latter of which uses the themes outlined here). The IFIs and the neoclassical economic advisors lined up behind the Russian strategy; the Chinese went their own way—having already learned the hard way about Bolshevik-style social engineering.

> Russia leaned on lawyers, economists, and bankers from the West for advice on how to privatize state firms, develop capital markets, and reform the legal system . . . China by contrast called little on foreign consultants. (McMillan 2002, 207–8; quoted in Mankiw 2003, 257)

Professor Mankiw spells out the stakes in this natural experiment.

> If McMillan is right that shock therapy was the problem, then the economics profession must accept some of the blame. Our profession lent some of its best and brightest to the transition effort, such as my former colleague Jeffrey Sachs. Most of these advisors pushed Russia to embrace a rapid transition to capitalism. If this was a mistake, as McMillan suggests, its enormity makes it one of the greatest blunders in world history.[14] (Mankiw 2003, 257)

The greatest *institutional* responsibility must lie with the major development agencies, the World Bank and the IMF with the strong support of the U.S. government, which gave the advice and funds that underwrote the Russian debacle.

> McMillan doesn't come right out and tell foreign governments to ignore the experts from the IMF and other first-world institutions, but it would an easy inference to draw. (Mankiw 2003, 257)

And our case study indicates that the inference would be correct.

9

Hirschmanian Themes of Social Learning & Change

The Balanced Growth Debate

Within development theory, the best exposition of the alternative approach espoused here is the still classic work of Albert Hirschman. My purpose in this chapter is to revisit Hirschman along with some related thinkers from adjacent fields to see if new light can be thrown on the current debate about the methods of development assistance. Today, the term *development planning* is officially dead, but the dream of socially engineering economic development on a broad scale lives on in the programs of the major agencies such as the World Bank, the IMF, the regional development banks, and the major bilateral aid agencies. Debate rages about these agencies and about their structural adjustment programs, policy-based loans accompanied by a "Christmas tree" of conditionalities, project loans, and technical assistance or training programs. To map these issues back into Hirschman's early work on economic development, we must revisit the theories that led to the idea of a "big push" to achieve "balanced growth."

Perhaps the golden thread starts with Adam Smith's theory that development, as evidenced by the extension of the division of labor, was limited by the extent of the market. The modern treatment of this theme dates from Alfred Marshall's notion of external economies (e.g., in his treatment of industrial districts (1961, chap. 10) and from Allyn Young's seminal 1928 paper on increasing returns. Nicholas Kaldor studied with Young in the 1920s and was later one of the principal exponents of Young's view that "increasing returns is a 'macro-phenomenon'" (Kaldor 1966, 9) (in addition to any increasing returns at the firm level).[1]

In the development literature, these increasing returns themes are emphasized by Paul Rosenstein-Rodan (1943) and Ragnar Nurkse (1967) in the concept of balanced growth. The economic interdependence expressed in the notion of balanced growth was not as controversial as the policy implications. "Whether the forces of economic progress are to be deliberately organized or left to the action of private enterprise—in short, whether balanced growth is enforced by planning boards or achieved spontaneously by creative entrepreneurs—is, of course, a weighty and much debated issue" (Nurkse 1967, 16).

The first line of thought was based on development planning using the idea of a "big push." The theorists of the big push had carried out the intellectual exercise of imagining all the mutually reinforcing economic processes that would seemingly need to be jump-started in a small time period to promote the liftoff to balanced growth. Hirschman perceptively criticizes the big push idea at the time, noting that if a country had the capacity to successfully carry out a big push industrialization program, then "it would not be underdeveloped in the first place" (1961, 54).[2] Existing developed countries had not followed that imaginative route, so it might be more fruitful to attend to the actual processes of development and how they might be assisted or catalyzed.

Nurkse himself broaches an alternative to the centralized big push using Joseph Schumpeter's (1934) emphasis on entrepreneurship in the market process. "Schumpeter's creative entrepreneurs seem to have what it takes, and as they move forward on a broad front, their act of faith is crowned with commercial success" (Nurkse 1967, 15). Hirschman agrees on entrepreneurship and vastly generalized the notion of entrepreneurship as induced decision making to mobilize often scattered and hidden developmental resources where the "inducing mechanisms" (rather than acts of faith) are provided by the same linkages or interdependencies emphasized in the increasing returns literature.

Far from denying the interdependencies, Hirschman notes how the impulses of economic change were in fact transmitted through these endogenous linkages (as opposed to the exogenous push supplied by a central government or an international development agency). Rather than imagining fission by having the state somehow coordinating the big push of splitting many atoms at once, the state might try to design its interventions to catalyze a sequential chain reaction using the linkages—and thus getting entrepreneurial forces moving "forward on a broad front."[3] Hirschman develops a similar metaphor:

> In other words, I do not deny by any means the interrelatedness of various economic activities of which the balanced growth theory has made so much. On the contrary, I propose that we take advantage of it, that we probe into the structure that is holding together these interrelated activities. As in the atom, there is much energy here that can be and is in fact being utilized in building up economic development nuclei. *Later on* these nuclei look as though they could never have been separated even for a single instant when in actual fact they might never have been assembled had not a sequential solution, i.e., an unbalanced growth sequence been found, by accident, instinct, or reasoned design. To look at unbalanced growth means, in other words, to look at the dynamics of the development process *in the small*. But perhaps it is high time that we did just that.[4] (Hirschman 1961, viii–ix)

The big push language is now passé, but that does not mean that the lessons of Hirschman's unbalanced growth vision of development have been taken to heart in the large development agencies.[5] The language has changed more than the substance. It has been argued throughout this book that the social engineering mentality and the organizational imperatives of the World Bank and the other large development agencies are quite at odds with the indirect approach expressed in Hirschman's ideas about the relationship between development advisor and country. Nevertheless, there always seems to be a hardy band of Hirschmanians within the World Bank. President Wolfensohn himself has long been a board member of the Institute for Advanced Studies in Princeton (where Hirschman has been for three decades), and Wolfensohn considers Hirschman along with Sen as his principal intellectual mentors. Nicholas Stern, the chief economist following Stiglitz, had more of a Hirschmanian bent than probably any previous chief economist. However Wolfensohn and the others of similar persuasion in the Bank have not made much progress in getting the elephant to dance. Within development economics, Hirschman's interdisciplinary style of thought, Old World intellectual sophistication, and lack of "buttoned-down, mathematically consistent analyses" (Krugman 1994, 40) have not been the mainstream—much to the detriment of the latter.

Conditionality-Based Development Aid: The New Big Push

Conditionalities on development loans or donor grants are much like the plan specifications in a model of centrally planned and socially engineered reforms.[6] In the literature on aid for economic development, a substantial body of research now questions the effectiveness of conditionalities in policy-based lending such as structural adjustment loans.[7] The doubts apply less to the "pro forma," "stroke-of-the-pen," or price-based conditionalities than to those aimed at institutional reforms. In the face of these doubts, what is to be done?

Some practitioners plod onward, thinking that they only need to make conditionalities tougher and more performance based—to just get the incentives right. Such advice does little to address some of the basic reasons for the ineffectiveness. Tougher performance-based conditionalities do not solve the basic motivational problem. This may seem strange from the narrow economic viewpoint (e.g., agency theory). Doesn't the carrot of aid provide the motivation? In psychological terms, the problem is that the aid only provides extrinsic or externally sourced motivation. Real reforms beyond the stroke-of-the-pen variety will usually require some "own reasons" or more intrinsic motivations for successful implementation. Otherwise there is only the motivation to make the minimal outward changes to get the aid. In addition, there is a negative reactance against the attempt to externally impose changes. Making conditionalities tougher and more performance based does not even attempt to address these underlying motivational problems. More assistance based on improved conditionalities is reminiscent of the endless attempts to improve central planning under socialism.

Another approach to the doubts about aid-baited conditionalities is to emphasize that aid works best in countries that have good policies and that aid is largely wasted in countries with poor policies. In light of the doubts about conditionalities turning around poor policies, it is suggested that aid should be focused where it is most effective, independent of conditionalities (i.e., on the countries with good policy environments). This might be interpreted as suggesting a good-policy screen as one large *ex ante*, or "front-loaded," conditionality so that other conditionalities are not needed thereafter. But this would more finesse the problem than solve it. The problem is the social learning process to get a country from poor policies to better policies. This one-big-carrot approach has the same if not worse motivational problems as the many-small-carrots approach. Moreover it is doubtful that it would be sustained under real-world conditions of partial fulfillment. If the list of good policies was partly but not completely fulfilled, then strong political and disbursement pressures would build (from both sides) to give at least "half a carrot," and we would be in effect back to the many-small-carrots approach.

Aid agencies have their preconceptions of "virtue" in the sense of good policies. They try "to buy virtue" by imposing conditionalities on program aid geared to "virtuous behavior" defined by various outward acts of allegiance to and implementation of "good policies." But if we take virtue as being defined not just by behavior but also by the right internal motives, then aid can only buy a faux virtue. Such aid pushes the external motive of receiving the aid into the motivational fore-ground and thus establishes external control—the lack of autonomy.

Where the internal motive was already present, autonomy-respect-ing aid could remove impediments and thus enable "virtuous action." "In these situations, the donor would set himself the task of rewarding virtue (or rather, what he considers as such) *where virtue appears of its own accord*."[8] This leads straightaway to the "paradox" that aid is only autonomy respecting when it does not do what is conventionally taken as a major purpose of program aid—to tip the balance of motives in favor of reforms and good policies.

> Paradoxically, therefore, program aid is fully effective only when it does not achieve anything—when, that is, no quid pro quo (in the sense of a policy that would not have been undertaken in the absence of aid) is exacted as the price of aid. (Hirschman and Bird 1971, 204)

The point about conditionalities is not simply that they might be ineffective but that they undermine the goal of autonomous develop-ment. Suppose that a government is facing pressing problems to finance better schooling or health care and realizes that it must clean up tax collection in order to raise the funding. In this case, we might say that the government has "internal motivation" to improve tax collection. But then a development agency (always in need of "moving the money") arrives to offer to finance the improvements in schooling or health care. Since this relaxes the internal pressures to improve tax collection, the agency substitutes its conditionalities by requiring a program of improving tax collection as a condition for the loan and its various tranches (e.g., a structural adjustment program).

Reformers in the government who have been pushing for tax reform may even welcome the conditionalities to strengthen their hand and to provide leverage and a commitment mechanism to ensure that the government will make the reforms. But the net effect is to externalize the reform motivation with the attendant effects of reactance, foot-dragging, and sabotage—and to train governments that the way to resolve pressing problems is to solicit long-term development loans or grants and then to play the conditionalities game with the agencies rather than undertake the difficult reforms on their own.[9]

External interventions by other people intended to change a person's behavior pose a threat to autonomy. The threat-to-autonomy or reactance effect results from using external motivators—carrots and sticks—to shift the locus of causality from internal to external. The effect shows itself in a poor quality and low-effort performance, in sullen and perfunctory behavior fulfilling the letter but not the spirit of an agreement, and perhaps even in the urge to defiantly do the opposite just to show one's autonomy.[10] Hirschman refers to these effects as the "hidden costs" of program aid (1971, 207), while Lepper and Greene (1978) call them the "hidden costs of rewards."

In the aid context, "good policies" bought by conditioned aid are usually not effective. If the policies were not adopted by the government independently of the aid, then the policies would tend to be

> adopted by aid-hungry governments in spite of continuing doubts of the policy makers themselves, resistance from some quarters within the government, onslaught against the "deal" from the opposition, and general distaste for the whole procedure.
>
> Naturally, doubts and reservations are not voiced at the moment of the aid compact; hence the delusion on the part of the donor that there has been a full meeting of minds. But soon after virtue has been "bought" through aid under these conditions, the reservations and resistances will find some expression—for example, through half-hearted

implementation or sabotage of the agreed-to policies—and relations between donor and recipient will promptly deteriorate as a result. (Hirschman and Bird 1971, 205)

The debate about conditionalities is to some extent ill posed. In psychological terms, the question is how to best indirectly foster the country's intrinsic motivation for reforms as opposed to the agency theory question of how to best impose carrots and sticks (extrinsic motivation) to promote reforms.

Unbalanced Growth Processes

This critique of conventional development assistance directs our attention back to the themes of the increasing returns and economic interdependence literature considered earlier—the linkages, internal pressures, or pressing problems in a country along with efforts already afoot to address the problems. The best way to ensure that a reform process has some internal motivation in a country is not to start it but to *find* it.[11]

> I began to look for elements and processes . . . that *did* work, perhaps in roundabout and unappreciated fashion. [T]his search for possible *hidden rationalities* was to give an underlying unity to my work. . . . [T]he hidden rationalities I was after were precisely and principally *processes of growth and change already under way* in the societies I studied, processes that were often unnoticed by the actors immediately involved, as well as by foreign experts and advisors. (Hirschman 1984a, 91–93)

Not all problems can be attacked at once, so attention is first focused *in the small* on the sectors or localities where some of the preconditions are in place and where initiative is afoot on its own. The initial small successes will then create pressures through the forward and backward linkages to foster both learning and change that is nearby in sectorial or locational terms—all of which might lead to a "growth pole" or local industrial district.[12] The successes when broadcast horizontally to those facing similar problems will start to break down the paralyzing beliefs that nothing can be done and will thus fuel broader initiatives that take the early wins as their benchmark.[13] Unlike a model that assumes large-scale organized social action directed by an external agency, the parties are responding to endogenous pressures and inducements from their economic partners or to opportunities revealed by others in a similar position.

One thing leads to, induces, elicits, or entrains another thing through chains of tensions, disproportions, and disequilibria. Hirschman at one point refers to the principle of unbalanced growth as "the idea of maximizing induced decisionmaking" (1994a, 278). The problem-solving pressures induced by unbalanced growth will call forth otherwise unused resources and enlist otherwise untapped energies. As a project moves from one bottleneck and crisis to another (in comparison with the smooth planned allocation of resources in a project), then "resources and abilities that are hidden, scattered, or badly utilized" will be mobilized (1961, 5). Hirschman (1984a, 95) notes the connections with Richard Cyert and James March's notion of "organizational slack" (1963) based on Herbert Simon's theory of "satisficing" (1955), with Nathan Rosenberg's theory (1969) that technological innovation is strongly influenced by "inducing" or "focusing" events such as strikes and wars, and, above all, with Harvey Leibenstein's theory of X-inefficiency (1966). Edmund Burke reiterates the ancient Greek theme of contests and struggle (agōn):

> [Difficulty] has been the glory of the great masters in all the arts to confront, and to overcome; and when they had overcome the first difficulty, to turn it into an instrument for new conquests over new difficulties. . . . He that wrestles with us strengthens our nerves, and sharpens our skill. Our antagonist is our helper. This amicable conflict with difficulty obliges us to an intimate acquaintance with our object, and compels us to consider it in all its relations. It will not suffer us to be superficial. (Burke [1790] 1937, 299–300)

Within economics, this is related not to the neoclassical notion of competition (not being able to affect price) but to the Austrian notion of the rivalry that elicits the best efforts of the competitors.[14]

One of Hirschman's best-known theories, the exit-voice analysis (1970), is concerned with the problem of eliciting or inducing decision making, particularly when organizations face decline. Many change processes can be parsed into two moments. Starting with some given, there are two general options: the transformation of the given by working to improve it or the replacement of the given option by another option that is improved. In Hirschman's formulation of the two moments of change, replacement is exit and transformation is voice. A customer dissatisfied with a company's product can exit to a competing product or can complain to the company (exercise voice) to try to get it to transform the product. In an organization, a dissatisfied member has the choice to exit (migrate) to another organization or to exercise voice to try to change the organization. Each potential migrant worker faces a choice: to exit to find a better home or to commit to making the home better. Two such general strategies of change are ubiquitous: fight (fight rather than switch) or flight (switch rather than fight), repair or replace, climb this hill or jump to another hill, and even "fix-it or nix-it" (a slogan used by protestors about the World Bank and IMF).

Conventional economists are trained (some would say hardwired in graduate school) to think primarily in terms of exit-based policies since that is the logic of the market (e.g., the "Wall Street rule" to sell shares rather than vote shares). Voice- or transformation-based strategies tend to get short shrift in the economic way of thinking. Exit-based reasoning may backfire. Hirschman's original example was the dismal performance of the Nigerian railroads in spite of the protests (voice) of many dissatisfied customers. In the usual monopoly versus competition reasoning, things would improve if the railroads had competition, and that eventually came from the trucking industry. But the effect was that the most dissatisfied and vocal customers (who required more reliable or time-sensitive transportation services) exited to trucking so that there was even less pressure on the railroads to improve. Since the railway ministry could not go bankrupt, the net effect was to go from bad to worse.

The same logic plays itself out in the school voucher debate or in the migration/brain-drain debate. Foster exit from where there is low performance, and it should lead to either improved performance or bankruptcy in the low-performing unit. But many of the people who are most likely to spur or enable change will be the first to exit, so improved performance is not the likely outcome. And if the schools or countries cannot go bankrupt, then the outcome in both cases may be a self-reinforcing downward spiral to "ghettoized" schools or "ghettoized" countries.

In order to yield responsible general advice, the economic way of thinking needs not only to go beyond extrinsic motivation but to go beyond exit-based reasoning to try to better understand how organizations work and how they might be transformed. But all too often, the advice is simply to change organizations to fit the Procrustean bed of the exit-based market reasoning (e.g., privatization in its various forms). Hirschman also makes the further point that even the exit-based reasoning is incomplete since it essentially ignores the question of how transformation to improve performance takes place under the pressure supplied by the exit.

Cognitive Side of Unbalanced Growth

This brings us to the cognitive version of unbalanced growth as a learning process. Many economists first saw Hirschman's vision of unbalanced growth as being about incentives or volitional impulses—but the ideas also have a cognitive side about the social learning process.

One can draw analogies to the process of unbalanced growth that takes place in individual learning. Suppose one took a static snapshot of a person's beliefs before and after learning some new and complex interconnected subject matter. The older set of beliefs might have certain self-reinforcing properties. It might at first seem difficult to change one part of the set of beliefs since one would then have some cognitive dissonance with the remaining older beliefs. One could imagine simply changing all the beliefs at once, a cognitive big push, to arrive at a new self-reinforcing set.

But that is rarely how learning takes place. Against the forces of self-preservation of the "whole cloth" of older beliefs, there are the incentives to solve problems for which the old beliefs may be inadequate. Change might start in the small, where problem-solving progress might be made by unraveling and changing some of the beliefs. But now the interconnections could help to unravel the older cloth. Bottlenecks or inconsistencies would appear between the old and new beliefs, and problem-solving pressures would be transmitted forwards, backwards, and sideways to adjust other beliefs. "One thing would lead to another," and eventually the person would arrive at a new set of interconnected beliefs.[15]

Now consider the viewpoint of the knowledgeable outsider, a teacher or trainer, who understood all along the problem-solving superiority of the new set of beliefs. Why couldn't the trainer just give a core course to impart the new knowledge to the student and thereby save the pupil all the time, energy, and pain of learning the hard way? Carrots and sticks, aid and conditionalities, could even incentivize the learning process. While a veneer of some "knowledgeable behaviors" might be incentivized–particularly in "good students"—by such carrots and sticks, learning that transforms older beliefs does not take place in that manner. In order for learners to have an ownership of new knowledge and for the new knowledge to have a transformative effect, the knowledge must be more the fruits of the learners' own activities. Such knowledge comes out of a constructivist active learning process, not out of a pedagogy of teaching, imparting, transmitting, disseminating, or pouring new knowledge into passive students.

Returning to the general theme of balanced versus unbalanced development, there is an interesting parallel with the thought patterns in the "Darwin wars" between creationists and evolutionists. From the old example of the optical eye to the modern example of the whole biochemical mechanism of DNA and RNA, there are living systems that are so complexly interdependent that it is quite difficult for the lay observer to imagine how the systems could have evolved sequentially. Seemingly everything has to be in place at once in order for the system to work and thus exhibit any evolutionary advantage. Hence this thought pattern pushes toward a creationist conclusion that there must be some Central Guiding Hand to explain such a complex, interdependent system.

In the thought patterns of the big push school, the complex interdependence of a modernizing economy also drives toward the conclusion that there needs to be a central guiding hand to jump-start the balanced growth miracle. Evolutionary biologists and the theorists of the unbalanced development school thus need to pay close empirical attention to the actual evolutionary histories in order to dispel the a priori thought patterns arguing for a central guiding hand. Much of that thought pattern seems based on taking snapshots before and after some large change and then not being able to readily imagine a step-by-step process to go from one to the other.

Hirschman uses the metaphor of solving a jigsaw puzzle for the unbalanced growth version of dealing with the set of problems facing a developing country (1961, 81–82). One can imagine a rather superhuman act of putting all the pieces together at once to solve the puzzle. Indeed don't the experts who have seen and studied seemingly similar puzzles put together elsewhere have that knowledge? That is the comforting fantasy of those who promote comprehensive, integrated, and balanced reform programs. "Do all these things together (so that it looks like the 'picture on the puzzle box'), and you will solve your problems!"

For the variety of reasons outlined in the preceding, countries cannot just solve all their problems at once. They must start with a few pieces that fit together and try to work outward to find other pieces that fit. Not all starting points are equal. Certain pieces of the puzzle might have nearby connections and linkages that allow building that part of the puzzle quickly—as opposed to parts whose solution might give little insight or impetus to solving the nearby parts. Perhaps someone who has seen similar puzzles solved would be a good coach to suggest promising starting points or fruitful directions for progress. Perhaps it would be helpful to study the "picture on the box," but a better metaphor might be putting together a puzzle when one doesn't know what the final picture will be. The actual solving of the puzzle is a piecemeal process starting in one or more propitious places and working outward through fruitful linkages to finally arrive at the new overall configuration.

We might also consider the analogy with the way an entrepreneur might develop a business. Success in an initial effort will create bottlenecks and pressures upstream or downstream that need to be resolved—as well as opportunities that can be captured. One thing leads to another in an evolutionary process of groping, adaptive learning, and experimentation. Each step is driven by the local needs to relieve pressures or grab opportunities. It is rather different from following the imposed performance incentives to move step-by-step through an engineering plan to construct a building or build a bridge. By studying the successful development of a complex, multifaceted business, would-be entrepreneurs might gain much insight into the process, which is very different from following a checklist-style business plan, or blueprint. If entrepreneurial business development is too fraught with uncertainties, complexities, instabilities, and incomplete knowledge to submit to technocratic planning, then one might well expect the same to hold for the larger processes of social reform, change, and development in a country.

In summary, learning, experimentation, and pragmatism are basic to any alternative to the command and control models of development assistance. The limited powers of cognition and the limited capacity for implementation of central authorities in the face of the complexity of organizational, institutional, and social realities do not give much hope for social engineering approaches. Hirschman, as a keen observer of the development process, sees successes as taking place in a rather different way, and he recommends that development projects attend to those "hidden rationalities" more than to the dreams of technocratic rationality entertained by social engineers. Initiatives need to find and enlist local energies and knowledge for trial-and-error problem solving. But each problem solved brings to the foreground other problems and opportunities through forward and backward linkages. Change unfolds because "one thing leads to another"—not because a given rational plan can be implemented through centrally coordinated action.

Bridges to Other Thinkers

Given the multidisciplinary nature of Hirschman's approach and of the approach taken here, an all-too-brief look at some bridges to other thinkers may nevertheless help to triangulate on Hirschman's ideas and to encourage profitable two-way traffic over these bridges.

Herbert Simon's Theory of Bounded Rationality

One generative metaphor for Herbert Simon's work on bounded rationality is the labyrinth, or maze.[16] We are in the maze, not helicoptering over the maze surveying all the options from an Olympian perspective. We do not see all the possibilities at any one time, we do not know the probabilities of the outcomes given our choices, and we do not have the computational capacity to determine an optimal outcome even if we had this information. Thus our capacity for "rational" behavior is bounded in many dimensions.

While Simon does not directly address the problems of economic development, his work has pioneered the critique of the substantively rational decision maker that is manifested in planning models, big push models, and, more generally, the ambitions of technocratic reason. The contrast of being in the maze instead of over it is a useful mental model to use in comparing realistic unbalanced growth strategies with the dreams of comprehensive development programs.

Another important connection is between Hirschman's emphasis on voice (transformation) and Simon's emphasis on organizations. Hirschman points out that exit-based strategies to improve performance are far from universal, and even where exit can generate pressure for improvement, exit-based reasoning has little to offer as to how organizations can restructure to improve their performance. Economists tend to have a cognitive map of the world (like Saul Steinberg's famous *New Yorker* cover) where markets dominate the landscape except for small market failures (small "lumps in a pail of buttermilk") known as *organizations* off in the distance. Having studied both organizations and markets throughout his career, Simon finds that the reality in the advanced economies is almost the opposite. Instead of thick markets connecting small organizational dots, Simon sees a world of organizations with thin markets connecting them. Indeed, he objects to the very term *market economy*.

> The economies of modern industrialized society can more appropriately be labeled organizational economies than market economies. Thus, even market-driven capitalist economies need a theory of organizations as much as they need a theory of markets. The attempts of the new institutional economics to explain organizational behavior solely in terms of agency, asymmetric information, transaction costs, opportunism, and other concepts drawn from neo-classical economics ignore key organizational mechanisms like authority, identification, and coordination, and hence are seriously incomplete. (Simon 1991a, 42)

This helps to restore some balance and bring some focus on voice and organizational transformation in contrast to a monoeconomics focused on markets and exit-based reasoning.

Charles Lindblom's Theory of Incrementalism and Muddling Through

Charles Lindblom (1990) considers a "scientific" model for governing society that in a modern form might be based on some assumed "social welfare function," "social choice rule," or "game solution concept" and juxtaposes it to the alternative model of a self-guiding society based on the use of "reflective intelligence" (Dewey), the competition of ideas, and government by discussion.[17] To quickly see the distinction, Lind-

blom suggests to "compare Marx with Franklin Roosevelt or Jan Tinbergen with Saul Alinsky" (Lindblom 1990, 216). In the "scientific"
model, the "correct solutions" are already defined but unknown. If "scientific" techniques could uncover those answers independent of any
political process, then the answers could be whispered into the ear of
the prince. However, in the model of a self-guiding society, preferences
and volitions are endogenous to the social/political process.

> As for ends—usually standing volitions—the self-guiding model neither
> takes any as given, as in some versions of the scientific model, nor
> regards them as discoverable. For no one can dis- or uncover a volition;
> and instead people form, chose, decide upon, or will. This they do
> through a mixture of empirical, prudential, aesthetic, and moral probes.
> Among more numerous lesser questions, probing pursues great existen-
> tial and moral questions, working answers to which join with the unex-
> pected to shape people and society. (Lindblom 1990, 216)

Economists such as Jan Tinbergen (1956) tend to view public policy-making as a comprehensive technocratically rational process of surveying the feasible alternatives, evaluating them according to some
agreed upon objective or welfare function, and choosing the most preferred alternative. In contrast, Lindblom argues that limited cognitive
capabilities, complexity, uncertainty, and conflicting values excluded
any such "synoptic" policy-making process.[18] For those reasons, actual
policy-making is better described as "disjointed incrementalism" and
"muddling through."

The similarities between Lindblom's process of incremental muddling through in policy-making and Hirschman's theory of unbalanced
growth are so striking that they authored a joint article pointing out
the convergence. Both approaches are skeptical of order, balance, and
detailed programming based on expert foresight, centralized direction,
and integrated overviews.

> [Both] agree it is most important that arrangements exist through which
> decision makers are sensitized and react promptly to newly emerging
> problems, imbalances, and difficulties; this essential ability to react and
> to improvise readily and imaginatively can be stultified by an undue pre-
> occupation with, and consequent pretense at, advance elimination of
> these problems and difficulties through "integrated planning."
> (Hirschman and Lindblom, 1971, 77)

One of the popular themes today in aid agencies is knowledge-based development assistance conceived of as the agency "giving" or disseminating the solution to a problem to a developing country. Yet Hirschman and Lindblom agree that this will "often result in complicating the problem through mistaken diagnoses and ideologies," and thus they argue that "the much maligned 'hard way' of learning by experiencing the problems at close range may often be the most expeditious and least expensive way to a solution" (1971, 77). Where conflict arises, they see the "mutual adjustment" of the participants as achieving a kind of coordination that could not have been anticipated or centrally planned. Similar processes of mutual adjustment without central control are evidenced in the procedures of common law (coordinated by precedents set by different judges), in Michael Polanyi's theory of coordination in science,[19] and in Mary Parker Follett's notion of horizontal coordination by reciprocity in organizations.[20] Finally, they see in this "political adjustment and strife analogues to self-interested yet socially useful adjustment in the market" (1971, 78).

Burton Klein's Vision of Dynamic Economics

The joint paper by Hirschman and Lindblom (1971) also discusses similarities with the work of Burton Klein. In an early work on technology development, Burton Klein and William Meckling (1958) contrast dynamic development strategies with the usual Olympian or "synoptic" approach of operations research. In the usual approach, the analyst, Mr. Optimizer, would gather the best current views, perhaps a consensus of the experts, as to what was the best option and then plans would be drawn to rationally allocate resources to develop that option—much like a development program based on the Official Views determined by the consensus of experts at elite development agencies. Klein and Meckling propose an alternative approach of Mr. Skeptic: parallel experimental development of several main options with early prototyping "to see what works" and then later allocation decisions guided by the results of these experiments. Thus they see the problem as "*not* one of choosing among specific end-product alternatives, but rather a problem of choosing a course of action initially consistent with a wide range of such alternatives; and of narrowing the choice as development proceeds" (Klein and Meckling 1958, 352).

They [Klein and Meckling] allege that development is both less costly and more speedy when marked by duplication, "confusion," and lack of communication among people working along parallel lines. Perhaps more fundamentally, they are against too strenuous attempts at integrating various subsystems into a well-articulated, harmonious, general system; they rather advocate the full exploitation of fruitful ideas regardless of the "fit" to some preconceived pattern of specifications. (Hirschman and Lindblom 1971, 66–67)

In his later work, Klein develops this analysis of parallel experimentation in the presence of genuine uncertainty into a full-fledged vision of dynamic economics (1977, 1984). Klein, like many others, wanted to develop Schumpeter's vision of a truly dynamic economy driven by entrepreneurial energies to continuously innovate and to create a perennial gale of creative destruction. While Klein's theory is couched in terms of a developed economy, the synergy with Hirschman's work is still evident. Klein focuses on rivalry between firms threatening each other's market shares as the driving force of dynamics. Hirschman sees unbalanced growth being driven not only by commercial rivalry but by a broader set of inducement mechanisms where innovative decisions are induced by the opportunities offered and the pressures applied by forward and backward linkages between firms or sectors; by the barriers (bottlenecks) or breaking of barriers that galvanize otherwise scattered, frustrated, or dormant energies; and, within organizations, by the pressures of exit and voice.

Klein specifically sees rivalry as promoting innovative effort (e.g., the X-efficiency of galvanizing scattered energies) and plays down the static notion of allocative efficiency. Klein notes that Louis Brandeis used a similar argument in favor of rivalrous competition in spite of the wastes or duplication that might be involved. In 1912, when economists were still perfecting the notion of allocative efficiency, Brandeis gave an X-efficiency argument in favor of the "wastes" of rivalrous competition in contrast to the static efficiency of big combines and trusts.

Incentive and development which are incident to the freer system of business result in so much greater achievement that the waste is relatively insignificant. The margin between that which men naturally do, and that which they can do, is so great that a system which urges men on to action and develops individual enterprise and initiative is preferable, in spite of the wastes that necessarily attend the process. (Brandeis quoted in Mason 1946, 382)

In planning a forest, static efficiency would suggest planting trees in openings for best access to sunlight; diminishing returns would set in as trees began to shade one another. But as mentioned in the preceding, Immanuel Kant, writing in 1784, sees that it was the rivalry of trees competing for sunlight that would make them "grow beautiful and straight" (Kant [1784] 1991a, 46). Starting with Alfred Marshall's metaphor of the various firms in an industry as being like young, middle-aged, and old trees in a forest (1961, 315), Klein finds, perhaps unknowingly, Kant's metaphor to illustrate dynamic efficiency.

And to put my proposition in terms of [Marshall's] analogy: when business firms compete by imposing risk upon each other they contribute not only to their own success but to the growth of the forest. One the other hand, when they fail to compete in deeds and seek the help of the government in exempting them from risk-taking, a few old trees can jeopardize the growth of an entire forest. (Klein 1977, 233–34)

In Klein's later work, he develops a notion of dynamic stability that is based not on rigidity or stasis but on conflict and constant problem solving at the microlevel. The flavor of the idea is given by a domestic example.

For example, which marriages are more likely to remain stable, those in which the marriage partners can be counted upon to never change their initial ideas, or those in which new "inventions" are constantly made to resolve matrimonial dilemmas? And the same is true in everything, from employing inventiveness to preventing a machine from breaking down often to constructing a new scientific theory. (Klein 1984, 182)

Likewise, Hirschman sees this continuous problem solving necessitated by dilemmas and conflict as the source of vitality and macrostability.

The secret of the vitality of pluralist market society and of its ability to renew itself may lie in this conjunction and in the successive eruption of problems and crises. The society thus produces a *steady diet of conflicts* that need to be addressed and that the society learns to manage. Correspondingly, the basic reason for the deterioration and loss of vitality of the Communist-dominated societies may reside in the success these societies had in suppressing overt social conflict. (Hirschman 1995, 243)

Jane Jacobs's Vision of Development

Although working well outside the confines of the "professional" study of economies known as *economics*, Jane Jacobs's voraciously eclectic work (1969, 1984) contributes to the tradition emphasizing increasing returns, agglomeration, and diversification. Indeed, those processes describe cities, and cities are her focus beginning with her best-known book *The Death and Life of Great American Cities* (1961). As professional economists paid more attention to the increasing returns processes so central to development, her work was better appreciated. In his work on endogenous growth theory, Robert E. Lucas notes: "I will be following very closely the lead of Jane Jacobs, whose remarkable book *The Economy of Cities* seems to me mainly and convincingly concerned (although she does not use this terminology) with the external effects of human capital" (Lucas 1988, 37).

I have focused on Hirschman's critique of the big push approach (and its latter-day forms in conditionality-based development programs) and his alternative vision of a more endogenous unbalanced growth process. Jane Jacobs has always been *the* antagonist to the technocratic city-planning tradition exemplified, for example, by the "High Modernism" of Le Corbusier.[21] Thus it should not be surprising that interesting parallels should exist with Hirschman's work.

She arrives at a similar vision of an unbalanced growth process by focusing on how old work leads to new, diversified work within cities and on the volatile trade between cities. To become more ramified and complex, an economic settlement should have multiple uses for imports to produce diversified and multistaged products with a significant portion for local use. In a complex environment, growth is not just an amplified throughput operation; it can lead to development. Each specialization of old work to achieve efficiency will soon lead to new work as the diversification of outputs into various product niches, to backward integration to produce previously imported inputs, and perhaps to unexpected "matings" with nearby processes and products to produce novel offspring. This is the sort of innovation that tends to happen when diverse people with various skills and complementary knowledge jostle together in companies and when companies jostle together in cities. "This process in which one sort of work leads to another must have happened millions of times in the whole history of human economic development" (Jacobs 1969, 53).

Given these processes of old work leading to new work within cities, the cities can grow through a process of dynamic interaction with each other by direct or indirect rivalry. To play in the "game," a city must produce something that it can export—perhaps based on its natural endowment. That is its "challenge" to other cities. The export earnings can then buy imports from other cities that are not produced in the given city. But if the other cities are not too advanced, then the import will present a plausible challenge to be replaced through learning and improvisation and perhaps improved upon within the city. Since the wealth to buy the imports may have been earned productively (not a gift), the city may already have some productive capacity that may begin to improvise and differentiate to produce and replace the import.

In the meantime, the other cities may be replacing the original exports of the city; its temporary advantage may be competed away. Now the domestic and perhaps improved version of the originally imported products can then be reexported perhaps to the original supplier city or more likely to other cities that are less developed or have different specializations. The new export earnings will then purchase other, more challenging imports, and the process can repeat itself ratcheted up at a higher level. In this matter, a diversified group of innovative cities can through trade learn from each other and are "developing on one another's shoulders" (Jacobs 1984, 144). This could well be called the "Jacobs's ladder" mechanism of development through volatile intercity trade.

> To rulers who want to know and control, as far as they can, what is going to be produced five years in the future and where it is going to be produced and how, and then five years beyond that, and so on, volatile intercity trade, forever unpredictably and opportunistically changing in content, represents sheer chaos. Of course it is not chaos. It is a complex form of order, akin to organic forms of order typical of all living things, in which instabilities build up (in this case, funds of potentially replaceable imports) followed by corrections, both the instabilities and the corrections being the very stuff of life processes themselves. (Jacobs 1984, 144–45)

Jacobs also develops her version of Hirschman's vision of the innovative developmental process of problem solving leading to more problems and pressures, which in turn calls forth more problem solving and so on.

> Earlier I defined economic development as a process of continually improvising in a context that makes injecting improvisations into everyday life feasible. We might amplify this by calling development an improvisational drift into unprecedented kinds of work that carry unprecedented problems, then drifting into improvised solutions, which carry further unprecedented work carrying unprecedented problems. (Jacobs 1984, 221–22)

Instead of a vision of integrated rational planning based on a comprehensive overview, Jacobs and Hirschman, as well as Lindblom and Klein, all envisage a process driven by endogenous pressures that call forth innovative problem solving, which, in turn, creates counterpressures—moves and countermoves ratcheting forward through seesaw advances.

Donald Schön's Theory of Decentralized Social Learning

Although not explicitly developed as a theory of learning, Hirschman's theory of unbalanced growth can be usefully seen as a theory of decentralized social learning (see Schön 1994) in a manner that will induce decision making by the "doers of development," will collect and release scattered and dormant local energies, and will instill "ownership" in the learners. The default theory of social learning on the part of development agencies whose counterparts are governments is that the central government makes policy innovations—with the help of its advisors—which are then transmitted to the rest of the country.

> [The standard approach] treats government as center, the rest of society as periphery. Central has responsibility for the formation of new policy and for its imposition on localities at the periphery. Central attempts to "train" agencies at the periphery. In spite of the language of experimentation, government-initiated learning tends to be confined to efforts to induce localities to behave in conformity with central policy. (Schön, 1971, 177)

But social learning can take place in a decentralized bottom-up manner with centralized coordination. In large multiplant companies, innovation may take the form of new ways of socially organizing and structuring productive processes (e.g., quality circles or self-managed work teams). Separate plants may perform pilot experiments to find out "what works and what doesn't." The headquarters office frames the experiments, detects the successes, and plays the knowledge broker to help other plants cross-learn from the successful ones. Schön describes a similar process between the government and the periphery of local units trying to carry out a certain social reform.

> Government cannot play the role of "experimenter for the nation," seeking first to identify the correct solution, then to train society at large in its adaptation. The opportunity for learning is primarily in discovered systems at the periphery, not in the nexus of official policies at the center. Central's role is to detect significant shifts at the periphery, to pay explicit attention to the emergence of ideas in good currency, and to derive themes of policy by induction. The movement of learning is as much from periphery to periphery, or periphery to center, as from center to periphery. Central comes to function as facilitator of society's learning, rather than as society's trainer. (Schön, 1971, 177–78)

Social learning is often very different from laboratory learning. Novel complexity, genuine uncertainty, conflict of values, unique circumstances, and structural instabilities mitigate against "laboratory conditions" for discovery and learning. Decentralized parallel experimentation with centrally sponsored framing and quality benchmarking followed by peer-to-peer cross-learning in the periphery is a more appropriate model than research at a central facility followed by the teaching, or dissemination, of the results.

Everett Rogers's Theory of Decentralized Innovation and Diffusion

In Everett Rogers's early work on the diffusion of innovations, he focuses on the classical hub-and-spokes or center-periphery model of diffusion.

> In this classical diffusion model, an innovation originates from some expert source (often an R&D organization). This source then diffuses the innovation as a uniform package to potential adopters who accept or

reject the innovation. The role of the adopter of the innovation is that of a passive accepter. (Rogers 1983, 333)

Spurred on by Schön's work (1971), he became aware of decentralized diffusion systems with horizontal diffusion between peers (which might involve partial reinvention of the model) rather than vertical transmission from experts to adopters.

> During the late 1970s I gradually became aware of diffusion systems that did not operate at all like the relatively centralized diffusion systems that I had described in my previous books. Instead of coming out of formal R&D systems, innovations often bubbled up from the operational levels of a system, with the inventing done by certain users. Then the new ideas spread horizontally via peer networks, with a high degree of reinvention occurring as the innovations are modified by users to fit their particular conditions. . . .
> Gradually, I began to realize that the centralized diffusion model was not the only wheel in town. (Rogers 1983, 334)

Perhaps the best example of a centrally sponsored system of decentralized innovation and diffusion in a developing country is in China over the last quarter of a century. Contrary to the classical model of reform models being established in the center and disseminated to the periphery, the Chinese recognized local reform models that could be in a region, county, commune, or even brigade. The local model could be in any sector or area such as administration, health, education, or industry and could be visited by groups from all over China who wanted to make a similar reform in their locality.

> The diffusion of innovations in China is distinctive in that it is (1) more horizontal in nature, (2) less dependent upon scientific and technical expertise, and (3) more flexible in allowing re-invention of the innovation as it is implemented by local units. These aspects of decentralized diffusion are facilitated by China's use of such diffusion strategies as models and on-the-spot conferences. The "learning from others" approach to decentralized diffusion in China was adopted officially as a national policy in the national constitution in 1978. (Rogers 1983, 340–41)

The same period marks the beginning of China's historic record of growth and development at the end of the twentieth century.[22]

Just-in-Time Inventory and Continuous Improvement Systems

The Japanese just-in-time (JIT) inventory system can be viewed as a system of dynamic production learning—not just a system of cutting inventory costs. Buffer inventories in production might be analogized to loans from international development agencies that allow one to get by current difficulties without necessarily solving the underlying problems. But with a JIT system, the costs of the problem are evident, and attention is then focused on solving the problem so that it does not recur again. Hirschman has praised the low tolerance for error and narrow latitude of some technical systems (e.g., aircraft maintenance or road surfaces where the low maintenance will show up as destructive potholes), which thus serve as inducement or pacing mechanisms for maintenance and learning. High tolerance for error or wide latitude for maintenance would operate like high inventory levels to weaken the incentives for corrective actions.

Just as a lowering of the water in a canal will reveal obstacles to navigation, so a systematic reduction in the levels of inventories will bring problems to the surface so that this created necessity will be the mother of invention to resolve the problems. Then with a continuous reduction in inventory levels, other problems will come to the surface and be resolved in a *kaizen* process of continuous improvement.

> This successive removal of inventories creates bottlenecks in production that make it possible to identify each work station's weaknesses; and in this way it is analogous to the potentially informative disruptions of production caused by, say, the construction of a new steel plant in stories of unbalanced growth. (Sabel 1994, 240)

Hirschman has been asked if he would actually advocate "unbalanced growth" in view of the "efficiency" properties of the formal models of balanced growth,[23] and one of his responses is that in the JIT inventory system "the Japanese initiate and induce it" (Hirschman, 1994b, 319).

Charles Sabel's Theory of Learning by Monitoring

The Japanese system of just-in-time inventories, local problem solving by teams, benchmarking between teams, and continuous improvement can be seen as a system of systematic learning in production that induces decision making, problem solving, and ownership by the participants. Charles Sabel has developed this and other examples in his theory of learning by monitoring (1994).

Often development strategies are flawed by implicitly assuming that which needs to be created. This often takes the form of assuming an effective governance system is in place so that a development advisor simply has to pour some new wine into the sound bottle (e.g., design a comprehensive set of conditionalities to be implemented by a developing country). In large organizations, top managers often adopt new strategic plans as if the problems lay in the specifics of the plan rather than in the lack of capacity to implement management's writ. The implicit assumption of an effective governance system imputes to the government of a country or to the management of a company a capacity to resolve coordination and collective action problems by command and control.

In contrast, Hirschman and Sabel ask how collective action problems are solved in the small and how change does take place—without assuming an effective fiat from the center. By developing a more realistic theory of change, they can then "back out" a more reasonable description of what the center can do to catalyze, assist, and broker the process—rather than trying to finesse the problem by assuming ab initio that the center can effectively implement its plans.

Sabel's treatment of collective action problems through learning by monitoring is particularly fruitful by showing important ways in which trust and "social capital" are developed without falling back on the conventional banalities about cultural inheritance and education. Individuals are assumed to have some sociability, some powers of reflection and discussion, and incomplete identities always in the process of formation and change (incompletely specified preference orderings in economists' terms). They are often in problematic situations where some collective action will benefit the group but where each may be vulnerable to the noncooperation of others (which can be defection or simply error). The problem being discussed is the group members' own common problem so that they will be involved in implementing any proposed solution (the "learning") and will thereby be monitoring the actions of others and hence the description "learning by monitoring." The discussion to arrive at a collective action plan must also include discussion of how to apportion the gains from cooperation and how to adjudicate differences that will arise.

So far the description of learning by monitoring does not differ substantially from the repeated games treatment of the evolution of "cooperation" (e.g., Axelrod 1984). Sabel goes beyond the game-theoretic treatment by assuming that the self-definitions and identities of the participants are changed by the discussion and cooperative efforts. Part of the discussion is to reinterpret and reframe their past, to discover and clarify their interests, and to establish a group identity with which the members can start to identify so that the cooperation is based more and more on "who they are" than on a tenuous game-theoretic modus vivendi (cooperating today only to avoid punishment tomorrow). The reciprocal belief that others also cooperate partly on the basis of identification (rather than strategy and guile) will lead to giving others some benefit of the doubt by interpreting occasional noncooperation by members as error rather than betrayal. In such a manner, trust and the norms of reciprocity (social capital) can be developed.

Central managers or coordinators, instead of being assumed as a deus ex machina, can be seen as agents of the group facilitating the "government by discussion" within the group and helping to minimize the vulnerabilities of cooperative action—while through benchmarking and other means of competitive stimulus helping to ensure that the group continues to face the problems that come to light. Where a set of people have interdependent opportunities and fates, the group members through initial problem-solving discussion and action accompanied by mutual monitoring can start to bootstrap a new collective identity that can help to stabilize future cooperative problem solving and learning.

Game theory and social choice theory transfer the economic model of fixed-preference exchange contracts from the marketplace to broader social and political settings. This leads to the idea of socially engineering the right contracts and institutions as an attempt to generate a semblance of "trust" through repeated prisoner's dilemma games. The alternative approach is through social processes wherein the parties, through discussion and joint activity, transform themselves to construct cooperative solutions to collective action problems. In terms of the intersecting circles that define "self" and "other," the alternative to "cooperation" based on the future threat potential of the "other" is a process that results in redefining a circle so that one who was previously "other" becomes a tentative part of a group with which one identifies.

[T]he rules of unbalanced growth transform what contractarians see as a chain of exchanges or an infinitely repeated game into a continuous discussion of joint possibilities and goals, where the parties' historical relation defines their mutual expectations. . . . Just as in a discussion, they must accept the possibility that their views of themselves, of the world, and the interests arising from both—their identities, in short—will be changed unexpectedly by those explorations. (Sabel 1994, 247–48)

Sabel gives a number of illuminating applications to production, science, and politics. For these processes to be transformative, participants must approach them with a vulnerability and a reflexive sociability—a mutual acceptance that participation may transform beliefs and preferences. In the preceding I note that the kaizen process of continuous improvement is the workplace version of Hirschman's theory of "unbalanced" development, which sees "the task of development policy [as] to maintain tensions, disproportions, and disequilibria" where "each move in the sequence is induced by a previous disequilibrium and in turn creates a new disequilibrium that requires a further move."[24]

John Dewey saw this species of pragmatism as being exemplified in scientific communities and democratic polities. Indeed, an example used by Sabel (1994, 269) and by Lindblom (1990, 266) is the Popper-Lakatos-Feyerabend concept of science driven by open discussion and the competition of theories underpinned by a rough agreement about the standards of argument and evidence in each domain of inquiry.[25] And, finally, the old notion of government by discussion is for Sabel a "deliberative constitutionalism [which] takes continuing differences of opinion as constitutive of a process of self-(re)definition, not an obstacle to it" (Sabel 1994, 269).[26]

Dewey and other American pragmatists following him saw social interchange as an active and constitutive process wherein people constructed cooperative solutions and simultaneously transformed themselves in the process. We have seen Hirschman's notion of disequilibria-induced social learning, the Japanese notion of just-in-time methods and continuous improvements, the Popper-Lakatos-Feyerabend notion of science, and the venerable notion of democratic government by discussion all as examples of these self-directed social learning processes.

Learning by monitoring is . . . an institutional device for turning, amidst the flux of economic life, the pragmatic trick of simultaneously defining a collective-action problem and a collective actor with a natural interest in addressing it. The disequilibria created by learning by monitoring are informatively effective for the same reasons as scientific experiments and democratic rule; and under these conditions the differences between the disciplines of the factory and laboratory dwindle in the face of the similarities. (Sabel 1994, 272)

Parallel Experimentation as a Basic Scheme
for Learning under Uncertainty

From a number of the Hirschmanesque thinkers being surveyed (e.g., Jacobs, Schön, Everett Rogers, and Sabel), it would seem that one basic idea about social learning has emerged—fostering parallel experimentation, comparison of results, and cross-learning between experiments to ratchet up the performance of the whole group. The parallel experimentation scheme could be seen as a proactive version of Hirschman's "search for possible *hidden rationalities* [which] was to give an underlying unity to my work" (1984a, 91).

In fact, the parallel experimentation scheme may be the way in which natural evolution itself operates. Any evolutionary change process has two basic moments: (1) variation (exploration or branching) to expand the range of possibilities and (2) selection (exploitation or pruning) to narrow down the range of possibilities (e.g., selection by survival of the fittest). These two moments occur in any optimization process (such as optimizing "fitness"). If we think of optimizing as maximizing altitude on a rugged multipeaked landscape (e.g., a "fitness landscape"), then the two moments are selection or exploitation in the sense of climbing up a given hill and variation or exploration in the sense of jumping to other hills.

Darwin's theory of evolution was actually only a theory about one of the moments, the theory of natural selection. There was no Darwinian theory of variation, and the role of variation remains a point of controversy in evolutionary theory to this day. We know that variation can be introduced by mutation, sexual reproduction ("crossover"), and genetic drift. In a multipeaked fitness landscape, a large interbreeding population might get stuck at a local peak; the variation might be too swamped by the selective pressure of a large population that it could not go downhill and cross the fitness valley to a higher peak on the other side.

It is interesting that one of the principal refinements of evolutionary theory in biology fits the framework of finding variation through parallel experimentation. Since Darwin extrapolated the notion of selection from the artificial selection done by animal breeders, it might be useful to see how breeders treat this problem of variation. Artificial breeders divide their herds into small, but not too small, subherds that, in effect, make separate parallel experiments and where the usual random variation will have more effect due to the smaller size of the herd. When there is a clearly successful innovation in a subherd, then those genes are transmitted to the other subherds (cross-learning) to ratchet up the desired characteristics of the whole herd.

One of the founders of modern population genetics, Sewall Wright (1931, 1986), carried over this idea from the practice of artificial selection to arrive at his "shifting balance theory" of natural evolution.[27]

> Judging from animal breeding, [Wright] thought that natural populations must be subdivided into small-enough partially isolated subgroups to cause random drifting of genes but large-enough subgroups to keep random drifting from leading directly to fixation of genes, for this was the road to degeneration and extinction. Mass selection within subgroups was followed by selective diffusion from subgroups with successful genetic combinations. The final step was the transformation of all subgroups by the immigration of organisms with a superior genotype and subsequent crossbreeding. (Provine 1986, 236)

The analogy between this evolutionary scheme and parallel experimentation to generate and share good ideas is not lost on biologists. Richard Dawkins illustrates evolution with a computerized model of spiders evolving with fitness determined by the fly-catching properties of their various webs. The spiders are divided into three subpopulations "evolving in parallel."

> These were thought of as evolving independently in three different geographical areas. But—here's the point—not *completely* independently. There is a trickle of genes, meaning that an individual occasionally migrates, from one local population to another. The way I put it was that these migrant genes were a kind of injection of fresh "ideas" from

another population: "almost as though a successful sub-population sends out genes that 'suggest' to a less successful population a better way to solve the problem of building a web." (Dawkins 1996, 136)

The smallness of the subpopulations plays a role in promoting greater variety in the experiments. In the biological case, the random genetic drift in a small inbred population may cause the loss of an adaptation characteristic of the current fitness hill of the overall population.

> But the impoverished genetic legacy of random drift could prove to be a bonus. Being unable to take the sub-population back to where the parent population had been, natural selection would be forced into other options. Selection could set the population on a new path that would eventually lead to an even higher peak of adaptedness. (Cronin 1991, 285)

The idea that semi-isolation from the fitness pressures in a larger population in order to pass through a valley of reduced fitness and then climb a higher peak elsewhere is the same root idea expressed by Burton Klein in his dynamic analysis of technology development decisions in contrast to the conventional "economizing" decisions to maximize the use of existing resources.

> He . . . advocates looseness in goal-setting and gradual, oblique, or multiple approaches to the goal. . . . In addition, he argues that it is rather secondary interest to the developer to achieve an efficient combination of inputs. His main interest is achieving a breakthrough to a new product or to radically improved performance characteristics. (Hirschman and Lindblom 1971, 69)

By having only a secondary interest in (semi-isolation from) the static hill-climbing pressure for an "efficient combination of inputs," the development effort might cross a valley to a higher peak on the other side (i.e., find "radically improved performance characteristics").

With this evidence, I would conjecture that the basic parallel experimentation idea, that is,

- different experiments running concurrently with some common goal (rather than focusing resources on what currently seems like the best option),

- with some semi-isolation from the pressure of immediate success,
- with benchmarking comparisons made between the experiments, and
- with the "migration" of discoveries between experiments wherever possible to ratchet up the performance of the whole population,

is a fundamental scheme for learning and change in the presence of real uncertainty.

The basic idea of parallel experimentation applied to social learning is that when a central agency does not know the answer (almost always the case in questions of development), then its best strategy is to sponsor a program of parallel decentralized experiments with discussion, benchmarking, and horizontal learning between the experimenters—all of which will tend to ratchet up the performance of the whole group.

Recently, Charles Sabel and Sanjay Reddy have proposed just such a mechanism of parallel experimentation for social learning for development.

> From these general considerations it is possible to sketch the kernel of a two-level economic-development framework that encourages constraint-relaxing learning—offered only as an example. At the "top" a benchmarking committee of the relevant government entities and qualified private actors, collaborates with potential users to establish the initial substantive and procedural criteria for participation, and defines the initial metrics by which applications are to be ranked. At the "bottom" project groups—whose members can be public or private entities or partnerships of both—compete to present projects that score highly under the emergent criteria. . . . After each round the selection criteria, benchmarks and institutional arrangements are adjusted to reflect improved measures of performance and a richer understanding of success. There is thus public or state learning as well as publicly available learning by private agents. Because the implicit theory of economic development—expressed in the selection criteria—is revised in the light of the means chosen to pursue them—the pooled experience of actual projects—we can call these arrangement[s] experimentalist. (Sabel and Reddy 2003, 10)

Start with a persistent social problem in a developing or transitional country (e.g., how to conduct bankruptcies and industrial restructuring, how to promote small private firms in a corrupt environment, how to fight endemic corruption, how to provide public services, and so forth). The agency (e.g., some appropriately local development agency) proposes a competition (e.g., between national regions, states, cities, etc.) for the best approach to addressing the problem. To qualify, entrants must make public the "theory" or ideas behind their approach. Moreover, they must agree to be judged by certain public benchmarking criteria (which they might themselves propose).

Based on the proposals, some of which could describe already existing programs, the agency will select a certain number of winners and will provide material assistance in some form (e.g., a block grant). The assistance will always require a substantial matching contribution (which could be a prior investment) from the entrants to ensure that they want to solve the problem and are not just in it to get the assistance. In any case, the aid provided by the agency is the least important part of the parallel experimentation scheme. The more the aid, the more a central agency will be emboldened to start dictating "answers," so the aid should be unobtrusively small so as not to interfere with the primary motivation of the public hunt for solutions to address a pressing problem.

The others in the contest will learn the winning theories as to how the problem can be addressed, and they may choose to adapt their own mode of operation. After a certain time period, the results are assessed according to the previously agreed upon benchmarks to see who the real winners were. There may be a second round of assistance where aid will go to those who did well in the first round (whether they previously received assistance or not). The point is to encourage horizontal or cross-learning between those who did well and those who didn't. Project funds may also be used to sponsor visits or secondments so that the laggards can learn directly from the emerging success stories. The public benchmarking establishes a rolling standard that will ratchet up as social learning improves performance (continuous improvement). Matters of local pride and prestige will play a role.

The public benchmarking between parallel experiments and ratcheting up of standards of performance are the heart of a real-time notion of parallel evaluation that stands in sharp contrast to the traditional notion of evaluation. Conventionally, the experts decide on the One Best Way that was supposed to be implemented. Then after a number of years, an evaluation is performed to learn from the results. Leaving aside all the enormous problems in the objectivity of evaluations and the resistance of bureaucracies to learning (due to the implication of prior error), the idea is that experts will take the "learnings" to heart to give still better redesigned recommendations the next time. But under conditions of uncertainty and acknowledged ignorance (not knowing the One Best Way), the best approach seems to be parallel experimentation and the real-time evaluation of benchmarking and communication of ideas between the experiments.

Sponsoring schemes of parallel experimentation is an important social learning methodology by which development agencies can, in an autonomy-respecting way, help doers who undertake the experiments to address common pressing problems.

10

Conclusions

Concluding the Example of the World Bank

Can the World Bank Change?

In this concluding chapter, I conclude the example of the World Bank and provide some reasonable summary and conclusion to the alternative philosophy of development assistance based on autonomy-respecting help.

Communism, as it actually existed, was not an alternative to a modern industrial society but a proposed alternative route to industrialization (see Griffin 1989). The route to industrialization provided by the West in the post–World War II period was "development" as engineered by all the assistance and aid agencies of the last half century. Each side in this developmental cold war offered the Third World its blueprints for accelerating history and making a jump over the chasm to modernity.

The communist path ignominiously failed. My reluctant conclusion is that the West's development institutions are also a failed dream, albeit in a less obvious manner. Where there has been development, it has been more as a do-it-yourself project (e.g., in East Asia), not by following the best-practice nostrums of the agencies. Development cannot be externally social engineered by either the communist or the West's blueprints.

After a half century on the path of official development assistance, we find ourselves lost, "wandering in a dark wood." Development will not yield to social engineering no matter how much aid is provided. A fundamentally different philosophy of development assistance is needed than that implemented—regardless of the rhetoric—by the World Bank and the other major development agencies.

Can the Bank change? Is it a matter of more enlightened leadership or is it a matter of structurally determined outcomes regardless of the leadership? My conclusion is that it is not a problem of leadership. James Wolfensohn is as "enlightened" a president as the Bank has ever had—or is likely to have in the future. The problems are structural, not managerial.

Structural Problem 1: Monopolistic Power

If in fact development were the sort of thing that could be engineered, then there would be a good case to have a very powerful global development agency. But we have surveyed the theories of various types of assistance—helper-doer relationships—across the fields of human endeavor, and we have found rather consistent results. Wherever the desired outcomes require sustainable changes in the actions and beliefs of the doers—unlike the "vaccination of children" model of assistance—then the engineering approach subtly fails to achieve thoroughgoing and long-lasting results.[1] The externally sourced pressures of the direct engineering approach can only create the external show of results that provides a type of short-term pseudo-verification for the aid bureaucracies. Genuine internal change in the doers requires internally sourced motivation and active learning by the doers—all of which requires a fundamentally different approach on the part of the helpers.

One problem lies in the imperatives of the organizations themselves. Individuals in large or small aid organizations need "to move money" and "to show results" for their bosses, sponsors, or donors. Hence the would-be helpers will try to take over, control, and own the interaction with the doers in order to deliver the desired results. The more powerful the helping organization, the more damaging is this organizational drive. It is not a matter of learning to behave differently since any "new strategies" or heroic individual efforts will soon be overwhelmed by the imperatives of organizational power. Smaller assistance organizations such as NGOs are subject to much the same dynamics but may cause less damage due to less power differential with the doers.

On the whole, the conundrum of actually helping people help themselves is so basic and subtle that trying to get a large development agency to operate on that basis is akin to trying to get an elephant to dance or a gorilla to knit a sweater. Regardless of the rhetoric and the genuine good intentions, it is not going to happen.

The alternative approach is based on respect for the own motivation and own powers of learning of the doers. Autonomy-respecting assistance essentially inverts the power dynamics between helper and doer. The more powerful and well-heeled is the helper, the less likely is the assistance to respect the autonomy of the doers. While I will catalogue a number of reasons why the World Bank cannot really implement autonomy-respecting assistance, let there be no doubt about the fundamental problem—the power of the Bank over its clients. Many of the other temptations and corruptions (e.g., the Bank-as-church imprimatur on Official Views) follow from the power differential.

The World Bank is now an economists' bank, not a civil engineers' bank. One might think that all the economists in positions of power in the Bank would recall their catechisms about the problems of monopoly. But it would seem that they are more attracted to the notion of "global" than they are repelled by the notion of "monopoly." All the rhetoric about a *global agency* having a *global role* to gather *global knowledge* to solve *global problems* seems to be so much *globaloney* to justify the monopolistic worldwide role of the World Bank.

Structural Problem 2: Affiliation with U.S. Policies and Interests

All this would be true of the World Bank if it were located in a neutral city like Geneva or, if one can imagine it, in the developing world (e.g., in Africa). But in fact, the World Bank and the IMF are located a few blocks from the White House in Washington, DC. Most of the communist countries during the cold war period, like North Korea or Cuba today, were not members of the Bretton Woods institutions, so the International Bank for Reconstruction and Development and the International Monetary Fund were not "international" in the sense of the United Nations. Instead they were part of the "West," led by the United States.

Today after the collapse of the Communist bloc, the United States has emerged as a relatively unchallenged global power, and the Bank and IMF have kept their roles as team players headquartered a few blocks from the White House. By arrangement, the president of the

Bank is always an American national selected by the U.S. president, while the Fund has always been led by a European.[2] Both institutions are thoroughly imbued with an American perspective as expressed in the "Washington consensus" (e.g., Stiglitz 2002) and in the cheerleading for increased American hegemony under the label *globalization*. Thus on many issues, the U.S. government does not need to exercise direct control. But on the major issues of the day, the Bank and Fund twist and turn according to the twists and turns of American foreign policy.[3]

A few years ago, pressures were building up from the Left (worldwide protests) and from the Right (the administration of President George W. Bush) to change the Bank, but all that changed after the events of September 11, 2001. After this date, the Bank eagerly played the role of shoring up the U.S. antiterror coalition by discovering new pockets of poverty so that more money could be moved to such star performers as Uzbekistan and Pakistan. And the Bank has dutifully played the camp-follower role in following U.S. armed forces into Afghanistan and Iraq (in the latter case, even without the United Nations) to further embellish its track record in social engineering and nation building. Protests against the Bank and Fund have continued but at a more subdued level after September 11. It would seem that the protests against the Bank in the past were based as much on its perceived role as an instrument of U.S. hegemony as on its performance as a development agency. In any case, our task to try to evaluate the Bank as a development assistance agency is much complicated by its close de facto identification with U.S. political and economic interests.

There are three other structural problems in the Bank aside from the number one problem of its monopolistic power differential over its less-developed clients and its number two problem of the de facto affiliation with the United States.

Structural Problem 3: Money Is Not the Key to Development Assistance

The third problem is that the Bank is a bank. The idea that money is key to development goes back to the original idea of the Bank as financing civil engineering projects, a role now largely taken over by the private sector. When the Bank then turned to policy-based lending and institutional development projects, it of course did not cease to function as a bank. While capital may indeed have been the missing ingredient necessary to build a dam or power station, it is by no means clear that money can buy real changes in policies or can build institutions. Indeed, I have argued that the availability of large amounts of money to developing countries overrides their other motivations and redirects their attention to playing whatever game is necessary to get the money. Money is the magnet that sets all compasses wrong; it is the root of much unhelpful help. Decades of experience in Africa and elsewhere have made it crystal clear that money is not the key missing ingredient in institutional development (as it might be in building an airport). The implicit assumption that a development agency should function as a money-moving machine has little to support it and much evidence against it.

Structural Problem 4: Working through Governments That Are Part of the Problem

The fourth structural problem is that in the Bank's helper-doer relationships, the doer is the government of the developing country. Needless to say, the governments of developing countries are made up more of the rich than the poor and more of the powerful than the powerless.[4] Yet the mission of the Bank is to enrich the impoverished and to empower the disempowered. Putting the mission together with the modus vivendi yields the unlikely strategy of working through the rich and powerful to help the poor and disempowered people of a country. But making any fundamental changes in the economic, political, and social relationships could not be further from the intentions of the rich and powerful elites in these countries.[5] Since these elites are more a part of the problem than a part of the solution, it should be no surprise that this strategy has shown meager results.[6] And the current calls to pour still more aid money through the usual channels do not address the problem. Loan monies to the governmental elites will be used mostly for their own benefit with at best some trickle down to the poor—feed enough oats to the horse and some will pass through to the road for the sparrows.

Structural Problem 5: Trying to Control Bad Clients Rather Than Exit Relationship

The fifth structural problem is the organization of the Bank as helper in its helper-doer relationship. The Bank is essentially a financial cooperative of its member countries, the developed "part 1" countries that participate mightily in Bank governance but do not borrow and the developing "part 2" countries that can borrow from the Bank. The problem with the borrowers being members is the way the voice-exit dynamics play out. A commercial bank does not have to make loans to any specific potential clients; it has no fixed set of "members." While a commercial bank may try to work with a potential client to improve its borrowing capacity, there are limits on that relationship. When the potential borrower shows little inclination to reform or restructuring, then the commercial bank can exit the relationship.

But the World Bank is locked into a relationship with the worst borrowing countries in the world. As these countries are in the most need of help, the Bank is constantly torn between the desire to help the poorest of the poor countries and to walk away from the oppressive and kleptocratic governments of those countries. While the Bank can in some cases reduce its involvement to a legal minimum, it cannot just walk away like a commercial bank. Hence the exit-voice dynamic works in the other direction of the Bank, trying to exercise more voice in the country—in effect trying to run the country in a state of tutelage (probably in conjunction with the IMF). If the experience in sub-Sahara Africa is any guide, the Bank's tutelage is not very effective. In many of the poorest countries, the lack of state capacity along with the AIDS crisis and the "no exit" condition on the Bank have transformed the Bank's aid program from social engineering for development toward the model of long-term charitable relief (the second form of unhelpful help). Indeed, if I was to make a "cynical prediction" about the future trajectory of the Bank, then the prediction is that the Bank will be both pushed and pulled to become a hospital for the "basket cases" of development assistance (e.g., "low-income countries under stress" or postconflict countries). Then the Bank will slowly switch from the first form of unhelpful help (social engineering) to the second form of unhelpful help (long-term charitable relief). But I have an alternative proposal.

A Modest Proposal for the World Bank:
Decentralization with Extreme Prejudice

My main goal has been to argue for an alternative philosophy of development assistance—the indirect approach of autonomy-respecting assistance. The World Bank, as the premier development agency, has been the principal case study. For reasons of the power differential and the other structural problems cited in the preceding, it does not seem that the World Bank could be retooled or restructured as a global agency to implement autonomy-respecting development assistance.

Agencies such as the World Bank and the IMF are now almost entirely motivated by big power politics and their own internal organizational imperatives. Much of their energies are consumed in doing whatever is necessary to perpetuate their global status. Intellectual and political energies spent trying "to reform" these agencies are largely a waste of time and a misdirection of energies. Dominant global institutions, like monopolies or dominant oligopolies in the private sector, can be counted on to use the power to maintain their dominance—and yet that dominance or monopolistic power is the number one problem.

I have no magical master plan to solve the problem. But in the spirit of "the king is naked" observations, it does not seem to me that one needs eight-thousand-plus elite development workers headquartered two blocks from the White House to provide the sort of genuine development assistance that is so badly needed. Perhaps this was not obvious fifty years ago, but it is obvious now.

Autonomy-respecting help can only come from agencies much closer to the ground where there is relatively little power differential between the helper and doer. This rules out the very idea of a powerful world development agency, but it leaves some hope at the city, state, national, or, perhaps, regional level (e.g., an "Asian IMF" in addition to other regional development agencies). Today, with the wonders of telephones, jet travel, videoconferencing, and the Internet, networks of more local agencies and institutions can do as good or even a much better job of international communication and coordination than a unified global agency—and can at the same time avoid the inevitable temptations of their own power and the inevitable pressure to be instruments of global hegemony.

The idea is to move from a global agency to global networks of local agencies where the latter includes not only governmental agencies but foundations, think tanks, university institutes, and the whole range of NGOs (see Fisher 1997). Applied to the World Bank, this strategy might be called "decentralization with extreme prejudice." For example, one way to start to seriously regionalize, if not localize, development assistance would be to redirect the repayment of Bank loans to regional development banks and agencies to be thereafter recycled in the regions and then to redeploy the people from the Bank who actually want to help those regions to those regional/local agencies.

But restructuring the current helper-doer relationship also requires major changes on the doers' side. The development assistance "industry" has succeeded in the last fifty years in creating a huge "moral hazard" problem in developing countries. Development aid has become not a way to help people solve their own problems but a way for governments to alleviate symptoms and to postpone problems to beyond their political horizon. Developmental problem solving requires a long confrontation with a problematic situation, but that encounter is often cut short by arrival of well-intended aid and magical "solutions" to postpone the confrontation to the future.[7] By undercutting the difficult process of people learning to help themselves, such help is ultimately unhelpful.

The overall change must shift the balance of initiative, responsibility, and ownership from the helpers to the doers. Rhetoric aside, the major development agencies will be the last ones to actually inaugurate such a basic change in strategy for the structural reasons already cited. Changes must start in the political processes of the developing countries to vigorously oppose further indebtedness or aid addiction under the current system of development finance. For their own good, the doers must undertake the daunting process of weaning themselves away from the financial and other "help" of the major agencies starting with the Bretton Woods institutions, the World Bank, and the IMF.[8] Only then can the doers begin to take charge of their own affairs and begin to help themselves.

With strong signals coming from the demand side of the assistance relationship, pressures will mount on the supply side for something like the decentralization-with-extreme-prejudice strategy to transform the powerful global agencies into global networks of local agencies that can provide autonomy-respecting assistance.

Concluding Remarks

Our main effort has been to delve into the intellectual and theoretical roots of a development philosophy based on the idea of helping people help themselves. The applications are much broader than development assistance; indeed the general ideas of "helping theory" apply to all helping relationships that attempt to affirm the potential autonomy of the doers. Interdisciplinary triangulation was used to elucidate the main ideas.

It is time to draw together the implications of the alternative philosophy described here for development assistance. The first but not last step is to follow the Hippocratic maxim of "Do no harm." After criticizing the conventional pedagogy of drilling answers into students' heads, John Dewey complained that many people then concluded that the alternative was for teachers to do nothing and let children play on their own. We have a similar problem after the critique of unhelpful help in conventional development assistance. Indeed, the first step toward a new strategy is a "radical reduction in development assistance" (Dichter 2003, 286) so as to do less harm and so that the locus of initiative can shift from the would-be helpers to the doers of development. After decades of addiction to getting (and giving) aid, this "radical reduction" is no simple matter for the doers or the helpers (e.g., the decentralization-with-extreme-prejudice strategy).

But there are ways in which development assistance can be genuinely helpful if done in an entirely different way. The alternative path of indirect autonomy-respecting help is a subtle and humble path that cannot be reduced to a checklist to be mechanically implemented. Some rough principles of the alternative path have been spelt out throughout the book in the five themes (the two Don'ts and the three Dos), each of which has a volitional and cognitive side (as stated in table 4 and summarized in table 7).[9]

There is nothing magic about these five themes; they serve largely to help organize thought and to organize the quotations from the eight thinkers in the appendix. There could be fewer themes (e.g., by combining the first and second Dos), or there could be more (e.g., by adding the sixth theme of the helper observing the limits of autonomy-respecting help by withdrawing or exiting when the helper is starting to control the doer or when the doer is incorrigibly corrupt). Our expository strategy has been to provide as many threads of Ariadne as possible so that, whatever the starting points, the readers can construct their own paths by finding and following some threads leading into the rich corpus of thinking about autonomy-respecting help in the different disciplines.

In development assistance, providing money and providing answers should not be the leading edge. Indeed, externally supplied money and answers are the volitional and cognitive instruments of heteronomy.

To start where the doers are and to see the world through their eyes requires a significant investment of time on the part of the helpers. In this case the helper could be a single community organizer, animator, or field educator.[10] For example, Muhammad Yunus immersed himself in the villages near his University of Chittagong and started lending his own money before arriving at the methods that were to become Grameen Bank.[11] Savings-based microcredit, pioneered by Grameen Bank, is a good example of the type and scale of help that is autonomy respecting. Since it enables people to do what they were trying to do anyway, it avoids the first form of unhelpful help, and since it is based on savings rather than external gifts of loanable funds, it also avoids the second form of unhelpful help. That case and other similar ones are drawn from an anthology of eighteen "instructive experiences in rural development" that illustrate autonomy-respecting methods (Krishna et al. 1997).[12]

When money can be provided, the amounts must be small enough relative to the doer's contribution (e.g., through matching grants or second-stage funding) so that the doer has to embark on the project for own motives and not just to get the aid. The Inter-American Founda-

TABLE 7. Summary of Volitional and Cognitive Version of Themes

General theme in helper-doer relation	Volitional Side	Cognitive Side
First do: Helper starting from doer's position	Help in actions that start from the doer's present situation in the world	Help that starts with the learner's present knowledge, not from a tabula rasa
Second do: Helper seeing through doer's eyes	Help with actions guided by doer's own perceptions of the world	Help with learning that starts with how the learner sees the world (e.g., helper "giving reason" to learner)
First don't: Distortionary assistance	Conditional aid to induce a certain action by doer	Giving biased information and one-sided arguments to induce a certain belief by learner
Second don't: Giving results to doer as a gift	Doing action for the "doer" so results are a gift	Giving the answers to the "learner" so beliefs are at best borrowed opinions, not knowledge
Third do: Autonomous activity of doers	Own-motivated action resulting in owned product of one's autonomous action	Self-directed learning resulting in owned knowledge (able to give reasons, arguments, and evidence)

tion was a good example of a money-moving agency with the self-limiting discipline so this could be done well (e.g., Breslin 1987; Glade and Reilly 1994). In 1983, the Inter-American Foundation supported Albert Hirschman for a tour of grassroots efforts in Latin America. The examples and accompanying analysis were published as *Getting Ahead Collectively* (Hirschman 1984b).

Of our eight thinkers, the others, aside from Hirschman, who worked on development assistance or community organizing are Paulo Freire, Fritz Schumacher, and Saul Alinsky. Other people who have worked in their tradition are Raff Carmen and Miguel Sobrado (2000) on Clodomir Santos de Morais's Organization Workshops, Myles Horton (Horton 1998) on the Highlander Folk School, and John Kretzmann and John McKnight (1993) on urban community organizing. Further examples of people who have worked on and described various aspects of what I have called "autonomy-respecting development assistance" are Denis Goulet (1971), Leopold Kohr (1973), Johan Galtung and colleagues (1980), Robert Chambers (1983), Koenraad Verhagen (1987), Anisur Rahman (1993), Allan Kaplan (1996), Raff Carmen (1996), Judith Tendler (1997), Deborah Eade (1997), Norman Uphoff, Martin Esman, and Anirudh Krishna (1998), and Jan Knippers Black (1999). The list could go on and on.

I have also paid special attention to the cognitive side of development assistance. Here again, the conclusions have pushed toward global networks of local agencies rather than powerful global agencies. Power corrupts, and we have accordingly seen how the most powerful agencies such as the World Bank and IMF cannot stop themselves from trying to play the role of the teacher who has the Official Answers. This in turn undercuts the freedom of inquiry of their own research staff that is the foundation of intellectual integrity. But for most development knowledge, the devil is in the details of local adaptation and tacit practicality, matters that cannot be solved by getting enough PhDs under the same roof in Washington, DC. It is not powerful global agencies that can be helpful but global networks of more local agencies. The key knowledge-based development assistance roles are

- helping to build local learning capacity in government and in local think tanks, institutes, and universities,
- brokering peer-to-peer learning between those who are trying to do something and those who have done it, and

- sponsoring schemes of parallel experimentation for decentralized social learning.

My purpose has been to lay an interdisciplinary intellectual foundation for this alternative tradition of development assistance. The ideas are not new. They are found across the disciplines of human endeavor and across the centuries. The root problem is the helping self-help conundrum that is fundamental to the fields of education, management, psychology, and all the other disciplines centered on some helper-doer relationship such as our topic of development assistance. In all these fields, virtually the same debate has raged over the years (or centuries) between the direct approach based on power and authority to improve the behavior of the doers and the indirect approach based on methods aiming to respect and enhance the autonomy of the doers.

From this broader perspective, those who labor to find alternative indirect and autonomy-respecting methods of development assistance are far from being alone. It is a grand tradition from Socrates in antiquity down through Kant to the eight thinkers we take as modern representatives. In Kantian terms, the root norm of respecting the autonomy of others is expressed as the principle to always treat others as ends in themselves, never simply as means—a principle that decides against the direct approach and in favor of the indirect approach. In Amartya Sen's terms, this is the constitutive role of development as freedom (or autonomy in our terms, see Sen 1999 and Alkire 2002), but we have emphasized along with Sen that it also plays an instrumental role. Development assistance based on direct methods ultimately fails instrumentally since it focuses on short-term changes in outward behavior. It constantly becomes undone and has to be done over again. Autonomy-respecting indirect methods seemingly take longer and are more subtle, but change based on the own motives and active learning of the doers is what is sustainable in the longer term.

Thus there are two intertwined arguments for autonomy-respecting assistance. One is normative or "constitutive," and it would hold even if people were, against much evidence, sufficiently docile and plastic so that social engineering could be "successful." The second argument is the instrumental one that, assuming people are in essence active, creative, and free, it is autonomy-respecting assistance that facilitates deep-lying and sustainable change.

The debate will go on, but it should be carefully noted that the development establishment does not disagree with the norm of helping people help themselves. The counterarguments are twofold. The first argument is that the major agencies already are helping people help themselves; indeed, that concept is routinely identified with any form of "help." Hence much of our analysis and case study has focused on explaining the prevalence of unhelpful help. The second argument is that helping people help themselves is fine, but it is a council of perfection in a world where many countries are falling to pieces. Hence the major agencies such as the World Bank may opt to reinvent themselves as global welfare agencies and call urgently for even greater sums to feed through their channels.

In other words, failure at the first form of unhelpful help (social engineering) may lead to a shift to long-term charitable relief, the second form of unhelpful help, with autonomy-respecting help put on a pedestal as an impractical ideal. But, to unpack the argument, the point is that autonomy-respecting assistance is indeed an impractical and well-nigh impossible ideal for the thundering dinosaurs of today's development establishment. That's not how it is done. The organizational prerequisite is to move from powerful global agencies to global networks of local agencies. The counterargument is that such less powerful and more local agencies cannot do what the powerful global agencies can "do"—an argument that contains much truth, albeit ironically, and that is part of our point.

Genuine development assistance requires quite different indirect methods posited on respect for the autonomy of the doers. And it is part of the wisdom of the indirect approach to know its limits. Helpers cannot and should not try "to do development." Helpers can at best use indirect, enabling, and autonomy-respecting methods to bring doers to the threshold. The doers have to do the rest on their own in order to make it their own. The doers will acquire development only as the fruits of their own labor.

Appendix

Eight Thinkers on the Five Themes

First Do: Starting from Where the Doers Are

This appendix simply pulls together quotations from eight thinkers on the five themes so that one can directly see the parallels in autonomy-respecting assistance across a range of helper-doer relationships (some quotations are repeated from the text). For each thinker, the helper-doers appear in a different role:

- development advisor-government for Albert Hirschman,
- development agency-developing country for E. F. Schumacher,
- organizer-community for Saul Alinsky,
- educator-community for Paulo Freire,
- teacher-learners for John Dewey,
- manager-workers for Douglas McGregor,
- therapist-clients for Carl Rogers, and
- spiritual teacher-learners for Søren Kierkegaard.

Albert Hirschman on the First Do

I began to look for elements and processes . . . that *did* work, perhaps in roundabout and unappreciated fashion. . . . [T]his search for possible *hidden rationalities* was to give an underlying unity to my work. . . . [T]he hidden rationalities I was after were precisely and principally *processes of growth and change already under way* in the societies I studied, processes that were often unnoticed by the actors immediately involved, as well as by foreign experts and advisors. (Hirschman 1984a, 91–93)

E. F. Schumacher on the First Do

It is quite wrong to assume that poor people are generally unwilling to change; but the proposed change must stand in some organic relationship to what they are doing already, and they are rightly suspicious of, and resistant to, radical changes proposed by town-based and office-bound innovators. (Schumacher 1973, 200)

Saul Alinsky on the First Do

As an organizer I start from where the world is, as it is, not as I would like it to be. That we accept the world as it is does not in any sense weaken our desire to change it into what we believe it should be—it is necessary to begin where the world is if we are going to change it to what we think it should be. That means working in the system. (Alinsky 1971, xix)

Paulo Freire on the First Do

In contrast with the antidialogical and non-communicative "deposits" of the banking method of education, the program content of the problem-posing method—dialogical par excellence—is constituted and organized by the students' view of the world, where their own generative themes are found. (Freire 1970, 101)

John Dewey on the First Do

Is it the pupil's own problem, or is it the teacher's or textbook's problem, made a problem for the pupil only because he cannot get the required mark or be promoted or win the teacher's approval, unless he deals with it? . . . Is the experience a personal thing of such a nature as inherently to stimulate and direct observation of the connections involved, and to lead to inference and its testing? Or is it imposed from without, and is the pupil's problem simply to meet the external requirement? (Dewey 1916, 155)

Douglas McGregor on the First Do

It is one of the favorite pastimes of headquarters groups to decide from within their professional ivory tower what help the field organization needs and to design and develop programs for meeting these "needs." . . . If the staff is genuinely concerned with providing professional help to all levels of management it will devote a great deal of time to exploring "client" needs directly. (McGregor 1960, 168–69)

Carl Rogers on the First Do

I have not found psychotherapy or group experience effective when I have tried to create in another individual something that is not already there; I have found, however, that if I can provide the conditions that allow growth to occur, then this positive directional tendency brings constructive results. (Rogers 1980, 120)

Søren Kierkegaard on the First Do

That if real success is to attend the effort to bring a man to a definite position, one must first of all take pains to find HIM where he is and begin there. That is the secret of the art of helping others. Anyone who has not mastered this is himself deluded when he proposes to help others. (Kierkegaard in Bretall 1946, 333)

Second Do: Seeing through the Doers' Eyes

Albert Hirschman on the Second Do

But word soon came from World Bank headquarters that I was principally expected to take . . . the initiative in formulating some ambitious economic development plan that would spell out investments, domestic savings, growth, and foreign aid targets for the Colombian economy over the next few years. . . .

My instinct was to try to understand better *their* patterns of action, rather than assume from the outset that they could only be "developed" by importing a set of techniques they knew nothing about. (Hirschman 1984a, 90–91)

E. F. Schumacher on the Second Do

If the people cannot adapt themselves to the methods, then the methods must be adapted to the people. This is the whole crux of the matter. (Schumacher 1973, 192)

Saul Alinsky on the Second Do

An organizer can communicate only within the areas of experience of his audience; otherwise there is no communication. . . .

Through his imagination he is constantly moving in on the happenings of others, identifying with them and extracting their happenings into his own mental digestive system and thereby accumulating more experience. It is essential for communication that he know of their experiences. (Alinsky 1971, 69–70)

Paulo Freire on the Second Do

I repeat: the investigation of thematics involves the investigation of the people's thinking—thinking which occurs only in and among men together seeking out reality. I cannot think *for others* or *without others*, nor can others think *for me*. (Freire 1970, 100)

John Dewey on the Second Do

When the parent or teacher has provided the conditions which stimulate thinking and has taken a sympathetic attitude toward the activities of the learner by entering into a common or conjoint experience, all has been done which a second party can do to instigate learning. . . . In such shared activity, the teacher is a learner, and the learner is, without knowing it, a teacher—and upon the whole, the less consciousness there is, on either side, of either giving or receiving instruction, the better. (Dewey 1916, 160)

Douglas McGregor on the Second Do

Perhaps the most critical point—and the one hardest to keep clearly in mind—is that help is always defined by the recipient. Taking an action with respect to someone because "it is best for him," or because "it is for the good of the organization," may be influencing him, but it is not providing help *unless he so perceives it*. (McGregor 1960, 163)

Carl Rogers on the Second Do

This formulation would state that it is the counselor's function to assume, in so far as he is able, the internal frame of reference of the client, to perceive the world as the client sees it, to perceive the client himself as he is seen by himself, to lay aside all perceptions from the external frame of reference while doing so, and to communicate something of this empathic understanding to the client. (Rogers 1951, 29)

Søren Kierkegaard on the Second Do

Instruction begins when you, the teacher, learn from the learner, put yourself in his place so that you may understand what he understands and in the way he understands it, in case you have not understood it before. (Kierkegaard in Bretall 1946, 335)

First Don't: Don't Try to Impose Change on Doers

Albert Hirschman on the First Don't

I reacted against the visiting-economist syndrome; that is, against the habit of issuing peremptory advice and prescription by calling on universally valid economic principles and remedies—be they old or brand new—after a strictly minimal acquaintance with the "patient." . . . I tried to identify progressive economic and political forces that deserved recognition and help. This position put me at odds with those who judged that the present society was "rotten through and through" and that nothing would ever change unless everything was changed at once. But this utopian dream of the "visiting revolutionary" seemed to me of a piece with the balanced growth and integrated development schemes of the visiting economist. (Hirschman 1984a, 93–94)

E. F. Schumacher on the First Don't

[If] the rural people of the developing countries are helped to help themselves, I have no doubt that a genuine development will ensue. . . . [But it] cannot be "produced" by skillful grafting operations carried out by foreign technicians or an indigenous elite that has lost contact with the ordinary people. (Schumacher 1973, 204)

Saul Alinsky on the First Don't

If you respect the dignity of the individual you are working with, then his desires, not yours; his values, not yours; his ways of working and fighting, not yours; his choice of leadership, not yours; his programs, not yours, are important and must be followed; except if his programs violate the high values of a free and open society. (Alinsky 1971, 122)

Paulo Freire on the First Don't

Unfortunately, those who espouse the cause of liberation are themselves surrounded and influenced by the climate which generates the banking concept, and often do not perceive its true significance or its dehumanizing power. (Freire 1970, 66)

John Dewey on the First Don't

We are even likely to take the influence of superior force for control, forgetting that while we may lead a horse to water we cannot make him drink; and that while we can shut a man up in a penitentiary we cannot make him penitent. . . . When we confuse a physical with an educative result, we always lose the chance of enlisting the person's own participating disposition in getting the result desired, and thereby of developing within him an intrinsic and persisting direction in the right way. (Dewey 1916, 26–27)

Douglas McGregor on the First Don't

[The manager's] task is to help [workers] discover objectives consistent both with organizational requirements and with their own personal goals, and to do so in ways which will encourage genuine commitment to these objectives. . . . He will not help them if he attempts to keep direction and control in his own hands; he will only hamper their growth and encourage them to develop countermeasures against him. (McGregor 1960, 152)

Carl Rogers on the First Don't

The scientist with the divided sea urchin egg . . . could not cause the cell to develop in one way or another, but when he focused his skill on providing the conditions that permitted the cell to survive and grow, the tendency for growth and the direction of growth were evident, and came from within the organism. I cannot think of a better analogy for therapy or the group experience, where, if I can supply a psychological amniotic fluid, forward movement of a constructive sort will occur. (Rogers 1980, 120–21)

We cannot teach another person directly; we can only facilitate his learning.
. . . "You can lead a horse to water but you can't make him drink."
(Rogers 1951, 389)

Søren Kierkegaard on the First Don't

A direct attack only strengthens a person in his illusion, and at the same time embitters him. There is nothing that requires such gentle handling as an illusion, if one wishes to dispel it. If anything prompts the prospective captive to set his will in opposition, all is lost. (Kierkegaard in Bretall 1946, 332)

Second Don't: Don't Give Help as Benevolence

Albert Hirschman on the Second Don't

[T]hey will be supplied with a great many ideas, suggestions, plans, and ideologies, frequently of foreign origin or based on foreign experience. . . . Genuine learning about the problem will sometimes be prevented not only by the local policy-makers' eagerness to jump to a ready-made solution but also by the insistent offer of help and advice on the part of powerful outsiders. . . . [S]uch practices [will] tend to cut short that "long confrontation between man and a situation" (Camus) so fruitful for the achievement of genuine progress in problem-solving. (Hirschman 1973, 239–40)

E. F. Schumacher on the Second Don't

A gift of material goods can be appropriated by the recipient without effort or sacrifice; it therefore rarely becomes "his own" and is all too frequently and easily treated as a windfall. (Schumacher 1973, 197)

Saul Alinsky on the Second Don't

Self-respect arises only out of people who play an active role in solving their own crises and who are not helpless, passive, puppet-like recipients of private or public services. To give people help, while denying them a significant part in the action, contributes nothing to the development of the individual. In the deepest sense it is not giving but taking—taking their dignity. Denial of the opportunity for participation is the denial of human dignity and democracy. It will not work. (Alinsky 1971, 123)

Paulo Freire on the Second Don't

[O]ppressors use the banking concept of education in conjunction with a paternalistic social action apparatus, within which the oppressed receive the euphemistic title of "welfare recipients." They are treated as individual cases, as marginal men who deviate from the general configuration of a "good, organized, and just" society. (Freire 1970, 60)

John Dewey on the Second Don't

To "make others happy" except through liberating their powers and engaging them in activities that enlarge the meaning of life is to harm them and to indulge ourselves under cover of exercising a special virtue. . . . To foster conditions that widen the horizon of others and give them command of their own powers, so that they can find their own happiness in their own fashion, is the way of "social" action. Otherwise the prayer of a freeman would be to be left alone, and to be delivered, above all, from "reformers" and "kind" people. (Dewey 1957, 270)

Douglas McGregor on the Second Don't

Management has . . . successfully striven to give more equitable and more generous treatment to its employees. . . . [B]ut it has done all these things without changing its fundamental theory of management. (McGregor 1960, 45–46)

Carl Rogers on the Second Don't

A further element that establishes a climate for self-initiated, experiential learning is empathic understanding. . . . This kind of understanding is sharply different from the usual evaluative understanding, which follows the pattern of, "I understand what is wrong with you." (Rogers 1980, 272)

Søren Kierkegaard on the Second Don't

But all true effort to help begins with self-humiliation: the helper must first humble himself under him he would help, and therewith must understand that to help does not mean to be a sovereign but to be a servant, that to help does not mean to be ambitious but to be patient, that to help means to endure for the time being the imputation that one is in the wrong and does not understand what the other understands. (Kierkegaard in Bretall 1946, 334)

Third Do: Respect Autonomy of the Doers

Albert Hirschman on the Third Do

In recent years, the concept of *dependencia*—perhaps best translated as lack of autonomy—has been intensively studied in Latin America. . . . With the brightest members of [Brazil's] younger generation almost all going abroad for graduate studies, they assume upon returning (if they return at all) that, having sat at the feet of true knowledge in the university of some advanced country, they no longer need to bother with what their elder compatriots have to offer as a result of experience and mature reflection. . . . I was struck and disturbed by the prevalence, in Latin America, of a style of policy-making and problem-solving that ostensibly denied the existence or even possibility of a cumulative learning process. . . . It is possible that this style . . . arises once again out of the lack of internal communication characteristic of countries that . . . continue to rely in policy-making on economic and social ideas imported from abroad. It is not an accident that the style is often abetted by the foreign expert who is one of its principal beneficiaries. (Hirschman 1973, v–vi)

E. F. Schumacher on the Third Do

The alternative to coercion cannot be found when spiritual realities are dismissed as being of no account or treated as merely subservient to economic aims. It cannot be found when the people are considered as objects to be driven, cajoled, or manipulated. Perhaps the best—perhaps even the only—effective slogan for aid is: "Find out what the people are trying to do and help them to do it better." (Schumacher 1961, 421)

Saul Alinsky on the Third Do

After all, the real democratic program is a democratically minded people—a healthy, active, participating, interested, self-confident people who, through their participation and interest, become informed, educated, and above all develop faith in themselves, their fellow men, and the future. The people themselves are the future. The people themselves will solve each problem that will arise out of a changing world. They will if they, the people, have the opportunity and power to make and enforce the decision instead of seeing that power vested in just a few. (Alinsky 1969, 55)

Paulo Freire on the Third Do

Authentic liberation—the process of humanization—is not another deposit to be made in men. Liberation is a praxis: the action and reflection of men upon their world in order to transform it. Those truly committed to the cause of liberation can accept neither the mechanistic concept of consciousness as an empty vessel to be filled, nor the use of banking methods of domination (propaganda, slogans—deposits) in the name of liberation. (Freire 1970, 66)

John Dewey on the Third Do

The essentials of the method are therefore identical with the essentials of reflection. They are first that the pupil have a genuine situation of experience—that there be a continuous activity in which he is interested for its own sake; secondly, that a genuine problem develop within this situation as a stimulus to thought; third, that he possess the information and make the observations needed to deal with it; fourth, that suggested solutions occur to him which he shall be responsible for developing in an orderly way; fifth, that he have opportunity and occasion to test his ideas by application, to make their meaning clear and to discover for himself their validity. (Dewey 1916, 163)

Douglas McGregor on the Third Do

The important theoretical consideration, derived from Theory Y, is that the acceptance of responsibility (for self-direction and self-control) is correlated with commitment to objectives. (McGregor 1960, 68)

Carl Rogers on the Third Do

Individuals have within themselves vast resources for self-understanding and for altering their self-concepts, basic attitudes, and self-directed behavior; these resources can be tapped if a definable climate of facilitative psychological attitudes can be provided. . . .

These conditions apply whether we are speaking of the relationship between therapist and client, parent and child, leader and group, teacher and student, or administrator and staff. (Rogers 1980, 115)

Søren Kierkegaard on the Third Do

For my own Error is something I can discover only by myself, since it is only when I discover it that it is discovered, even if the whole world knew of it before. (Kierkegaard in Bretall 1946, 158)

Notes

1. One of the bad habits I picked up in the World Bank was referring to it simply as the Bank. Similarly, the International Monetary Fund, or IMF, is referred to as the Fund.

2. As in the case of the Soviet Union, much insight can be gained into the Bank by listening to the jokes. In this case, the joke was: "What's the difference between Stiglitz and God?" Answer: "God is everywhere—including Washington."

3. The joke is that after Joe's last trip before his resignation, Joe was as usual called to Jim's office. Jim said: "Joe, you missed the last management meeting!"—to which Joe replied: "Jim, I certainly would have made it if I knew it was the Last Management Meeting."

4. One joke about the Joe and Jim show went as follows. Joe arrived to find the Bank divided into operations types (represented by Jim)—who built "cathedrals in the desert"—and research types (to be represented by Joe)—who built "castles in the air." As the protests mounted, the external affairs (PR) department decided to take a page out of Jimmy Carter's book and do a video of Joe and Jim building a house together to show the Bank doing good work. Jim supervised, and Joe was given a hammer and a box of nicely laid out nails. As the cameras rolled, Joe took out a nail and hammered it in and then took out the next nail and threw it away. After seeing this repeated several times, Jim intervened to ask why Joe was throwing away every other nail. Joe pointed out that if Jim had read any of Joe's papers, then he would know that everything comes in two classes—and that those were the nails with the heads on the wrong end. Jim said: "Aha, now we see the superiority of the Bank's operations people. We know there is nothing wrong with those nails; they are just for the opposite side of the house." The video was never released.

5. For Joe's farewell party, his staff put together a top ten list of reasons

why he resigned. The top reason was "He had just seen one too many 'hot Summers' in Washington."

6. I contributed to five out of the nine speeches selected for the volume *Joseph Stiglitz and the World Bank: The Rebel Within* (Chang 2001), representing Stiglitz's years in the Bank.

7. When Joe got the Nobel prize, his ex-staff put together another top ten list of reasons why Joe got the Nobel prize in economics, and the top reason was "Because there is no Nobel Prize in Organizational Management."

8. Joe had renewed my three-year fixed-term contract while he was chief economist; I was never a regular "tenured" Bank staff member.

9. Many of the original memos are posted on my website www.ellerman.org under the heading "Notes, Memos, and other Rants from the World Bank."

10. The partnership with Gheorge Efros in Moldova was particularly fruitful (see Ellerman and Kreacic 2002).

11. The managers who rise through the ranks (particularly vice presidents) often were in the Young Professionals (YPs) program. The YPs form an elite corps in the Bank that can only be likened to the Janissaries in the Ottoman Empire (see Coser's 1974 study of the Janissaries and of other "Patterns of Undivided Commitment"). They were "kidnapped" out of (graduate) school and then raised up in the "sultan's palace" so they had the total allegiance necessary to be the "elite managers" in the "empire," and so they literally knew of no other way of doing things.

CHAPTER 1

1. See www.worldbank.org and Oxfam 1985, 14.

2. Truman 1956, 227. Quoted in Dichter 2003, 286.

3. In the preface to their book, Dewey and Tufts identify which author wrote which chapter. All the quotes from Dewey and Tufts are from the chapters by Dewey.

4. Note the rephrasing that changes the people from being passive recipients of teaching to being active learners with some facilitation or help from others.

5. The latest are the Millennium Development Goals, or MDGs. See the World Bank's site: www.worldbank.org. The suggestions for changing development assistance to reach the MDGs run the whole gamut from more money to still more money.

6. See Easterly 2001 and Dichter 2003 generally and Van de Walle 2001 specifically on Africa.

7. The "business" of development assistance is to be distinguished from

humanitarian disaster relief. The latter always has a valid claim but should nevertheless be administered in ways that do not undercut development (e.g., it should be limited in time and should maximally involve the victims of disasters in the reconstruction of their lives).

8. Doing includes thinking; "doer" is not juxtaposed to "thinker." Instead, the "doers of development" (Wolfensohn 1999b) actively undertaking tasks are juxtaposed to the passive recipients of aid, teaching, or technical assistance. See Holt 1976 for an example of the "doer" terminology in the helper-doer relationship.

9. While our focus is not on *personal* self-help, some of the self-help literature has a similar perspective; see Deci 1995 for a treatment similar in spirit to this book and see Combs et al. 1971 or Egan 1990 for excellent overviews and bibliographies.

10. The phrase is from Uphoff, Esman, and Krishna 1998.

11. The phrase is from McClelland 1970.

12. The Bourbaki series of books in mathematics has the practice of marking a particularly difficult or tricky point with the S-shaped symbol from a dangerous bend road sign printed in the margin of the book.

13. For the parallel point in the management literature, see Ackoff 1977, 1986, or 1994 on the distinction between growth and development. It is less a matter of what one has than what one can do—given the material means to do it. Since one cannot transfer the capability to do something as one can transfer wealth, we see immediately the fallacy in many notions of development assistance (e.g., as the *transfer* of resources and knowledge). See Kohr 1973 on "development without aid."

14. Many helpers seem to use an implicit model of something like "vaccinating children" as the paradigm of development assistance. It is not important whether the vaccination is done autonomously or not—but that it is done. Or if the model is that of an expert doctor intervening to perform an operation, then the patient may be (or might as well be) unconscious. The important thing is "to get it done," and then people will supposedly be better off. And the helpers will have the moral satisfaction of having "made people better off." A cruder metaphor would be herding cattle or sheep through a narrow chute so they have to jump into a dip vat. The parasites (e.g., ticks) are killed just as well if the animals go willingly or have to be forced.

15. Albert Memmi found essentially the same two forms of an unhelpful helper-doer relationship. In the social engineering case, the helper is the dominator or colonizer, while the doer is the subjugated one or the colonized (Memmi 1967). In the case of "oppressive benevolence" (to use John Dewey's phrase), the helper is the provider, and the doer is the dependent (Memmi 1984).

16. And all who have visited the main building in Washington, DC, will

recognize the magnificent atrium as the secular equivalent of St. Peter's Cathedral in the Vatican.

17. See part two of Hayek 1979 for an intellectual history of the secular religion of social engineering that predates the modern form of social engineering based on the content and prestige of economics.

18. I say "in theory" since it is only the money that moves that generates income for the IFIs, so the interpretation of "sufficient progress" in satisfying the conditionalities is quite elastic in practice. This in turn allows would-be reformers who do not see beyond the conventional direct approach to say: "There is nothing wrong with the approach; we just need to be really tough in enforcing the conditionalities"—as if it were a question of getting the contractors to more closely follow the specifications in an engineering project. In cruder terms, it is as if the cattle or sheep were getting out of the narrow chute leading to the dipping vat—in which case the solution is to strengthen the chute to better channel their behavior.

19. Over the years there has been a huge literature analyzing the World Bank by critics and by reformers suggesting how the elephant might learn to dance (e.g., Caufield 1996; Griesgraber and Gunter 1996; World Bank 1998a; Easterly 2001; and Pincus and Winters 2002).

20. There is a corresponding cognitive point about the unteachability of significant truths: "A novel or a work of history in the humanistic sense does not and cannot directly teach truth or wisdom. It offers us a process, a series of events in our minds, which will tend to bring a responsive individual nearer to his own truth and his own wisdom by recognition or anticipation of his own experience" (Shattuck 1988, 144).

21. Kierkegaard uses a variation on the metaphor. The Socratic helper is like the driver of horses who can "help them by applying the lash" (Bretall 1946, 157) but cannot pull the load.

22. Jean-Jacques Rousseau points out that the problem starts in child rearing to "disentangle the secret intention which dictates the gesture or the scream" ([1762] 1979, 66).

23. In an analogy with statistics, a type 2 error would be accepting a false-motive project whereas a type 1 error would be rejecting a true-motive project.

24. See "Problems Encountered in Buying Virtue through Aid" in Hirschman and Bird 1971, 205–7.

25. "Large amounts of aid delivered over long periods, create incentives for governments and donors that have the potential to undermine good governance and the quality of state institutions" (Bräutigam 2000, 1).

26. *Moral hazard* here refers to the opportunistic commissions or omissions by the doers because of an arrangement that protects them from the full consequences.

27. Not surprisingly, the debate about moral hazard and dependency in

international development assistance has strong parallels with the domestic debates about welfare reform (e.g., see Murray 1984 or Ellwood 1988 on the "helping conundrums"). The philosophical analysis goes back at least to Rousseau's analysis in books one and two of *Emile* of the potential change in causality in children crying: "The first tears of children are prayers. If one is not careful, they soon become orders. Children begin by getting themselves assisted; they end by getting themselves served" ([1762] 1979, 66).

28. John Stuart Mill supported help "always provided that the assistance is not such as to dispense with self-help, by substituting itself for the person's own labour, skill, and prudence, but is limited to affording him a better hope of attaining success by those legitimate means. This accordingly is a test to which all plans of philanthropy and benevolence should be brought (Mill [1848] 1970, book 5, chap. 11, §13). Note the similarity to the opening quotation from John Dewey.

29. See, for example, the approach to community development in Kretzmann and McKnight 1993.

30. Among development economists, the late Peter Bauer (1976, 1981, and 2000) developed these arguments about aid with particular force.

31. One sees the evidence every day in calls by leaders of the development industry to address this or that development problem with $X billions more funds—rather than undertaking the difficult and subtle reforms for a more effective approach where money has at most only a background role.

32. The original Say's Law in economics is usually paraphrased "Supply creates its own demand."

33. "All ironic observing is a matter of continually paying attention to the 'how,' whereas the honorable gentleman with whom the ironist has the honor of dealing pays attention only to the 'what'" (Kierkegaard 1992, 614). In our case, the "gentleman" is the conventional helper who focuses on getting the doers to do the right "what."

34. Immanuel Kant emphasizes the use of practical reason and critical reason giving rise, respectively, to autonomous will and autonomous reason. As Marx notes, there is both "describing the world" and "changing the world." In biology, organisms have sensory (afferent) and motor (efferent) systems.

35. See, for example, the Comprehensive Development Framework (CDF) outlined in Wolfensohn 1997, 1998, 1999a, and 1999b and in Stiglitz 1998.

36. The self-help theme is ancient, particularly the idea that "the gods help those who help themselves," which is found in Aesop, Aeschylus, Sophocles, and Euripides (see Bartlett 1968). And the Koran attests that "Verily never will God change the condition of a people until they change it themselves, with their own souls."

37. The principle that people should appropriate the (positive as well as

negative) fruits of their labor (or expressed as the juridical principle that legal responsibility should be assigned according to de facto responsibility) has been developed at some length in Ellerman 1992 and 1995 (and in earlier journal articles cited therein such as Ellerman 1985 or, within a Kantian—"treating people as persons rather than things"—framework, Ellerman 1988b or chap. 4 in Ellerman 1995).

38. Sen's *Development as Freedom* (1999) gives a comprehensive review of this approach, and Alkire 2002 gives a more recent treatment. See Sen 1982 and 1984 for earlier work.

39. See Roe 1998 on using triangulation to approach complex policy issues.

CHAPTER 2

1. This is at least one meaning of Jean-Paul Sartre's quip in *No Exit:* "Hell is other people."

2. For surveys and applications, see Pratt and Zeckhauser 1991, Eatwell et al. 1989, or Campbell 1995. For earlier critical analysis of agency theory, see Perrow 1972, Hirsch, Michaels, and Friedman 1987, Pfeffer 1994, and the references contained in Eisenhardt 1989. For our purposes, *agency theory* refers to the broad attempt to design contracts and organizations to use economic motives to mold people's behavior.

3. In the legal relationship, the agent takes on a legal role to act in the interests of the principal, but economists now use the terminology in a broader context where the agent is not necessarily under any legal obligation to act in the interests of the principal.

4. Apologies to J. L. Austin (1970, 252), who made a similar point about oversimplification and philosophers.

5. See Piore for the contrast, "Quality versus cost: the high road and the low road" (1995, 78), and see Simmons and Mares 1983 for a description of some transformations to high-performance quality-oriented companies.

6. For instance, many corporate reformers, buttressed by the intellectual prestige of economics and particularly agency theory, try to address the separation of ownership and control in publicly traded companies by putting managerial stock options in the motivational foreground. Then they seem to be surprised when managerial professionalism is eclipsed and, instead of building more companies of lasting value, there is a flood of accounting tricks, stock option games, and share price manipulations.

7. The notion of a nondistortionary intervention is related to the end-independence of rules of just conduct as emphasized by Rousseau, Hume, Kant, and particularly Friedrich Hayek (e.g., Hayek 1978, 77). In a similar

vein, Michael Polanyi uses the metaphor of providing "fuel and oil for a machine, the operation of which is not controlled by the [provider]" (1951, 41).

8. This type of independence between intervention and motivation is essentially due to the fact that the slope of a mathematical function is independent of its constant term. Moving a graph vertically does not change the slope associated with any horizontal coordinate. In more general mathematical terms, suppose the decision problem is to maximize an objective function subject to some constraints. An intervention would then be nondistortionary if it relaxed some constraints ("enabling") but did not affect the first-order marginal conditions for optimization (not "controlling"). Thus an ND intervention could enable one to do what one already wanted to do.

9. See Harrold 1995 and Jones 2000 for a related "sectorwide" approach.

10. To enable doer autonomy, the desired independence applies to cognitions as well as volitions. Information and knowledge provided as a form of assistance should be unbiased (i.e., showing all sides to a question), and aid should not be tied to assent to specific opinions. In proposing an earlier related plan, Hirschman and Richard Bird note that "elaborate arrangements should be made to divorce the exchange of opinions about suitable economic policies from the actual aid-giving process" (1971, 211).

11. Thomas Schelling (1992) suggests a broader application of this model to climate change and other multilateral allocation issues.

12. Rousseau points out the classic example in the raising of children—"in making the child keep quiet today one is encouraging him to cry more tomorrow" ([1762] 1979, 69).

13. Charles Murray traces this failure to "The Law of Unintended Rewards. Any social transfer increases the net value of being in the condition that prompted the transfer" (1984, 212). "Persons who are in the unwanted condition *completely involuntarily* are not affected by the existence of the reward. . . . But the number of such pure examples is very small. . . . The program that seeks to change behavior must offer an inducement that unavoidably either adds to the attraction of, or reduces the penalties of engaging in, the behavior in question" (Murray 1984, 213–15).

14. For instance, Francis Fukuyama notes that there "is little doubt that welfare benefits create what economists call 'moral hazard' and discourage work" (1999, 71) and cites Moffitt 1992. "When you give people money, food, or housing, you reduce the pressure on them to work and care for themselves. No one seriously disputes this proposition" (Ellwood 1988, 19).

15. Aid is not the only source of this problem. The term *Dutch disease* originally referred to the purely economic phenomenon where the discovery and sale of new natural resources caused a country's currency to appreciate to the detriment of the country's manufactured exports. But the term might also

describe the generalized moral hazard phenomenon in which natural resources may blunt the incentives and impede the rallying of forces necessary for genuine development efforts (Russia and Nigeria are apt contemporary examples of resource-rich "rent economies," whereas Japan, Korea, Israel, and Singapore are resource-poor)—not to mention the effects of resource riches on bringing into the motivational foreground the pecuniary motivations that breed corruption.

16. While libertarians (or classical European-style liberals) may understand well the perversity of unhelpful help (Hirschman 1991 surveys the older literature on perversity; see Murray 1984, 1988, or 1997 for a recent libertarian example), the problems are not resolved by the approach of world-weary cynicism and no aid (just as the original problem of moral hazard due to overinsurance is not best solved by having no insurance). The cold turkey approach of no help may have a bracing remedial effect after a long addiction to unhelpful help, but our task is to find forms of help that enable self-reliance and autonomy rather than just assume that such capabilities will be forthcoming in the absence of help.

17. "At present much of the foreign aid is a welfare gesture rather than a development measure. It tends to postpone, if not outright prevent, the emergence of a social dynamic that can enable these [African] countries to move towards greater self-reliance" (Hyden 1983, 180).

18. The idea is captured by a statement by a campesino organizer about the Inter-American Foundation, "'The Foundation is not the push that gets you going, but the push that keeps you going'" (Breslin 1987, 114). I first heard the "moving train" metaphor from my World Bank colleague Peter Miovic.

19. The most notorious example of this was the World Bank's two-volume (over 1,200-page) *Sourcebook for Poverty Reduction Strategies* providing suggestions about what a country might come up with in its very own "poverty reduction strategy" (World Bank 2002). Thus the autonomy-respecting "country in the driver's seat" plank in the Bank's well-intended Comprehensive Development Framework tended to be overridden by the inherent social engineering tendencies of a large and very powerful agency (Wolfensohn 1999a). There is an old joke, "When the Revolution comes, you will get peaches and cream—and you will like them." The updated version is "When you follow this checklist to develop 'your' poverty reduction strategy, you will come up with the 'right' policies—and you will 'own' them."

20. Apropos illusion, see Caufield 1996 for the earlier World Bank history as the "Masters of Illusion."

21. In the original model of moral hazard in insurance, the insured party might also try "to game" the co-payments and deductibles requirements by having multiple insurance policies. The insurance companies or legal authorities would reply with exclusivity requirements. In quite an analogous manner,

aid recipients might try to seek multiple funding for a project (e.g., cover one donor's matching requirement with a grant from another donor), and the donors would reply with donor coordination efforts.

22. See Deci and Ryan 1985; Elster 1983; Lane 1991, 2000; Candy 1991; Kohn 1993; and Deming 1994.

23. See, for example, Ruskin (1862) 1985. Lutz 1999 discusses J. C. L. Simonde de Sismondi, Thomas Carlyle, and John Ruskin.

24. See Titmuss 1970, Arrow 1972, Scitovsky 1976, Hirsch 1976, Sen 1982, Schelling 1984, Akerlof 1984, Hirschman 1992 (where intrinsically motivated activities are called *noninstrumental activities,* e.g., p. 148), Kreps 1997, and Prendergast 1999.

25. Many analyses of aid problems (e.g., Ostrom et al. 2001) do not make the explicit distinction between internal and external motivation, but then it quietly enters the analysis in the clothing of "ownership" questions. Being motivated to do something with ownership is closely related to having internal motivation to do it.

26. See Maslow 1968 and 1998 for this type of hierarchy of needs model.

27. Unconditional aid can be used for any end, so the locus of that decision remains with the doer. Cognitively, having the doer hear arguments on all sides of a question leaves the locus of deciding which argument to accept with the doer.

28. A crude macroexample would be the West's introduction of opium into old China so that the West would then have a lever for external intervention. Getting Native Americans hooked on "firewater" (whiskey) played a similar role. Managers waving money or other strong incentives in the face of subordinates plays a similar role in trying to establish an external locus of causality—and agency theory is the theory of such interventions. Critics of the international finance institutions argue that the IFIs use easy loans in a similar way to establish a lever for autonomy-incompatible external interventions such as structural adjustment programs. Once the country is deeply indebted, then the social engineers have the levers to get it "to do the right thing"—as if "doing the right thing" were simply a matter of "what" and not "how."

29. See Deci and Ryan 1985 for the notion of locus of causality. They differentiate it from the notion of locus of control (see Lefcourt 1976) by interpreting the latter as dealing with the outcomes rather than sources of action. Nevertheless, one may find the notion of "locus of control" often used to indicate the source of actions. We use the notions of having an internal locus of causality, self-determination, and autonomy as being synonymous for our purposes.

30. See Hirschman 1977.

31. "It is no more [the merchant's or manufacturer's] function to get profit

for himself out of that provision than it is a clergyman's function to get his stipend. This stipend is a due and necessary adjunct, but not the object of his life, if he be a true clergyman, any more than his fee (or honorarium) is the object of life to a true physician" (Ruskin [1862] 1985, 178). Note the foreground-background distinction where the clergyman's stipend is a "due and necessary adjunct" (i.e., in the background), "not the object of his life."

32. A classic example where economics has ignored crucial questions of motives for behaviors is the economic treatment of cooperation and trust based on repeated prisoner's dilemma games (Axelrod 1984 is the *locus classicus*). When a prisoner's dilemma game is repeated, the credible threat of being punished by the other party's defecting tomorrow may elicit cooperative behavior today. But this sort of cooperative behavior is quite different from cooperation and trust motivated by some fellow feeling for the other parties or some identification with the broader group that includes the other parties. Institutional design based on threat-induced cooperation would be rather different from design based on fellow feeling or identification where the penalties attached to noncooperation were not eliminated but played a secondary role as motivational backstops. This criticism of the repeated games treatment of cooperation was first pointed out to me by Ronald Dore (see Dore and Whittaker 1994).

33. "Yet although reverence is a feeling, it is not a feeling *received* through outside influence, but one *self-produced* by a rational concept, and therefore specifically distinct from feelings . . . which can be reduced to inclination or fear" (Kant [1785] 1964, 69).

34. See Elster 1983, chapter 2, "States That Are Essentially By-Products," and also Lane 2000, 265, 276.

35. "Here is the radical fallacy of those who urge that people must use promises and threats in order to encourage opinions, thoughts, and feelings which they think good, and to prevent others which they think bad. Promises and threats can influence acts. Opinions and thoughts on morals, politics, and the rest, after they have once grown in a man's mind, can no more be influenced by promises and threats than can my knowledge that snow is white or that ice is cold" (Morley 1928, 203).

36. Kierkegaard uses similar stories of putting a cap on a certain type of elf (1989, 12, 468) or putting special armor on the god Mars to see how they looked (1992, 174), but in each case the act made them invisible. Elster points out similar notions in Gregory Bateson's double-bind theory (1972) and in the work of Watzlawick 1976 and Farber 1976.

37. These insightful phrases, originating with Ezra Taft Benson, have been popularized and expanded upon by Stephen Covey (1990).

38. For example, suppose one buys a townhouse in the middle of winter and is looking forward to spring to spruce up the poorly attended front yard.

But the Townhouse Association Beautification Committee (a.k.a. Lawn Nazis) arrives before spring to inform the new owners that they must attend to the yard or face certain penalties. Instead of just thinking, "Now we have two reasons to spruce up the lawn," the new owners might well resent the attempt to externalize their motivation.

39. Even a dog is supposed to know the difference between being stumbled over and being kicked.

40. See Frey 1997.

41. "The first [effect] is the expected deterrent effect: the fear of getting caught and the severity of sanctions motivate taxpayers to comply with the law. However, the retroactive, confrontational, and coercive aspects of a deterrence approach to law enforcement also have an indirect, negative effect by alienating taxpayers and lowering their willingness to comply voluntarily with the law" (Kinsey 1992, 259).

42. In like manner, an antipoverty agency with elite salaries, perquisites, and prestige cannot just assume that its members are motivated primarily by a dedication to the poor. The idea that top salaries must be paid to attract "the best people" (or at least the best "hirelings") to an organization dedicated to the pursuit of intrinsic motives betrays a misunderstanding both of such organizations and human motivation, a misunderstanding that seems to be widespread.

43. This tendency for the helper to increasing takeover responsibility and control over the doer is investigated later as the "Tendler effect."

44. See Tendler 1997 for a description of public workplace reforms in a developing country based on building internal motivation and using the insights of the workplace transformation movement represented here primarily through the pioneering work of McGregor. See also Murray 1988 and Uphoff 1994.

45. "Property systems are in general not completely self-enforcing. They depend for their definition upon a constellation of legal procedures, both civil and criminal. The course of the law itself cannot be regarded as subject to the price system. The judges and police may indeed be paid, but the system itself would disappear if on each occasion they were to sell their services and decisions. Thus the definition of property rights based on the price system depends precisely on the lack of universality of private property and of the price system. . . . The price system is not, and perhaps in some basic sense cannot be, universal" (Arrow 1972, 357).

46. In the promiscuous atmosphere of ancient Rome, when noblemen went off with their escorts or concubines, they might leave guards to watch over their wives. The Roman satirist Juvenal (circa 60–130) needled them by remarking, "But who is to guard the guards themselves? Your wife arranges accordingly and begins with them" (Juvenal, *Satire VI*, 347).

CHAPTER 3

1. There are other metaphors that could be used as ladders to be climbed and then thrown away. Medawar (1960) contrasts a jukebox (with the musical records taken as internal) with a record player (with the records taken as external). The jukebox has a set of preexisting options, one of which is selected by the simple pushing of a button, whereas when a record player plays music, the set of external instructions must be supplied in the form of a record. Another metaphor is that one goes to a department store to select a pair of pants from among a preexisting set of options, whereas one instructs a tailor to make a suitable pair of pants.

2. Jerne also notes the connection with a modern version of the innate ideas scheme in Noam Chomsky's theory of generative grammar (1960), and thus Jerne's Nobel lecture is entitled "The Generative Grammar of the Immune System" (Jerne 1993). When a child learns a language, the child "learns" far more than was ever received in linguistic data. Chomsky's account is that the received data select how the innate linguistic capacity will unfold, perhaps not unlike the way that Medawar describes the development of the embryo: "Embryonic development . . . must therefore be an unfolding of preexisting capabilities, an acting-out of genetically encoded instructions; the inductive stimulus is the agent that selects or activates one set of instructions rather than another" (1982, 295).

3. McGregor 1948, reprinted in 1966, 152.

4. Peter Drucker (1954) developed essentially the same Theory Y ideas in his management by objectives (MBO) (also called "management by objectives and self-control") approach as opposed to "management by control" (as noted in McGregor 1966, 15–16, and in Drucker 1973). But the MBO theory was so popularized (indeed, vulgarized) by Drucker and others apparently in order to reach a mass market that it is commonly interpreted to mean "management by results" in a manner quite along the lines of Theory X and agency theory. Hence we rely more on McGregor's treatment of these ideas.

5. These five chronological steps are not to be confused with our five themes (the two Don'ts and the three Dos)—although some steps and themes are essentially the same.

6. In the same spirit, George Bernard Shaw quips, "if you teach a man anything he will never learn it" (1961, 11), in the sense that if you force a boy to eat broccoli, then he will probably not want to eat it on his own later on.

7. Everett Rogers's seven roles for a change agent (1983, 315–17) have some similarity to McGregor's five steps. McGregor's last step is also Rogers's last role. "The end goal for a change agent is to develop self-renewing behavior on the part of the client system. The change agent should seek to put him or herself out of business by developing the clients' ability to be their own

change agents. In other words, the change agent must seek to shift the clients from a position of reliance on the change agent to self-reliance" (Rogers 1983, 316–17). See Eugster 1966 for an excellent case study of the "field educator" as a change agent operating in an autonomy-respecting manner.

8. One common metaphor is the two-sided "letting go" problem of the grown teenager leaving the parents' nest. The teenager needs self-confidence to release the parental hand, and the parents need trust (and the willingness to forsake dependency and control) to let go of the grown teenager's hand.

9. Charles Handy notes the parallels between management consulting and psychotherapy (represented in our Parthenon of eight thinkers by Douglas McGregor and Carl Rogers). "Internalization . . . means that the individual recipient of influence adopts the idea, the change in attitude or the new behaviour, as his own. Fine. He will act on it without pressure. The change will be self-maintaining to a high degree. . . . The successful psychotherapist is the one whose patients all believe they cured themselves—they internalized the therapy and it thereby became truly an integral part of them. Consultants suffer much the same dilemma of the psychotherapist—the problem of internalization. If they wish the client to use the right solution with full and lasting commitment then they must let him believe it is *his* solution" (1993, 145).

10. For the general role of self-fulfilling prophecies in social affairs, see Merton 1968, or Rosenthal and Jacobson 1968, or Rist 1970 with a focus on schooling. The work of the Santa Fe school (e.g., Arthur 1994) on self-reinforcing processes has emphasized the multiplicity of equilibria (e.g., Theory X and Theory Y).

11. Recall the earlier discussion about the "universal solvent" problems in basing institutional design solely on material motivation.

CHAPTER 4

1. Zen Buddhism is another example, but Taoism has temporal priority.

2. See Csikszentmihalyi 1990 for extensive examples of this "flow" phenomena.

3. Laszlo Versényi has an excellent treatment of the Socratic method (1963, 110–24). The cognitive version of the "activity = behavior + motive" scheme is "belief = proposition + grounds for belief." Just as an activity might have an external or internal motive, so a belief might be held for external reasons such as conformity to authority or conventional wisdom, or a belief might be rationally grounded in evidence and argumentation as described by Versényi. In the former case, Mill notes that "Truth, thus held, is but one superstition the more, accidentally clinging to the words which enunciate a truth" (Mill [1859] 1972, 103). "A man may be a heretic in the truth; and if he

believe things only because his pastor says so, or the Assembly so determines, without knowing other reason, though his belief be true, yet the very truth he holds becomes his heresy" (Milton [1644] 1957a, 739). This was a major theme in the work of Søren Kierkegaard—not the "what" of belief but the "how."

4. This too was ancient Eastern wisdom. "When you know a thing, to recognize that you know it, and when you do not know a thing, to recognize that you do not know it. That is knowledge" (Confucius, *Analects*, bk. 2, 17). "To know you don't know is best. Not to know you don't know is a flaw" (Lao-Tzu 1989, chap. 71).

5. In the questions of human affairs, there is little reason then or now for this "ignorance" or intellectual humility to be just ironic.

6. "The chief aspirations of a person are aspirations to freedom—I do not mean that freedom which is free will and which is a gift of nature in each of us, I mean that freedom which is spontaneity, expansion, or autonomy, and which we have to gain through constant effort and struggle" (Maritain 1943, 10–11). "All this boils down to the fact that the mind's natural activity on the part of the learner and the intellectual guidance on the part of the teacher are both dynamic factors in education, but that the principal agent in education, the primary dynamic factor or propelling force, is the internal vital principle in the one to be educated; the educator or teacher is only the secondary— though a genuinely effective—dynamic factor and a ministerial agent" (Maritain 1943, 31).

7. The theme that practicality was the road to engaging the interest and initiative of the students played a major role more recently in John Dewey's pragmatic philosophy of education. Interpreters of Dewey's pedagogy often think that his purpose was to urge "practical training" rather than to simply use practical problems as the source of student engagement so that the student's faculties of critical reason and social sympathy would be improved through active use.

8. For instance, the Cambridge Platonist Ralph Cudworth, writing in the late 1600s, notes that "knowledge was not to be poured into the soul like liquor, but rather to be invited and gently drawn forth from it; nor the mind so much to be filled therewith from without, like a vessel, as to be kindled and awakened" ([1731] 1996, 78). Cudworth also saw clearly the active nature of learning: "knowledge is an inward and active energy of the mind itself, and the displaying of its own innate vigour from within, whereby it doth conquer, master, and command its objects" ([1731] 1996, 73).

9. This can't-push-on-a-string asymmetry was reflected in our previous discussion of external and internal motivation. External motivation can override and crowd out own motivation to control behavior, but removing the former will not automatically supply the latter. One cannot externally bring

about internally motivated action just as opening a faucet cannot itself supply water pressure. The oft-repeated ("warhorse") metaphor for this insight is "While we may lead a horse to water we cannot make him drink" (Dewey 1916, 26).

10. The aid agencies who want to pour more aid into the usual methods "to overcome the barriers" resemble the archetypical American tourist who simply shouts louder at an uncomprehending foreigner. A different approach is needed. See the discussion in chapter 3 about how what is first seen as an instructionist process is later discovered to be a selectionist process.

11. "[The teacher] does not give knowledge. Knowledge cannot be *given*. If you ask me a question all I can do in my reply is to try to put into words a part of my experience. But you get only the words, not the experience. *To make meaning* out of my words, you must use your own experience. . . . But to the extent that you do share some of my experience, then by talking about my experience, by throwing a light on part of it, I may reveal to you something *in your experience* that you had not seen before, or help you to see it in a new way, to make, in David Hawkins's words, 'transitions and consolidations'" (Holt 1976, 85). The referenced passage by Hawkins is "The teacher offers the learner some kind of loan of himself or herself, some kind of auxiliary equipment which will enable the learner to make transitions and consolidations he could not otherwise have made. And if this equipment is of the kind to be itself internalized, the learner not only learns, but begins, in the process, to be his own teacher—and that is how the loan is repaid" (quoted in Holt 1976, 60; from Hawkins 1973 and reprinted in Hawkins 2000, 44). Polya's notion of "inside help" (1965, 137; quoted in chap. 1) is very similar.

12. Ortega y Gasset makes a similar point. "It is a magisterial forest; old, as teachers should be, serene and complex. In addition it practices the pedagogy of suggestion, the only delicate and profound pedagogy. He who wishes to teach us a truth should not tell it to us, but simply suggest it with a brief gesture, a gesture which starts an ideal trajectory in the air along which we glide until we find ourselves at the feet of the new truth" (1961, 67).

13. This Chicago tradition of community organizing was developed further by Saul Alinsky and more recently by John McKnight and his colleagues (see Kretzmann and McKnight 1993).

14. See also Hirschman's foreword to this book.

15. "Yes, but then one can in turn learn the 'how' . . . by rote and recite it" is almost a perfect description of the training programs and dissemination of "best practices" programs of the major development agencies.

16. This also relates to one interpretation of Socratic ignorance: "Plato . . . would be very firmly insistent that even if he did know the answers [to questions about beauty, courage, friendship, and so forth], if he told us them they wouldn't do us any good. I mean, it's in the nature of these questions that you

have to puzzle them out for yourself. An answer is worth nothing unless it has come through your own thinking" (Burnyeat 1987b, 17).

17. See the discussion of codified versus tacit knowledge in chapter 6.

18. Note that this is the volitional counterpart to the cognitive theme that the best way for a teacher "to teach" a truth is to put the learner in a situation to learn it by him- or herself.

19. This might be compared with Polanyi's description of end-independence in a spontaneous order: "The actions of such individuals are said to be free, for they are not determined by any *specific* command, whether of a superior or of a public authority; the compulsion to which they are subject is impersonal and general" (Polanyi 1951, 159). The idea goes back to Rousseau's theme that it is not coercion if the "necessity [is] in things, never in the caprice of men" ([1762] 1979, 91).

20. If conditionalities were not imposed and the doers still made the reforms (for their own reasons), then the response might be: "Why were Bank resources used to fund something they were going to do anyway? The Bank's scarce resources should be used for maximum effect." It is very hard to reconcile the mentalities of the direct and indirect approaches.

21. Kierkegaard, the master psychologist of the indirect method, makes the same point about the shy withdrawal of external pressure so that a change in belief will be genuine: "This is what is achieved by the indirect method which, loving and serving the truth, arranges everything dialectically for the prospective captive, and then shyly withdraws (for love is always shy), so as not to witness the admission which he makes to himself alone before God— that he has lived hitherto in an illusion" (Bretall 1946, 332). This withdrawing or exiting when an indirect approach threatens to revert to a direct approach is a particularly subtle aspect of the indirect approach.

22. In case the reader feels it is a stretch to present both Gandhi's nonviolent satyagraha strategy and Liddell Hart's analysis of the best military strategies (chap. 3) as indirect approaches, it should be noted that J. Nehru (1956, 457–58) quotes exactly the same passages from Liddell Hart when discussing Gandhi's strategies.

23. In view of the connection with Kierkegaard, we might say that this treatment of B-ing and non–B-ing is existentialism in a nutshell.

24. We focus on actions (volitional activities), but there is always an analogous argument about judgments (cognitive activities). A judgment or belief can be analyzed into the asserted proposition plus the grounds for the belief. An asserted belief based on considerations of ideology or organizational conformity would only be an inauthentic pseudojudgment (even if the asserted statement is true). For instance, when organizational pressure is explicitly or implicitly exerted on the researchers in a development agency "to play with the team" and "speak with one voice," then that tends to undercut the

authenticity and intellectual integrity of the research results produced by the agency—regardless of the truth or falsity of the results. It is for precisely these reasons that external observers will tend to give more credence to research results that run against organizational views than those results that corroborate the party line—in spite of the heartfelt protests of the researchers about their personal intellectual integrity. Chapter 7, on learning in development agencies, explores these themes.

25. See James Scott's description of the government's attempt "to scale up" bottom-up village development in Tanzania (1998).

26. A similar analysis applies to the inauthentic cooperation based on the threat of punishment in the next round of a repeated prisoner's dilemma game (see Dore and Whittaker 1994).

CHAPTER 5

1. See Arrow 1963 or Pauly 1980.

2. "The more workable and more popular commitments are precisely those that are highly visible, verifiable, measurable and, at their best, irreversible. One thinks of a revision of the customs tariff, of the imposition of credit restrictions in order to curb inflation, or, most typically perhaps, of a devaluation" (Hirschman and Bird 1971, 206). In Arturo Israel's ranking of reforms by specificity (1987), these are the reforms with high specificity.

3. This theme is well developed at length in De Soto 2000.

4. Success for a leader or, in general, a helper may be paradoxical in the sense that the helper creates the situation where the doers take success as *their* own accomplishment (see Black 1999 or Edmunson 1999 for a practical overview of such paradoxes). David McClelland notes the "ultimate paradox of social leadership and social power: to be an effective leader, one must turn all of his so-called followers into leaders" (1970, 40). This echoes the notion of the Taoist ruler who governs in such a way that when the task is accomplished, the people will say, "We have done it ourselves" (Lao-Tzu, chap. 17).

5. This assumes inter alia that the NGO has internal motivation to supply its own autonomy-respecting assistance to the ultimate doers. If, however, the NGO is driven largely by funding pressures, then lump-sum funding of its core budget will more likely sponsor and prolong the self-indulgence of the NGO leadership and staff (see Dichter 2003).

6. Wilhelm von Humboldt, the founder of the University of Berlin, wrote an essay in the 1790s outlining the limits of state action in view of the active learning theory—a theory later developed in his work in linguistics (1963, [1836] 1997). His remarks provide a general cautionary tale about the limitations of externally imposed change. "The cultivation of the understanding, as

of any of man's other faculties, is generally achieved by his own activity, his own ingenuity, or his own methods of using the discoveries of others. Now, State measures always imply more or less compulsion; and even where this is not directly the case, they accustom men to look for instruction, guidance, and assistance from without, rather than to rely upon their own expedients" (Humboldt [1854] 1969, 25).

7. Previous work on the direction of autonomous and self-reliant development includes Goulet 1971, Kohr 1973, Galtung et al. 1980, Gran 1983, Korten and Klauss 1984, Verhagen 1987, Rahman 1993, Kaplan 1996, Eade 1997, Carmen 1996, Uphoff et al. 1998, Black 1999, and Carmen and Sobrado 2000.

8. "There is only one axiom that never changes at Highlander: *learn from the people; start their education where they are*" (Adams 1975, 206).

9. Quoted in Braybrooke and Lindblom 1963, 71–72, in the context of their treatment of "disjointed incrementalism." Also quoted in Hirschman 1973, 249.

10. See Stiglitz 2001, Reddaway and Glinski 2001, and Ellerman 2001a.

11. "The change agent must psychologically zip him or herself into the clients' skins, and see their situation through their eyes" (Rogers 1983, 316).

12. "You must find a way to determine what their perception is. You can't do it by psychoanalyzing or being smart. You have to ask yourself what you know about their experience and cultural background that would help in understanding what they're saying. You need to know more about them than they know about themselves. This sounds like a paradox, but the reason they don't know themselves fully is that they haven't learned to analyze their experience and learn from it. When you help them to respect and learn from their own experience, they can know more about themselves than you do" (Horton 1998, 70–71).

13. See Salmen 1987, Slim and Thompson 1993, and Narayan 2000 for a development of this theme in development assistance.

14. In a footnote, Donald Schön and Martin Rein attribute the phrase "giving reason" to a 1979 report on "The Teacher Project" by Eleanor Duckworth and Jeanne Bamberger. See also Duckworth 1987.

15. In the first Citizenship School started by the Highlander School, the literacy pedagogy was described by one of the first teachers: "They tell me a story, a story which I write down, then they learn to read the story. It's their story in their words, and they are interested because it's theirs" (quoted in Horton 1998, 103).

16. See Ellerman 1992 for a modern development of this theory.

17. Hutcheson is important for another reason. The American Declaration of Independence is one of the high points of the inalienable rights tradition. The conventional scholarly view has been that "Jefferson copied Locke"

(Becker 1958, 79). But Locke had no serious theory of inalienability, and he in fact condoned a limited voluntary contract for slavery, which he nicely called "Drudgery." In his important study *Inventing America*, Garry Wills reinvents Jeffersonian scholarship concerning the intellectual roots of the Declaration of Independence. Wills convincingly argues that the Lockean influence was more indirect and even to some extent resisted by Jefferson, while Hutcheson's influence was central and pervasive. In particular, "Jefferson took his division of rights into alienable and unalienable from Hutcheson, who made the distinction popular and important" (Wills 1979, 213).

18. Such a person would be the cognitive equivalent of the person who responds primarily like a marionette only to external incentives.

19. In addition to being wary of "Greeks bearing gifts," Henry David Thoreau notes, "If I knew for a certainty that a man was coming to my house with the conscious design of doing me good, I should run for fear that I should have some of his good done to me" (see Carmen 1996, 47). For a further development of this theme, see Gronemeyer 1992.

20. In 1784, Immanuel Kant wrote a short but influential pamphlet, *What is Enlightenment?* "Enlightenment is man's release from his self-incurred tutelage. Tutelage is man's inability to make use of his understanding without direction from another. Self-incurred is this tutelage when its cause lies not in lack of reason but in lack of resolution and courage to use it without direction from another. *Sapere aude!* 'Have the courage to use your own reason!'—that is the motto of enlightenment" (see Schmidt 1996).

21. See Illich 1978a for an extensive treatment of dependency creation in modern civilization, and see Prebisch 1984, Furtado 1987, and Evans 1979 on dependence in the political economy of development.

22. Imagine how long a company would remain in business if it interpreted "demand for its products" to mean that people would accept the products if given to them essentially for free.

23. An impact evaluation is used to evaluate social funds by comparing communities that received the funds with the communities that didn't. "A good impact evaluation asks the question: What would the status of the beneficiaries have been without the program? 'Counterfactuals' are usually constructed through the use of control/comparison groups. . . . The general evaluation design is a matched comparison between social fund communities or beneficiaries and others with similar characteristics that did not implement a social fund project" (Social Protection Unit 2000, 42). The outcome of such a "good impact evaluation" is that those who get resources or training generally do better than those who don't. Hence agency task managers conclude that they should continue such programs—even though an impact evaluation does not consider the costs or alternative uses of the same resources. Research economists in the agency sell their staff-weeks to use flashy e-con-ometrics to

compare funded communities with "counterfactual" communities that receive no funds. When asked about a real counterfactual of communities with the same resources used in an alternative way, they plead "no data." Thus the game goes on, and agencies request more money for "successful programs" with "good evaluations."

24. Dichter (2003, 98) quotes from Charles Dickens's *Bleak House* on "rapacious benevolence."

25. Or as Jane Jacobs has put it with brevity and clarity: "Development cannot be given. It has to be *done*. It is a process, not a collection of capital goods" (1984, 119). "Development is a do-it-yourself process; for any economy it is either do it yourself or don't develop" (1984, 140).

26. Project managers in development agencies sometimes unfortunately view projects with autonomous initiative (a "moving train") as "not invented here" and not a result of *their* efforts. "Our resources should be used in situations where we can really turn things around and make a big difference." Moreover, unlike agency-initiated projects, such indigenous projects might evolve in ways that are outside the perceived policy guidelines of the development agency. Agency-initiated pseudoprojects with little legitimacy or embeddedness can still be presented to one's superiors as "our project" in which "we can take pride—it would not have happened without our help." Indeed.

CHAPTER 6

1. Indeed, much of the analysis in this chapter is a slightly abstract "case study" based on my five years in the Economic Development Institute, or EDI (now the World Bank Institute, or WBI), the wing of the World Bank that should be concerned with capacity-building. After that I moved to become an advisor to the chief economist, Joseph Stiglitz. In this position knowledge and research issues were paramount (see the next chapter), and I was somewhat involved in the 1998 *World Development Report* (World Bank 1998b) on the "knowledge for development" theme.

2. See Argyris and Schön 1978 for the distinction between the "espoused theory" and the actual theory-in-use.

3. In the biological learning example this corresponds to the genes transmitting the hardwired behavior, as is the case for insects, rather than transmitting the learning mechanism so the organism can learn in its own environment. One of my "attack memos" (2000) in the Bank explained this distinction and was entitled "Getting the Bugs out of the Knowledge Bank Idea."

4. The rush to show results has many sources. When a new chief comes to the top of a subunit in an organization, then during the early part of his or her

tenure, there is the rush to show that this person is making a difference. In the latter part of the chief's tenure, it is "legacy time," so the failure to get sustainable results from the first half of his or her tenure must be compensated for by the renewed rush to establish a legacy. Then this person is promoted to employ the skills for which he or she was promoted on an even broader scale.

5. See Hyden (1983, 178–79) for a description of these "organizational imperatives of donor agencies" in the African context.

6. See chapter 14 on "localness" in Senge 1990; chapter 9 on "self-attribution: market influences" in Lane 1991; and chapter 6 on self-respect in Murray 1988 or the discussion of self-efficacy in Bandura 1995.

7. Sen 1999, 11. Hence the oft-noted view of development agency and developing country as doctor and patient.

8. Similar dynamics can result when responsibility is shifted to consultants. See the analysis of "shifting the burden" as the "generic dynamics of addiction" in Senge 1990, 104–13.

9. See Candy 1991, 60, for various descriptions of cognitively dependent, cue-seeking students.

10. For instance, at the end of the 1990s and beginning of the twenty-first century, the Bank was involved in funding satellite-based worldwide video hookups in what was called the Global Development Learning Network, or GDLN. The first director of the GDLN was a mature individual with educational experience outside the Bank who understood that the important thing was to allow competition in the use of the channel capacity. But there was strong pressure to restrict the use of the facilities to Bank-provided materials and events—all in the name of "quality assurance." It was questioned why the Bank should allow materials to be transmitted over its network that are not up to its quality standards. Thus as the directors change, one can foresee a focus on transmitting Bank-supplied canned materials and on transmitting important talking heads from Washington, DC, to the benighted regions of the world in an electronic caricature of the standard methodology of transmitting development knowledge.

11. But in some cases the client is asked at least to rewrite the letter in his or her own words since the resultant broken English will enhance the authenticity and pathos of the request for aid. This problem is writ large in the countries' "own" Poverty Reduction Strategy Papers (PRSPs) that often seem to be written in such impeccable bureaucratic Bankese that they appear to have been written or edited inside the World Bank, written by Bank retirees as consultants, or culled directly from previous Bank documents.

12. For a critique of considering capacity building as just strengthening the capacity to deliver donor-defined programs, see Eade 1997.

13. Unfortunately, this sort of irony seems to be completely lost inside the large training agencies.

14. Take the example of the Joint Vienna Institute (JVI). In the early 1990s, the JVI was hurriedly set up in Vienna by the IMF Institute (the training wing of the Fund), EDI, EBRD, and other agencies since there was no time to set up training centers in the transition economies. The development of capacity in the postsocialist countries would supposedly take place within five years, so there was a JVI sunset clause to that effect. Of course, nothing happened about building capacity in the transition economies since both the trainers and trainees enjoyed the paid vacations in Vienna. At the end of the sunset clause, EDI led the charge to get it overturned so that the "successful programs" could continue. The evaluations showed that both trainers and trainees wanted it to continue, so the agencies were just responding to demand! All the people who might have benefited in the transition economies if the millions had been spent on capacity building (rather than long vacations in Vienna) were not asked to fill in evaluation forms.

15. For example, one public relations document from the training wing of the Bank brags: "A 1996 evaluation found that . . . trained women had systematically better business practices, higher business incomes and felt more empowered than control groups without access to . . . training."

16. The older and now apparently obsolete pattern of human affairs was that people or organizations make certain accomplishments and then they might eventually have public recognition for their accomplishments. In the new world of public relations, the idea is to directly affect and manage the public perceptions so as to avoid the difficult intermediate step of genuine accomplishments. When successful, one has Daniel Boorstin's (1980) wonderful definition of a celebrity as one who is well-known for being well-known.

17. *Learning delivery* is one of my favorite oxymoronic phrases used by the training wing of the Bank. Training is the sort of thing that can be delivered, and learning may or may not take place, but learning cannot be delivered. The notion of "delivering learning" shows a failure to understand the basics of education.

18. The World Bank recently undertook a multiyear study on quality assurance in ESW, and the eventual report, "Fixing ESW," barely mentioned the capacity-building function of ESW. Even the old dichotomy between due diligence and capacity-building ESW was replaced by new categories of due diligence, diagnostic, and customized ESW with no mention of capacity building.

19. Currently the ESW products in the World Bank include the Country Economic Memorandum (CEM), Country Financial Accountability Assessment (CFAA), Country Procurement Assessment Review (CPAR), Country Profile of Financial Accountability (CPFA), Financial Sector Assessment (FSA), Poverty Assessment (PA), Public Expenditure Review (PER), Social and Structural Review (SSR), Development Policy Review (DPR), cus-

tomized Nonlending Services (NLS) reports, and various ad hoc sector studies—all of which can be done for each country and repeated every few years.
"Inputs" into Country Assistance Strategies (CAS) and "editing" of Poverty
Reduction Strategy Papers (PRSPs) are not counted as ESW activities,
although they also help to keep staff busily working.

20. This cliché is now giving clichés a bad name. Even those who think
that everyone should wear a three-piece suit will still loudly proclaim that one
size does not fit all.

21. "It is a time-honored Japanese gardening technique to prepare a tree
for transplanting by slowly and carefully binding the roots over a period of
time, bit by bit, to prepare the tree for the shock of the change it is about to
experience. This process, called *nemawashi*, takes time and patience, but it
rewards you, if it is done properly, with a healthy transplanted tree" (Morita
1986, 158).

22. This is a variation on the Chinese story of the farmer who pulled up
the stalks of his plants a few inches to help them grow faster and taller but
found them all withered the next morning.

23. "As paradoxical as it may seem to people accustomed to equating bor-
rowing with imitative copying, *borrowing is, above all, an act of social invention*"
(Cole 1989, 125). "Every alleged example of local implementation of central
policy, if it results in significant social transformation, is in fact a process of
local social discovery" (Schön 1971, 161). The United Nations Development
Program (Fukuda-Parr et al. 2002, 185) has used the title of one of Stiglitz's
Bank speeches, "Scan Globally, Reinvent Locally," as a slogan or epigram (see
Chang 2001, chap. 6).

24. When language has been debased by bureaucratic double-talk and public relations banalities ("We have learned that X alone is not enough; X + Y is
needed"), then one strategy to try to recover some meaning is to state what is
ruled out. But if most everyone on the planet agrees with a statement, then it
is also a waste of time (e.g., banal throw-away criticisms of "weak institutions,"
"poor governance," and "unsound policies"). Analysis needs to be pushed at
least to the point where it has enough "edge" that someone will disagree. As
Lawrence Summers, the former chief economist of the World Bank, used to
say, "If you don't have an edge, you don't have a point."

25. Gunnar Myrdal has described how certain black "leaders" served as
gatekeepers to the black community in the American South during the early
twentieth century.

> For this [white authorities] need liaison agents in the persons of Negro
> "leaders." . . . They have, therefore, an interest in helping those leaders
> obtain as much prestige and influence in the Negro community as possi-
> ble—as long as they cooperate with the whites faithfully. . . .

Under these circumstances it is understandable that the individual
Negro who becomes known to have contact with substantial white people gains prestige and influence with Negroes for this very reason. Correspondingly, an accommodating Negro who is known to be influential
in the Negro community becomes, because of this, the more useful to
the whites. The Negro leader in this setting serves a "function" to both
castes and his influence in both groups is cumulative—prestige in the
Negro community being an effect as well as a cause of prestige among
the whites. (Myrdal [1944] 1972, 721–22)

Roughly the same dynamics played out in the relationship between the
Russian reformers and the international aid community during most of the
1990s.

26. When Count Potemkin accompanied Catherine the Great on boat
trips on the Volga, there were mobile groups of actors dressed as peasants who
would assemble and disassemble "villages" periodically along the river to show
the passing empress how happy her subjects were. That organizational logic is
unchanged today. The "field trips" of the top officials of large development
agencies are highly choreographed stage plays. For example, World Bank President James Wolfensohn, like Catherine, wanted to get out of the capital to
see the real Russia, so a visit was arranged to a typical small Russian city. The
training wing of the Bank got an advance notice of his travel plans, quickly
planned a training event in the city at the same time, and invited the president to drop by. President Wolfensohn, a graduate of the Harvard Business
School, arrived to find Russian students from that esteemed school flown in to
lecture on business in that small Russian city. Count Potemkin would be
impressed at how the Bank has modernized this indigenous Russian tradition—instead of importing a foreign model of a pseudo-event.

27. "Powerful institutions—the state bureaucracies, the corporations, and
the professions—have an inherent antagonism toward self-help efforts
because such activities pose a challenge to the existing order" (Stokes 1981,
136).

28. See Schön's treatment (1983) of the technical expert in contrast with
the reflective practitioner.

29. See Ryle 1945–46 for the earlier distinction between knowing how
and knowing that, Oakeshott 1991 for a treatment of practical knowledge versus technical knowledge, Schön 1983 for a related treatment of professional
versus instrumental knowledge, Marglin 1990 on *techne* versus *episteme*, and
Scott 1998 on *metis* versus episteme/techne (see p. 425 on the terminological
differences of Marglin's usage). The tacit/codified distinction looms large in
Nonaka and Takeuchi 1995, and the authors note that Squire 1987 gives a
dozen labels for similar distinctions. See Davenport and Prusak 1998 on the

importance of tacit knowledge in organizational knowledge management. See Scott 1998 for a progressive critique of "high-Modernist" social engineering also based on an appreciation of the embedded practical knowledge that he calls *metis*.

30. Even the codified part may suffer from the "Rashomon effect" described in Schön 1971.

31. The baseball metaphor was used by the Texan populist and political commentator Jim Hightower to describe the first President George Bush.

32. "Natural-born development experts" seem to be a particularly American affliction. But one might include people born in developing countries whose principal intellectual formation has been in the United States or in their former colonizer, such as the United Kingdom or France.

33. This belief in the ultimate efficacy of political will to force institutional change is characteristic of the Bolshevik or Jacobin mentality (see chap. 8).

34. See Wedel 1998, Ellerman 2001a and 2003, and chapter 8 on the role of the Harvard wunderkinder in Eastern Europe and in Boris Yeltsin's Russia.

35. See the chapter on cargo cult science in Feynman 1985.

36. See the foreword by J. K. McCarthy in Lawrence 1979 for the cargo cult formulation of the question of development assistance: "Where is the road that leads to cargo?" Jan Knippers Black also uses the cargo cult metaphor for some recent development thinking (1999, 137 or 280).

CHAPTER 7

1. See Morley 1928, 218.

2. The root heresy was Stiglitz's view that the client countries should hear the best arguments on all sides of the difficult development issues—thereby shifting the locus of decision making and ownership to the country.

3. Max Planck once quipped that even physics only progresses funeral by funeral.

4. In fact this practice of pseudoverification is the heart of the recurring fad of "results-based management," "output-based aid," and the like.

5. See John Stuart Mill's extended argument in *On Liberty* ([1859] 1972, 120).

6. I am focusing on the Bank's intellectual control over its own research staff. On a few occasions, the attempted control extended to outsiders with politically incorrect views who were inadvertently invited to speak at the Bank, for example, at the Annual Bank Conference on Development Economics (ABCDE). After Jeffrey Sachs had sided with the Republican majority in the Congressional Meltzer Commission findings quite critical of the Bank and Fund, Sachs was invited to give an ABCDE address while Larry

Summers was still secretary of the treasury. While visiting the Bank on the day before Sachs's talk, Summers noticed the signs announcing the talk posted around the Bank and "ordered" them torn down. Of a less comical nature was an intervention by the board of directors of the Bank to suppress a paper at the post–September 11 ABCDE conference in 2002. A distinguished Princeton economist, Alan Krueger, was commissioned to give an empirical paper on the roots of terrorism. The Bank had a clear Official View that terrorism was rooted in poverty so that some of the huge funds for the war on terrorism could be channeled to the Bank. When Krueger's paper arrived so that it could be printed for distribution at the conference, its conclusions were quite the opposite. Little connection between terrorism and poverty or education was found. Instead evidence pointed to "political conditions and long-standing feelings of indignity and frustration that have little to do with economics" (Krueger and Malecková 2003, 119). The Board representatives from the Gulf States were particularly upset at the mention of political conditions and at the fact that the Bank would commission a study of terrorism in the first place. They managed to have the paper completely suppressed at the conference and airbrushed out the conference program (see http://econ.worldbank.org/abcde/) and publications. It was later published in the prestigious *Journal of Economic Perspectives* (Krueger and Malecková 2003) with no mention of the incident or of the Bank.

7. Universities, like development agencies, now have public relations or external affairs offices. But in the case of universities, they have the good sense to stay out of intellectual questions. One can imagine the intellectual distortions that would result from, say, the Harvard public relations office touting a faculty member's theory as "the Harvard theory" so that other faculty members would then be pressured "to play with the team," "not embarrass the organization by publicly airing differences," and "coordinate results" so as "not to reduce the franchise value of our reputation" by publishing contradictory results. Yet such behavior is *routine* in the research departments of the major development agencies such as the World Bank and the IMF. See Ellerman 2002.

8. Now that the historical moment for voucher privatization has passed (see chap. 8), the leading institutions of the stock market cargo cult—the Bank, the Fund, and USAID—are promoting mandatory defined-contribution pension plans in order to rekickstart the moribund securities markets in the transition and developing economies. Such plans are funded with obligatory deductions from workers' pay, and the funds are invested with workers bearing the risk. Thus these agencies "promote free markets" with schemes that force people to indirectly "buy" securities that they would not buy voluntarily. For example, as if the Bank-sponsored voucher privatization was not enough of a disaster in Kazakhstan, the World Bank and USAID sponsored a

100 percent "second-pillar" pension system in that country, a system that has already put over a billion dollars from workers' pay into the private "pension funds" to be invested in Kazakh securities. But, as a new pension system, it will take more than a generation for this debacle to unfold, long after the relevant Bank/USAID officials have retired on their defined-benefit pensions. Then it will be time to further "help" the country by indebting it with another pension loan. In this way, the government could meet its "implicit pension liability" to the workers whose forced savings would then have disappeared in the maw of the cargo cult securities market.

9. When predictions fail, then skewed perceptions and rationalizations are a likely outcome. See Festinger, Riecken, and Schachter 1956, Festinger 1957, part 2 in Lane 1991, and Elster 1983. See Akerlof and Dickens 1982 for an economic treatment of cognitive dissonance, and see Hirschman and Bird 1971, 206, for applications in development.

10. For instance, in the World Bank, the research department is the Development Economics vice presidency, and its head is the Bank's chief economist. But there is no such recognition of the other fields that might have some relevance for development such as political science, law, administrative science, sociology, anthropology, education, and management theory.

11. Leaving aside questions of ideology, Kanbur (2001) argues that economists taking a "finance ministry" perspective will disagree with those who are closer to the ground since the former tend to think in terms of aggregates and averages (trying to wade across a river with an "average" depth of three feet), medium-term equilibrium (when the poor might be dead in the short run), and competitive markets.

12. Frederick Taylor's One Best Way mentality expressed in his *Principles of Scientific Management* showed a remarkable misunderstanding of the intellectual methodology of science. Perhaps it was no surprise that his thought was much appreciated by Lenin and was influential in later Soviet management thinking.

13. See Hirschman 1973, 238–40.

14. Recall that the universal recommendation that everyone wear a three-piece suit is always tempered by the slogan "one size does not fit all."

15. Some of the best computer-based training programs have "experts" popping up on the screen giving contradictory advice. "In other words, the program communicates that there's not always one right answer. It invites trainees to learn to use their own judgment rather than rely on someone else's—especially when the someone else isn't as close to the situation as you are. Organizations today are facing increasingly complex situations where there are many possible answers. Traditional training that insists on right and wrong answers disempowers the individual—it robs people of their decision-making ability" (Schank 1997, 24).

16. See Rondinelli 1983 on an adaptive approach.

17. In chapter 3, the "insect theory" points out that in the higher animals (unlike insects) the genes transmit the learning mechanisms rather than just the specific learnings. See Ellerman 2000.

18. One might be amazed at the "trainers" in development agencies who would not think of giving the answers to their own children struggling with homework problems because they understand the importance of the learning experience but then in their day job will design and implement "training programs" "to disseminate development knowledge" from the agency to the developing countries.

19. J. Hart 1926, 148–49. Quoted in *Unearthing Seeds of Fire*, a book on the Highlander Folk School in Tennessee, a school that was modeled in part on the Danish Folk High Schools (Adams 1975, 23). See Horton 1998 for more on the former and Borish 1991 on the latter.

20. This is expressed in the "marketplace of ideas concept—the proposition that truth naturally overcomes falsehood when they are allowed to compete. . . . The belief that competing voices produce superior conclusions [is] . . . implicit in scientific reasoning, the practice of trial by jury, and the process of legislative debate" (Smith 1988, 31).

21. Unfortunately developing countries were routinely put "under the knife" of structural adjustment programs or shock therapy programs while being actively discouraged from "getting a second opinion" since that might only be confusing and weaken the resolve to enforce the programs.

22. Devil's advocacy (see Schwenk 1984) is interpreted broadly to include a number of related techniques to better elicit the main policy alternatives. A *Cassandra's advocate* (Janis 1972, 217) is a person who emphasizes alternative interpretations of data and focuses on all the things that can go wrong ("Murphy's Law-yer"). The *Rashomon effect* (see Schön 1971, 210) illustrates that the same set of circumstances and events can be interpreted very differently by different people. Discussion organized as a debate between the proposed policy and the best alternative has been called the *dialectical method* (see Schwenk 1989; or Tung and Heminger 1993). *Multiple advocacy* (Haas 1990, 210), *equivocality* (Weick 1979, 174), and *double visioning* (see Schön 1983, 281) refer to the practice of not only allowing but fostering the presentation of two or more policy options.

23. See Ellerman 2001b and 2002.

24. See Levy 1985, Smith 1988, and Sunstein 2003.

25. Jefferson echoes John Milton's defense of intellectual freedom in *Areopagitica*. "And though all the winds of doctrine were let loose to play upon the earth, so Truth be in the field, we do injuriously, by licensing and prohibiting, to misdoubt her strength. Let her and Falsehood grapple; who ever knew Truth put to the worse, in a free and open encounter?"

26. When other possibilities are being realized simultaneously with the given project—as in parallel experimentation—then evaluation can be based on direct comparison and benchmarking between the parallel experiments.

27. Davenport and Prusak 1998, 113.

28. "True Socraticism represents first and foremost an attitude of mind, an intellectual humility easily mistaken for arrogance, since the true Socratic is convinced of the ignorance not only of himself but of all mankind. This rather than any body of positive doctrine is the contribution of Socrates" (Guthrie 1960, 75).

29. Holt's use of "do-ers" (with the hyphen) denotes autonomous individuals engaged in active learning by doing. "The point is that it is the do-er, not someone else, who has decided what he will say, hear, read, write, or think or dream about. He is at the center of his own actions. He plans, directs, controls, and judges them. He does them for his own purposes—which may of course include a common purpose with others. His actions are not ordered and controlled from outside. They belong to him and are a part of him" (Holt 1976, 5).

30. See McGregor 1960 and chapter 3 on McGregor's Theory Y for this management theory, where "controlling boss" = "theory X manager" and "enabling boss" = "theory Y manager." See a similar distinction between enabling and coercive bureaucracies in Adler and Borys 1996.

31. The most famous example is between the IMF and China. China never agreed to an IMF program, so without IMF money, it had to stumble along with the "wrong" reforms, which led over the last twenty years to what seems to be the largest growth episode in recorded history. See Stiglitz and Ellerman 2001 and the next chapter.

32. As a "school" for the Third World, the World Bank has had no recent graduates (not counting Korea or Cyprus as Third World). Among transition countries, the only country graduating to nonborrowing status is a country that had no real reason to join as a borrowing country in the first place (Slovenia).

33. *Conned* is a reference to the remark of Anatoly Chubais, the top Russian "reformer," about how he conned or cheated the international financial institutions out of $20 billion. See Reddaway and Glinski 2001, 600.

CHAPTER 8

1. My main focus is on privatization prior to the Russian reformers' "loans-for-shares" scheme—the latter of which played a major role in creating today's oligarchs and which was not publicly opposed by the IFIs. Many commentators seem to avoid learning difficult lessons from the earlier voucher pri-

vatization by focusing on the loan-for-shares scheme as the "Mother of all Debacles" instead of simply as "Dream Team: The Sequel."

2. Jeffrey Sachs was the first young tenured Harvard economics professor to gain notoriety in this regard, but he was soon eclipsed by his colleagues Larry Summers (who during the early 1990s became chief economist of the World Bank and later secretary of the treasury in the U.S. government) and Summers's protégé Andrei Shleifer (who was born in Russia but emigrated to America as a teenager). While there were some sharp divisions between the wunderkinder, they and the IFIs were united on the shock therapy strategy and voucher schemes analyzed here.

3. The Harvard funds had no more relationship to Harvard University than the Federal Express company has to the U.S. Postal Service—just good advertising.

4. Quoted in Harding 1987, 318. Thus do Chinese socialists instruct market bolsheviks on the non-Bolshevik methods of institutional transformation. A related "pave the paths" metaphor is used by Christopher Williams (1981, 112). In a complex of new buildings, let grass grow between them, see where footpaths develop, and then pave the paths. While voicing Hayek's ideas about the market as a spontaneous order, many market bolsheviks (such as Václav Klaus) labored to totally stop spontaneous privatization instead of trying to find the closest socially acceptable channel so that those market forces might swell from a stream to a river (see Ellerman 1993).

5. "Dual pricing avoided the chain-reaction disruption that shock therapy generated. Permitting the state-owned firms to sell extra outputs and to buy extra inputs in markets allowed new interfirm relationships *to grow around the stable platform of the existing ways of doing business*" (McMillan 2002, 204, with italics added).

6. Deng Xiaoping's pragmatism, "It is not important if the cat is black or white, but that it catches the mice," was echoed by Ralf Dahrendorf's call "to work by trial and error within institutions" (1990, 41; quoted in Sachs 1993, 4). Dahrendorf's book *Reflections on the Revolution in Europe* was a deliberate updating of Edmund Burke's anti-Jacobin tract *Reflections on the Revolution in France* ([1790] 1937). Sachs argues against Dahrendorf's pragmatism, noting, "If instead the philosophy were one of open experimentation, I doubt that the transformation would be possible at all, at least without costly and dangerous wrong turns" (Sachs 1993, 5). To avoid "costly and dangerous wrong turns," the then–Harvard wunderkind promoted the scheme of mass privatization through voucher investment funds.

7. An "agency chain" is a multilinked chain of principal-agent relationships. For instance, in the large publicly traded U.S. companies, the theory is that the shareholders are the ultimate principals who "supervise and control" the board of directors as their agents (in theory through board elections but, in

fact, dissidents tend to use exit—selling shares—rather than voice). The board, in turn, is supposed to select and supervise the top managers (rather than the other way around) in another link in the agency chain. Then the top managers supervise the middle managers and so forth eventually down to the workers on the office or shop floor. In voucher schemes designed by the experts, there were even more layers of principals and agents: citizens as VIF shareholders, the VIF board of directors, the fund management company, boards of directors of portfolio companies, and finally managers and workers of the portfolio companies—all of which, after being legislated, was supposed to work overnight after many decades of communism. Meanwhile, after a century of trying to get multilayered agency chains to work, the West still has plenty of Enron-type scandals and out-of-control executive compensation packages.

8. There is a side theme that might be explored. Youthful prodigies are typically in activities based on abstract symbol manipulation (e.g., mathematics, computer programming, music, or chess), where subtle and often tacit background knowledge obtained from years of human experience is not so relevant (see Scott's 1998 wonderfully relevant discussion of *metis*). As economic theory has become more mathematical, there is now the phenomenon of wunderkind professors in economics (e.g., Jeffrey Sachs, Larry Summers, and Andrei Shleifer were all prodigy professors at Harvard) who are then unleashed—with the compounded arrogance of youth, academic credentials, and elite associations—into the real world as ersatz policy "experts." Paul Starobin (1999) contrasts the wunderkinder of Big Bangery with the mature pragmatists behind the Marshall Plan and notes the striking difference in results. When wunderkinder cast long shadows in development agencies, then it must be late in the day for those agencies.

9. *Shrink-wrapped ownership* is a metaphor denoting a structure where owners are those "stakeholders" who—independently of any formal ownership—have an up-close functional relationship to the operations of a firm that would include the staff and major suppliers (including finance) or customers and perhaps local authorities but not, say, absentee buyers of secondhand shares. The idea is to match ownership to function with the firm rather than treat ownership as a tradable commodity that can be bought by otherwise unrelated parties. By *firm* I mean the de facto firm that meets every working day, not the formal legal entity that meets once a year. The strikingly successful Chinese TVEs function with a shrink-wrapped ownership/control structure (see Weitzman and Xu 1994) even without Western-style formal ownership—much to the bewilderment of the Western experts.

10. In a lease buyout, the enterprise staff—who developed de facto property rights in the decentralizing reforms—were allowed to proceed "straight to the market" by purchasing the company with seller-supplied credit on an

installment or lease-purchase basis. As in U.S.-style leveraged buyouts, the installment payments are made by the company (not the individuals) to the seller. The lease buyouts worked best as medium-sized (or smaller) firms. But the Soviet dinosaurs typically needed to be busted up anyway into a related set of medium-sized firms, so lease-buyout "spin-offs" or "breakaways" could also be used to restructure and privatize large firms.

11. See the debate in Dabrowski, Gomulka, and Rostowski 2001 and Stiglitz and Ellerman 2001.

12. The failure of elite academic and bureaucratic economists to understand this mutual hostage argument surely derived in part from their fundamental antiworker animus. This was clearly shown in the behind-the-scenes archpaternalist view that worker ownership would just lead to workers destroying their own livelihood by stripping the assets of their own firms. They argued for strong absentee owners who would be interested in maintaining the long-run health of the assets and who would act as "asset advocates." And then the elite advisors supported voucher investment funds—funds that, together with Enron-style managers, showed their great devotion to assets by promptly tunneling them out of the firms. However, some Polish critics of the "Stiglitz perspective" (Dabrowski et al. 2001) allow that "workers' self-management played an important part in limiting the fall in output and the amount of criminal asset stripping in the state sector in Poland," and thus they are "Not Poles Apart" on the short agency chain and mutual hostage arguments (Stiglitz and Ellerman 2001).

13. The idea that the more powerful the helper, the more help that can be provided has been argued against throughout this book. In fact, the more powerful the helper, the more the doers will have their autonomy overridden or undercut by the helper. Unfortunately, powerful development agencies tend to think in linear terms—the more aid they push into one end of the pipeline, the more "development" that comes out the other end.

14. Of the three Harvard wunderkinder, Larry Summers and Andrei Shleifer made more direct contributions to the Russian debacle than Jeffrey Sachs. Shleifer was a colleague of Mankiw's at Harvard, and Summers was the president of Harvard University. Sachs now has a reinvented persona at Columbia University.

CHAPTER 9

1. *Increasing returns* means that a scale increase in inputs gives a more than proportional increase in outputs.

2. A more recent corollary is that if the postcommunist countries actually

had the state capacity to somehow change all their institutions at once according to the plans of the institutional shock therapists, then they would have had the state capacity "to make" communism successful in the first place.

3. More recently, Nicholas Stern (2001) has argued that public action to improve the investment climate may have the public goods or atmospheric effect of a coordinated push of entrepreneurs, investors, and managers toward a high equilibrium of self-reinforcing expectations.

4. Jane Jacobs has made a similar point. "Possibly because so many ambitious and expensive attempts to force or coax economic expansion have failed during the second half of the twentieth century, it has finally become permissible to say that the emperor has no clothes—that economic theory can't explain economic expansion." After dismissing the question of what governments must do to spur growth as the "wrong way" to approach the matter, she argues that the real question is the "question of what *economies* do" (2000, 158).

5. See also Streeten 1959 on the pressures and impulses that drive unbalanced growth sequences.

6. A policy-based conditionality ("you get aid X if you adopt policy Y") is sometimes repackaged as a "mutual commitment mechanism" ("to show the depth of the development agency's commitment to policy Y, it is willing to provide aid X if you are willing to also commit to policy Y").

7. See the discussion and references in Mosley et al. 1991, World Bank 1998a, Killick 1998, Gwin and Nelson 1997 (particularly Collier 1997), Tarp and Hjertholm 2000, and Van de Walle 2001.

8. Hirschman and Bird 1971, 204. Italics added.

9. "We will pretend to make best efforts to fulfill your conditionalities, and you will pretend that you don't have to move the money anyway."

10. Wilhelm von Humboldt (1767–1835) gave an early expression of this contrast between internal and external motivation. "Whatever task is not chosen of man's own free will, whatever constrains or even only guides him, does not become part of his nature. It remains forever alien to him; if he performs it, he does so not with true humane energy but with mere mechanical skill" (Humboldt 1963, 47).

11. "But, though a nation may borrow its tools from abroad, for the energy to handle them it must look within. *Erquickung hast du nicht gewonnen, Wenn sie dir nicht aus eigner Seele quillt*" (Tawney [1932] 1966, 194). The quote from Goethe's *Faust* (part 1) might be translated as "You have not gained refreshment if it does not come out of your own soul" (Terrill, 1973, 69).

12. See Perroux 1953.

13. In some cases knowledge of others' successful models is necessary even for possible learners to formulate their own problems. "Managers don't know

what they want until they see what they can get; in this sense, solutions are used to formulate problems" (Cole 1989, 36). This mutual influence of means and ends is characteristic of the attitude of pragmatism.

14. Similarly, allocative efficiency can be contrasted with X-efficiency. In the previous quote from Kant, he describes what we might call the X-efficiency of the rivalry between trees competing for sunlight to grow tall and straight. Neoclassical theory would take the growth properties of the trees as given and focus on reallocating the trees to the open spots where sunlight was more available. That would maximize the growth on the standard assumption of diminishing returns to the crowding or rivalry of trees in one area.

15. Hirschman's treatment of similar questions also involves the interplay between beliefs and actions. Actions can lead to cognitive dissonance with old beliefs, and thus a change in beliefs, just as new beliefs can lead to new actions. See the excellent discussion in Meldolesi 1995, 56–67.

16. See Simon 1991b, chapter 11, "Mazes without Minotaurs".

17. For instance, as espoused by Francis Bacon, the Marquis de Condorcet, Jeremy Bentham, Claude-Henri Saint-Simon, Auguste Comte, Sidney and Beatrice Webb, or Marx—see Hayek 1979 for a similar notion of scientism.

18. See Lindblom 1959, 1990, and Braybrooke and Lindblom 1963.

19. See Polanyi 1966, 70–74, 217, in addition to Polanyi 1951 as well as Lavoie 1985 on spontaneous order.

20. See Metcalf and Urwick 1942, 297–314, cited in Lindblom 1965, 8.

21. The contrast between these two traditions is extensively and provocatively analyzed in the context of social and economic development by James Scott (1998).

22. See the discussion of the Chinese experience in chapter 8.

23. Here again we see a contrast between a neoclassical view of static efficiency (e.g., JIT inventory as saving inventory costs in a "given" process) and a more Schumpeterian or dynamic efficiency (e.g., JIT inventory as problem-based innovation and learning to change the process of production).

24. Hirschman 1961, 66–67. See the chapter entitled "Social Conflicts as Pillars of Democratic Market Societies" in Hirschman 1995 on the positive role of conflict and discussion to build trust and cohesion in a democracy—a theme well developed by Niccolò Machiavelli about the Roman republic in his *Discourses*.

25. See Popper 1965 and Lakatos and Musgrave 1970.

26. See, for example, John Stuart Mill ([1859] 1972), Walter Bagehot ([1869] 1948), James Bryce ([1888] 1959), John Dewey (1927, 1939), Ernest Barker ([1942] 1967), Frank Knight (1947), James Buchanan (1954), Bernard Crick (1962), Charles Lindblom (1990), and Jurgen Habermas (1990).

27. While the shifting balance theory is rather difficult to test in a natural setting, the success of the ideas in animal breeding has been supplemented

recently with success in improving performance of computerized genetic algo-rithms by introducing parallel or distributed subpopulations. See Toquenaga and Wade 1996.

CHAPTER 10

1. John Locke makes this distinction well: "I may be cured of some disease by remedies that I have not faith in; but I cannot be saved by a religion that I distrust and by a worship that I abhor" (Locke [1689] 1990, 41; quoted in Mor-ley 1928, 222).

2. Hence the highest-ranking American in the Fund is typically in the number two position of deputy managing director. When Stanley Fischer, the deputy managing director of the IMF during the contentious late 1990s and a previous chief economist for the World Bank, retired from the IMF, he imme-diately took the yellow brick road from Nineteenth Street (IMF headquarters) to Wall Street to become a vice chairman of Citigroup. That was certainly congruent with the hypothesis that the IMF sees the world through a Wall Street lens.

3. See Freeland 2000, Blustein 2001, and Stiglitz 2002 on how the Bank and Fund functioned as junior partners in U.S. foreign policy in Russia and in the East Asian crisis during the 1990s. Following is a small personal example of microcontrol: I was working with moderates and reformers in Iran in the early 1990s preparing and giving some Bank seminars on privatization and related economic restructuring. Then for whatever reason the U.S.-Iran rela-tionship hit another bump in the road, and the United States decided that Iran should be more isolated. The phone calls were made to the Bank, and the word was passed down the ranks to stop the program, including the seminars. Since Iran, however, was a fully qualified member of the Bank, the program was only reduced down to the bare minimum (e.g., a sewer project in Tehran).

4. And the staff members in the Bank and Fund from developing coun-tries are drawn from the middle and upper classes.

5. Charitable programs focused on individuals or families are fine, but the elites would not support help to the poor and disenfranchised to organize themselves socially and politically to collectively act on their own behalf.

6. "The basic fallacy in official development aid is, as a commentary on foreign aid underscores (Lappé et al. 1980), that it can reach the powerless by going through the powerful. As long as foreign aid is being channeled through recipient governments its chances of reaching the poor or stimulating popular participation are pre-empted by the structural constraints prevailing on the [African] continent" (Hyden 1983, 182).

7. It is amusing and perhaps illuminating to suppose that the large devel-

opment agencies were present during the era of historical events such as the American or French Revolution. Perhaps after the Boston Tea Party or the storming of the Bastille, a new World Bank loan could have been quickly arranged to alleviate the social pressures and thus to stabilize the Bank's client government.

8. When South Africa renewed its membership in the Bank and Fund after the democratic elections in 1994, there was considerable political opposition in South Africa to becoming indebted to the Bretton Woods institutions. Over the next years, the Bank launched a remarkable and modestly successful campaign to get South Africa to borrow. In addition to the usual Bank approaches, a high-level retreat was held between leaders of the Bank and the South Africa government, and the South Africa finance minister was even made the head of the Development Committee that oversees the governance of both the Bank and Fund and whose annual meeting each year is the principal official business of the annual Bank/Fund meetings.

9. See also Douglas McGregor's five-step program described in chapter 3.

10. Carla Eugster (1966) tells her remarkable story of a union organizer turned housewife and then field educator on her own initiative in a nearby impoverished black community. The case exemplifies autonomy-respecting assistance as she constantly walked on the edge, catalyzing action in a community of which she was not a part while observing the limits of the autonomy-respecting helper role by withdrawing whenever it seemed that she was taking ownership or leadership or that people were only doing things to please her rather than for their own motives. It was a subtle, time-consuming process that was full of pitfalls even when she brought no money. If she had a large wealth or power differential with respect to the doers, then it would have been near impossible to prevent the overriding or undercutting forms of unhelpful help.

11. And the founder of the successful Academy for Rural Development in Comilla (in what used to be eastern Pakistan) first lived in a village for two years to learn about rural life firsthand. Later, the same person, Akhtar Hameed Khan, lived a year in Orangi before starting up the Orangi Pilot Project. P. A. Kiriwandeniya returned to his home village for a year to learn about rural credit problems before starting SANASA in Sri Lanka.

12. One of the cases, the Philippine National Irrigation Administration, is extensively analyzed by Frances Korten, Robert Siy, and others in *Transforming a Bureaucracy* (1989). David Korten and Rudi Klauss (1984) have collected together cases and analyses in autonomy-respecting assistance under the title *People Centered Development*.

Bibliography

Abrams, M. H. 1953. *The Mirror and the Lamp: Romantic Theory and the Critical Tradition*. London: Oxford University Press.

Ackoff, Russell L. 1977. "National Development Planning Revisited." *Operations Research* 25, no. 2 (March–April): 212–18.

———. 1986. *Management in Small Doses*. New York: John Wiley.

———. 1994. *The Democratic Corporation*. New York: Oxford University Press.

Adams, Frank, with Myles Horton. 1975. *Unearthing Seeds of Fire*. Winston-Salem, NC: John F. Blair.

Addams, Jane. 1965. "A Modern Lear." In *The Social Thought of Jane Addams*, edited by Christopher Lasch, 105–23. Indianapolis: Bobbs-Merrill.

Adler, Paul S., and Bryan Borys. 1996. "Two Types of Bureaucracy: Enabling and Coercive." *Administrative Science Quarterly* 41: 61–89.

Akerlof, George. 1984. *An Economic Theorist's Book of Tales*. New York: Cambridge University Press.

Akerlof, George, and William Dickens. 1982. "The Economic Consequences of Cognitive Dissonance." *American Economic Review* 72 (June): 307–19. Reprinted in Akerlof 1984.

Alinsky, Saul. 1969. *Reveille for Radicals*. New York: Vintage.

———. 1971. *Rules for Radicals*. New York: Vintage.

Alkire, Sabina. 2002. *Valuing Freedoms: Sen's Capability Approach and Poverty Reduction*. New York: Oxford University Press.

Andreski, Stanislaw. 1972. *Social Sciences as Sorcery*. New York: St. Martins.

Argyris, Chris, and Donald Schön. 1978. *Organizational Learning: A Theory of Action Perspective*. Reading, MA: Addison-Wesley.

Arrow, Kenneth. 1963. "Uncertainty and the Welfare Economics of Medical Care." *American Economic Review* 53: 941–73.

———. 1972. "Gifts and Exchanges." *Philosophy and Public Affairs* 1: 343–62.

Arthur, Brian. 1994. *Increasing Returns and Path Dependence in the Economy*. Ann Arbor: University of Michigan Press.

Ashby, W. Ross. 1960. *Design for a Brain*. 2d ed. London: Chapman and Hall.

———. 1963. *An Introduction to Cybernetics*. New York: John Wiley and Sons.

Augustine. 1948. *Basic Writings of Saint Augustine*. Edited by Whitney J. Oates. New York: Random House.

Austin, J. L. 1970. *Philosophical Papers*. 2d ed. London: Oxford University Press.

Axelrod, Robert. 1984. *The Evolution of Cooperation*. New York: Basic Books.

Bagehot, Walter. [1869] 1948. *Physics and Politics*. Reprint, New York: Knopf.

Bandura, Albert, ed. 1995. *Self-Efficacy in Changing Societies*. Cambridge: Cambridge University Press.

Barker, Ernest. [1942] 1967. *Reflections on Government*. Reprint, London: Oxford University Press.

Bartlett, John. 1968. *Familiar Quotations*. 14th ed. Boston: Little, Brown.

Bateson, Gregory. 1972. *Steps to an Ecology of Mind*. New York: Ballantine.

Bauer, P. 1976. *Dissent on Development*. Cambridge: Harvard University Press.

———. 1981. *Equality, the Third World, and Economic Delusion*. Cambridge: Harvard University Press.

———. 2000. *From Subsistence to Exchange and Other Essays*. Princeton: Princeton University Press.

Becker, Carl. 1958. *The Declaration of Independence*. New York: Vintage Books.

Bennett, W. J., ed. 1993. *The Book of Virtues*. New York: Simon and Schuster.

Benziger, V. 1996. "The Chinese Wisely Realized That They Did Not Know What They Were Doing." *Transition* 7, nos. 7–8 (July–August): 6–7.

Berger, Peter. 1976. *Pyramids of Sacrifice*. Garden City, NY: Anchor Books.

Berlin, Isaiah. 1969. *Four Essays on Liberty*. Oxford: Oxford University Press.

———. 1980. *Against the Current: Essays in the History of Ideas*. New York: Viking.

Black, Bernard, Reinier Kraakman, and Anna Tarassova. 2000. "What Went Wrong with Russian Privatization." *Stanford Law Review* 52: 1–84.

Black, H. 1968. *Black's Law Dictionary*. St. Paul: West Publishing.

Black, Jan Knippers. 1999. *Development in Theory and Practice: Paradigms and Paradoxes*. 2d ed. Boulder: Westview.

Blustein, Paul. 2001. *The Chastening: Inside the Crisis That Rocked the Global Financial System and Humbled the IMF*. New York: PublicAffairs.

Bondurant, Joan. 1958. *Conquest of Violence: The Gandhian Philosophy of Conflict*. Princeton: Princeton University Press.

Boorstin, Daniel. 1980. *The Image: A Guide to Pseudo-Events in America*. New York: Atheneum.

Borish, Steven M. 1991. *The Land of the Living: The Danish Folk High Schools and Denmark's Non-violent Path to Modernization.* Nevada City, CA: Blue Dolphin.

Bräutigam, Deborah. 2000. *Aid Dependence and Governance.* Stockholm: Almqvist and Wiksell International.

Braybrooke, David, and C. Lindblom. 1963. *The Strategy of Decision.* New York: Free Press.

Brehm, Jack. 1972. *Responses to the Loss of Freedom: A Theory of Psychological Reactance.* Morristown, NJ: General Learning Press.

Breslin, Patrick. 1987. *Development and Dignity.* Rosslyn, VA: Inter-American Foundation.

Bretall, Robert, ed. 1946. *A Kierkegaard Anthology.* Princeton: Princeton University Press.

Bryce, James. [1888] 1959. *The American Commonwealth.* Reprint, New York: G. P. Putnam's Sons.

Buber, Martin. 1965. *Between Man and Man.* New York: Macmillan Publishing.

Buchanan, James. 1954. "Social Choice, Democracy, and Free Markets." *Journal of Political Economy* 62 (April): 114–23.

———. 1977. "The Samaritan's Dilemma." In *Freedom in Constitutional Contract,* edited by J. Buchanan, 169–80. College Station: Texas A&M University Press.

Buchanan, Scott. 1970. *Embers of the World.* Edited by Harris Wofford. Santa Barbara: Center for the Study of Democratic Institutions.

Burke, Edmund. [1790] 1937. "Reflections on the French Revolution: In a Letter Intended to Have Been Sent to a Gentleman in Paris." In *The Harvard Classics: Edmund Burke,* edited by C. Eliot, 143–378. Reprint, New York: Collier.

Burnet, Macfarlane. 1959. *The Clonal Selection Theory of Acquired Immunity.* Cambridge: Cambridge University Press.

Burnyeat, Myles. 1987a. "Wittgenstein and Augustine *De Magistro.*" *Proceedings of the Aristotelian Society* supp., 61: 1–24.

———. 1987b. "Plato: Dialogue with Myles Burnyeat." In *The Great Philosophers,* edited by Bryan Magee, 14–30. Oxford: Oxford University Press.

Campbell, Donald. 1995. *Incentives: Motivation and the Economics of Information.* New York: Cambridge University Press.

Campos, Jose Edgardo, and Hilton L. Root. 1996. *The Key to the Asian Miracle: Making Shared Growth Credible.* Washington, DC: Brookings Institution.

Candy, Philip. 1991. *Self-Direction for Lifelong Learning.* San Francisco: Jossey-Bass.

Carmen, Raff. 1996. *Autonomous Development.* London: Zed Books.

Carmen, Raff, and Miguel Sobrado, eds. 2000. *A Future for the Excluded: Job Creation and Income Generation for the Poor. Clodomir Santos de Morais and the Organizational Workshop*. London: Zed.

Caufield, Catherine. 1996. *Masters of Illusion: The World Bank and the Poverty of Nations*. New York: Henry Holt.

Chambers, Robert. 1983. *Rural Development: Putting the Last First*. Essex, UK: Longman Scientific and Technical.

Chang, Ha-Joon, ed. 2001. *Joseph Stiglitz and the World Bank: The Rebel Within*. London: Anthem.

Chomsky, Noam. 1966. *Cartesian Linguistics*. New York: Harper and Row.

———. 2000. "Propaganda and Indoctrination." Znet Commentary, December 10, 2000. http://www.zmag.org.

Coburn, Kathleen, ed. 1968. *Inquiring Spirit: A Coleridge Reader*. New York: Minerva Press.

Cole, Robert E. 1989. *Strategies for Learning*. Berkeley: University of California Press.

Collier, Paul. 1997. "The Failure of Conditionality." In *Perspectives on Aid and Development*, edited by Catherine Gwin and Joan Nelson, 51–77. Washington, DC: Overseas Development Council.

Combs, Arthur W., Donald L. Avila, and William W. Purkey. 1971. *Helping Relationships: Basic Concepts for the Helping Professions*. Boston: Allyn and Bacon.

Confucius. 1938. *The Analects of Confucius*. Translated by Arthur Waley. New York: Vintage.

Coser, Lewis. 1956. *The Functions of Social Conflict*. New York: Free Press.

———. 1974. *Greedy Institutions: Patterns of Undivided Commitment*. New York: Free Press.

Covey, Stephen. 1990. *The Seven Habits of Highly Effective People*. New York: Simon and Schuster.

Crick, Bernard. 1962. *In Defense of Politics*. Chicago: University of Chicago Press.

Cronin, Helena. 1991. *The Ant and the Peacock*. Cambridge: Cambridge University Press.

Csikszentmihalyi, Mihaly. 1990. *Flow: The Psychology of Optimal Experience*. New York: Harper and Row.

Cudworth, Ralph. [1731] 1996. *A Treatise Concerning Eternal and Immutable Morality*. Edited by S. Hutton. Reprint, Cambridge: Cambridge University Press.

Cyert, Richard, and James March. 1963. *Behavioral Theory of the Firm*. Englewood Cliffs, NJ: Prentice-Hall.

Cziko, Gary. 1995. *Without Miracles: Universal Selection Theory and the Second Darwinian Revolution*. Cambridge: MIT Press (a Bradford Book).

Dabrowski, Marek, Stanislaw Gomulka, and Jacek Rostowski. 2001. "Whence Reform?: A Critique of the Stiglitz Perspective." *Journal of Policy Reform* 4, no. 4: 291–324.

Dahrendorf, Ralf. 1990. *Reflections on the Revolution in Europe: In a Letter Intended to Have Been Sent to a Gentleman in Warsaw*. New York: Random House.

Datta, Dhirendra Mohan. 1961. *The Philosophy of Mahatma Gandhi*. Madison: University of Wisconsin Press.

Davenport, Thomas, and Laurence Prusak. 1998. *Working Knowledge*. Boston: Harvard Business School Press.

Dawkins, Richard. 1996. *Climbing Mount Improbable*. New York: W. W. Norton.

Deci, Edward, with Richard Flaste. 1995. *Why We Do What We Do*. New York: Penguin Books.

Deci, Edward, and Richard Ryan. 1985. *Intrinsic Motivation and Self-Determination in Human Behavior*. New York: Plenum Press.

De Grazia, Alfred. 1975. *Eight Bads—Eight Goods: The American Contradictions*. Garden City, NY: Anchor Books.

Deming, W. Edwards. 1994. *The New Economics for Industry, Government, Education*. Cambridge: MIT Center for Advanced Engineering.

Dennett, Daniel. 1995. *Darwin's Dangerous Idea: Evolution and the Meanings of Life*. New York: Touchstone.

DePree, Max. 1989. *Leadership Is an Art*. New York: Dell.

de Soto, Hernando. 2000. *The Mystery of Capital*. New York: Basic Books.

Dewey, John. 1916. *Democracy and Education*. New York: Free Press.

———. 1927. *The Public and Its Problems*. Chicago: Swallow Press.

———. 1939. *Freedom and Culture*. New York: Capricorn.

———. 1957. *Human Nature and Conduct: An Introduction to Social Psychology*. New York: Modern Library.

Dewey, John, and James Tufts. 1908. *Ethics*. New York: Henry Holt.

———. 1932. *Ethics*. Rev. ed. New York: Henry Holt.

Dichter, Thomas. 2003. *Despite Good Intentions: Why Development Assistance to the Third World Has Failed*. Amherst: University of Massachusetts Press.

Donovan, Suzanne, John Bransford, and James Pellegrino, eds. 1999. *How People Learn: Bridging Research and Practice*. Washington, DC: National Academy Press.

Dore, Ronald. 1976. *The Diploma Disease: Education, Qualification, and Development*. Berkeley: University of California Press.

Dore, Ronald, and Hugh Whittaker. 1994. "Introduction." In *Business Enterprise in Japan: Views of Leading Japanese Economists*, edited by Kenichi Imai and Ryutaro Komiya, 1–15. Cambridge: MIT Press.

Drucker, Peter. 1954. *The Practice of Management*. New York: Harper and Row.

———. 1973. *Management: Tasks, Responsibilities, Practices*. New York: Harper and Row.

Duckworth, Eleanor. 1973. "Language and Thought." In *Piaget in the Classroom*, edited by M. Schwebel and J. Raph, 132–54. New York: Basic Books.

———. 1987. *"The Having of Wonderful Ideas" and Other Essays on Teaching and Learning*. New York: Teachers College Press, Columbia University.

Dunn, Edgar. 1971. *Economic and Social Development: A Process of Social Learning*. Baltimore: Johns Hopkins Press.

Eade, Deborah. 1997. *Capacity-Building, an Approach to People-Centered Development*. Oxford: Oxfam.

Easterly, William. 2001. *The Elusive Quest for Growth: Economists' Adventures and Misadventures in the Tropics*. Cambridge: MIT Press.

Eatwell, John, Murray Milgate, and Peter Newman, eds. 1989. *The New Palgrave: Allocation, Information, and Markets*. New York: W. W. Norton.

Edelman, Gerald. 1992. *Bright Air, Brilliant Fire: On the Matter of the Mind*. New York: Basic Books.

Edelman, Gerald, and Giulio Tononi. 2000. *A Universe of Consciousness*. New York: Basic Books.

Edmunson, Charles. 1999. *Paradoxes of Leadership*. Cambridge, MA: Edmunson.

Egan, Gerard. 1990. *The Skilled Helper: A Systematic Approach to Effective Helping*. 4th ed. Pacific Grove, CA: Brooks/Cole.

Eisenhardt, Kathleen. 1989. "Agency Theory: An Assessment and Review." *Academy of Management Review* 14, no. 1: 57–74.

Ellerman, David. 1985. "On the Labor Theory of Property." *Philosophical Forum* 16 (summer): 293–326.

———. 1988a. "The Legitimate Opposition at Work: The Union's Role in Large Democratic Firms." *Economic and Industrial Democracy: An International Journal* 9, no. 4 (November): 437–53.

———. 1988b. "The Kantian Person/Thing Principle in Political Economy." *Journal of Economic Issues* 22, no. 4: 1109–22.

———. 1990. *The Democratic Worker-Owned Firm*. London: Unwin-Hyman Academic.

———. 1992. *Property and Contract in Economics: The Case for Economic Democracy*. Cambridge, MA: Blackwell.

———. 1993. "Management and Employee Buy-Outs in Central and Eastern Europe: Introduction." In *Management and Employee Buy-Outs as a Technique of Privatization*, edited by D. Ellerman, 13–30. Ljubljana: Central and Eastern European Privatization Network. Available at www.ellerman.org.

————. 1995. *Intellectual Trespassing as a Way of Life: Essays in Philosophy, Economics, and Mathematics*. Lanham, MD: Rowman and Littlefield.

————. 2000. "Getting the Bugs out of the Knowledge Bank Idea." World Bank Memo. http://www.ellerman.org/Davids-Stuff/Memos/Insect-Theory.pdf

————. 2001a. "Lessons from East Europe's Voucher Privatization." *Challenge: The Magazine of Economic Affairs* 44, no. 4 (July–August): 14–37.

————. 2001b. "Guest Editorial: Mixing Truth and Power: Implications for a Knowledge Organization." *Newsletter of World Bank Group Staff Association*, November–December, 3.

————. 2002. "Should Development Agencies Have Official Views?" *Development in Practice* 12, no. 3: 285–97.

————. 2003. "On the Russian Privatization Debates: What Has Been Learned a Decade Later?" *Challenge: The Magazine of Economic Affairs* 46, no. 3 (May–June): 6–28.

Ellerman, David, and Vladimir Kreacic. 2002. "Transforming the Old into a Foundation for the New: Lessons of the Moldova ARIA Project." Policy Research Working Paper 2866. Washington, DC: World Bank.

Ellwood, David. 1988. *Poor Support: Poverty in the American Family*. New York: Basic Books.

Elmore, R. 1991. Foreword. In *Education for Judgment*, edited by C. R. Christensen, D. A. Garvin, and A. Sweet, ix–xix. Boston: Harvard Business School Press.

Elster, Jon. 1983. *Sour Grapes: Studies in the Subversion of Rationality*. Cambridge: Cambridge University Press.

Elster, Jon, C. Offe, and U. Preuss. 1998. *Institutional Design in Post-Communist Societies: Rebuilding the Ship at Sea*. Cambridge: Cambridge University Press.

Erikson, Erik. 1964. *Insight and Responsibility*. New York: Norton.

————. 1969. *Gandhi's Truth: On the Origins of Militant Nonviolence*. New York: Norton.

Esman, Milton, and Norman Uphoff. 1984. *Local Organizations: Intermediaries in Rural Development*. Ithaca: Cornell University Press.

Estes, Ralph. 1996. *Tyranny of the Bottom Line: Why Corporations Make Good People Do Bad Things*. San Francisco: Berrett-Koehler.

Eugster, Carla. 1966. "Field Education in West Heights: Equipping a Deprived Community to Help Itself." In *Sociology in Action*, edited by Arthur Shostak, 208–25. Homewood, IL: Dorsey Press. Originally published in *Human Organization*, fall 1964.

European Bank for Reconstruction and Development (EBRD). 1993. *Management and Employee Buy-Outs in Central and Eastern Europe—An Introduction*. London: EBRD.

Evans, Peter. 1979. *Dependent Development: The Alliance of Multinational, State, and Local Capital in Brazil*. Princeton, NJ: Princeton University Press.

Farber, Leslie. 1976. *Lying, Despair, Jealousy, Envy, Sex, Suicide, Drugs, and the Good Life*. New York: Basic Books.

Feshbach, Murray. 2003a. *Russia's Health and Demographic Crises: Policy Implications and Consequences*. Washington, DC: Woodrow Wilson International Center.

———. 2003b. "A Country on the Verge." *New York Times*, May 31.

Festinger, L. 1957. *A Theory of Cognitive Dissonance*. Stanford: Stanford University Press.

Festinger, L., H. Riecken, and S. Schachter. 1956. *When Prophecy Fails*. New York: Harper Torchbooks.

Feynman, Richard. 1985. *Surely You're Joking Mr. Feynman*. New York: W. W. Norton.

Fisher, Julie. 1993. *The Road from Rio: Sustainable Development and the Nongovernmental Movement in the Third World*. Westport, CT: Praeger.

———. 1997. *Nongovernments: NGOs and the Political Development of the Third World*. West Hartford, CT: Kumarian Press.

Follett, Mary Parker. [1926] 1992. "The Giving of Orders." In *Classics of Public Administration*, edited by J. Shafritz and A. Hyde, 66–74. Reprint, Pacific Grove, CA: Brooks/Cole.

Freeland, Chrystia. 2000. *Sale of the Century: Russia's Wild Ride from Communism to Capitalism*. New York: Crown Business.

Freire, Paulo. 1970. *Pedagogy of the Oppressed*. New York: Continuum.

Frey, Bruno. 1997. *Not Just for the Money: An Economic Theory of Personal Motivation*. Cheltenham, UK: Edward Elgar.

———. 2001. *Inspiring Economics: Human Motivation in Political Economy*. Cheltenham, UK: Edward Elgar.

Friedman, Maurice. 1960. *Martin Buber: The Life of Dialogue*. New York: Harper Torchbooks.

Froebel, Friedrich W. 1954. "Froebel." In *Three Thousand Years of Educational Wisdom*, edited by Robert Ulich, 523–76. Cambridge: Harvard University Press.

Fukuda-Parr, Sakiko, Carlos Lopes, and Khalid Malik, eds. 2002. *Capacity for Development: New Solutions to Old Problems*. New York: United Nations Development Programme and Earthscan.

Fukuyama, Francis. 1999. *The Great Disruption*. New York: Free Press.

Furtado, Celso. 1987. "Underdevelopment: To Conform or Reform." In *Pioneers in Development: Second Series*, edited by G. Meier, 205–27. New York: Oxford University Press.

Galtung, Johan, Peter O'Brien, and Roy Preiswerk, eds. 1980. *Self-Reliance: A Strategy for Development*. Geneva: Institute for Development Studies.

Gandhi, Mohandas K. 1957. *An Autobiography: The Story of My Experiments with Truth*. Boston: Beacon Press.

———. 1961. *Non-violent Resistance (Satyagraha)*. New York: Schocken.

Gilbert, Christopher, and David Vines, eds. 2000. *The World Bank: Structure and Policies*. Cambridge: Cambridge University Press.

Gilbert, Christopher, A. Powell, and D. Vines. 2000. "Positioning the World Bank." In *The World Bank: Structure and Policies*, edited by Christopher Gilbert and David Vines, 39–86. Cambridge: Cambridge University Press.

Glade, William, and Charles Reilly, eds. 1994. *Inquiry at the Grassroots: An Inter-American Foundation Fellowship Reader*. Arlington, VA: Inter-American Foundation.

Goulet, Denis. 1971. *The Cruel Choice*. New York: Atheneum.

Gran, Guy. 1983. *Development by People*. New York: Praeger.

Griesgraber, Jo Marie, and Bernhard Gunter, eds. 1996. *The World Bank: Lending on a Global Scale*. London: Pluto Press.

Griffin, Keith. 1989. *Alternative Strategies for Economic Development*. New York: St. Martin's Press.

Gronemeyer, Marianne. 1992. "Helping." In *The Development Dictionary: A Guide to Knowledge as Power*, edited by Wolfgang Sachs, 51–69. London: Zed Books.

Guthrie, W. K. C. 1960. *The Greek Philosophers: From Thales to Aristotle*. New York: Harper and Row.

Gwin, Catherine, and Joan Nelson, eds. 1997. *Perspectives on Aid and Development*. Washington, DC: Overseas Development Council.

Haas, E. B. 1990. *When Knowledge Is Power: Three Models of Change in International Organizations*. Berkeley: University of California.

Habermas, Jurgen. 1990. *Moral Consciousness and Communicative Action*. Cambridge: MIT Press.

Hamilton, Alexander, James Madison, and John Jay. [1788] 1961. *The Federalist Papers*. New York: New American Library.

Handy, Charles. 1989. *The Age of Unreason*. Boston: Harvard Business School Press.

———. 1993. *Understanding Organizations*. 4th ed. London: Penguin.

Harding, Harry. 1987. *China's Second Revolution: Reform after Mao*. Washington, DC: Brookings Institution.

Harrold, P. 1995. "The Broad Sector Approach to Investment Lending: Sector Investment Programs." World Bank Discussion Paper 302.

Hart, B. H. Liddell 1941. *The Strategy of Indirect Approach*. London: Farber and Farber.

———. 1963. Foreword. In *Sun Tzu: The Art of War*, edited by S. B. Griffith, v–vii. London: Oxford University Press.

———. 1967. *Strategy*. New York: New American Library.

Hart, Joseph K. 1926. *Light from the North: The Danish Folk High Schools—Their Meanings for America*. New York: Holt.

Hawkins, David. 1973. "What It Means to Teach." *Teachers' College Record* 75, no. 1: 7–16.

————. 2000. *The Roots of Literacy*. Boulder: University Press of Colorado.

Hayek, Friedrich. 1960. *The Constitution of Liberty*. Chicago: University of Chicago Press.

————. 1978. *New Studies in Philosophy, Economics, and the History of Ideas*. Chicago: University of Chicago Press.

————. 1979. *The Counter-Revolution of Science: Studies on the Abuse of Reason*. Indianapolis: Liberty Fund.

————. 1992. *The Fortunes of Liberalism: Essays on Austrian Economics and the Ideal of Freedom*. Edited by Peter Klein. Chicago: University of Chicago Press.

Heyes, Cecilia, and David Hull, eds. 2001. *Selection Theory and Social Construction*. Albany: State University of New York Press.

Hirsch, Fred. 1976. *Social Limits to Growth*. Cambridge: Harvard University Press.

Hirsch, P., S. Michaels, and R. Friedman. 1987. "'Dirty Hands' versus 'Clean Models': Is Sociology in Danger of Being Seduced by Economics?" *Theory and Society* 16, no. 3: 317–36.

Hirschman, Albert O. 1961. *The Strategy of Economic Development*. Paperback ed. 1958. Reprint, New Haven: Yale University Press.

————. 1970. *Exit, Voice, and Loyalty*. Cambridge: Harvard University Press.

————. 1971. *A Bias for Hope: Essays on Development and Latin America*. New Haven: Yale University Press.

————. 1973. *Journeys toward Progress*. New York: Norton.

————. 1977. *The Passions and the Interests*. Princeton: Princeton University Press.

————. 1981. *Essays in Trespassing: Economics to Politics and Beyond*. Cambridge: Cambridge University Press.

————. 1984a. "A Dissenter's Confession: 'The Strategy of Economic Development' Revisited." In *Pioneers in Development*, edited by G. Meier and D. Seers, 87–111. New York: Oxford University Press.

————. 1984b. *Getting Ahead Collectively: Grassroots Experiences in Latin America*. New York: Pergamon Press.

————. 1991. *The Rhetoric of Reaction: Perversity, Futility, Jeopardy*. Cambridge, MA: Belknap Press.

————. 1992. *Rival Views of Market Society*. Cambridge: Harvard University Press.

————. 1994a. "A Propensity to Self-Subversion." In *Rethinking the Development Experience: Essays Provoked by the Work of Albert O. Hirschman*, edited

by L. Rodwin and D. Schön, 277–83. Washington, DC: Brookings Institution.

———. 1994b. "Hirschman: Responses and Discussion." In *Rethinking the
Development Experience: Essays Provoked by the Work of Albert O.
Hirschman*, edited by L. Rodwin and D. Schön, 314–21. Washington, DC:
Brookings Institution.

———. 1995. "Social Conflicts as Pillars of Democratic Market Societies." In
A Propensity to Self-Subversion, 231–48. Cambridge: Harvard University
Press.

Hirschman, Albert O., and Richard M. Bird. 1971. "Foreign Aid: A Critique
and a Proposal." In *A Bias for Hope*, edited. by Albert O. Hirschman,
197–224. New Haven: Yale University Press.

Hirschman, Albert O., and Charles E. Lindblom. 1971. "Economic Develop-
ment, Research and Development, and Policy Making: Some Converging
Views." In *A Bias for Hope*, edited. by Albert O. Hirschman, 63–84. New
Haven: Yale University Press. Reprint of Albert O. Hirschman and Charles
E. Lindblom. 1962. *Behavioral Science* 7: 211–22.

Holt, John. 1976. *Instead of Education: Ways to Help People Do Things Better*.
New York: Delta.

Horton, Myles, with Judith Kohl and Herbert Kohl. 1998. *The Long Haul: An
Autobiography*. New York: Teachers College Press.

Hull, David L. 2001. *Science and Selection*. New York: Cambridge University
Press.

Humboldt, Wilhelm von. 1963. *Humanist without Portfolio*. Translated by
Marianne Cowan. Detroit: Wayne State University Press.

———. [1854] 1969. *The Limits of State Action*. Edited by J. W. Burrow.
Reprint, Cambridge: Cambridge University Press.

———. [1836] 1997. "The Nature and Conformation of Language." In *The
Hermeneutics Reader*, edited by Kurt Mueller-Vollmer, 99–105. Reprint,
New York: Continuum.

Hutcheson, Francis. 1755. *A System of Moral Philosophy*. London.

Hyden, Goran. 1983. *No Shortcuts to Progress: African Development Management in Perspective*. Berkeley: University of California Press.

Illich, Ivan 1972. *Deschooling Society*. New York: Harper and Row.

———. 1976. *Medical Nemesis: The Expropriation of Health*. New York: Pantheon.

———. 1978a. *Toward a History of Needs*. New York: Pantheon Books.

———. 1978b. *The Right to Useful Unemployment and Its Professional Enemies*.
London: Marion Boyars.

Ionescu, G., and I. de Madariaga. 1972. *Opposition: Past and Present of a Political Institution*. Harmondsworth, UK: Penguin.

Israel, Arturo. 1987. *Institutional Development: Incentives to Performance.* Washington, DC: World Bank.

Jacobs, Jane. 1961. *The Death and Life of Great American Cities.* New York: Vintage.

———. 1969. *The Economy of Cities.* New York: Random House.

———. 1984. *Cities and the Wealth of Nations: Principles of Economic Life.* New York: Random House.

———. 2000. *The Nature of Economies.* New York: Modern Library.

Janik, Allan, and Stephen Toulmin. 1973. *Wittgenstein's Vienna.* New York: Touchstone.

Janis, I. L. 1972. *Victims of Groupthink.* Boston: Houghton Mifflin.

Jerne, Niels K. 1955. "The Natural Selection Theory of Antibody Formation." *Proceedings of the National Academy of Sciences U.S.A.* 41: 849.

———. 1967. "Antibodies and Learning: Selection versus Instruction." In *The Neurosciences: A Study Program,* edited by G. C. Quarton, T. Melnechuk, and F. O. Schmitt, 200–205. New York: Rockefeller University Press:

———. 1993. "The Generative Grammar of the Immune System." In *Nobel Lectures in Physiology or Medicine, 1981–1990,* edited by J. Lindstern. Singapore: World Scientific. Available at http://www.nobel.se/medicine/laureates/1984/jerne-lecture.html.

Jones, Stephen. 2000. "Increasing Aid Effectiveness in Africa? The World Bank and Sector Investment Programmes." In *The World Bank: Structure and Policies,* edited by Christopher Gilbert and David Vines, 266–81. Cambridge: Cambridge University Press.

Juvenal. *Satire VI.* Available at http://www.fordham.edu/halsall/ancient/juvenal-satvi.html.

Kaldor, Nicholas. 1966. *Causes of the Slow Rate of Economic Growth of the United Kingdom.* Cambridge: Cambridge University Press.

Kamii, Constance. 1973. "Pedagogical Principles Derived from Piaget's Theory: Relevance for Educational Practice." In *Piaget in the Classroom,* edited by M. Schwebel and J. Raph, 199–215. New York: Basic Books.

Kanbur, Ravi. 2001. "Economic Policy, Distribution, and Poverty: The Nature of Disagreements." *World Development* 29, no. 6: 1083–94.

Kanbur, Ravi, and Todd Sandler with Kevin Morrison. 1999. *The Future of Development Assistance: Common Pools and International Public Goods.* Washington, DC: Overseas Development Council.

Kanbur, Ravi, and David Vines. 2000. "The World Bank and Poverty Reduction: Past, Present, and Future." In *The World Bank: Structure and Policies,* edited by Christopher Gilbert and David Vines, 87–107. Cambridge: Cambridge University Press.

Kanigel, Robert. 1997. *The One Best Way: Frederick Winslow Taylor and the Enigma of Efficiency*. New York: Viking.

Kant, Immanuel. [1785] 1964. *Groundwork of the Metaphysic of Morals*. Translated by H. J. Paton. Reprint, New York: Harper Torchbooks.

———. [1784] 1991a. "Idea for a Universal History with a Cosmopolitan Purpose." In *Kant Political Writings*, edited by H. Reiss, 41–53. Reprint, New York: Cambridge University Press.

———. [1797] 1991b. *The Metaphysics of Morals*. Translated by M. Gregor. Reprint, New York: Cambridge University Press.

———. [1786] 1991c. "What Is Orientation in Thinking?" In *Kant: Political Writings*, edited by H. Reiss, 237–49. Reprint, Cambridge: Cambridge University Press.

Kaplan, Allan. 1996. *The Development Practitioners' Handbook*. London: Pluto Press.

Keynes, John Maynard. 1933. "National Self-Sufficiency." In *The Collected Writings of John Maynard Keynes*, edited by D. Moggeridge, 233–46. London: Cambridge University Press. Originally published in the *Yale Review*, 1933.

Kierkegaard, Søren. 1989. *The Concept of Irony with Continual Reference to Socrates*. Edited and translated by Howard Hong and Edna Hong. Princeton: Princeton University Press.

———. 1992. *Concluding Unscientific Postscript to Philosophical Fragments*. Edited and translated by Howard and Edna Hong, vol. 1. Princeton: Princeton University Press.

Killick, Tony, with R. Gunatilaka and A. Marr. 1998. *Aid and the Political Economy of Policy Change*. London: Routledge.

Kinsey, Karyl. 1992. "Deterrence and Alienation Effects of IRS Enforcement: An Analysis of Survey Data." In *Why People Pay Taxes: Tax Compliance and Enforcement*, edited by J. Slemrod, 259–85. Ann Arbor: University of Michigan Press.

Klein, Burton. 1977. *Dynamic Economics*. Cambridge: Harvard University Press.

———. 1984. *Prices, Wages, and Business Cycles: A Dynamic Theory*. New York: Pergamon Press.

Klein, Burton, and W. Meckling. 1958. "Application of Operations Research to Development Decisions." *Operations Research* 6: 352–63.

Knight, Frank. 1947. *Freedom and Reform*. New York: Harper and Row.

Kohn, Alfie. 1993. *Punished by Rewards: The Trouble with Gold Stars, Incentive Plans, A's, Praise, and Other Bribes*. Boston: Houghton Mifflin.

———. 1999. *The Schools Our Children Deserve*. Boston: Houghton Mifflin.

Kohr, Leopold. 1973. *Development without Aid: The Translucent Society*. Carmarthenshire, UK: Christopher Davies.

Korten, David C. 1983. "Social Development: Putting People First." In *Bureaucracy and the Poor: Closing the Gap*, edited by David Korten and Felipe Alfonso, 201–21. West Hartford, CT: Kumarian Press.

———. 1984. "Rural Development Programming: The Learning Process Approach." In *People-Centered Development*, edited by D. Korten and R. Klauss, 176–88. West Hartford, CT: Kumarian Press.

Korten, David C., and Rudi Klauss, eds. 1984. *People-Centered Development*. West Hartford, CT: Kumarian Press.

Korten, Frances F., and Robert Y. Siy, eds. 1989. *Transforming a Bureaucracy: The Experience of the Philippine National Irrigation Administration*. Manila: Ateneo De Manila University Press.

Kreps, David. 1997. "Intrinsic Motivation and Extrinsic Incentives." *American Economic Review* 87: 359–65.

Kretzmann, John P., and John L. McKnight. 1993. *Building Communities from the Inside Out: A Path toward Finding and Mobilizing a Community's Assets*. Evanston, IL: Institute for Policy Research.

Krimerman, L. I. 1972. "Autonomy: A New Paradigm for Research." In *Philosophical Redirections of Educational Research*, edited by L.G. Thomas. Chicago: National Society for the Study of Education.

Krishna, Anirudh, Norman Uphoff, and Milton Esman, eds. 1997. *Reasons for Hope: Instructive Experiences in Rural Development*. West Hartford, CT: Kumarian Press.

Krueger, Alan, and Jitka Malecková. 2003. "Education, Poverty, and Terrorism: Is There a Causal Connection?" *Journal of Economic Perspectives* 17, no 4 (fall): 119–44.

Krugman, Paul. 1994. "The Fall and Rise of Development Economics." In *Rethinking the Development Experience: Essays Provoked by the Work of Albert O. Hirschman*, edited by L. Rodwin and D. Schön, 39–58. Washington, DC: Brookings Institution.

Lakatos, Imre, and Alan Musgrave, eds. 1970. *Criticism and the Growth of Knowledge*. Cambridge: Cambridge University Press.

Lane, Robert E. 1991. *The Market Experience*. New York: Cambridge University Press.

———. 2000. *The Loss of Happiness in Market Democracies*. New Haven: Yale University Press.

Lao-Tzu. 1989. *Te-Tao Ching*. Translated by Robert Henricks. New York: Ballantine.

Lappé, Frances Moore, Joseph Collins, and David Kinley. 1980. *Aid as Obstacle*. San Francisco: Institute for Food and Development Policy.

Lasch, Christopher. 1995. *The Revolt of the Elites and the Betrayal of Democracy*. New York: Norton.

Lau, Lawrence, Ying-Yi Qian, and Gerard Roland. 2000. "Reform without Losers: An Interpretation of China's Dual-Track Approach to Transition." *Journal of Political Economy* 108, no. 1: 120–43.

Lavoie, Don. 1985. *National Economic Planning: What Is Left?* Cambridge, MA: Ballinger.

Lawrence, Elizabeth. 1970. *The Origins and Growth of Modern Education*. Baltimore: Pelican.

Lawrence, Peter. 1979. *Road Belong Cargo: A Study of the Cargo Movement in the Southern Madang District New Guinea*. Atlantic Highland, NJ: Humanities Press.

Lefcourt, Herbert. 1976. *Locus of Control*. Hillsdale, NJ: Erlbaum/Wiley.

Leibenstein, Harvey. 1966. "Allocative Efficiency versus X-Efficiency." *American Economic Review* 56, no. 3: 392–415.

———. 1980. *Beyond Economic Man: A New Foundation for Microeconomics*. Cambridge: Harvard University Press.

Lepper, Mark R., and David Greene, eds. 1978. *The Hidden Costs of Rewards: New Perspectives on the Psychology of Human Motivation*. Hillsdale, NJ: Erlbaum.

Levy, Leonard. 1985. *Emergence of a Free Press*. New York: Oxford University Press.

Lilienthal, David. 1944. *TVA-Democracy on the March*. New York: Harper.

———. 1967. "Overseas Development as a Humanist Art." In *Management: A Humanist Art*. New York: Columbia University Press.

Lin, Yutang, ed. 1948. *The Wisdom of Laotse*. New York: Modern Library.

Lindblom, Charles. 1959. "The Science of 'Muddling Through.'" *Public Administration Review* 19: 79–88.

———. 1965. *The Intelligence of Democracy: Decision Making through Mutual Adjustment*. New York: Free Press.

———. 1979. "Still Muddling, Not Yet Through." *Public Administration Review* 39 (November–December): 222–33.

———. 1990. *Inquiry and Change*. New Haven: Yale University Press.

Lloyd, Geoffrey E. R. 1996. *Adversaries and Authorities: Investigations into Ancient Greek and Chinese Science*. Cambridge: Cambridge University Press.

Lloyd, Richard. 1993. "Pilot Privatizations and Management-Employee Buy-Outs in Russia, 1991–92." In *Management and Employee Buy-Outs as a Technique of Privatization*, edited by D. Ellerman, 150–58. Ljubljana: Central and Eastern European Privatization Network.

Locke, John. [1689] 1990. *A Letter Concerning Toleration*. Reprint, Buffalo, NY: Prometheus Books.

Lucas, Robert E. 1988. "On the Mechanics of Economic Development." *Journal of Monetary Economics* 22, no. 1: 3–42.

Luther, Martin. [1522] 1942. "Concerning Secular Authority." In *Readings in Political Philosophy*, ed. F. W. Coker, 306–29. Reprint, New York: Macmillan.

Lutz, Mark. 1999. *Economics for the Common Good*. London: Routledge.

Mankiw, N. Gregory. 2003. "Review of: Reinventing the Bazaar (Book by John McMillan)." *Journal of Economic Literature* 41 (March): 256–57.

Maren, Michael. 1997. *The Road to Hell: The Ravaging Effects of Foreign Aid and International Charity*. New York: Free Press.

Marglin, Stephen. 1990. "Losing Touch: The Cultural Conditions of Worker Accommodation and Resistance." In *Dominating Knowledge: Development, Culture, and Resistance*, edited by Frederique Marglin and Stephen Marglin, 217–82. Oxford: Clarendon.

Maritain, Jacques. 1943. *Education at the Crossroads*. New Haven: Yale University Press.

Marjolin, Robert. 1989. *Architect of European Unity: Memoirs, 1911–1986*. Translated by William Hall. London: Weidenfeld and Nicolson.

Marshall, Alfred. 1961. *Principles of Economics*. London: Macmillan.

Maslow, Abraham. 1968. *Toward a Psychology of Being*. New York: Van Nostrand.

Maslow, Abraham, with D. Stephens and G. Heil. 1998. *Maslow on Management*. New York: John Wiley and Sons.

Mason, Alpheus Thomas. 1946. *Brandeis: A Free Man's Life*. New York: Viking Press.

Mason, Edward S., and Robert E. Asher. 1973. *The World Bank since Bretton Woods*. Washington, DC: Brookings Institution.

Matson, Floyd. 1966. *The Broken Image: Man, Science, and Society*. Garden City, NY: Anchor Books.

McClelland, David C. 1970. "The Two Faces of Power." *Journal of International Affairs* 24, no. 1: 29–47.

McClintock, Robert. 1982. "Reaffirming a Great Tradition." In *Invitation to Lifelong Learning*, edited by R. Gross, 46–78. Chicago: Follett. Originally published as Robert McClintock. 1971. "Toward a Place of Study in a World of Instruction." *Teachers College Record* 73, no. 2 (December): 161–205.

McGregor, Douglas. 1948. "The Staff Function in Human Relations." *Journal of Social Issues* 4, no. 3: 5–22. Reprinted in McGregor 1966, 145–71.

———. 1960. *The Human Side of Enterprise*. New York: McGraw-Hill.

———. 1966. *Leadership and Motivation*. Cambridge: MIT Press.

———. 1967. *The Professional Manager*. Edited by Caroline McGregor and Warren Bennis. New York: McGraw-Hill.

McKnight, John. 1995. *The Careless Society: Community and Its Counterfeits*. New York: Basic Books.

McMillan, John. 2002. *Reinventing the Bazaar: A Natural History of Markets*. New York: Norton.

Medawar, Peter B. 1960. *The Future of Man: Reith Lectures, 1959*. London: Methuen.

———. 1982. *Pluto's Republic*. Oxford: Oxford University Press.

Medawar, Peter B., and Jean S. Medawar. 1977. *The Life Science*. New York: Harper and Row.

Meldolesi, Luca. 1995. *Discovering the Possible: The Surprising World of Albert O. Hirschman*. Notre Dame: University of Notre Dame Press.

Memmi, Albert. 1967. *The Colonizer and the Colonized*. Boston: Beacon Press.

———. 1984. *Dependence: A Sketch for a Portrait of the Dependent*. Translated by Philip A. Facey. Boston: Beacon Press.

Merton, Robert K. 1968. "The Self-Fulfilling Prophecy." In *Social Theory and Social Structure* 475–90. New York: Free Press.

Metcalf, Henry, and L. Urwick, eds. 1942. *Dynamic Administration: The Collected Papers of Mary Parker Follett*. New York: Harper.

Michels, R. 1962. *Political Parties*. New York: Collier Books.

Mill, John Stuart. [1848] 1970. *Principles of Political Economy*. Reprint, Harmondsworth, UK: Penguin.

———. [1859] 1972. "On Liberty." In *J. S. Mill: Utilitarianism, on Liberty and Considerations on Representative Government*, edited by H. B. Acton, 69–185. Reprint, London: J. M. Dent and Sons.

Milton, John. [1644] 1957a. "Areopagitica." In *John Milton: Complete Poems and Major Prose*, edited by Merritt Hughes, 716–49. Reprint, New York: Odyssey Press.

———. [1659] 1957b. "To Remove Hirelings out of the Church." In *John Milton: Complete Poems and Major Prose*, edited by Merritt Hughes, 856–79. Reprint, New York: Odyssey Press.

Moffitt, Robert. 1992. "Incentive Effects of the United States Welfare System: A Review." *Journal of Economic Literature* 30: 1–61.

Montaigne, Michel de. [1595] 1958. *Essays*. Translated by J. M. Cohen. Reprint, Harmondsworth, UK: Penguin.

———. [1595] 1991. *The Complete Essays*. Translated by M. A. Screech. Reprint, London: Penguin.

Moore Jr., Barrington. 1972. *Reflections on the Causes of Human Misery and upon Certain Proposals to Eliminate Them*. Boston: Beacon Press.

Morita, A. 1986. *Made in Japan*. New York: E. P. Dutton.

Morley, John. 1928. *On Compromise*. London: Macmillan.

Mosley, Paul, Jane Harrigan, and John Toye. 1991. *Aid and Power: The World Bank and Policy-Based Lending*. London: Routledge.

Murray, Charles. 1984. *Losing Ground: American Social Policy, 1959–1980*. New York: Basic Books.

———. 1988. *In Pursuit of Happiness and Good Government*. New York: Simon and Schuster.

———. 1997. *What It Means to Be a Libertarian: A Personal Interpretation*. New York: Broadway Books.

Murrell, Peter. 1992. "Conservative Political Philosophy and the Strategy of Economic Transition." *Eastern European Politics and Societies* 6, no. 1: 3–16.

Myrdal, G. [1944] 1972. *An American Dilemma*. 2 vols. Reprint, New York: Pantheon.

Narayan, Deepa, with P. Raj, K. Schafft, A. Rademacher, and S. Koch-Schulte. 2000. *Voices of the Poor: Can Anyone Hear Us?* Washington, DC: Oxford University Press for the World Bank.

Nehru, J. 1956. *The Discovery of India*. London: Meridian.

Nelson, Leonard. 1949. *Socratic Method and Critical Philosophy*. Translated by T. K. Brown. New York: Dover.

Nonaka, I., and H. Takeuchi. 1995. *The Knowledge-Creating Company*. New York: Oxford.

Nurkse, Ragnar. 1967. *Problems of Capital Formation in Underdeveloped Countries and Patterns of Trade and Development*. New York: Oxford University Press.

Nussbaum, Martha. 1994. *The Therapy of Desire: Theory and Practice in Hellenistic Ethics*. Princeton: Princeton University Press.

———. 1997. *Cultivating Humanity: A Classical Defense of Reform in Liberal Education*. Cambridge: Harvard University Press.

———. 2000. *Women and Human Development: The Capabilities Approach*. Cambridge: Cambridge University Press.

Oakeshott, Michael. 1991. *Rationalism in Politics and Other Essays*. Indianapolis: Liberty Fund.

OED (Operations Evaluation Department). 2000. *Kazakhstan Country Assistance Evaluation* (draft). Washington, DC: World Bank.

Ortega y Gasset, Jose. 1961. *Meditations on Quixote*. New York: Norton.

———. 1966. *Mission of the University*. New York: Norton.

Ostrom, Elinor, Clark Gibson, Sujai Shivakumar, and Krister Andersson. 2001. *Aid, Incentives, and Sustainability: An Institutional Analysis of Development Cooperation*. Bloomington, IN: Workshop in Political Theory and Policy Analysis.

O'Toole, James. 1995. *Leading Change: Overcoming the Ideology of Comfort and the Tyranny of Custom*. San Francisco: Jossey-Bass.

Oxfam. 1985. *The Field Directors' Handbook: An Oxfam Manual for Development Workers*. Edited by Brian Pratt and Jo Boyden. Oxford: Oxford University Press.

Patterson, Orlando. 2002. Beyond Compassion: Selfish Reasons for Being Unselfish. *Daedalus*, winter: 26–38.

Pauly, Mark. 1980. *Doctors and Their Workshops: Economic Models of Physician Behavior*. Chicago: University of Chicago Press.

Perroux, Francois. 1953. "Note sur la notion de 'pole de croissance.'" *Economie appliquee* 8 (January–June): 307–20.

Perrow, Charles. 1972. *Complex Organizations: A Critical Essay*. New York: McGraw-Hill.

Pfeffer, Jeffrey. 1994. *Competitive Advantage through People*. Boston: Harvard Business School Press.

Piaget, Jean. 1955. *The Language and Thought of the Child*. New York: Meridian.

———. 1970. *Science of Education and the Psychology of the Child*. New York: Orion Press.

Pincus, Jonathan, and Jeffrey Winters, eds. 2002. *Reinventing the World Bank*. Ithaca: Cornell University Press.

Piore, Michael. 1995. *Beyond Individualism*. Cambridge: Harvard University Press.

Plato. 1961. *The Collected Dialogues of Plato*. Edited by Edith Hamilton and Huntington Cairns. New York: Pantheon Books.

Polanyi, Michael. 1951. *The Logic of Liberty*. Chicago: University of Chicago Press.

———. 1962. *Personal Knowledge: Towards a Post-Critical Philosophy*. Chicago: University of Chicago Press.

———. 1966. *The Tacit Dimension*. Garden City, NY: Doubleday.

Polya, George. 1965. *Mathematical Discovery: On Understanding, Learning, and Teaching Problem Solving*. Vol. 2. New York: John Wiley and Sons.

Popper, Karl R. 1962. *The Open Society and Its Enemies: The High Tide of Prophecy: Hegel, Marx, and the Aftermath*. New York: Harper and Row.

———. 1965. *Conjectures and Refutations: The Growth of Scientific Knowledge*. New York: Harper and Row.

Pratt, John W., and Richard J. Zeckhauser, eds. 1991. *Principals and Agents: The Structure of Business*. Boston: Harvard Business School Press.

Prebisch, Raúl. 1984. "Five Stages in My Thinking on Development." In *Pioneers in Development*, edited by G. Meier and D. Seers, 175–91. New York: Oxford University Press.

Prendergast, Canice. 1999. "The Provision of Incentives in Firms." *Journal of Economic Literature* 37 (March): 7–63.

Provine, W. B. 1986. *Sewall Wright and Evolutionary Biology*. Chicago: University of Chicago Press.

Rahman, Md Anisur. 1993. *People's Self-Development*. London: Zed Books.

Reddaway, Peter, and Dmitri Glinski. 2001. *The Tragedy of Russia's Reforms:*

Market Bolshevism against Democracy. Washington, DC: U.S. Institute of Peace Press.

Rist, Ray C. 1970. "Student Social Class and Teachers' Expectations: The Self-Fulfilling Prophecy in Ghetto Education." *Harvard Educational Review* 40: 411–50.

Robertson, D. H. 1921. "Economic Incentives." *Economica,* October, 231–45.

Roe, Emery. 1998. *Taking Complexity Seriously: Policy Analysis, Triangulation, and Sustainable Development.* Boston: Kluwer.

Rogers, Carl R. 1951. *Client-Centered Therapy.* Boston: Houghton Mifflin.

———. 1969. *Freedom to Learn.* Columbus, OH: Charles Merrill.

———. 1980. *A Way of Being.* Boston: Houghton Mifflin.

Rogers, Everett. 1983. *Diffusion of Innovations.* 3rd ed. New York: Free Press.

Rohr, Janelle, ed. 1989. *The Third World: Opposing Viewpoints.* Opposing Viewpoints, edited by D. Bender and B. Leone. San Diego, CA: Greenhaven Press.

Rondinelli, Dennis. 1983. *Development Projects as Policy Experiments: An Adaptive Approach to Development Administration.* London: Methuen.

Rosenberg, Nathan. 1969. "The Direction of Technological Change: Inducement Mechanisms and Focusing Devices." *Economic Development and Cultural Change* 18, no. 1: 1–24.

Rosenstein-Rodan, Paul. 1943. "Problems of Industrialization of Eastern and South-Eastern Europe." *Economic Journal* 53 (June–September): 202–11.

Rosenthal, Robert, and Lenore Jacobson. 1968. *Pygmalion in the Classroom.* New York: Hold, Rinehart, and Winston.

Ross, Stephen. 1973. "The Economic Theory of Agency: The Principal's Problem." *American Economic Review* 63:134–39.

Rota, Gian-Carlo. 1997. *Indiscrete Thoughts.* Edited by F. Palombi. Boston: Birkhäuser.

Rousseau, Jean-Jacques. [1762] 1979. *Emile, or on Education.* Translated by Allan Bloom. Reprint, New York: Basic Books.

Ruskin, John. [1862] 1985. *Unto This Last.* Reprint, London: Penguin.

Ryle, Gilbert. 1945–46. "Knowing How and Knowing That." *Proceedings of the Aristotelian Society* 46: 1–16.

———. 1967. "Teaching and Training." In *The Concept of Education,* edited by R. S. Peters, 105–19. London: Routledge and Kegan Paul.

Sabel, Charles. 1994. "Learning by Monitoring: The Institutions of Economic Development." In *Rethinking the Development Experience: Essays Provoked by the Work of Albert O. Hirschman,* edited by Lloyd Rodwin and Donald Schön, 231–74. Washington, DC: Brookings Institution.

Sabel, Charles, and Sanjay Reddy. 2003. "Learning to Learn: Undoing the Gordian Knot of Development Today." Mimeo. http://www2.law.columbia.edu/sabel/papers.htm

Sachs, Jeffrey. 1993. *Poland's Jump to the Market Economy*. Cambridge: MIT Press.

Salmen, Lawrence F. 1987. *Listen to the People*. New York: Oxford (a World Bank publication).

Santayana, George. [1922] 1962. *Reason in Common Sense*. 2nd ed. Reprint, New York: Collier Books.

Schank, Roger. 1997. *Virtual Learning: A Revolutionary Approach to Building a Highly Skilled Workforce*. New York: McGraw-Hill.

Schelling, Thomas C. 1984. *Choice and Consequences: Perspectives of an Errant Economist*. Cambridge: Harvard University Press.

———. 1992. "Some Economics of Global Warming." *American Economic Review* 82, no. 1: 1–20.

Schmidt, J., ed. 1996. *What Is Enlightenment? Eighteenth-Century Answers and Twentieth-Century Questions*. Berkeley: University of California Press.

Schön, Donald A. 1971. *Beyond the Stable State*. New York: Norton.

———. 1983. *The Reflective Practitioner: How Professionals Think in Action*. New York: Basic Books.

———. 1987. *Educating the Reflective Practitioner*. San Francisco: Jossey-Bass Publishers.

———. 1994. "Hirschman's Elusive Theory of Social Learning." In *Rethinking the Development Experience: Essays Provoked by the Work of Albert O. Hirschman*, edited by L. Rodwin and D. Schön, 67–95. Washington, DC: Brookings Institution.

Schön, Donald A., and Martin Rein. 1994. *Frame Reflection: Toward the Resolution of Intractable Policy Controversies*. New York: Basic Books.

Schumacher, E. F. 1961. "A Humanistic Guide to Foreign Aid." *Commentary* (November): 414–21.

———. 1973. *Small Is Beautiful: Economics as If People Mattered*. New York: Harper and Row.

———. 1997. *This I Believe and Other Essays*. Devon, UK: Resurgence Books.

Schumpeter, Joseph. 1934. *The Theory of Economic Development*. London: Oxford University Press.

Schwartz, Benjamin I. 1978. "The Rousseau Strain in the Contemporary World." *Daedalus* 107, no. 3 (summer): 193–206.

Schwenk, C. R. 1984. "Devil's Advocacy in Managerial Decision Making." *Journal of Management Studies*, April, 153–68.

———. 1989. A Meta-Analysis of the Comparative Effectiveness of Devil's Advocacy and Dialectical Inquiry. *Strategic Management Journal* 10, no. 3: 303–6.

Scitovsky, Tibor. 1976. *The Joyless Economy: An Inquiry into Human Satisfaction and Consumer Dissatisfaction*. Oxford: Oxford University Press.

Scott, James C. 1998. *Seeing Like a State: How Certain Schemes to Improve the Human Condition Have Failed*. New Haven: Yale.

Sen, Amartya. 1982. *Choice, Welfare, and Measurement*. Oxford: Blackwell.

———. 1984. *Resources, Values, and Development*. Cambridge: Harvard University Press.

———. 1999. *Development as Freedom*. New York: Knopf.

Seneca. 1969. *Letters from a Stoic*. Translated by Robin Campbell. London: Penguin.

Senge, Peter. 1990. *The Fifth Discipline: The Art and Practice of the Learning Organization*. New York: Currency Doubleday.

Shattuck, Roger. 1988. "Thoughts on the Humanities." *Daedalus*, summer, 143–49.

Shaw, Clifford R. 1944. *Memorandum Submitted to the Board of Directors of the Chicago Area Project*. Mimeo. Chicago: Chicago Area Project.

Shaw, G. B. 1961. *Back to Methuselah*. Baltimore: Penguin.

Simmons, John, and William Mares. 1983. *Working Together*. New York: Knopf.

Simon, Herbert. 1955. "A Behavioral Model of Rational Choice." *Quarterly Journal of Economics* 69, no. 1: 99–118.

———. 1991a. "Organizations and Markets." *Journal of Economic Perspectives* 5, no. 2 (spring): 25–44.

———. 1991b. *Models of My Life*. New York: Basic Books.

Slim, Hugo, and Paul Thompson, eds. 1993. *Listening for a Change: Oral Testimony and Development*. London: Panos.

Smith, Adam. [1759] 1969. *The Theory of Moral Sentiments*. Reprint, New Rochelle, NY: Arlington House.

Smith, Jeffery A. 1988. *Printers and Press Freedom: The Ideology of Early American Journalism*. New York: Oxford University Press.

Smullyan, Raymond. 1977. *The Tao Is Silent*. San Francisco: Harper and Row.

Social Protection Unit. 2000. "The End of Charity: How Social Funds Empower Communities." *Spectrum*, summer/fall. Washington, DC: World Bank.

Söderqvist, T. 2002. "The Life and Work of Niels Kaj Jerne as a Source of Ethical Reflection." *Scandinavian Journal of Immunology* 55, no. 6: 539–45.

Squire, L. R. 1987. *Memory and Brain*. New York: Oxford University Press.

Starobin, Paul. 1999. "What Went Wrong." *National Journal*, December 4, 3450–57.

Stern, Nicholas. 2001. *A Strategy for Development*. Washington, DC: World Bank.

Stern, Susan. 1997. "The Marshall Plan, 1947–1997: A German View." http://www.germany-info.org/newcontent/ff/ff_6c.html.

Stiglitz, Joseph. 1998. "Towards a New Paradigm for Development: Strategies,

Policies, and Processes." Raúl Prebisch Lecture at United Nations Conference on Trade and Development (UNCTAD), Geneva, October 19. Reprinted in Chang 2001.

———. 2001. "Whither Reform? Ten Years of the Transition." In *Joseph Stiglitz and the World Bank: The Rebel Within*, edited by Ha-Joon Chang, 127–71. London: Anthem.

———. 2002. *Globalization and Its Discontents*. New York: Norton.

Stiglitz, Joseph, and David Ellerman. 2001. "Not Poles Apart: 'Whither Reform?' and 'Whence Reform?'" *Journal of Policy Reform* 4, no. 4: 325–38.

Stokes, Bruce. 1981. *Helping Ourselves: Local Solutions to Global Problems*. New York: Norton.

Storm, D. Anthony. 1999. "Kierkegaard's Pseudonymous Method of Authorship." http://209.63.222.24/dstorm/sk/author.htm

Streeten, Paul. 1959. "Unbalanced Growth." *Oxford Economic Papers* 11 (June): 167–90.

Sullivan, William M. 1995. *Work and Integrity: The Crisis and Promise of Professionalism in America*. New York: Harper.

Sunstein, Cass. 2003. *Why Societies Need Dissent*. Cambridge: Harvard University Press.

Tarp, Finn, and Peter Hjertholm, eds. 2000. *Foreign Aid and Development: Lessons Learnt and Directions for the Future*. London: Routledge.

Tawney, Richard H. 1964. *The Radical Tradition*. New York: Minerva Press.

———. [1932] 1966. *Land and Labor in China*. Reprint, Boston: Beacon Press.

Tendler, Judith. 1975. *Inside Foreign Aid*. Baltimore: Johns Hopkins University Press.

———. 1997. *Good Government in the Tropics*. Baltimore: Johns Hopkins University Press.

———. 2000. "Why Are Social Funds So Popular?" In *Local Dynamics in the Era of Globalization*, edited by S. Yusuf and S. Evenett, 114–29. Oxford: Oxford University Press for the World Bank.

Terrill, Ross. 1973. *R. H. Tawney and His Times*. Cambridge: Harvard University Press.

Tinbergen, Jan. 1956. *Economic Policy: Principles and Design*. Amsterdam: North-Holland.

Titmuss, Richard. 1970. *The Gift Relationship*. London: Allen and Unwin.

Toquenaga, Y., and M. J. Wade. 1996. "Sewall Wright Meets Artificial Life: The Origin and Maintenance of Evolutionary Novelty." *Trends in Ecology and Evolution* 11: 478–82.

Truman, Harry. 1956. *Years of Trial and Hope: Memoirs*. Vol. 2. Garden City, NY: Doubleday.

Tung, L. L., and A. R. Heminger. 1993. "The Effects of Dialectical Inquiry,

Devil's Advocacy, and Consensus Inquiry Methods in a GSS Environment." *Information and Management* 25: 33–41.

Ul Haq, Mahbub. 1982. *Oral History Interview of Mahbub Ul Haq by Robert Asher (Dec. 3, 1982)*. Washington, DC: World Bank Archives.

Ulich, Robert, ed. 1954. *Three Thousand Years of Educational Wisdom*. Cambridge: Harvard University Press.

Uphoff, Norman. 1985. "Fitting Projects to People." In *Putting People First*, edited by Michael Cernea, 359–95. Washington, DC: Oxford University Press for the World Bank.

———, ed. 1994. *Puzzles of Productivity in Public Organizations*. San Francisco: ICS Press.

Uphoff, Norman, M. Esman, and Anirudh Krishna. 1998. *Reasons for Success: Learning from Instructive Experiences in Rural Development*. West Hartford, CT: Kumarian Press.

Van de Walle, Nicolas. 2001. *African Economies and the Politics of Permanent Crisis, 1979–1999*. New York: Cambridge University Press.

Verhagen, Koenraad. 1987. *Self-Help Promotion: A Challenge to the NGO Community*. Amsterdam: Royal Tropical Institute.

Versényi, Laszlo. 1963. *Socratic Humanism*. New Haven: Yale University Press.

Wade, Robert. 1996. "Japan, the World Bank, and the Art of Paradigm Maintenance: *The East Asian Miracle* in Political Perspective." *New Left Review* 217 (May–June): 3–36.

Waismann, Friedrich. 1967. *Ludwig Wittgenstein und der Wiener Kreis*. Oxford: Basil Blackwell.

Watzlawick, Paul. 1976. *How Real Is Real?* New York: Vintage.

Wedel, Janine. 1998. *Collision and Collusion*. New York: St. Martin's Press.

Weick, Karl. 1979. *The Social Psychology of Organizing*. New York: Random House.

Weitzman, Martin. 1993. "How Not to Privatize." In *Privatization Processes in Eastern Europe*. Edited by M. Baldassarri, L. Paganetto, and E. S. Phelps, 249–69. New York: St. Martin's Press.

Weitzman, Martin, and Chenggang Xu. 1994. "Chinese Township-Village Enterprises as Vaguely Defined Cooperatives." *Journal of Comparative Economics* 18: 121–45.

Westbrook, Robert. 1991. *John Dewey and American Democracy*. Ithaca: Cornell University Press.

Whyte, William Foote. 1955. *Money and Motivation: An Analysis of Incentives in Industry*. New York: Harper and Row.

Wiener, Norbert. 1954. *The Human Use of Human Beings*. Garden City, NY: Doubleday Anchor.

———. 1961. *Cybernetics: Or Control and Communication in the Animal and the Machine*. 2d ed. Cambridge: MIT Press.

Williams, Christopher. 1981. *Origins of Form*. New York: Architectural Book Publishing.

Wills, Garry. 1979. *Inventing America*. New York: Vintage Books.

———. 1994. *Certain Trumpets: The Call of Leaders*. New York: Simon and Schuster.

Wittgenstein, Ludwig. 1922. *Tractatus Logico-Philosophicus*. Translated by C. K. Ogden. New York: Harcourt Brace.

Wolfensohn. James D. 1997. "Annual Meetings Address: The Challenge of Inclusion." Given in Hong Kong, September 23. Available at www.worldbank.org/.

———. 1998. "Annual Meetings Address: The Other Crisis." Given in Washington, DC, October 6. Available at: http://www.worldbank.org/.

———. 1999a. "A Proposal for a Comprehensive Development Framework (a Discussion Draft)." Washington, DC.

———. 1999b. "Annual Meetings Address: Coalitions for Change." Given in Washington, DC, September 28. Available at http://www.worldbank.org.

World Bank. 1993. *East Asian Miracle: Public Policy and Economic Growth*. Washington, DC: World Bank and Oxford University Press.

———. 1996. *The World Bank Participation Sourcebook*. Washington, DC.

———. 1998a. *Assessing Aid: What Works, What Doesn't, and Why*. Washington, DC.

———. 1998b. *World Development Report: Knowledge for Development*. New York: Oxford University Press.

———. 2000. *World Development Report 2000/1: Attacking Poverty*. Washington, DC: Oxford University Press for the World Bank.

———. 2002. *A Sourcebook for Poverty Reduction Strategies*. Vols. 1 and 2. Washington, DC.

Wortman, Tunis. [1800] 1966. "A Treatise Concerning Political Enquiry." In *Freedom of the Press from Zenger to Jefferson: Early American Libertarian Theories*, edited by Leonard Levy, 230–84. Reprint, Indianapolis: Bobbs-Merrill.

Wright, Sewall. 1931. "Evolution in Mendelian Populations." *Genetics* 16: 97–159.

———. 1986. *Evolution: Selected Papers*. Edited by William B. Provine. Chicago: University of Chicago Press.

Young, Allyn. 1928. "Increasing Returns and Economic Progress." *Economic Journal* 38 (December): 527–42.

Index